NOTE TO READERS

The Civil Procedure Rules 1998 (made pursuant to the Civil Procedure Act 1997 and the Woolf Committee's Report) came into force on April 26, 1999. One of the changes so effected is in legal terminology. It is still correct to use the old terminology in relation to cases decided under the old procedure, but increasingly the new terminology will be that which must be used, as we have more and more decisions under the new procedure. For the convenience of readers, we are therefore including a list of the new terms they are most likely to encounter.

Old term	New term
plaintiff	claimant (in Scotland "pursuer")
minor/infant	child
next friend/guardian *ad litem*	litigation friend
writ	claim form
pleading	statement of case
in camera	in private
ex parte	without notice
inter partes	with notice
Mareva injunction	freezing injunction
Anton Piller order	search order

UNDERSTANDING LAW
Series Editor: Roger Brownsword

Understanding Law
John N. Adams and Roger Brownsword

Understanding Contract Law
John N. Adams and Roger Brownsword

Understanding Criminal Law
C.M.V. Clarkson

Understanding Equity and Trusts
Jeffrey Hackney

Understanding EU Law
Erika Szyszczak and Adam Cygan

Understanding Family Law
Michael Freeman

Understanding Property Law
W.T. Murphy, Simon Roberts and Tatiana Flessas

Understanding Public Law
Gabriele Ganz

Understanding Tort Law
Carol Harlow

ownsword

UNDERSTANDING
LAW

Fourth Edition

LONDON
SWEET & MAXWELL
2006

Published by Sweet & Maxwell Limited
of 100 Avenue Road, Swiss Cottage, London, NW3 3PF
(http://www.sweetandmaxwell.co.uk)

First Edition 1992
Second Edition 1999
Third Edition 2003
Fourth Edition 2006

No natural forests were destroyed to make this product; only farmed
timber was used and replanted

ISBN 978–0–421–96060–2
ISBN 0–421–960–604

Typeset by J&L Composition, Filey, North Yorkshire
Printed in Great Britain by Ashford Colour Print, Hants

ACKNOWLEDGEMENTS

We have received much help in producing this book and it is a pleasure to acknowledge this assistance.

First, because the book has had a long gestation period, we have a number of background debts to record: to Deryck Beyleveld and Tony Bottoms (who played a major part in setting the framework for the introductory law course at Sheffield) as well as to Mick Cavadino, Jim Dignan, and Tony Richardson (who have been involved in teaching the course since its inception over ten years ago).

Secondly, during the actual writing-up of the book a number of persons made helpful comments and suggestions, provided useful materials, and read through various parts of the manuscript. It is invidious to identify particular individuals but special thanks are due to Martin Foreman of the Crown Prosecution Service; Richard de Friend of the University of Kent; Robert Harrison of Vizzards, solicitors; Simon Johnson, barrister; Gerry Maher of the University of Glasgow; Iain Patton of the Crown Prosecution Service; and a clutch of colleagues at the University of Sheffield, especially Cosmo Graham, Ian Harden, Vanessa Laird, Norman Lewis, Tim Murphy, and Tony Prosser.

Thirdly, work on the book was facilitated by a brief period of study-leave (for Roger Brownsword) as well as by supportive intellectual milieu in what is now the Centre for Socio-Legal Studies at Sheffield.

Last, but by no means least, we are indebted to John Griffith, not only for lending his support to this project but for steering us through from start to finish. Needless to say, responsibility for errors and omissions is ours.

John N. Adams and
Roger Brownsword
1992.

PREFACE

This book is primarily concerned with the English legal system, but it is not a "nuts and bolts" description of it. Rather, our intention is to encourage readers to achieve an understanding of law in general and to develop a critical view of the institutions, processes, and materials, which comprise the English legal system in particular.

Now, it might seem fairly obvious, indeed trite, to declare that our purpose is to promote an understanding of law. What else, one might ask, could law books and legal education possibly be about? The fact is, however, that, in this country at least, law books and law schools have tended to be more concerned with expounding "black-letter" legal doctrine than with encouraging the development of a broader understanding of law and legal systems. Moreover, as legal doctrines and subject-areas have burgeoned, so students have been asked to absorb more and more black-letter materials without cultivating an improved understanding of law. This is not to say, of course, that the black-letter tradition is wrong in treating the exposition of legal doctrine as important. Rather, its error is to concentrate too narrowly on the exposition of legal doctrine to the exclusion of all other concerns about law. Accordingly, the underlying purpose of this book is to rectify the black-letter bias by encouraging an approach which stimulates inquiry into both doctrine and practice with a view to evaluating and explaining what is going on under the banner of "law".

Our interpretation of what is involved in "understanding law" has three salient characteristics. Firstly, an inquiring approach must be cultivated; to inquire is to question. This means that, in addition to pursuing black-letter "questions of law" (i.e. seeking to ascertain the legal position in relation to particular issues), a wide range of "questions about law" must be asked. In Chapter Two, we sketch a range of such questions (questions of conceptualisation, description, evaluation, and explanation). However, this particular set and sequence of questions about law should not be treated as fixed; for, our intention is not to replace one constraining framework (black-letterism) with another. Secondly, we must, so far as possible, establish a reasoned basis for our understanding. To form a critical view of law is to develop a reasoned position about the nature, legitimacy, and operation of the practice (*cf.* Ch.10). Thirdly, whilst the law has its own distinctive institutions and discourse, its own idiosyncrasies and rituals, it is essentially just one of the many practices—albeit a particularly significant practice—which comprise the fabric of social life. Accordingly, we must be prepared to have recourse to those disciplines—particularly, philosophy, sociology, history, economics, and psychology—which are concerned with understanding human social conduct in general. The study of law, in other words, must become an integrated multi-disciplinary enterprise.

Whilst our discussion of the English legal system is guided by these methodological principles, it is far from being the last word on understanding law. In fact, very much as with our *Understanding Contract Law* (first published in 1987), our concern is to address law in such a way that ideas will be stimulated and questions provoked. Nevertheless, in taking these steps we have encountered a number of recurrent substantive themes. It is as well, therefore, to indicate two of these themes at the outset.

First, it is apparent that modern legal systems are subject to a number of competing demands. This results in a variety of tensions. For example, judges are expected to apply "the law"; but they are also expected to achieve just and reasonable decisions. Where, in a particular case, application of "the law" would produce an unjust outcome, there is clearly a dilemma for the judge (see Chs 4 and 5). Similarly, whilst we demand that our systems of criminal, civil, and administrative justice should be designed to promote "justice", we also demand that these systems should be workable, relatively speedy, and efficient (see Chs 6, 7, and 8). Thus, to take perhaps the starkest illustration of this tension, whilst some may demand that no evidence obtained unlawfully by the police should be admissible (in the interests of justice and due process), others may insist that where evidence conclusively and reliably indicates guilt then it should be admitted (in the interests of efficient control of crime) even though it might have been obtained unlawfully. Arbitrating competing demands of this kind is no easy task; and there is no reason to suppose that the particular accommodation of such demands to be found in legal doctrines, and in the practice of legal officials, is necessarily the best one.

This leads to our second main theme. Whilst English society and its legal system in the twenty-first century might reflect a particular mix of values and attitudes, this needs to be put into both historical and comparative perspective, since, at different times and in different places, very different values and practices have prevailed. For example, as we point out in our discussion of criminal justice (see Ch. 6), imperial Chinese law in the eighteenth and nineteenth centuries was underpinned by general subscription to a notion of collective responsibility. Thus, when a salute fired by a British ship accidentally killed a Chinese bystander, the authorities demanded that a gunner be surrendered to them for execution. Whilst we would have little hesitation today in condemning such a response as irrational, the progressive rationalisation of modern societies has led, not to a consensus on questions of value, but, as we have said already, to serious conflicts whose resolution is sought in our hard-pressed legal system. Hence, even if we agree that the Chinese doctrine of collective responsibility was irrational, we might have conflicting views about a doctrine of vicarious criminal liability under which, for example, parents would be liable for the crimes of their children, and company executives liable for the crimes of their employees.

In these introductory remarks, it remains only to confess our own theoretical predilections. Broadly speaking, our position is underpinned by a synthesis of Immanuel Kant's rationalist philosophy and Max Weber's sociological method. This yields inter alia a concern that reason should be pressed to its limits, that individual rights should be taken seriously, that explanation should start with the reasons and purposes of individual actors, and that it makes sense to think that law can be "correctly" understood. If readers, having considered these matters, have reason to believe otherwise, so be it. Again, as with *Understanding Contract Law*, our ambition is not so much that readers should agree with our answers, but that questions should be posed and pursued. In the final analysis, therefore, what matters is that an attempt to understand law should be made, not that our particular understanding of law should be adopted.

* * *

Since we wrote the first edition of this book, nothing has happened to alter our view that an understanding of law implies a grasp of the values underlying particular institutional designs and doctrinal choices, as well as an appreciation of both historical and comparative context. However, the educational manifesto that we set out in the book now looks rather less radical than it did a decade ago. Indeed, the idea that law school education should encourage an active engagement with the materials, that the emphasis should be on understanding rather than rehearsal, and that law should be placed in its ethical and social context could plausibly claim to have become the received wisdom (see, e.g. Oliver, 1994; Brownsword, 1996; Carnie, 2004). Orthodoxy, however, is not necessarily a bad thing—at any rate, it is no bad thing so long as it places the idea of understanding at the heart of the law school mission.

CONTENTS

1

WHAT IS LAW?

As a first step towards "understanding law", we need to be clear about two things: the object of our inquiry, the idea of "law", and the sense in which our inquiry is concerned with "understanding". In the first part of this book, we address these two issues, concentrating in this chapter on the question of how we are to conceive of law.

1. TOWARDS A CONCEPT OF LAW

There is no difficulty in specifying our field of interest: quite simply, it is law and legal systems in general, and the English legal system (the legal system in England and Wales) in particular. At the present day, the English legal system is taken to comprehend the activities of Parliament, the courts, judges and juries, barristers and solicitors, and policemen and the like, together with the statutes and case-law precedents which govern these activities. Although this suffices to convey a sense of the subject matter of this book, there is a difference between having some familiarity with the activities of those who are engaged in the practice of law and having a *conceptual* understanding of law. Even if we know a policeman when we see one, we might lack any general idea of law itself. For example, we might have no sense of how law relates to power and authority, politics, religion, and morality, and the like. If law has a defining "essence", what is it? How do we determine whether some activity is of a "legal" character?

The most important way in which a conceptual framework organises our thinking is by establishing categories. Thus, once we have a concept of law (in which the essence of law is identified), we have a basis for discriminating between law and non-law. For example, with a concept of law, we are in a position to respond to the old chestnut of whether so-called "international law" really is law. If international treaties, courts, custom, and the like, meet the conceptual requirements for law, then it is appropriate to view such phenomena as examples of law. However, if these phenomena do not meet the conceptual requirements, then it is inappropriate to treat them as though they did—rather as it is inappropriate to shelve a philosophy text in the geography section of a library. Of course, conceptual propriety aside, some will see political advantage in clothing their operations in the *language* of law and legality. However, it is important to appreciate that, in principle, there is a clear distinction between words and concepts. The object of conceptualising law is not to play around with the word "law", but to clarify our thinking by drawing a map in which the differences between various kinds of phenomena are charted.

To clarify this further, imagine that an anthropologist wishes to present the results of a study of the way in which disputes are settled in a simple island community (*cf.* Roberts, 1979). Firstly, she outlines the general field of her inquiry—dispute-settlement in an island community. Secondly, she considers where the dispute-settling practices of the island community stand in relation to a coherent conceptual framework. Are these practices instances of law? If she believes that a coherent concept of law treats all attempts at dispute-settlement (whatever their form and regardless of whether court-like institutions are involved) as instances of law, then the anthropologist must regard her research as a study of legal processes. In these circumstances, it would be natural to present the research as a study of "law". However, whether or not she used the word "law", her *conceptual* position would be that the phenomena studied fell within the same category, the category of law, as equivalent phenomena in more complex societies.

In the remainder of this chapter, we will make a start on conceptualising law, particularly with a view to considering whether modern so-called legal systems should be treated as co-extensive with the concept of law.

2. LAW AS A SYSTEM OF RULES

For conceptual purposes, a promising starting point seems to be the network of rules which is characteristic of modern legal systems (or, more accurately, those systems which we call "legal systems" and which are widely assumed to be instances of the concept of law). A plausible hypothesis, therefore, is that the pattern, or essence, of law is to be located in its distinctive structure of rules. This is precisely the view elaborated by H.L.A. Hart in his celebrated book *The Concept of Law* (1961).

According to Hart, the distinctive feature of modern legal systems is not simply that they have complex rule structures, but that the rules relate to one another in a hierarchical fashion. At the foundations of modern legal systems can be found what Hart terms the "secondary rules" of the system, representing the constitutional arrangements of the particular society. Under these secondary rules, certain persons or bodies will be authorised to make law (to introduce, amend, and repeal legal rules), and to adjudicate on disputes arising under the law. The rules so made by the authorised persons or bodies (in the prescribed manner) are what Hart calls the "primary rules" of law. According to Hart:

"[So] many of the ideas which constitute the framework of legal thought, require for their elucidation reference to one or both of these two types of rule [i.e. primary and secondary rules], that their union may be justly regarded as the 'essence' of law, though they may not always be found together wherever the word 'law' is correctly used. Our justification for assigning to the union of primary and secondary rules this central place is not that they will there do the work of a dictionary, but that they have great explanatory power." (p.151)

Thus, the more obvious kinds of rules of law—for instance, the rules of the criminal law, the rules of the law of torts (this being concerned with such matters as road accidents, nuisance, and libel and slander), and the rules relating to the making of contracts and wills—are examples of primary rules. Whilst there is some disagreement about whether all primary rules have precisely the same character, the important point is that all such rules—whether they are duty-imposing, duty-releasing, power-conferring, or whatever—must originate from one of the law-making persons or bodies recognised by the secondary rules. And this is where such persons as judges and Parliamentarians, and such bodies as the courts and the legislature (Parliament in the United Kingdom) come in; for, within Hart's conceptual scheme, the courts and the legislature (and their respective personnel) are established by the secondary rules, under which they are authorised to carry out certain operations in relation to primary rules.

One of the virtues of Hart's conceptual scheme is that it underlines the importance of the secondary rule structure. Whilst the citizens of the United Kingdom do not carry around in their pockets copies of a constitution, the fact is that their encounters with the primary rules (with "the law" as it would commonly be perceived) are shaped by the background constitutional arrangements, by the panoply of secondary rules. Although this secondary rule structure may remain largely hidden, in one respect at least its influence is highly visible. For, in modern legal systems, it is hard not to notice the omnipresence of legal "officials", of judges and legislators, policemen and prison officers, taxmen and traffic wardens, all of whom are placed by the secondary rules in some "official" position for the purposes of performing some function in relation to the primary rules. The significance of this is that modern legal systems, through their secondary rule structures, not only draw a sharp distinction between officials and non-officials, but also create a sophisticated division of labour between the various officials.

The cornerstone of the secondary rules (and, indeed, of the primary rules) is what Hart terms the rule (or rules) of recognition. What Hart has in mind is the idea that, amongst the secondary rules, there is a master rule which provides a definitive test of whether a particular rule qualifies as a rule of the legal system in question (and, in this sense, is a legally valid rule). In principle, such a master rule could take a number of different forms, but in a developed legal system it will comprise a statement of the authoritative sources of law. Moreover, it will rank in order the official sources of law so that, in cases of conflict, it is clear which rule of law prevails. We need to say a little more about this important concept of a rule of recognition.

Typically, law courses open by familiarising students with the sources of law within their jurisdiction. Without saying as much, this involves setting out the content of the rule of recognition. Thus, in England, law students are told that the principal sources of law in our legal system are the rules made by Parliament (in the form of statutes and statutory instruments), the rules made by courts and tribunals (in the form of precedents), and, since the accession of the United Kingdom to the European Economic Community in 1972, various rules, regulations, directives, and decisions made by the Community's law-making institutions. In other jurisdictions, this list of sources might include such items as Constitutions, Bills of Rights, Codes, textbooks, and so on. Not only is it drilled into novice law students that the official sources are the only sources that matter—hence, in England, the speculations of eminent law professors, however interesting, are strictly unofficial—but also that the sources are ranked. Accordingly, in England, Community law outranks all other legal rules, and statutes and statutory instruments outrank domestic judicial precedents.

We now have an outline of the idea that law is a system of rules. A legal system is to be viewed as akin to a pyramid of rules, the secondary rules (crowned by the rule of recognition) at the top, with the primary rules beneath. Whilst the secondary rules define the officials within the legal system (and are essentially addressed to those officials), the primary rules are addressed to all citizens. Moreover, given the rule of recognition, it should be possible at any given time to identify the complete set of rules laid down by statutes, judicial decisions and the like, and, in this sense, to proffer a comprehensive statement of the law of the jurisdiction (hence the common practice of textbook writers to purport to declare the law as at a particular date).

3. LAW AS A PURPOSIVE ENTERPRISE

Although the rule model fits pretty well with many of the ideas that we have about law, its tendency to focus on formal features invites two concerns about its adequacy.

First, it may be argued that the key to law lies in the purpose, not the form, of the practice. And, whilst it would be wrong to accuse the rule model of lacking altogether a functional dimension, it is basically a formal account. In consequence, it is not really designed to answer the question of why we need law. Secondly, if the essential characteristic of law is that it is a regime of primary and secondary rules, it follows that any phenomenon lacking this feature is not truly a case of law. Indeed, Hart underscores just this point by saying that the introduction of secondary rules, to support a regime of primary rules, may "be considered a step from the pre-legal into the legal world . . . [converting a] regime of primary rules into what is indisputably a legal system" (Hart, 1961, p.91). Accordingly, the system of "international law" and the "law" of simpler societies, allegedly lacking fully-developed secondary rule structures, arguably fail to qualify as cases of law. Given that Hart is not attempting to pre-empt our use of the word "law", this may be thought to be a trivial concern about the rule model. For, if we so wish, we can continue to talk about "international *law*" (including violations of, or compliance with, "international *law*", which may be important in the context of international relations: see Koskenniemi, 2002; Sands, 2006); and, similarly, if we so wish, we can talk about the "law" amongst the Barotse and the Cheyenne, or whoever. This, however, confuses linguistic and conceptual matters and misses the thrust of Hart's argument, which is that, no matter how we employ the word "law", there will always remain a critical distinction between, on the one hand, regimes of primary and secondary rules and, on the other hand, regimes of primary rules alone (or, of course, non-rule regimes). In other words, for Hart, while the *linguistic* boundaries can be drawn wherever we wish, the *conceptual* boundaries of law must be drawn around regimes of primary and secondary rules. The objection to the rule model, then, is that it attaches too much weight to form rather than function in setting the conceptual framework for law. After all, if the purposes underlying "international law" and the "law" of simpler societies are the same as those underlying modern "indisputable" legal systems, why make so much of their different formal manifestations?

In the light of these concerns, we need to address the matter of the purpose of law directly. Here, a helpful analysis is presented by the American writer, Karl Llewellyn, in the form of his "law-jobs" theory (see Llewellyn, 1940). According to Llewellyn, no group can survive and flourish as a group unless what he calls the "law-jobs" are properly performed. Moreover, when Llewellyn insists that "no group" can flourish without attending to the law-jobs, he really means no group—the Cheyenne Indians just as much as a scout troop or the commuter society of south-east England. In Llewellyn's view, the effective functioning of all groups, from the scout troop up to wider political society, and beyond to the international community, is contingent upon proper attention to the law-jobs. The law-jobs, then, hold a key to successful group life and, with that, a key to understanding the purpose of law.

Essentially, Llewellyn identifies four law-jobs as follows: (i) adjustment of what he calls the "trouble case"; (ii) preventive channelling of conduct and expectations (and preventive re-channelling of conduct and expectations to adjust to change); (iii) the allocation of authority; and (iv) the provision of direction and incentive within the group (what Llewellyn calls the job of "net drive"). This sets a fourfold task for law.

First, law must establish mechanisms for settling disputes and conflicts as they arise between members of the group (the "trouble case"). If A alleges that B has broken his arm, or has made off with some of his property, or has failed to repay a debt, but B denies A's allegations, there must be some recognised way in which A and B can resolve the matter. Whether the recognised process involves talking of some kind (e.g. by way of mediation or conciliation, or some form of arbitration or adjudication), or splitting (i.e. A and B go their different ways), or fighting, or whatever, the imperative for the group is that the dispute is settled. For group life cannot flourish where A and B (and their respective supporters) maintain a vendetta against one another. As modern forms of centralised government emerge, dispute settlement becomes more complex. Sometimes the State initiates a claim or complaint against a citizen (as with much of the criminal law, *cf.* Ch.6); sometimes one citizen makes a claim against another citizen (as with the civil law, *cf.* Ch.7); and sometimes a citizen makes a complaint against the State (as with public law, *cf.* Ch.8). In each case, a variety of forms and techniques, more or less formal, more or less coercive, is available (see Mackie, 1991). However, the fundamental point remains that, as in simpler societies, it is imperative that the legal mechanisms for resolving such disputes are regarded as authoritative.

Secondly, group life must be regulated. Just as there have to be rules of the road, otherwise motorists are liable to collide, there must, more generally, be rules regulating social intercourse. At a minimum, the citizen's interests in physical integrity must be regulated. Moreover, if citizens wish to trade with one another, to buy and sell goods and services, there must be property rules and the ground rules for making exchanges need to be established. Admittedly, such a regulatory framework does not guarantee that disputes will not arise. B may still deny that he broke A's arm, or stole his property, or failed to repay a debt, for these denials concern questions of fact. Nevertheless, the existence of an accepted regulatory framework significantly reduces the scope for conflict about the relevant rules. It is not enough, however, that a regulatory regime is instituted. As Llewellyn says, the regulatory job includes preventive re-channelling of conduct and expectations to adjust to change. The social and the physical (natural) environments do not stand still. In the social world, for example, attitudes change. At the beginning of the twenty-first century, attitudes towards such matters as abortion, divorce, and suicide, and towards women, children, and consumers are radically different from the views which prevailed at the end of the nineteenth century. If the regulatory framework is to be accepted, the law must reflect such changes—there remains more than a lingering regard for capital punishment, but few of its supporters would wish to hang someone for stealing a sheep or for attempting to commit suicide.

Thirdly, authoritative procedures must be established identifying who is to resolve disputes (and how) and who is to lay down the regulatory framework (and how). Indeed, the creation of constitutional arrangements is the most urgent task for law. As John Finnis remarks:

"Once the problems of social order, and of authority as a rational response to such problems, have become the object of practically reasonable reflection in a community, 'constitutional' provision for the location of authority becomes a first priority. If the ruler does not make it his business to determine the location of authority for later times (not to mention for lower levels), thoughtful members of such societies will commonly make it their business to try, as best they can, to reach some understanding about it". (1980, p.250)

The point is that, in any group, someone must be recognised as having the authority to make the rules for the group and to settle disputes (or, at least, to lay down how disputes are to be settled). As groups become more complex, no individual will be in a position to carry this burden alone, so that such authority will have to be shared. In other words, complex groups will call for sophisticated structures of delegated authority. Moreover, these structures will have to be such that continuity of authority is maintained despite particular individuals coming and going. Thus, in the United States, for example, even the assassination or impeachment of a president, does not undermine the essential continuity of the Constitution and of the legal system; that is, presidential authority survives even where particular presidents perish or resign. Above all, however, the constitutional arrangements must provide the foundation of authority. The more that these arrangements are accepted, the better the prospects for effective regulation and dispute-settlement within the community; the less that they are accepted, the worse the prospects, not only for the law-jobs, but for civilised life in general.

Finally, it falls to the law to make arrangements for setting goals and policies within the community. In some groups (such as a chess club), the goals define the group and are non-contentious. Quite simply, one does not join if one does not have an interest in the goals which provide the *raison d'etre* of the group. In some simpler societies, survival may be the overriding goal, so that policy questions (if any) are about means rather than ends. However, in complex modern societies, community goals and policies are the very stuff of which political debate is made. Indeed, this is the "trouble-case" writ large. Once again, the law must identify who is to set policy (and how), and a community will flourish only where the legal framework for policy-setting is authoritative. It can be argued that the modern malaise of British political life, its resemblance in Lord Hailsham's (1976) striking phrase to "an elective dictatorship", stems from precisely this problem. Government policy is set in and around Cabinet by a handful of Ministers (and their advisers) drawn from the ruling party; the content of such policies is not significantly restricted by a legal framework commanding general respect; such policies as are adopted in Cabinet are then rubber-stamped by a legislative assembly in which the ruling party has a majority despite (usually) representing only a minority of the electorate; and, from this production-line process, the policies of the ruling caucus emerge as laws. Not surprisingly, adherence to such laws is by no means automatic—as the problems with the introduction of the community charge (or "poll tax"), in both Scotland and England, vividly illustrated in the early 1990s.

What, then, are we to make of the law-jobs theory? As with the rule model of law, we can use it to map out some legal landmarks. For instance, we can associate the judiciary with the job of dealing with the "trouble-case", the legislature with the job of preventive channelling, and the executive with the job of net drive. Moreover, the Constitution fits well with the job of allocating authority. However, does Llewellyn's theory assist, as we hoped that it might, in throwing some light on the purpose of law? The central thrust of the law-jobs theory is that group life is problematic, potentially conflictual, potentially chaotic, potentially destructive. The blunt answer to the question of what law is for, is that law's purpose is to address these problems. The form of law's response varies from one group to another, from one society to another. In simpler societies, law tends to respond less formally; in more complex societies, legal responses tend to be more formal, more like the elegant rule structure depicted by Hart. However, whatever the form of law's response, its purpose is always the same: to set up authoritative mechanisms whereby social order can be established and maintained, social change managed, disputes settled, and policies and goals for the community adopted.

4. LAW AS A TYPE OF DOMINATION

The law-jobs theory suggests that we should view modern legal systems as a particular kind of attempt to grapple with the regulation of social life. This is not to deny that Hart is right in identifying the intersection of primary and secondary rules as distinctive of modern law. Rather, the law-jobs theory invites us, first, to locate regimes of primary and secondary rules in a broader framework of social regulation, and, secondly, to appreciate that such rule-regimes are only one instance of systems where "the law-jobs get done".

However, before we jump to the conclusion that, once we realise that modern legal systems are merely one manifestation of the attempt to establish social order (to regulate social intercourse, to settle disputes, and so on), we have the whole picture, we might consider the views of German sociologist Max Weber. One of the central themes of Weber's sociology is that modern societies distinguish themselves from their predecessors by their progressive rationalisation. In the sphere of law, such rationalisation is evidenced by the subjection of legal discourse and decision-making to a framework of rules. Whilst this is very much in line with Hart's conception of modern legal systems as regimes of primary and secondary rules, Weber adds a fresh dimension to the rule-model of law. For, the point emphasised by Weber is not simply that modern legal systems are rule-regulated but that their rule-regulation founds a particular kind of claim to legitimate domination—the claim that the (primary) rules of law should be regarded as authoritative because they are the outcome of recognised rule-governed processes (and, similarly, that the officials administering such rules should be recognised as authoritative because they occupy positions designated by the secondary rule structure). Bearing in mind that the allocation of authority is one of the key law-jobs, Weber's introduction of the idea of legitimate domination is of considerable importance. In fact, Weber develops a threefold typology of domination, possible claims to legitimacy (and acceptance of authority) being of a charismatic, traditional, or legal-rational type.

The *charismatic* structure of domination, Weber says, "rests upon that authority of a concrete individual which is based neither upon rational rules nor upon tradition" (Weber, 1954, p.337). It is the primitive sense of the sacredness of an object (e.g. an idol or a totem), or a place, but it is equally applicable to offices and institutions. It cannot be explained entirely in terms of material or ideal factors. Although Weber sees charismatic authority as having declining importance in modern legal systems, it remains critical to understanding some legal regimes (e.g. the judicial systems of some Islamic states) and, in our own constitutional history, it is relevant to understanding such matters as the position of the Crown, and the royal prerogative (*cf.* Ch.3). Like charismatic domination, *traditional* domination is a form of personal authority. However, the basis of traditional domination is custom and practice. For instance, if tradition prescribed that the line of Rex I should rule, than Rex III would claim to be (and would be) recognised as the legitimate ruler on the ground that he was the eldest son of Rex II (who was the eldest son of Rex I). Finally, legitimate domination may assume a *rational-legal* form. In this type of domination, authority is of a rule-governed, not a personal, nature. Thus, in the legal-rational type, the reason why, say, Lord Denning's judgments should be regarded as authoritative is not because he was a judge with a certain charisma, nor because tradition accords legitimacy to judicial decisions, but simply because he was occupying an official decision-making position under the (secondary) rules. As Weber puts it:

"[In the legal-rational type of domination] every single bearer of powers of command is legitimated by that system of rational norms, and his power is legitimate in so far as it corresponds with the norms. Obedience is thus given to the norms rather than to the person." (1954, p.336)

The significance of this is that, where the legal-rational form prevails (and, as we have said, Weber sees this form as characteristic of modern legal systems), it contains, as it were, the basis of its own claim to legitimacy. Compliance with the law is demanded not on the ground of personal authority, of charisma or tradition, but on the ground that we should submit ourselves to the impartial authority of the rule-system (i.e. the regime of primary and secondary rules as Hart would have it). What Weber is suggesting, therefore, is that, with modern legal systems, a powerful legitimating symbol (law, or the Rule of Law) has emerged. The authority of legal officials is to be recognised, not because they have special powers or a unique sense of justice or the like, but purely and simply because they act in accordance with the law. In short, in modern legal systems, compliance with the primary rules is pressed simply because such rules are valid as "the law".

Although the charismatic, the traditional, and the legal-rational are three distinct types of domination, it should not be thought that particular social situations must embody only one of these types. Earlier forms of domination may residually survive in modern rational systems; or, conversely, rational elements may be present in predominantly charismatic or traditional regimes. Similarly, it should not be forgotten that respect for tradition may delay the open adoption of more efficient (rational) procedures.

In this light, consider the rise and fall of those two great fictitious characters in English law, John Doe and Richard Roe. Briefly, by the fifteenth century, the writs of right, which were the forms of action used to recover possession of freehold land, and which were of great antiquity, had become encrusted with procedural complexities. By contrast, the action of ejectment, which could be used to recover possession of leasehold land, was altogether more modern and efficient. In time, landowners came to wonder why they could recover their leasehold properties more expeditiously than their freeholds. The rational answer would have been to reform the writs of right; instead, these real actions being hallowed by tradition, the difficulty was side-stepped. What happened was that freeholders seeking to recover possession pleaded that the land had been leased to one (fictitious) John Doe who had been wrongfully ejected by one (fictitious) Richard Roe. Doe sued Roe in ejectment, and, on the latter's behalf, the real defendant (the real person in possession of the freehold land) was advised to intervene in the action and defend his title. Either he intervened (in which case he was obliged to accept the fiction and, effectively, Doe's leasehold title) or he did not (in which case judgment would be entered, and he would be turned off the land). By about 1575–80, the real action had been largely supplanted in practice. Even so, it was not until the nineteenth century that Doe and Roe could be dispensed with, and rationality supplant tradition and fiction.

Let us take stock. We can start by agreeing with Llewellyn that attempts to establish social order, attempts to perform the law-jobs, may manifest themselves in many different ways (the Eskimos sing nith-songs to resolve their disputes; the Nuer employ the "leopard-skin chief"; the English present arguments in a courtroom, with the lawyers often wearing eighteenth-century wigs; and so on). In this light, Hart may well be correct to pick out the intersection of primary and secondary rules as distinctive of modern legal systems, but, unless there is more to modern legal systems than this, they seem to be just one of the many types of attempts to establish social order. Weber, however, gives us pause to wonder whether modern legal systems are not after all rather special; for the modern practice of law is more than rule-governed—its rules are the basis of its legitimacy.

5. LAW AS THE RULE OF THE POWERFUL

Notwithstanding the insights offered by such abstract ideas as primary and secondary rules, law-jobs, and legal-rational domination, could it be that we have not yet identified what is really going on in modern legal systems? An important thread in our discussion is the idea that modern legal systems involve officials. Where there are rules to be made there must be official rule-makers; so, too, there must be official rule-interpreters and official rule-enforcers. To make an obvious point, such officials are in positions of power. If we do not have a clear idea about how such power is exercised (and, thus far, we lack any idea about this), then it is arguable that we do not really understand law. Of course, we can report the outcomes of specific occurrences—for example, that, in a particular case, a particular official applied a particular rule with a particular result. However, what we must consider is whether there is some pattern in the exercise of legal power—a pattern which may, in turn, disclose the essential nature of law.

Sociologists often draw a distinction between simpler societies (so-called *Gemeinschaft* societies), where social bonds are forged around shared values, and more complex, modern, societies (so-called *Gesellschaft* societies) in which individuals are economically inter-dependent but where there is no consensus about values (although there may be a consensus about the way in which disputes about values are to be arbitrated). If we assume that modern legal systems are located in *Gesellschaft* societies (*cf.* "*Gesellschaft* law" as Kamenka and Tay (1980) have called the legal analogue), what are the implications for the exercise of legal power? Can the law be in some sense "impartial"? Or, does it inevitably reflect certain sectional interests?

Granted that quite a number of legal rules are neutral, in the sense that we simply have to have a rule and it does not matter much what it is (e.g. if we want to have vehicles using roads, we have to decide on which side they will drive), nevertheless much law is not of this character. Accordingly, if we focus upon legislative assemblies, as the principal modern rule-making institutions, it seems fairly clear that legislative outcomes (statutes and the like) cannot be impartial as between competing interest groups. Indeed, the whole point of having legislative assemblies seems to be to enable one group (the ruling political party) to translate its sectional interests into a legal form. Thus, if Conservative and Labour governments in the United Kingdom enacted precisely the same laws with regard to such matters as, say, industrial relations and taxation, we would begin to wonder whether Parliamentary democracy was working. Furthermore, behind the façade of the political parties, we must assume that there are various networks of competing interests seeking to influence the ruling party's legislative programme. As Chambliss and Seidman observe:

"In all [*Gesellschaft*] societies, regardless of how the interest groups vary in number, those which are most likely to be effective are the ones that control the economic or political institutions of the society. The most influential groups will of course be those which control both. As a consequence, legislation typically favors the wealthier, the more politically active groups in the society. Not surprisingly, in America this means that the managers and owners of the large corporations and mammoth business complexes will enjoy more success in getting laws passed which benefit them than will the 'average citizen' or, in a more extreme contrast, the unemployed resident of a slum." (1971, p.65).

Given the undeniable fact that legislative outcomes reflect the preferences of certain interest groups, is it possible to salvage any kind of imparitiality thesis for law?

The obvious move is to argue that, whilst legislative assemblies are not impartial, the application and enforcement of the law is strictly impartial: judges apply the law, and policemen enforce it, without fear or favour. Indeed, such impartial application and enforcement of the law is the nub of the Rule of Law. There are, however, at least two difficulties with this contention. First, if the laws produced by legislative assemblies reflect particular sectional interests, then the "impartial" application and enforcement of these laws must simply reproduce such sectional interests. For example, if a statute regulates trade union activities in such a way as to reflect the interests of employers, the impartial application and enforcement of the statute does not mean that the interests of employers and organised labour are fairly balanced—it means that the interests of the former prevail. Secondly, the claim that the law is impartially applied and enforced is highly problematic. Whilst judges may be immune from the lobbying to which politicians are subject, they may be guided by sectional values when the facts or the interpretation of the law are in dispute (see further Chs 4 and 5). Equally, enforcement agencies must make decisions about which parts of the law are to be most rigorously enforced (e.g. white collar crime or social security fraud, drink-driving or kerb-crawling, possession of obscene publications or drugs, and so on), and individual enforcement agents must make decisions about such matters as who is to be arrested, who is to be detained in custody, and who is to be prosecuted. Once again, it is arguable that such background policy decisions and individual discretionary decisions cannot be strictly impartial, but must betray the attitudes and values of particular interest groups.

If the law is shot through, directly or indirectly, with the interests of various competing groups, then is there any pattern to such legal politics? One view, "pluralism", denies that any deeper pattern is to be discerned. *Gesellschaft* societies are made up of a multitude of interest groups (consumer, environmental, conservationist, transport, women's, and so on), individuals often being actively involved in a number of such groups. Some pressure groups are more effective than others, and groups which are effective in one quarter of legal practice may be quite ineffective in another quarter. Thus, the reflection of sectional interests in legal systems is a complex matter (*cf*. Macpherson, 1973; Held, 1987). Against this, however, a Marxist view would maintain that rules and decisions within legal systems can be traced to the interests of the ruling economic class (*cf*. Collins, 1984; Kairys, 1982). From this perspective, the only complexity in law lies, on the one hand, in its occasional strategic concessions to the interests of the proletariat, and, on the other hand, in its elaborate attempts to persuade the subservient classes that law is the epitome of justice and impartiality.

From a pluralist or a Marxist viewpoint, Hart, Llewellyn and Weber seem to put the emphasis in the wrong place. Indeed, from a Marxist perspective, Weber's highlighting of legal-rational domination seems to look at law through the wrong end of a telescope. For, whilst Weber appreciates that, in modern legal systems, citizens accept the legitimacy of law, he does not realise that this is the outcome of a confidence trick played on the proletariat by the ruling class.

With the introduction of pluralist and Marxist perspectives on law, a major conceptual division—between "law as authority" and "law as power"—comes into view. In the writing of Hart, Llewellyn, and Weber, we constantly run up against the idea that the concept of law is intimately connected with the idea of authority. Moreover, Hart in particular is keen to persuade his readers that law should be regarded in a relatively favourable light—that law is an affair of obligation, not of crude coercion (or of people being obliged to obey). However, this threatens to run together two distinguishable theses, the "political" thesis that those systems which are commonly viewed as "legal systems" merit some respect, and the "conceptual" thesis that law is to be conceived of in terms of moral authority and moral obligation. Now the pluralist and Marxist emphasis on the connection between law and power is of obvious relevance to one's assessment of the political thesis. However, this emphasis is important, too, for one's appreciation of the conceptual thesis. Crucially, whatever we make of the distinctively pluralist and Marxist accounts of how legal officials (as we currently conceive of such persons) operate as power-brokers, at one level these theories must be correct; for law, however conceived, surely must be seen as a vehicle for the organisation and exercise of power. Accordingly, the conceptual opposition between "law as authority" and "law as power" is not to be read in terms of a contrast between "law as a power-free zone" as against "law as a practice involving power". Rather, the relevant distinction is between "law as morally legitimate power" (i.e. as power backed by moral authority) and "law as naked power". If, then, power cannot be kept out of the concept of law, the question remains whether the essence of law is to be found in such notions as rules, sanctions, and effectiveness *simpliciter*, or whether the concept of law has a deeper connection with legitimacy and moral authority.

6. LAW AS A MORAL ENTERPRISE

One of the most lucid modern exponents of the claim that the concept of law is necessarily tied up with the idea of morality is the American jurist, Lon Fuller. In his book *The Morality of Law* (1969), Fuller argues that, if law is to realise its regulatory ambitions, legal officials must respect what he calls "the inner morality of law". This comprises a number of procedural ideals guiding any attempt to regulate human behaviour (at least, on the scale associated with a legal system). According to Fuller, rules of law should be general, promulgated, prospective, clear, non-contradictory, and relatively constant; they should not require the impossible; and there should be a congruence between the rules as promulgated and the rules as administered by the officials. There are two ways of interpreting this. On one view, the principles constituting the so-called "inner *morality*" of law are misleadingly characterised as such; for they are no more than the kind of considerations which would be taken into account by any competent legal official, anxious to secure the effective operation of the system. In other words, the Fullerian principles are principles of effectiveness, not principles of morality. The rival view, however, is that the characterisation is correct, the principles being of a moral nature.

Putting to one side Fuller's intentions, both interpretations can claim some degree of plausibility. For example, with regard to the principle that laws should take effect prospectively, what precisely is the objection to retroactive legal rules (at any rate, where such rules impose penalties)? Is it that retroactive rules are necessarily ineffective (because people cannot use them to guide their conduct)? Or, is it that such rules are perceived to be unfair, trapping those who, at the relevant time, were given no proper warning that they were violating the law? Neither account can be written off as absurd. (For a particularly interesting commentary on issues of retroactive application in recent case-law, see Harris, 2002). Similarly, in relation to the principle that the law should not require the impossible, consider the case of *R. v Larsonneur* (1933). Larsonneur, a French subject, having lawfully entered the United Kingdom, was required to leave no later than March 22, 1933. She complied with this requirement by going to the Irish Free State. However, the Irish authorities ordered her deportation and, in April 1933, the Irish police escorted her back to Holyhead where she was handed over to the English police. It was held that Larsonneur, being found in the United Kingdom after the date by which she had been required to leave, thus committed a criminal offence under the Aliens Order, 1920. If this decision seems objectionable, is it because it treats Larsonneur unfairly or because it violates a canon of effective regulation? Similarly, we might examine Fuller's other principles, in each case finding it equally possible to construct arguments both of effectiveness and of fairness in support of the particular principle. So, are the Fullerian principles to be read as a recipe for a functioning, by and large effective, order, or are they prescriptions for a fair legal order?

For Fuller, the answer is clear. The principles are not just about order, they are about just order. In Fuller's view, the crux of the inner morality is the principle of congruence, for this enshrines the idea of the Rule of Law, understood as a regime of fair play (of sticking to the rules) between legal officials and citizens. To underline this claim, Fuller invokes a distinction between law as a managerial enterprise and law as a reciprocal enterprise.

"Surely the very essence of the Rule of Law is that in acting upon the citizen (by putting him in jail, for example, or declaring invalid a deed under which he claims title to property) a government will faithfully apply rules previously declared as those to be followed by the citizen and as being determinative of his rights and duties . . .

The twin principles of generality and of faithful adherence by government to its own declared rules cannot be viewed as offering mere counsels of expediency. This follows from the basic difference between law and managerial direction; law is not, like management, a matter of directing other persons how to accomplish tasks set by a superior, but is basically a matter of providing the citizenry with a sound and stable framework for their interactions with one another, the role of the government being that of standing as a guardian of the integrity of this system." (1969, pp.209–10)

In the important case of _Bennett v Horseferry Road Magistrates' Court_ (1993), the House of Lords, operating with a distinctly Fullerian view, accepted that it was the responsibility of the judiciary "to oversee executive action and to refuse to countenance behaviour that threatens . . . the rule of law" (_per_ Lord Griffiths at 150). The question in _Bennett_ was whether it would be wrong to bring criminal proceedings (concerning alleged dishonesty in financing the purchase of a helicopter) against the appellant in circumstances where the English police, having traced the appellant (and the helicopter) to South Africa, did not initiate standard procedures for extradition—instead, the English police apparently colluded with their South African counterparts in having the appellant forcibly (and unknowingly) returned to England. For the majority of the House, this was such a clear abuse of process that, although the appellant could be assured of a fair trial in England, a stand had to be taken. As Lord Bridge put it (at 155):

"There is, I think, no principle more basic to any proper system of law than the maintenance of the rule of law itself. When it is shown that the law enforcement agency responsible for bringing a prosecution has only been enabled to do so by participating in violations of international law and of the laws of another state in order to secure the presence of the accused within the territorial jurisdiction of the court, I think that respect for the rule of law demands that the court take cognisance of that circumstance. To hold that the court may turn a blind eye to executive lawlessness beyond the frontiers of its own jurisdiction is, to my mind, an insular and unacceptable view."

Since *Bennett*, the House has underlined the extent of its duty to maintain the Rule of Law by adding "entrapment" (where law enforcement agents instigate the commission of a crime which would otherwise not have taken place) to its abuse of process jurisdiction (see *R. v Latif* (1996) and *R. v Loosely* (2001)).

Most recently, in one of the Belmarsh suspected terrorist cases, *A (FC) and others (FC) v Secretary of State for the Home Department* (2005), a seven-member panel of the House of Lords underlined the strength of its commitment to the Rule of Law. The question in this case was whether, in a context of heightened security and concerns about terrorist activities, the Special Immigration Appeals Commission (SIAC) may receive evidence which might have been procured by torture, the acts in question having been carried out by officials of a foreign State *without the complicity of the British authorities*. Of course, if British authorities had been complicit, there would be no support for such evidence being treated as admissible. However, there was a nice question where the evidence, so to speak, just fell into the hands of the British authorities. In a split decision, the Court of Appeal (2004) held that SIAC may receive such evidence. As Laws L.J. (in the majority) saw it:

"This case has concerned the means by which, in the acute setting created by the threat to the life of the nation which currently faces the United Kingdom, the State has sought to reconcile competing constitutional fundamentals. I do not say it has been done perfectly, or could not have been done better. But I do not think the executive or the legislature has at all lost sight of those constitutional principles which it is the court's special duty to protect: the rule of law, and the avoidance of arbitrary power." (para 282)

In other words, when the life of the nation is at stake, it would be an irresponsible exercise of power to stand on principles that might be applicable to less acute settings.

We might draw some parallels between the Court of Appeal's approach in *A (FC) and others (FC)* and its approach in *Burns* (2002)—a case where the alleged abuse concerned irregularities in deportation-cum-extradition proceedings leading to the appellant being returned from Venezuela to the United Kingdom to face charges relating to the importation of cocaine. On the facts of *Burns*, it was conceded that the Venezuelan authorities might not have acted in accordance with either local or international law; but, whilst the British authorities did nothing to discourage the Venezuelans from deporting Burns to the United Kingdom, they had not engineered the deportation or colluded with the Venezuelans in breaking the law—at worst, the British had allowed the Venezuelans to proceed in a way that suited British interests. Accordingly, the court held, there was no reason to think that by bringing Burns to trial (where he was duly sentenced to 14 years' imprisonment for importation of drugs plus 2 years for escaping from custody) the State had perpetrated an abuse of process that threatened the integrity of the system.

On the strength of these decisions, we might wonder whether, where the most serious and shocking of crimes are involved, the public interest in the integrity of the criminal justice system might be judged to be outweighed by the public interest in the apprehension of the most heinous of offenders—in other words, we might wonder whether the Rule of Law might be relaxed to make exceptions for the most serious of crimes (see, further, Ashworth, 2002, 108–118; and, generally, see Ch. 6). However, in *A (FC) and others (FC) v Secretary of State for the Home Department*, the Law Lords resoundingly dismiss any such thoughts: the integrity of the legal system remains paramount. As Lord Bingham puts it:

"It trivialises the issue before the House to treat it as an argument about the law of evidence. The issue is one of constitutional principle, whether evidence obtained by torturing another human being may lawfully be admitted against a party to proceedings in a British court, irrespective of where, or by whom, or on whose authority the torture was inflicted. To that question, I would give a very clear negative answer." (para.51)

Again, Lord Hoffmann is outright in his condemnation of torture and adamant that no system with Rule of Law commitments should touch evidence obtained by such means, even if, so far as the torture itself is concerned, the State has a clear conscience. Thus: "The use of torture is dishonourable. It corrupts and degrades the state which uses it and the legal system which accepts it" (para.82). The Fullerian principles, it seems, are alive and well at the highest level of the British judicial system—and, for those who argue that the judiciary need to have an unshakeable resolve in keeping faith with human rights and the vision of a just global order, this is indeed encouraging (see Brownsword, 2004; Kennedy, 2004; Gibb, 2005).

Whether one takes the view that the Fullerian principles represent the canons of effective management or the basis of a reciprocal moral compact between government and citizens, they offer an important watershed in our appreciation of the essential nature of law. For, even if governance in accordance with the (Fullerian) ideal of the Rule of Law does not meet the demands of all moral points of view, it is nevertheless transparent, calculable and accountable. On the one side, such governance is to be distinguished from regimes of pure terror and coercion—where the Rule of Law obtains, citizens at least know where they stand. On the other side, however, the Fullerian model of law does not align itself with any particular substantive morality. For Fullerians, law is to be identified with integrity of process, not with distinctive substantive values; law is to be defined in terms of its inner (procedural), not its "external" (substantive), morality.

These remarks take us to one of the central debates within legal theory, the debate between the legal positivists and the natural-law theorists. The nub of the dispute is the question of whether there is a necessary connection between the concept of law and the concept of morality. According to the legal positivist view—represented in the nineteenth century by such writers as Jeremy Bentham and John Austin, and in the twentieth century by such jurists as Hans Kelsen (1967), H.L.A. Hart (1961), and Joseph Raz (1979)—there is no such connection. As Austin succinctly put it: "The existence of law is one thing; its merit or demerit is another." (p.184) Of course, legal positivists do not deny that legal rules often coincide with moral principles, but they insist that such a connection with morality is not a necessary feature of the concept of law. Within legal positivism, a sharp line is to be drawn between legal validity and moral value, and between legal obligation and moral obligation. By contrast, in a tradition which stretches back to Aristotle and Aquinas, these "separation" theses are contested by natural-law theorists. Thus, hard-nosed natural-law theorists argue that legal validity is a species of moral validity, and legal obligation a species of moral obligation. Most dramatically, it is contended that no immoral rule should be regarded as a rule of law (see e.g. Beyleveld and Brownsword, 1986; 1994). Thus, putting this in Fullerian terms, whereas legal positivists view law as an exercise in managerial direction, natural-law theorists regard it as a reciprocal enterprise.

Whilst legal positivists regard Fuller as just confused or wrong, from the standpoint of Natural-Law Theory, he seems to be very much on the right track. However, as we have intimated, the more robust exponents of Natural-Law Theory may object that Fuller does not go far enough. For example, in a famous paper (Fuller, 1957–8), Fuller points out that, in Nazi Germany, the administration frequently relied upon secret rules and retroactive validation of acts taken by the Party; in short, the principles of the inner morality were regularly violated. Yet, would the position in Nazi Germany have been rectified legally speaking if the principles of the inner morality had been faithfully observed? Suppose that the purge of the Jews had taken place pursuant to prospective rules which had been promulgated. Some natural-lawyers would argue that such an immoral enterprise, despite its respect for the Fullerian principles, could not possibly qualify as a case of law.

Tying these ideas back to our concern about the notion of "law as authority", the position is as follows. If we adopt the legal positivist view, law is essentially a morally neutral functioning order. In line with this approach, acceptance of the secondary rules (or other legal phenomena) may be for any reason whatever, and legal rule structures are not necessarily compatible with any particular moral requirements. Thus, a legal positivist is able to reason that, just because a legal system has "authority" (i.e. is accepted), it does not follow that it is morally sound. By contrast, if we adopt a natural-law view, the essence of law is that it is a moral phenomenon, the legitimacy of which rests on its moral character. For a natural-law theorist, it is incoherent to believe that a morally illegitimate order can be legal, or have (moral) authority. On balance, Marxists might be expected to prefer the legal positivist view; for, whilst the natural-law position entertains the vision of a just order beyond existing regulatory orders (which idea certainly has appeal to some Marxists), it may be seen as something of a hostage to fortune, capable of being turned by ruling class apologists into an argument for the moral legitimacy of those existing orders which exercise coercion in the name of law (*cf.* Sypnowich, 1990).

7. FOUR CONCEPTIONS OF LAW

Our first steps towards conceptualising the field of law have unearthed two major dichotomies: first, whether law is to be characterised in formal or functional terms; and, secondly, whether law is to be characterised in morally neutral or moral terms. Arising from this, the concept of law may be formulated in one of four ways as follows:

(1) A formal morally neutral concept of law: for example, law may be conceptualised as a regime of rules (as Hart suggests), the rules (as legal positivists insist) having no necessary connection with morality.

(2) A functional morally neutral concept of law: for example, law may be conceptualised as an order seeking to perform various functions required for group life (as Llewellyn suggests), the order (as legal positivists insist) having no necessary connection with morality.

(3) A formal moral concept of law: for example, law may be conceptualised as a regime of rules (as Hart suggests), the rules (as natural lawyers insist) having a necessary connection with morality.

(4) A functional moral concept of law: for example, law may be conceptualised as an order seeking to perform various functions required for group life (as Llewellyn suggests), the order (as natural lawyers insist) having a necessary connection with morality.

As we have seen, the significance of different conceptualisations is that they offer competing frameworks for the classification of phenomena in the social world. Thus, if we apply a formal morally neutral concept of law, as in (1) above, to the field of our inquiry, we will treat the phenomena (i.e. modern so-called legal systems) as the paradigm of the concept of law. The modern practice of law, in other words, will seem co-extensive with the concept of law. By contrast, if we adopt a functional morally neutral concept of law, as in (2) above, we will treat the same phenomena as merely an instance (but not as the paradigm) of the concept of law. Of course, within such a conceptual framework, modern legal systems may be the paradigm of some other concept (e.g. as Weber suggests, of a particular type of domination), but they will not be the paradigm of the (broader) concept of law itself. The contrast becomes even stronger if we adopt either of the moral concepts of law (i.e. either (3) or (4) above), for these concepts will exclude from the category of law any rules or orders which fail to pass moral muster. Accordingly, within these morally-centred conceptual frameworks, there is no guarantee that those modern practices which we commonly call "law", and which represent the field of our inquiry, will be recognised as instances of law.

Alongside these four basic conceptual frameworks, we also have to reckon with the pluralist and Marxist views of law. To the extent that these views offer an account of how power is exercised in modern legal systems, they tend to presuppose a formal morally-neutral concept of law, as in (1) above. However, in principle, a pluralist or a Marxist could argue for a rival concept of law in which phenomena were grouped together depending upon the way in which power was exercised.

Again, to avoid any misunderstanding, it is worth reiterating the point we made at the outset, that conceptual choices are not to be confused with linguistic choices. Conceptualisation involves classifying phenomena, not making decisions about word-usage. The concepts we employ primarily shape the beliefs we hold, not the words we utter. Hence our concept of law determines our beliefs about whether or not a particular phenomenon qualifies as a case of law; and, as we have seen, different conceptual schemes generate different beliefs. If we were to continue with our attempts to conceptualise law, the next step would be to determine whether it is possible to make a reasoned choice between competing concepts of law. However, this raises complex philosophical questions which must await consideration in the next chapter.

8. DOES LAW HAVE A FUTURE?

On most conceptions of law, we think that it has both a present and a past; and we might think that law has an evolutionary trajectory that underlies its progression from the past to the present. Should we assume, though, that law has a future?

Recall Karl Llewellyn's law-jobs theory, according to which both simple and modern societies are seeking ways to regulate conduct, to channel behaviour towards certain acts and away from others. Different societies adopt different strategies for this purpose; and, indeed, in modern societies the State seeks to channel behaviour not simply by enacting legislation but also by tweaking the market or by fostering social pressure. For example, a law against smoking in public places might exist alongside a punitive tax on tobacco, a public information campaign that drills home the health hazards of smoking and background support for the pressure generated by the anti-smoking lobby. In the end, smokers might give up their habit not because of the legal restrictions but because of the cost, or concerns about their own health, or simply because of relentless peer pressure. If we conceive of law in a narrow Hartian way, we will say that law here exists alongside other measures of social control; if we conceive of law in broader functional terms, we might recognise all such measures as instances of law (or, possibly, "regulation").

Increasingly, however, the State relies on a quite different channelling strategy. What it tries to do is to design in the desired conduct or to design out undesired conduct. Where it proceeds in this way, the State does not attempt to give citizens reasons for acting in a particular way, the way that the State wants citizens to act is the only option that is available in practice. In his seminal book, *Code and Other Laws of Cyberspace* (1999), Lawrence Lessig identifies four modes of regulation, namely: the law, social norms, the market, and architecture (or, code). By way of an illustrative example, Lessig imagines that government wants to channel its citizens to wear seatbelts. It could proceed in more than one way, thus:

"It could pass a law to require the wearing of seatbelts (law regulating behavior directly). Or it could fund public education campaigns to create a stigma against those who do not wear seatbelts (law regulating social norms as a means to regulating behavior). Or it could subsidize insurance companies to offer reduced rates to seatbelt wearers (law regulating the market as a way of regulating behavior). Finally, the law could mandate automatic seatbelts, or ignition-locking systems (changing the code of the automobile as a means of regulating belting behavior). Each action might be said to have some effect on seatbelt use; each has some cost. The question for the government is how to get the most seatbelt use for the least cost." (93–94)

Now, if we imagine a high-tech future, it is conceivable that government might be able to channel conduct by a variety of such interventions. Some interventions might involve product design, or architectural features, or the development of intelligent environments, and the like. Others (and, here, we really are taking a leap) might involve coding citizens themselves (for example, by modifying their genetic make-up) so that they are disposed to act only in socially approved ways. With one step rapidly following another in taking forward both biotechnology and information and communication technology, and with significant developments in neurotechnology and nanotechnology, the prospect of a future of this kind is not altogether fanciful (see Brownsword, 2005)

What, though, does this have to do with the future of law? If we conceive of law in a way that embraces such technological fixes, we will continue to think that law regulates social life. However, law as we conceive of it today involves a definite engagement with the reasoning processes of its subjects; the Rule of Law is quintessentially about declaring the rules and administering them faithfully. If there is no longer any such declaration, because the technology is embedded, channelling seems to assume a radically different form. To be sure, if we want to apply the word "law" to such guiding and governing technology, we can do so. However, we should not kid ourselves: code really is something else.

2

THE IDEA OF UNDERSTANDING

An "understanding" of law is constituted primarily by an ability to conceptualise legal phenomena (*cf.* Ch.1), to account for the way in which law operates, and to evaluate its operation. In this chapter, we will elaborate upon this idea of understanding in three stages. First, we will distinguish between "questions of law" (roughly, questions calling for the exposition, interpretation, and application of legal materials) and "questions about law" (i.e. questions about any aspect of law and legal systems); secondly, we will consider a range of "first-order" inquiries about law (raising matters of description, explanation, evaluation, and conceptualisation); and, thirdly, we will sketch some "second-order" inquiries (i.e. inquiries concerning the status of our first-order understanding of law).

1. QUESTIONS OF LAW AND QUESTIONS ABOUT LAW

Where the study of law adopts a so-called "black-letter" approach, it concentrates narrowly on questions of law, on identifying and applying the relevant legal rules and principles to particular factual situations. But, what precisely is meant when it is said that a case raises "a question of law"? To answer this, we can look at two of the best known cases in English law, *R. v Dudley and Stephens* (1884) (which involved a question of criminal law) and *Donoghue v Stevenson* (1932) (which involved a question of civil law).

In *Dudley and Stephens*, the defendants were charged with the murder of a 17-year-old boy. They had been the crew of a yacht, the *Mignonette*, which had sunk in a storm on July 5, 1884, 1600 miles off the Cape of Good Hope. As a result, they had been compelled to put to sea in a small boat. This boat had no supply of food or water, except an 11 lb tin of turnips. They caught a turtle but, after the twelfth day, they had nothing left to eat. On July 24, it was proposed that lots should be cast as to who should be put to death to save the rest. The following day, the defendants determined to kill the boy (who was, by now, very weak). Dudley carried out this act, and the three remaining men fed on the body and blood of the boy for four days before being picked up by a passing vessel. It appeared that, if the men had not fed on the boy, they would probably not have survived, and the boy, being in a weak condition, was likely to have died before them. In other words, there was no appreciable chance of anyone surviving, unless one of the crew was killed and eaten by the survivors. Accordingly, the question of law for the court was whether killing in these circumstances was to be excused on the grounds of necessity. After an elaborate review of the authorities, going as far back as Bracton (*c.* 1210–68), Lord Coleridge C.J. concluded that the defence of necessity was not made out; the defendants, therefore, were guilty as charged.

Assuming that the defendants failed in *Dudley and Stephens* because the court rejected the very possibility of arguing a defence of necessity in murder cases, a host of questions of law— questions addressing what, in particular circumstances, the legal position might be—spring to mind. For example, if some passengers, trapped in a rapidly flooding part of a stricken vessel, were able to escape only by forcibly removing a person who, through fear, had frozen on the only ladder leading to safety, and if such forcible removal would result in the certain death of the person so removed, would a defence of necessity be available? In the light of *Dudley and Stephens*, presumably it would not. Yet, in *Re A (children)* (2000), the much-debated case of the conjoined twins, Jodie and Mary, where the Court of Appeal unanimously held that surgical separation would be lawful even though it would result in the death of Mary, Brooke LJ held that the medical team would have a defence based on necessity. According to Brooke LJ, the particular circumstances satisfied the test for necessity: the separation was needed to avoid inevitable and irreparable evil (the death of Jodie), it was no more than reasonably necessary for this purpose, and the evil inflicted (the death of Mary) was not disproportionate to the evil to be avoided (the death of both Jodie and Mary). It is true, of course, that the surgeons had no personal stake in this outcome (unlike the shipwrecked sailors) and that Mary was already a doomed life (akin, perhaps, to the person frozen on the ladder or a falling mountaineer); but, is the logic of Brooke LJ's approach that we should follow the Netherlands where, for many years, necessity has been treated as a defence to euthanasia carried out by doctors in accordance with approved medical criteria and guidelines? And, then, might the defence be available as an answer to a less serious charge (e.g. where a driver of an ambulance or a fire-engine committed a traffic violation), or in civil proceedings (e.g. if squatters were to cite their homelessness as a necessary reason for occupying vacant housing)? The decision in *Dudley and Stephens* also invites questions about the availability of defences which are similar to, but not identical with, necessity. For instance, what would have been the legal position in *Dudley and Stephens* if the boy had responded to Dudley's attack by killing him in self-defence? Or, what if Dudley had killed the boy under duress, one of the other crew members having threatened to kill him (i.e. Dudley) if he did not do the dirty deed? And, what if the threat had not been to kill Dudley, but to break his arm, or to burn his house down, or to kill one of Dudley's relatives (should the crew get back safely), and so on? From these various questions of law, we can turn to our second illustrative case, *Donoghue v Stevenson*, in which a quite different set of questions of law arose.

In *Donoghue*, a woman contracted gastroenteritis allegedly as a result of consuming a bottle of ginger beer, the drink having been purchased for her at a café in Paisley by a friend. She alleged that the ginger beer caused her illness because the bottle (which was opaque) contained the decomposed remains of a snail. Potentially, these facts gave rise to a number of questions of law. For example, did the woman have a claim against her friend, or against the café proprietors, or against the manufacturers of the drink? In the event, she chose to sue the manufacturers for £500, contending that the latter were negligent in that they had failed to take reasonable care to prevent snails or other noxious objects from getting into their products. In response, the manufacturers argued that, even if the facts as pleaded were true, they were still not liable to the pursuer. That is, the manufacturers maintained that, even if there had been a snail in the bottle, even if the woman's illness had been caused by the snail in the ginger beer, and even if proper precautions had not been taken at the factory, the law nevertheless did not require them to compensate the woman. Accordingly, the House of Lords (the supreme appeal tribunal for England, Wales, and Scotland) was asked to rule on the specific question of whether the law required a careless manufacturer of a product to compensate the ultimate consumer (or user) of the product where the consumer suffered illness or other personal injury. The House decided three to two in the pursuer's favour.

In his celebrated speech, expressing the majority view in *Donoghue*, Lord Atkin advanced a general answer to the question raised, the so-called "neighbour principle". The idea of this principle is that any person who fails to take reasonable care (whether this be a manufacturer of ginger beer or any other product, a repairer, a driver, a doctor, or whoever) is liable to compensate any injured "neighbour", the category of "neighbours" being those persons whom the careless party could reasonably foresee being so affected by his carelessness. In this sense, the pursuer in *Donoghue* was held to be a neighbour in relation to the manufacturers of the ginger beer. Although the neighbour principle answered the particular question raised on the facts of *Donoghue*, it opened the way to a further set of questions of law. In the light of the neighbour principle, what would be the position, for example, if the bottle of ginger beer had exploded, causing no physical injury to the purchaser or would-be consumer of the drink, but injuring another customer at the café? Or, what if the exploding ginger beer bottle caused no physical injury, but, instead, gave someone a nasty shock, or damaged someone's clothing or other property? Or, again, suppose that, in *Donoghue*, the pursuer's sole complaint was that the ginger beer had lost its "fizz". In principle, would a claim of this kind lie against the negligent manufacturers, or would this be a matter to be taken up (if at all) with the café proprietors?

No doubt, by fiddling around with the facts of *Dudley and Stephens* and *Donoghue*, many more questions of this kind could be formulated. However, the object of the exercise is not to draw up a comprehensive list of variations on the theme of either the shipwrecked sailors or the snail which may or may not have been in the ginger beer bottle, but to appreciate that, in each variation, our inquiry is directed at finding an answer to a question of law. In each case, in other words, we are inquiring about the legal position in relation to a specified factual situation. Now, to raise a question of law in this way is to pose a particular kind of question about law. When we consider what the legal position is in cases like *Dudley and Stephens* and *Donoghue* (and in hypothetical variations on such factual situations), our inquiry is directed at the materials associated with a particular legal system. However, this is not the only line of inquiry which may be pursued; and, indeed, the dominant theme of this book is precisely that we cannot hope to understand law if we limit ourselves simply to asking questions of this kind.

If, therefore, we return to *Dudley and Stephens* and *Donoghue*, what kind of questions about law (apart from questions of law) might these decisions prompt? Thinking about *Dudley and Stephens*, one obvious line of inquiry is to consider the merits of rejecting the defence of necessity. In the case itself, Lord Coleridge C.J. was emphatic about the defendants' obligations:

"To preserve one's life is generally speaking a duty, but it may be the plainest and the highest duty to sacrifice it. War is full of instances in which it is a man's duty not to live, but to die. The duty, in case of shipwreck, of a captain to his crew, of the crew to the passengers, of soldiers to women and children . . . these duties impose on men the moral necessity, not of the preservation, but of the sacrifice of their lives for others, from which in no country, least of all, it is to be hoped, in England, will men ever shrink . . ." (p.287)

Yet, this view was not uniformly shared in England, especially in nautical circles, where the custom amongst shipwrecked sailors in the dire straits of *Dudley and Stephens* was to draw lots as to who should be killed. Thus, many contemporaries thought that the defendants' real fault lay not so much in killing the boy, but in failing to follow the customary practice of drawing lots (see Simpson, 1984). From this standpoint, the decision to commute the death sentence imposed upon the defendants to a term of six months' imprisonment must have seemed eminently reasonable.

Similarly, we might question the merits of the majority view in *Donoghue*. In Lord Atkin's opinion, it would have been manifestly unjust if (assuming the facts were as pleaded) the pursuer were to be denied a remedy against the negligent manufacturers. But, would it actually have been so unjust to have decided against the pursuer? One of the central ideas of justice, surely, is the principle that "like cases should be treated alike". Prior to the decision in *Donoghue*, it is arguable that like injured parties were denied relief. So, as a matter of justice, should the House of Lords not have rejected the claim in order to maintain consistency with previous legal decisions? Moreover, it was argued by the dissenting Law Lords in *Donoghue* that, if the claim were allowed, it would be difficult to know where to draw the line on negligence actions in future. This could lead to injustice if judges failed to draw the line consistently in the same place. Further, it may be thought that Lord Atkin's reasoning was somewhat short-sighted. After all, if manufacturers were to be called to account for their negligence, might they not simply return to the customer their increased liability costs by raising the price of their products?

While we are pondering the merits of Lord Atkin's view, another thought may occur to us. Although the majority decision in *Donoghue* opens the door in principle for claims to be made against negligent manufacturers, it may not be that easy in practice to succeed in such a claim. If she had been put to proof, could the pursuer in *Donoghue* have shown on a balance of probabilities both that the manufacturers had failed to take reasonable care (that they were at fault in the legal sense) and that the consumption of the ginger beer had caused the gastroenteritis? For, without proof of both fault and cause, a claim in negligence will fail. This, of course, puts *Donoghue* in a somewhat different light. Whilst the decision in *Donoghue* undoubtedly assists present day pursuers or claimants in negligence, it appears that the law of negligence (requiring proof of both fault and cause) is pitched very much against pursuers and claimants. Accordingly, this raises the altogether larger question of whether it is right to make it so difficult for accident victims to recover. Why not make recovery easier for, say, the Thalidomide (or, more recently, the Opren) victims by dispensing with the fault requirement (*cf.* the Consumer Protection Act 1987)? Indeed, if we are dispensing with proof of fault, why not dispense with proof of cause too? Why not, for example, compensate children who are diagnosed as brain-damaged after vaccination, irrespective of whether it can be shown that the vaccine actually caused the brain damage? But, then, would a "no-fault no-cause" regime of this kind make sense in relation to accidents on the road or at work? Clearly, it would be a nonsense if victims of road accidents were able to recover compensation from any motorists who happened to be in the vicinity at the time—getting compensation to victims is one thing, determining *who* should bear the compensatory responsibility (and *why* and *on what terms*) is quite another (*cf.* Cane, 2002). Would it be more sensible, then, to follow the recommendation of the Pearson Royal Commission (Pearson, 1978) that road accident victims should be able to recover from an insurance fund financed by a small increase in the price of petrol?

In critically appraising *Dudley and Stephens* and *Donoghue*, and in thinking about the regulation of accident liability more generally, we are asking, not what the law is (in the sense of what the legal materials provide), but what the law ought to be. We might, however, address such matters in a rather different way. Our interest may lie in accounting for particular legal decisions, or for the emergence of particular legal doctrines at a particular time. For instance, why were the defendants in *Dudley and Stephens* brought to trial at all? In his fascinating study of the case, Brian Simpson (1984) reveals that the prosecution appears to have been partly the result of a dispute between the Admirality (who condoned the practice) and the Home Office (which did not). Equally, of course, we may be interested in the reasons why decisions not to prosecute are taken. For example, if—as many commentators believe—the law is "vigorously enforced against 'street criminals' [to whom we might add 'welfare scroungers' and shipwrecked sailors] but rarely applied to comparable corporate conduct" (Rudovsky, 1982, p.243), how do we account for this (*cf.* Cotterrell, 1984, Ch.8)? Turning to *Donoghue*, we may wonder why Lord Atkin decided in favour of the pursuer. Was it, as some suggest, because he discussed the case with his children who persuaded him of the simple justice of the pursuer's case (see Lewis, 1983)? Or, was it because he thought that the balance of the previous decisions lay in favour of the pursuer, or because he was conscious of developments in the law of negligence in the United States behind which English law was lagging? More generally, why do judges (similarly, other legal officials) make the decisions that they do? Do they act as "class warriors" handing down decisions which are consistent with the interests of ruling political and economic elites? Or, do they simply apply the law as they find it in the statutes and the precedents, or perhaps, like Plato's philosopher-kings, exercise independent judgment as to the rightness of a decision?

Similarly, we may question the reasons underlying a particular doctrinal development. For example, one feature of the law of negligence at the time of *Donoghue* was the so-called doctrine of "common employment". According to this doctrine, where one employee was injured at work as a result of the negligence of a fellow employee, the injured employee was unable to recover compensation from the employer (the employer otherwise being liable for the negligence of his employees under the principle of vicarious liability). Since accidents are to be expected at workplaces, and since such accidents will often be caused by the carelessness of a fellow employee, the doctrine of common employment seems extraordinarily harsh. How, then, might we account for its emergence and continued existence until well into the twentieth century (albeit in a somewhat modified form)? One view is that the doctrine of common employment and the law of negligence generally had to be framed in a way which would not retard the industrialisation of modern societies. If the law had been too safety-conscious, railways, canals, and the like, would not have been built so readily. Favourably interpreted, therefore, the law was designed to promote the longer-term public interest; interpreted less favourably, the explanation lay in the law serving the interests of the entrepreneurial classes (*cf.* Horwitz, 1977). Another view altogether, however, is that the explanation is more complex, lying in the conjunction of changing expectations (as fatalistic world views give way to more modern outlooks) together with the development of economic infrastructures (both private and State) able to meet expectations of compensation, and the law, somewhat belatedly, catching up with both.

To sum up, any attempt to understand law must establish a list of questions about legal systems. What is wrong with blackletterism is not that it fails to ask any questions about law, but that it concentrates too narrowly on just one such type of question, questions *of* law. Our field of inquiry must be opened up. Questions of evaluation and explanation, as we have seen, are just as much questions about law and are integral to our attempt to make sense of the practice. Moreover, we must consider the work of philosophers and sociologists, economists and historians, anthropologists and psychologists, and the like; for their questions, when focused on law, are our questions too.

2. FIRST-ORDER INQUIRIES

Black-letterism concentrates on the law as it is, not as it ought to be, nor on why it came to be as it is. However, to say that blackletterism is concerned with describing the operation of law would be to overstate its scope; for, what it purports to describe is the content of the formal legal materials (the content of the relevant statutes and precedents, and so on), not the operation of these materials in practice. Indeed, the standard criticism of black-letterism is not so much that it ignores questions of evaluation, explanation, and conceptualisation, but that it only partially describes the practice of law by screening off everything except the formal rules. In this section, we will consider the range of first-order inquiries which must structure any serious attempt to get to grips with law, but which are excluded from the black-letter lawyer's terms of reference.

(i) Description

Black-letterism, as we have just remarked, is commonly criticised as attempting only a partial description of the operation of law. Often, this criticism is expressed by saying that black-letterism overlooks the problem of the "gap", the possible disjunction between the law-in-the-books and the law-in-action. In some instances, the gap may be obvious. For example, we do not assume that everyone observes the rules of the criminal law: the law-in-the-books may prohibit murder, theft, rape, and so on, but we all know that crimes of this kind nevertheless are committed. Compare with this, however, our assumption that, even if criminals do not observe the law-in-the-books, police officers at least surely stick to the rules, complying with the procedures laid down by law when stopping and searching, arresting and questioning suspects. Researchers of police behaviour offer mixed reports about such matters (see e.g. White, 1991, Chs 3 and 4); but, for present purposes, it is unnecessary for us to consider this further. The point is that we cannot begin to understand the operation of the criminal justice system unless we know not only what the relevant law-in-the books prescribes, but also what actually happens in practice. To avoid any misunderstanding, we should say, of course, that this need for empirical investigation applies to all aspects of the operation of law, not exclusively in relation to the criminal justice system. Moreover, we are not implying that, if empirical research reveals a persistent disjunction between prescription and behaviour, we should necessarily alter the prescription—simply that we have taken a first step towards understanding the complex relationship between prescription and behaviour.

Descriptions of legal phenomena may be at different levels of generality. Some descriptions may be quite concrete. For example, in the most important English study of the choices made by defendants in the magistrates' courts (Bottoms and McClean, 1976), the researchers amassed a wealth of detailed information about the outcomes of the various choices made by the defendants observed. They provide many tables giving facts and figures, which reveal, inter alia, that over ninety per cent of the defendants in question elected to plead guilty to the charges. Other descriptions, however, may be pitched at quite an abstract level. For example, researchers may set up a range of "ideal-types" (like Weber's ideal-types of legitimate domination, or the *Gesellschaft* and *Gemeinschaft* models of society and of law, *cf.* Ch.1), the object of which is to facilitate the description of complex phenomena (by relating them to certain abstract features embodied in the ideal-types). An excellent example of this kind of approach is to be found in the work of Herbert Packer (1969). Packer, and many writers since him, have employed two ideal-types, the "crime control" and the "due process" models, to structure their descriptions of the criminal justice system (*cf.* King,

1981). Basically, the fewer the safeguards built in against the risk of convicting the innocent, the more a system will fit the model of crime control—the greater the safeguards, the more it will fit due process. (For further discussion of ideal-types as conceptual-descriptive resources, see pp.45–46).

Up to a point, the importance of descriptive inquiries is self-evident, for, without the benefit of empirical studies (predictable though their results sometimes may be), our knowledge of the operation of law is incomplete and unconfirmed. Moreover, the results of such studies may serve to rectify ("debunk", as some would put it) false assumptions which have hitherto been made about the practice. It should also be borne in mind, however, that descriptive inquiries may prompt evaluative and explanatory questions; for, once we discern how some aspect of the law *is*, we may feel compelled to consider whether this is really as it *ought to be* (i.e. evaluate the state of affairs), and to examine *how it came to be the way it is* (i.e. explain the state of affairs).

(ii) Evaluation

An evaluation of some feature of the legal system may be concerned with either its effectiveness or its moral legitimacy. For instance, suppose that, in an attempt to stop abortions, the law were changed so that it became a criminal offence for a person to carry out, or to have, an abortion. Some might condemn this on the grounds that it would simply drive women into the hands of back-street abortionists. Others, however, might condemn the law on the grounds that, effectiveness or ineffectiveness apart, it is immoral to interfere with a woman's freedom to have an abortion. Clearly judgments of effectiveness call for a rather different kind of inquiry to judgments of legitimacy. Evaluations of the former kind can only be reasoned where an impact study has been conducted, or where experience enables us to anticipate the likely impact. Evaluations of the latter kind, however, are quite another matter, and it is upon such moral judgments that we shall now concentrate.

Moral reasoning, in modern times, displays a fundamental tension between two schools of thought, the "teleological" and the "deontological". According to the teleological approach, an action is morally right if it promotes (at least as well as any alternative action) some specified goal. In principle, there are as many teleological theories as there are specifications of the goal to be promoted. However, by far the best known teleological position is Utilitarianism, which holds that actions are morally legitimate provided that they maximise "utility". In Jeremy Bentham's classical exposition of Utilitarianism, this means that the morally correct action is the one that produces the greatest net balance of pleasure over pain. It should perhaps be noted that although the slogan "the greatest happiness of the greatest number" has come to be associated with Bentham, this is not a wholly accurate representation of his brand of Utilitarianism. For, whilst classical Utilitarianism certainly aims for the greatest happiness, it places no restrictions on the way in which this happiness is distributed—happiness, in other words, does not have to be spread across the greatest number. In opposition to the teleologists, and particularly to Utilitarianism, there are a number of deontological positions. For the deontologist, a moral position is built around respect for the individual, not collective goals. Thus, deontologists generally start with Immanuel Kant's famous injunction to treat others always as ends and never simply as a means, this yielding a range of principles specifying an individual's prima facie rights and duties. Although modern deontologists, like John Rawls (1972), Ronald Dworkin (1978), and Alan Gewirth (1978), tend to emphasise rights rather than duties, the golden thread in deontological approaches is that goals cannot legitimately be pursued where this involves violating an individual's rights or duties. In Dworkin's evocative terminology, the rights of an individual act as "trumps" when the moral cards are played.

One of the standard illustrations (an illustration, it should be said, designed to present Utilitarianism in an adverse light) of the difference between a utilitarian and a right-and-duty approach concerns the legitimacy of framing an innocent scapegoat. The utilitarian argument is that, in order to maintain public confidence in the criminal justice system, it may sometimes be legitimate to arrest, and put up for trial, persons whom the authorities know could not have committed the crime. Indeed, at the time of the highly publicised release of those convicted as IRA terrorists for pub bombings in Guildford and Birmingham, the question was put, in a distinctly utilitarian spirit, if it would not really be better to refuse to re-open cases of this kind, even though innocent persons might have to remain in custody. Against this, a right-and-duty approach would insist that, irrespective of any utility flowing from such a victimisation, the State has no right to act in this way; for a more blatant example of treating someone simply as a means could scarcely be found.

Whilst it may be thought that innocent scapegoats figure more in the conjectures of *Guardian* readers than in the cells of English prisons, it is arguable that our criminal justice system is geared in such a way that unintentional victimisations occur a little too frequently for comfort. For example, in their defendants' study, Bottoms and McClean (1976) estimated that eighteen per cent of the guilty-pleaders might have been innocent of at least one of the relevant charges. If, in fact, the design of our criminal justice system means that cases are processed reasonably efficiently, but at the price of routinely convicting some innocent defendants, a utilitarian may judge that such arrangements are legitimate (and, indeed, will so judge if no alternative design of the criminal justice system promises to promote as much utility). On the other hand, anyone who takes the rights of individuals seriously will reject this kind of justification. Innocent persons have a right not to be convicted, and it simply will not do to argue that, by and large, the system works quite well, or that it would be expensive or inconvenient to effect improvements.

Recently, an important debate has begun concerning the breadth of police powers to take DNA samples from suspects and then to retain such samples in the National DNA Database (see, e.g. Kennedy 2004). Broadly speaking, under a clutch of controversial legislative provisions, the police may take a DNA sample from anyone who is arrested and detained (other than in connection with traffic offences). Furthermore, the sample that has been taken may be retained even though the person is not actually prosecuted or, if prosecuted, is acquitted. Hence, the National DNA Database, which already holds several million DNA profiles, includes a significant number of profiles of persons who have come into contact with the police but who are "innocent". The breadth of these powers offends civil libertarians, who note the far more restrictive powers generally available elsewhere in Europe; and, while the profile itself does not disclose sensitive (e.g. medical) information about the individual, the underlying sample (which is also retained) has such potential and, thus, raises questions about respect for an individual's right to privacy. Having said this, there is no doubting the utility of the collection in general (profiles of individuals being compared with samples collected from crime scenes both to eliminate and to identify suspects) and the retained profiles in particular, these having been linked with a significant number of murders, attempted murders, rapes, sexual offences, aggravated burglaries, and offences relating to the supply of drugs. In *R v Chief Constable of South Yorkshire*

Police, ex parte LS and Marper (2004), the House of Lords held that section 82 of the Criminal Justice and Police Act 2001, which authorises retention of the samples (both fingerprints and DNA samples) even where there is no prosecution or there is an acquittal, is compatible with the rights of privacy and non-discrimination as protected by the European Convention on Human Rights. However, their Lordships, although unanimous in the result, were not entirely at one on the question of whether the privacy right was engaged—whether or not a DNA profile that identifies a person (possibly linking a particular person to a particular crime scene) should be treated as information about that person is a nice point. At all events, the case has been taken on appeal to Strasbourg where the judgment of the European Court of Human Rights is awaited with interest.

By way of a footnote to *R v Chief Constable of South Yorkshire Police*, it is worth saying that, while our present concern is with the tension between utilitarian and right-and-duty thinking, DNA profiling and the like pose difficult questions even if respect for rights is the only criterion. On the one side, non-consensual taking and retention of samples might violate privacy rights; but, on the other side, the gains in police intelligence mean that rights to life and personal integrity, to property, and even to privacy might be more effectively protected. Faced with such a tension, it will not suffice to say that the National DNA Database has utility; rather a judgment has to be made about the relative importance of the rights involved, the necessity for impinging on a right (which is always a matter for regret), and the proportionality of the response (whether it is appropriate, for instance, to retain the profiles indefinitely).

Although the tension between goal-based and right-and-duty-based reasoning is particularly vivid in cases concerning the rights of suspects, it should not be thought that this phenomenon is restricted to the criminal justice system. The legal system, in all its facets, is riddled with this tension. Consider, for example, the dilemma faced by the courts in *Equal Opportunies Commission v Birmingham City Council* (1989). The question, there, was whether Birmingham City Council, as the local education authority, was in violation of the Sex Discrimination Act 1975. At the centre of this dispute were the eight single-sex selective grammar schools remaining in Birmingham (the council's general policy being to have non-selective secondary schools). Five of the grammar schools were for boys (admitting 542 pupils), and three for girls (admitting 360 pupils). It followed that it was more difficult for a girl than a boy to win a place at one of the grammar schools. Although the council was aware of this disparity, its intention was not to discriminate in favour of boys—it simply could see no satisfactory way of rectifying the disparity. To build another grammar school for girls would be wasteful when, with school rolls falling, there were already too many places for pupils in secondary schools; to alter the mix at the grammar schools would involve difficult dealings with the school governors; and to reduce the places for boys, down to 360, would prejudice the boys without assisting the girls. As Dillon L.J. put it:

"In truth the council's position really is that they are knowingly continuing their acts of maintaining the various boys' and girls' selective schools, which inevitably results in discrimination against girls in the light of the great disparity in the numbers of places available, because the only alternatives open to the council, even with the consent of the Secretary of State, are unattractive or difficult to apply." (1988, at 856).

Whilst sympathetic to the practical difficulties confronting the council, the Appeal Courts ruled in favour of the EOC, their Lordships being adamant that the girls in Birmingham had a right to enjoy the same educational opportunities as the boys, and that the courts had no dispensing power to relieve the council of its statutory duty. In short, Birmingham's utilitarian arguments were overridden by the rights of the girls.

The tension between utilitarian and right-and-duty approaches will be one of the recurring themes in the later chapters of this book, and its implications for judicial reasoning in particular is a matter to which we will return in Chapters 4 and 5.

(iii) Explanation

To demand an "explanation" from someone is sometimes to seek a justification rather than a causal account of that person's actions. For instance, if we were to ask a youth who had just smashed some windows to explain (meaning, justify) his actions, our demand would be that the window-breaker should offer good reasons (not any old reasons) justifying his conduct. Accordingly, if he responded that—like Belloc's John Vavassour de Quentin Jones—he was simply fond of throwing stones, we might regard this as a pretty poor justification (although a utilitarian might have to think twice about this); but at least the thrust of our question would seem to have been understood. Our concern in this section is not primarily with explanation in the sense of justification (for this takes us back to questions of evaluation), but with explanation in the sense of identifying the processes which result in some action or state of affairs (i.e. in our hypothetical case, with accounting for the youth's actions in breaking the window).

Whatever its particular focus, explanatory inquiry seeks to isolate background conditions and proximate causes so that the phenomenon in question is better understood. Of course, this quest for understanding is not entirely academic. If we understand why some event occurs, we may be able to make such an event happen again (where we make a positive judgment about the event), or we may be able to prevent such an event recurring (where we make a negative judgment about the event). In this sense, knowledge is power, the power to control social situations, and (possibly) to engineer social change through the law (but, for the limits of law's "engineering" potential, see e.g. Roshier and Teff, 1980, Ch.6; and Jenkins, 1980).

Where some major occurrence is regarded as "deviant" or "pathological" (e.g. disturbances in prisons or on the streets), an explanation will be demanded as a matter of urgency. Official investigators (who, often, will be senior judges) will be charged with isolating the causes and making recommendations with a view to preventing any repetition of the events. Lord Scarman's Report (Home Office, 1981), following his inquiry into the inner-city riots of 1981 (particularly in Brixton and Toxteth), is a model of this kind of explanatory enterprise. Scarman identified a background of inadequate housing, high unemployment, poor social amenities, poor educational opportunities, and so on. Into this cocktail of inner-city deprivation, stir a deteriorating relationship between the police and the public, together with a particularly aggressive style of policing, and the ingredients for a riot are nearly complete. On this view, all that is required now is some kind of "flashpoint" and disturbances will follow. Given this diagnosis, Scarman recommended that steps should be taken to re-establish a proper background relationship between the police and the policed (to re-establish policing by consent), to avoid flashpoints by increasing police awareness of the need for sensitive policing of inner-city communities (e.g. by striking a sensible balance between strict enforcement of the law and the need to maintain order), and to ameliorate the conditions of inner-city life.

Essentially, three kinds of factors are regularly highlighted in explanatory accounts. These are human biology (increasingly, one suspects, emphasising human genetics), the mental states of individual actors (encompassing an actor's attitudes and beliefs, his reasons for action, and psyche), and the social setting for action (including interaction with other actors, social status and role, and background social structures). On occasion, the explanatory emphasis is very much on "human nature", rather as some nineteenth-century criminologists contended that the causes of crime lay in human physiology, in the "born criminal". Modern explanatory accounts, however, tend to rely more often on either the mental states of various actors involved, or background structures and constraints. Of course, the explanatory background may be pitched at varying levels of generality. In the case of the Scarman Report, as we have seen, the explanatory context is relatively local, the social and economic setting in Brixton (in 1981). However, the context could be set at a more concrete level (e.g. as when Scarman describes the flashpoint events), or at a much more general level. Marxists, for example, operate within a very general explanatory framework, namely the structure of classes (membership of which is determined by one's position in relation to the means of production) and class conflict. From such a Marxist perspective, the particular context for the Brixton riots is relatively unimportant. Riots are to be explained in terms of an upsurge in revolutionary class-consciousness (and, of course, in this framework, riots are not at all to be seen as "pathological").

Although inquirers may lay particular emphasis on one or other of the basic explanatory factors, this is not to say that inquirers never mix their strategies. Indeed, many would argue that only a "rounded" explanation, involving a combination of strategies, is adequate. Thus, in their study of the magistrates' courts, Bottoms and McClean (1976) explain guilty-pleading from two perspectives—the defendants' own reasons for pleading guilty and the cultural context of the courts. From the former perspective, the phenomenon of defendants pleading guilty seems relatively straightforward, the majority saying that they so pleaded either because they were guilty (or, similarly, because they were caught red-handed), or because the police had a good case (or, similarly, because they had confessed to the police). Although ten per cent of the defendants said that they pleaded guilty in order "to get it over with quietly with less fuss", seven per cent because they were acting "on [their] lawyer's advice", and five per cent because they hoped "to get a lighter sentence", these reasons do not—at least, not in these numbers—suggest anything seriously amiss. However, once the contextual perspective is brought into play, matters seems less straightforward. What Bottoms and McClean suggest is that defendants in the criminal process find themselves caught in a cross-current of occupational cultures. On the one hand, the police endeavour to process suspects through to conviction as efficiently as possible; on the other hand, the personnel in the courts, while committed in principle to the ideal of a fair hearing, are under pressure to keep cases moving so that there is no serious backlog of business. In practice, this means that, in addition to the police attempting to channel suspects towards a guilty plea (by pressing for a statement or admission to be made), the courts offer various incentives for guilty-pleaders (most significantly, the prospect of a reduced sentence, the so-called "sentencing discount"). This structural account puts the reasons offered by guilty-pleaders in a rather different light. In particular, it suggests that those defendants who pleaded guilty because they had confessed, or because the police seemed to have a good case, might have been caught in the structural (crime control) currents; whereas, those who pleaded guilty to take advantage of the sentencing discount, and who acted on their lawyer's advice, might have seen the sense of swimming with, rather than against, the "bureaucratic" tide.

Finally, we should note a general issue about explanation which generates a cluster of difficult questions. Our interest is in explaining conduct which is associated with the operation of law (e.g. why defendants plead guilty, why magistrates give particular sentences, why prisoners and residents of inner-city areas sometimes riot, and so on). Although these phenomena take place within the physical world (the laws of gravity apply just as much in the magistrates' courts and in Brixton as elsewhere on our planet), our interest is in human behaviour as a social phenomenon (i.e. in the conduct of human beings located in particular social and cultural contexts). The general question, therefore, is whether explanations of such phenomena have the same formal characteristics as explanatory accounts of the behaviour of physical phenomena, where, rightly or wrongly, a certain model of "scientific explanation" is presupposed. Basically, this model envisages that an explanation will identify a cause and effect relationship between phenomenon PC and phenomenon PE, thereby yielding a scientific law of the form, "If PC, then PE". To what extent is this model applicable to the explanation of legal phenomena?

Certainly, some explanatory statements about the practice of law invite comparison with the scientific model. For example, some research suggests that during periods of economic recession crimes against property (including rioting) increase while, if anything, crimes of violence abate. It is tempting to convert such claims into either weak law-like statements of the form "If PC, then the probability of PE is raised", or into strong law-like statements of the form "If PC, then PE". If "PC" stands for a particular contextual or structural phenomenon, whereas a weak law-like statement implies that individual actors retain some autonomy, the entailment of a strong law-like statement is that the particular background conditions strictly determine conduct (i.e. render the occurrence of PE unavoidable). This raises a veritable hornet's nest of difficulties. For our purposes, however, what needs to be emphasised is simply that a hard-nosed structural-determinist approach undermines the significance of an action-based explanation. The point is that, if an actor's mental set merely reflects the outlook embodied in some (determining) background structure, the agent is not only not in control of his actions, his reasons are not the key to explaining his conduct. However, so long as matters of this kind remain controversial, inquirers who wish to play it safe must hedge their bets by considering both reasons for action and the impingement of background structures; while inquirers who believe that reasons and purposes are the key to explaining human social conduct must emphasise the "interpretive" nature of their enterprise and, possibly, take refuge in the idea that rational action is its own explanation (*cf.* Hollis, 1977; and see further p.42, and Ch.10).

(iv) Conceptualisation

We can deal with conceptualisation quite briefly. As we have seen (*cf.* Ch.1), a conceptual scheme is basically a classificatory framework. Hence, if we were to conceive of law as, say, "a, by and large effective, regime of primary and secondary rules, the rules having any content whatsoever", then we could sort out into the categories of "law" and "non-law" the various so-called legal systems of the world. Thus, on this basis, we might classify the legal systems of, say, Ancient Rome, the European Community, and the United States as clear examples of law. In this category, we might also include the legal system of Nazi Germany (immorality not counting against legal status), but we might exclude so-called international law (because of its inadequate secondary rule structure).

How, then, do conceptual schemes relate to schemes of ideal-types which, as we saw earlier on in this chapter, may be employed for descriptive purposes? Whilst some writers may wish to discriminate between "concepts" and "ideal-types", or reserve the label "ideal-type" for theoretical constructs which are precisely of the kind envisaged by Max Weber, for our purposes, concepts and ideal-types may be regarded as identical. It follows, therefore, that, if we had so wished, we could have presented the question in the previous chapter as one about an ideal-type (not a concept) of law, and we could have talked in this chapter about the concepts (not the ideal-types) of crime control and due process. More importantly, it follows that conceptual and ideal-typical schemes are equally concerned with classification and description of phenomena.

Whilst concepts and ideal-types are primarily descriptive and classifactory theoretical resources, they are not irrelevant to evaluative and explanatory lines of inquiry. Some concepts (e.g. "justice", "democracy", "freedom", and so on) pretty obviously bear an evaluative connotation. It is possible, of course, to declare that concepts of this kind are employed in a value-neutral way; but such a disclaimer apart, the assumption must be that such concepts are value-laden. Accordingly, if someone presents a concept of, say, democracy, and then classifies the political system in the United Kingdom as an instance of democracy, we assume that this both classifies the political system and signifies approval of it. In other words, the social facts under such a conceptualisation are neither theory-neutral, nor value-free. Perhaps this serves to draw more sharply into focus, the debate between the legal positivists and the natural-law theorists about the concept of law. Whereas the legal positivist concept of law is value-neutral, the natural-law concept is value-laden (giving law a positive valuation). Thus, when natural-lawyers classify phenomena as instances of "law" or "non-law", their classificatory descriptions bear a necessary evaluative connotation (positive or negative as the case may be).

Concepts and evaluations may become entwined in a rather different way. If we wish to evaluate a particular legal doctrine, this will often involve analysis of key conceptual components. For example, we might ask whether the legal concepts of *"mens rea"* (criminal intent, see Ch.6), "insanity" and "diminished responsibility", or the classification of epilepsy as a case of "insanity", or the doctrine that confessions (to be admissible in evidence) must have been given "voluntarily", are adequate in the light of a psychologist's understanding of these matters (see e.g. Blackman, 1981; Hill and Griffiths, 1982; Irving and Hilgendorf, 1980). Or, we might ask whether the legal concept of "causation" makes sense to a philosopher; or whether the concept of "economic duress" in the law of contract is intelligible to an economist, and so on. In other words, conceptual clarification may often be a prerequisite for, or an accompaniment to, doctrinal evaluation.

Concepts and ideal-types may also impinge in various ways upon explanatory inquiries. Recall, for example, Weber's typology of legitimate domination, each ideal-typical category of which reflects a particular kind of reason for respecting the authority of another and complying with his decrees. To determine whether a general situation of compliance, or a particular relationship of submission, is an instance of one of the ideal-types, it is essential to inquire into the thinking of those who claim authority and those who comply. In itself, such an inquiry does not explain anything. However, if one believes that reasons are a key factor in explaining conduct, then the application of Weber's typology not only classifies relationships of legitimate domination, it also suggests an explanation of the conduct of those who comply.

Finally, we can pick up and develop our earlier remark that reason-centred explanatory strategies may try to keep structural-determinism at arm's length by elaborating the idea of "rational action as its own explanation". Suppose, for example, that we go along with the natural-law view that so-called legal officials (judges, legislators, and the like) only truly act as legal officials (properly conceived) where they act in a morally appropriate fashion. As we have already seen, natural-law classifications and descriptions are rolled up with evaluations. However, they are also rolled up with explanations, for where a natural-lawyer classifies an official as having acted legally, this conceptualisation of the situation does three things: it describes the situation ("This is a case of law, or legal conduct"); it evaluates the conduct ("This official has behaved as he ought to behave, i.e. rationally"); and it explains the conduct ("This official has behaved rationally, as he ought to; therefore, his conduct requires no explanation—i.e. rational action is its own explanation"). In view of this, we should end this section with a caution: whilst it is helpful, for expository purposes, to separate out the various first-order questions, it does not follow either that first-order theorising can be neatly divided up into pigeonholes, or that theorists will share the same understanding of the relationships between the various first-order lines of inquiry.

3. SECOND-ORDER INQUIRIES

If readers expected the enterprise of understanding law to be a relatively simple matter of digging out the facts, they might be concerned about two aspects of our discussion. First, understanding law seems to call for a complex multi-disciplinary approach, drawing on the work of philosophers, sociologists, psychologists, historians, economists, and the like. Secondly, there seems to be a possibility that there might be precious few facts (or, at any rate, facts of any significance or interest) to be extracted. Taking up this second concern, the point is that all the interesting statements about law seem to be theory-dependent (and, in some cases, value-dependent too), dependent upon particular conceptual, evaluative, and explanatory frameworks. And, the problem is that, wherever we look, there are competing views about the appropriate theoretical frameworks for the pursuit of particular first-order questions.

Now, if particular accounts of legal phenomena depend upon the particular theoretical frameworks employed, a number of second-order questions present themselves. Such second-order questions invite reflection on the nature of our first-order understanding—a second-order understanding, as it were, of our first-order understanding. For example, to what extent can statements about law be true or false? To what extent can we have knowledge of legal phenomena? To be blunt, can our first-order understanding of law have any independent, or objective, validity? As a way of locating the many positions which can be taken in response to questions of this kind, two broad distinctions may be helpful. First, we can distinguish between those positions which maintain that it is possible to gain knowledge about legal phenomena by direct sense-experience (i.e. without the mediation of any theoretical framework) as opposed to those positions which accept that theoretical frameworks must be employed. This distinction, in other words, is between those who argue that there are theory-free facts in this field and those who deny this proposition. Secondly, amongst those who accept that there are no theory-neutral facts in relation to law, we can distinguish between those who argue that theoretical frameworks have only relative validity ("relativists") and those who maintain that they have absolute (or categorical, or objective) validity ("absolutists").

Dealing with the first of these distinctions, the implicit thrust of our discussion has been very much in favour of those who argue that social facts (including facts about law) are theory-dependent. To be sure, some factual statements may be relatively uncontroversial. However, it seems to us that even the simplest descriptive statements about law presuppose a stock of conceptual resources. Accordingly, the more important distinction is between the relativists and the absolutists, amongst whom it is common ground that there can be no understanding without theory, that legal facts are theory-dependent.

For a relativist, the adoption of a particular theoretical framework is, in the final analysis, a matter of choice, commitment, or preference. Particular theoretical frameworks (as between one another) are optional; one theoretical framework is no more valid than any other. On the relativist view, rival conceptual frameworks (e.g. Legal Positivism or Natural-Law Theory), rival evaluative frameworks (e.g. deontological or teleological), rival explanatory strategies (e.g. action-based or structural), are all equally valid perspectives. Accordingly, for the relativist, inquiries into the practice of law are capable of yielding only true statements, knowledge and facts, relative to a chosen theoretical framework—right answers, in other words, are right relative only to the particular theoretical framework within which the answers are generated. Although relativism entails that there is no way of conclusively arbitrating between competing theoretical perspectives, it should not be thought that this entails that there can be no serious assessment of the credentials of particular theories. For example, it is open to self-conscious relativists (or to those who, for the sake of argument, are prepared to concede relativism) to assess a particular theory by a process of so-called "immanent critique". This strategy basically involves drawing out contradictions within a theory (or between one part of an overall theoretical position and another), or teasing out some "questionable" implications of a position. Faced with such contradictions or questionable implications, one is invited to revise one's position; but, of course, given relativism, this can be no more than an invitation, albeit a persuasive one. By contrast, an absolutist holds that it is possible to arbitrate between competing theoretical frameworks, from which it follows that certain theoretical positions are rationally justifiable (i.e. correct), that proponents of rival theoretical positions can meaningfully debate the correctness of particular positions, and that correct theoretical positions, if correctly employed, will yield true statements and unqualified right answers.

Against this backcloth of relativism and absolutism, arguments in favour of particular theories assume many forms, resting on a variety of practical or yet further theoretical considerations. It may be argued, for example, that certain sorts of explanatory frameworks must be preferred (or must be correct) because they produce law-like statements which "work", in the sense that they enable us to predict the outcomes of particular situations (or enable us to intervene effectively in such situations). Or, again, it may be argued that various practical (political) considerations weigh in favour of certain conceptual positions (as, for instance, it is commonly argued in favour of Legal Positivism that it fosters a constructively critical view of the operations of governments). Alternatively, it may be argued that certain theoretical considerations offer reasons in favour of a particular theoretical position. Some moral philosophers, Alan Gewirth (1978) and R.M. Hare (1981) for example, have argued that our thinking involves contradictions if we do not adopt particular moral positions; and this kind of reasoning can be extended into a defence of particular conceptual and explanatory frameworks. Whether or not such ambitious defences can be made out, however, remains a highly controversial question (see further Ch.10).

Finally, it should be said that, throughout the last century, absolutist positions have been very much on the defensive. Indeed, relativism (sometimes shading off into nihilism) is quite clearly the dominant view today. Whilst the sceptical attitude which underpins relativism may be welcomed as an antidote to dogmatism and intolerance, its bottom line is stark: the idea of objective understanding is illusory, and, immanent critique apart, we can basically believe whatever we like about law. In other words, if we follow the relativist line, one person's understanding of law must be seen as precisely that—one person's understanding, and nothing more (see Fish, 1994).

3

LEGAL INSTITUTIONS AND THE RULE OF LAW

The institutional framework of the English legal system can be stated straightforwardly (if crudely) as follows. Parliament performs a legislative function (by enacting statutes and statutory instruments), the courts perform a judicial function by resolving disputes under the law and laying down precedents (see Chs 4 and 5). The judiciary is independent, but judicial decisions can be reversed by Parliament and statutes take priority over precedents in the case of conflict. Subject to any constraints arising from the United Kingdom's membership of the European Community, Parliament is sovereign and can enact what laws it chooses. Although the legal system operates in the name of the Crown, the monarch's role in practice is largely ceremonial. The object of this chapter is to sketch the emergence of the modern British state so that we can better appreciate its constitution in both an historical and a comparative context.

1. PATRIMONIAL GOVERNMENT

The government of England prior to the emergence of the modern state corresponded to what Weber called "patrimonial". In order to understand this term, we need also to understand the term "patriarchalism" which Weber used to characterise the authority of a master over his household (we will see later in this chapter an interesting use of a similar concept in the seventeenth century debates on the divine right of kings). The stability of a household arises from the fact that its members share lodgings, food, live together in close proximity and are mutually dependent. This is the form of social organisation corresponding to the pure type of traditional domination. The head of the household has no administrative staff, the members of the household are responsible to the head and obey his commands because this is part of an inviolable order of things depending on immemorial tradition. If we look at medieval castles, we will see that the great hall where communal eating and entertainment took place is a characteristic feature. The great hall was an essential part of this type of social organisation. Obviously, the social units which can operate in this way are limited in size. Where households expand, and the need to administer large territories emerges, patriarchal government transforms into the form Weber called "patrimonial". The need to administer large territories necessitates an administrative staff, but such administrative staff emerge from the household. Thus in England the chamberlain ceased to be a personal servant of the master (the king), and became an officer of state. Patrimonial government, being essentially a development from the patriarchal household, tends to instability as it expands, for the very fact of expansion weakens the authority of the head of the household. Moreover, other households within the realm, which have not over-expanded, may be in better shape than the dominant household, and able to challenge it. This happened repeatedly in France, for example, up to the seventeenth century, and also in medieval Scotland. To solve the problem of extending their authority beyond the household whilst counteracting the tendency towards decentralisation, patrimonial rulers resort to a number of strategies. For example, Anglo-Saxon kings held kinship groups responsible for the crimes of their individual members (and see Ch.6). As towns develop, trades are organised into guilds which are similarly held responsible for the services of their members, and in return enjoy a monopoly over the specialist trades which they represent (the organisation of the Bar in England at the present day is a direct reflection of such guild origins—see Ch.9). The central government under feudalism was essentially patrimonial, but feudalism was a system of economic organisation, which in its classical form enabled the patrimonial ruler to raise substantial armies. Under feudalism a villager's position was compulsory and hereditary giving him right to a share of land in return for a part of the yield. Some feudal tenants however held their land in return for specific military duties. Public finance was characteristically partly met by services rendered to the head of the household by the tenants in chief, and partly by making local groups responsible for the provision of services. Thus in England and Wales parishes were responsible for maintaining the roads in their locality (a disastrous system which persisted up to the Highways Act 1862 and which had the effect that many communities became inaccessible by road during winter months).

As time goes on, the raising of public revenues by taxation may come to be increasingly important, but a precondition for this is the emergence of a bureaucracy (see p.53) which can administer the collection of taxes.

A patrimonial government, like any other government, needs to maintain a monopoly on military force. One of the problems of such governments however is the tendency of other households within the realm to acquire such forces. The Wars of the Roses are an illustration of the results of this. Maintaining sufficiently large forces on a regular basis is difficult without an efficient government bureaucracy able to collect taxes. Characteristically, patrimonial rulers raise forces as needed, and disband them when the need is over. This pattern certainly subsisted in medieval England, and the disbanding of forces after various adventures in France was a major cause of social instability (see Hurnard, 1969). Stable patrimonial governments, however, do not depend on force, but upon the respect accorded to tradition. Indeed, the more dependent a ruler is on force, the more inherently unstable the regime, for the death of the ruler, or his loss of his forces' allegiance, is likely to result in the overthrow of the regime (readers might like to contemplate the fate of a number of modern dictatorships in this context which lacked the stabilising elements of charisma and tradition present in a patrimonial system).

The officials of a patrimonial state characteristically try to make their offices hereditary. This happened to a certain extent in England—the position of Earl Marshal, for example, is still hereditary—but to a much greater extent in France, where inheritance of benefices, and trading in them, extended through all ranks of officialdom. This is another aspect of the fragmentation of authority which is characteristic of patrimonialism.

As an attempt to counteract such fragmentation, rulers typically adopt three strategies:

(1) They personally visit different parts of their realms. As well as enabling the ruler to keep an eye on things, this enables them to distribute the costs of maintaining the royal household (usually a problem in the absence of taxation). This strategy was used by Anglo-Saxon kings; and we will recall the number of bedchambers around England where "Queen Elizabeth slept".

(2) They send members of their household to visit the various parts of the kingdom. The use of the General Eyre by English kings in the Middle Ages, and the emergence of the Assize Circuits of the common law courts are examples of this strategy.

(3) Key members of likely rival households are kept at court, in effect as hostages. This strategy was adopted in France, especially by Louis XIV whose palace at Versailles, as we will see, was built with this purpose in mind.

In this chapter, we will sketch the transformation of England from a patrimonial government to a modern state. Weber's preconditions for the emergence of such a state are: (1) the monopolisation of the means of domination and administration based on the creation of a centrally directed and permanent system of taxation, and a centrally directed and permanent military force in the hands of a central governmental authority; (2) the monopolisation of legal enactments and the legitimate use of force by the central authority; and (3) the organisation of a rationally orientated officialdom, whose exercise of administrative functions is dependent upon the central authority (Bendix, 1966, p.383). The satisfaction of these conditions is most likely under a money economy, something with which Anglo-Saxon England was blessed, and which, it seems, survived the Norman Conquest for the classic feudal system in which payments are made in the form of services rendered was never very pure or tenacious in England (see MacFarlane, 1973). The development of rationally orientated officialdom in England, as in the rest of Western Europe, was largely attributable to the Church which, administratively, was essentially a rational bureaucracy much influenced in its development by a rational legal system namely Roman law (see Ullmann, 1975). Finally, the expansion of bureaucratic administration into important departments of public life occurred quite soon after the Conquest. In England the royal household quickly established its control over important litigation (notably suits for the recovery of freehold land through the common law courts which emerged from the royal household (see p.264). Decentralised jurisdictions did exist (in the case of the County Palatines of Durham and Lancaster they existed until the Courts Act 1971, and there were others), but in essence the legal system was centralised. In many European countries, by contrast, significant judicial territories were "no go" areas for royal justice.

2. LEGAL DOMINATION AND THE BRITISH CONSTITUTION

According to Dicey, the famous Victorian jurist, a cornerstone of the British constitution was the assurance that all government powers depended upon the rule of law. This limitation of governmental powers he subdivided under three headings: the absence of arbitrary power in any individual or department of government; equality before the law, or the equal subjection of the officials of government to the courts and the ordinary common law applicable to all British subjects; the fact of the constitution being part of the ordinary law of the land (Dicey, 1885, pp.202–3). Now, to modern eyes, whilst this is a reasonable description of the constitution of Victorian Britain, it does not seem to explain why Victorian Britain (at least by the standards of the time) was a relatively liberal society. The French philosopher Montesquieu had, over a century earlier, attributed the relative freedom which prevailed in Britain in his day to the separation of state powers—legislative, executive and judicial—each checking and balancing the other. This theory was to have considerable influence upon the drafting of the United States' Constitution, a constitution that has, of course, survived undiminished for over two centuries. Yet we have only to contemplate the fate of many of the elaborate constitutions imposed by the British government on former colonies as they achieved independence to realise that, like the rule of law, the doctrine of the separation of powers is really only a subjective description, something Montesquieu merely *thought* he observed (and his report was not even particularly exact in the context of his own time). Something is missing: why do nationals of a country such as the United States respect their constitution, whilst those of many other former colonies did not, though they might observe their customary and religious laws quite rigidly?

We will here recall the way in which Weber addressed the question of why different types of law are obeyed in different societies. He considered how an individual's image of existence might ground different notions of legality (and with them different attitudes towards leadership and obedience). Hence, as we have seen, Weber's threefold typology of domination: charismatic, traditional and legal (see pp.10–12). Charismatic domination is important in our own constitutional history in understanding the position of the Crown, and the development of that elusive feature of the modern British constitution, the "royal prerogative". A single institution often exhibits more than one type of domination. Traditional domination is the legitimacy accorded to an authority which is perceived always to have existed. The British Crown derives a certain authority from the fact of its very antiquity, as well as from the charisma attaching to it. This element is also present in the development of the common law in the respect it accords precedent (though this aspect may also be justified by the rationalist view that like cases ought to be treated alike). This respect for tradition is well illustrated in the growth of legal fictions in the development of English common law. A legal response developed for one purpose could by these means readily be used for another (see our account of the side-stepping of the real actions on pp.11–12). By about 1575–80, as we have seen, the real actions had largely been supplanted. When Lord Ellesmere (?1541–1617) regretted their decay, he was expressing the veneration due to ancient institutions which is the essence of traditional domination.

This example is not the only one in English legal history and indeed Roman law went through a similar phase in its development. A further example of the strength of tradition is the way in which in both England, Wales and Scotland feudal forms persist in modern land law, though they are now stripped of virtually all their incidents, and in both cases the laws are entirely divorced from the feudal social relations which they once reflected. These feudal relations, tenures and estates, form the conceptual backbone of a rational modern law of real property in both countries.

The final form of domination is legal: it comprises obedience to a system of rules applied judicially and in accordance with established principles which are valid for all members of a society. Unlike in societies governed by charismatic and traditional domination, people obey the law *as such*. A large part of the legislation which makes up the fabric of a modern legal system is obeyed because it is perceived to be rational to do so (even if we disagree with it); it retains neither charismatic nor traditional elements, though they linger in the legislative imprimatur of Parliament and the Crown.

The older forms of domination still co-exist however in many of our present-day legal institutions, especially in the sphere of constitutional law. As suggested above, a system which exhibits the influence of charisma and tradition may nevertheless be rational as well. Roman law, like the common law of England, is a good illustration of this. It forms the basis of the law of all other European countries, including Scotland and eastern Europe. As codified by the Emperor Justinian in the sixth century, long after it had passed through its predominantly charismatic and traditional phases, it was adopted by these modern states largely because it was a coherent system when compared to the mass of often conflicting customary law which they had accumulated.

Armed with this conceptual apparatus we are in a position to sketch out the development of the British constitution so that we might explain how it came about that what we might call the "snapshots" taken by Montesquieu and Dicey in the eighteenth and nineteenth centuries could show (however fuzzily) what they did. First, however, since the events of the Revolution of 1688 are crucial to an understanding of these matters, we will give a short résumé of the historical events of that period.

The Civil War concluded with the defeat of Charles I and his subsequent execution on January 30, 1649. The period of the "Commonwealth" between then and the restoration of the monarchy in 1660 is interesting for the many legal reforms proposed by the Hale Commission, but it made no direct lasting impact because in constitutional theory, the legislation of the Commonwealth was without effect (see Veall, 1974).

Charles II, though by no means an honest dealer, was an astute politician, and when James II succeeded to the throne in February 1685, the monarchy was probably stronger than it had been at any time since the Tudors. There is little doubt that James could have enjoyed a peaceful and successful reign had he, like Charles II, been prepared to treat his religion as a private matter. Unfortunately, within three years, in his attempt to further the cause of Catholicism, he had nurtured a fatally substantial opposition. At the same time, William of Orange was attempting to organize an effective European alliance to oppose an increasingly powerful France. William could not secure the adherence of England to this alliance with James on the throne. James had no son; William's mother was Charles I's daughter, and his wife was James' eldest daughter. Many people disliked James and feared where he might take England; they were inclined therefore to believe the rumour that the son born so opportunely to him on June 10, 1688 had been smuggled into the queen's bedchamber in a warming pan. In this way, they were able to reconcile themselves to the succession of William and Mary on the basis that it was, as it were, merely an anticipation of the true succession.

The birth of James's son actually helped to precipitate the revolution, for he would certainly be brought up a Roman Catholic and thus perpetuate a Catholic dynasty. Thus William was invited to cross to England to preserve her statutory liberties and the Protestant religion. William accepted the invitation, since it meant that England could probably be drawn into the alliance against Louis XIV. Louis made the error of failing to invade Holland, and this, combined with fortuitously favourable winds, enabled William to make his landing on English shores. James attempted to escape to France (a fact which helped confirm his opponents in the belief that he intended to re-establish Catholicism, with French assistance if need be), but was captured. William, seeing the political advantage of James's flight to France, took every care to ensure that James might succeed in escaping a second time. James fell for this strategem, escaped, and duly left the way clear for William and Mary to claim the throne.

Parliament was summoned, and drew up a Declaration of Rights. It offered the throne to William and Mary who accepted it. The Parliament was then declared to be a true Parliament, in the same way as the Parliament which effected the restoration in 1660 had been. The Declaration of Rights was then turned into the Bill of Rights. This, together with the Toleration Act, and the Mutiny Act, laid the basis of the Revolution Settlement.

3. KEY FEATURES OF THE CONSTITUTIONAL SETTLEMENT

(i) *The independence of the judiciary*

One consequence of the Revolution was that the security of judges from dismissal at the will of the government was established. James had dismissed judges whom he considered opposed to his plans. The Act of Settlement provided that judges' commissions should be during good behaviour, and that they should be removable only upon the address of both Houses of Parliament. Salaries for judges were to be established and ascertained (12 & 13 William III c.2, s.3). In fact a bill to ascertain the commissions and salaries of judges was vetoed by William, and this situation was not remedied until the nineteenth century. A salary had been paid to judges since the thirteenth century (sometimes erratically), and in the late seventeenth century this was fixed at £1000, which was supplemented from court fees. This fee income was not taken away until 1826 when salaries were raised from £2400 to £5500 to compensate for its loss (HEL I 254–5). The rule that judges in superior courts are immune from liability for acts done in their judicial capacity had also become established by this time, though its basis was not properly stated until Willes J.'s judgment in *The Mayor of London v Cox* (1867).

(ii) The army

Control of force has proved a crucial factor in the ability of individuals and groups to dominate their countries throughout history. It was therefore prudently provided that "the raising or keeping of a standing army within the kingdom in time of peace unless it be with the consent of Parliament, is against the law" (I Wm. & M. sess. 2 c.2 s.i 6). To the present day, Parliament consents to the raising and keeping of the armed forces only on an annual basis.

(iii) Control of taxation

James had levied customs duties before they had been regularly granted to him by Parliament. Consequently, the levying of taxes without the consent of Parliament was prohibited (id.s.i.4). The settlement left the control of taxation firmly in the hands of Parliament, the Crown's expenses of maintaining the royal household being defrayed from taxation in the sums voted to it by Parliament as the "Civil List".

(iv) The suspending and dispensing powers

The sovereignty of Parliament entails that no one else can suspend or abrogate a law. Both of these powers were claimed by the Crown prior to 1688. The suspending power was the power to abrogate a statute so that it lost its binding force altogether, the dispensing power was the power to grant individual exemption from the application of a statute. The Act of Settlement declared that "the pretended power of suspending of laws, or the execution of laws, without the consent of Parliament, is illegal" (I Wm. & M. sess. 2 c.2 s.i 1). The dispensing power was only condemned "as it hath been assumed and exercised of late" (id. s.i 2). It was intended to regulate the matter by further legislation, but this was never done. Recent dispensations were declared invalid, and future dispensations were not to be valid unless it was specifically provided in the statute in respect of which the dispensation was given that this was permissible. In practice the Crown did not again assert these powers. The dispensing power should not be confused with the separate power of the Crown to pardon convicted criminals. This power is the result of the Crown's control over criminal procedure which is a consequence of the fact that all offences technically are either against the Queen's peace or her Crown or dignity (Blackstone I Comm. 268 and 408–9).

(v) Freedom of the press

Another consequence of the Revolution, which was to be important in the constitutional conflicts of the later eighteenth century and which helped to pave the way for the Reform Act of 1832, was England's acquisition of a press more uninhibited than its counterparts elsewhere in Europe at that time, complete with the first modern law of copyright. It is worth looking at this not only because it is important in itself, but because the nature of the law of copyright which emerged differed significantly from the French equivalent of *droit d'auteur* which was one by-product of the French Revolution.

The invention of printing in the fifteenth century afforded a means for the wider dissemination of ideas, and ushered in a revolution in the transmission of information which parallels in impact the broadcasting revolution in the twentieth century. The reluctance of some modern governments to accept absolute freedom of broadcasting or of information on the Internet, may help us to understand the reluctance of sixteenth-century governments to accept the freedom of the press. The Tudors controlled information in two ways: they passed specific laws making it an offence to publish treasonable, seditious, heretical or blasphemous works (compare modern disputes on blasphemy and pornography); and they gave large powers of control over printing and publishing to a guild, the Stationers' Company, backing this up with ordinances, largely based on the rules of that Company, for the organisation and control of printing. This in effect conferred on the Stationers' Company a valuable publishing monopoly, outside of which few could operate. In return for enjoying this monopoly, the Stationers were expected to prevent the publication of obnoxious works. A printer or publisher was required to register all books with the Company, and to pay a registration fee. The effect of registration was to confer on the printer or publisher who registered it title to the work. The origin of the word "copyright" lies not as many suppose in the fact that the copyright proprietor can stop others from copying his work, it originates in the registration procedure conferring on a person rights to the copy (in the same sense as journalists talk about "delivering their copy").

The licensing laws under which the Stationers' Company operated obviously gave large powers to the Crown, and interfered with individual liberty. Parliament finally refused to renew the licensing laws in 1694. Thereafter, many attempts were made by the book trade to recover its monopoly, but without success. Finally, the Stationers hit upon the strategy of adopting the arguments put forward by Daniel Defoe in favour of author's rights, as a way of pursuing their own interests (Rose, 1993, p.35). The result was a Bill which became the famous Copyright Act 1709–10 'for the Encouragement of Learning by Vesting the Copies of printed Books in the Authors or Purchasers of such Copies' (Deazley, 2004, Ch.2). This Act for the first time conferred upon authors the right to stop others from copying their works. It is important to note, however, that this right, which was an indirect product of the ideas thrown up by the Revolution of 1688, was from the outset regarded in economic terms, and as a result English law had little difficulty in applying it subsequently to a wide variety of works. It was but a short step to extend it to cover works of art, but eventually even engineering drawings came to enjoy copyright protection (see *British Leyland v Armstrong Patents* (1986) as did computer-generated works (Copyright Designs and Patents Act 1988, s.9(3)). By contrast, French *droit d'auteur*, also a product of revolution, came to be based on an author's natural rights to the creations of his or her mind, rather than on economic interest. The moral rights of an author, for example to object to derogatory treatment of his or her work, followed naturally from the initial premise. English law, on the other hand, considered that the recognition of the author's property, when combined with measures to facilitate dealings in that property through the preservation of sanctity of contract, would suffice. Indeed, only in 1988 did a UK Copyright Act introduce the concept of moral rights, as required by the Berne Copyright Convention (Art.6 *bis*), of which Great Britain is a participatory signatory.

The differing development of copyright law in England and France highlights the very different intellectual climates which existed in England and France following their revolutions. The lack of any coherent principle underlying the English constitutional settlement, and the relative lack of social disruption in England in 1688, meant that there was little incentive to do other than go on much as before. Indeed, at the time of the Restoration in 1660 the clock had actually been put back in that, as noted above, many useful legal reforms of the Commonwealth period which anticipated those of the nineteenth century were abrogated or not implemented (see Veall, 1974). Even the use of Norman French was reintroduced, and not abolished until 1731 (4 Geo II c.26). By contrast, the intellectual climate of the French Revolution was rationalist, and a large part of the old order (including the legal system) was swept away and replaced by new institutions.

4. CONSTITUTIONAL THEORY AND THE BILL OF RIGHTS

There is no statement of any overriding constitutional principle in the Bill. As will be apparent from the provisions noted above, it is rather a series of responses to the perceived abuses which had led to the Revolution. In part, this was because the fundamental principles governing the position of the Crown, the royal prerogative, the position and powers of Parliament and the Courts, and the rights and liberties of the subject, had largely been settled in the aftermath of the Civil War: they had not been the subject of controversy since the Restoration.

In particular, the Bill of Rights did not reflect Hobbes' theory of sovereignty. Thomas Hobbes (1588–1679) argued that in a state of nature "the life of man is solitary, poor, nasty, brutish and short". Eventually, people conclude that it would be better to live in peace, have covenants kept, and not do things to others they would not like done to themselves. But in a state of nature there are no laws which can secure this desirable state of affairs. In order to get security therefore people surrender their natural power and liberty to a sovereign. The sovereign as the ultimate source of law cannot be subject to it. Consequently there can be no limits to a sovereign's power. This theory was to prove influential in the nineteenth century. Jeremy Bentham (1748–1832) accepted Hobbes' theory of sovereignty, and advocated the use of a sovereign legislature as the best way of effecting the law reforms which his utilitarian theory (see p.37) demanded. The theory in this form was used to support the Whigs' passing of the Reform Act of 1832. It is also an early formulation of legal positivism which via John Austin (1790–1859) has been a major strand in jurisprudential thinking down to the present day especially in the writings of H.L.A. Hart (see Ch.1). Certainly statements that Parliament's powers are unlimited can be found in modern constitutional law textbooks. The Settlement was of a different age, however. It reflected the common law ideas of Matthew Hale

(1609–76), and the medieval idea of the supremacy of the law. In particular, the royal prerogative was subject to the law. This idea was to give rise to some exceptionally complex doctrines concerning the prerogative.

Under medieval English political theory, the king was regarded as a natural man who, under the law (ordained by God), was the head and representative of the state but not the sovereign power within it. The king was subject to the law (see Ullmann, 1975). The position of the king in feudal theory was simply that of the greatest feudal lord. Allegiance was also owed by the king to his subjects. Either party could renounce their allegiance, as did the barons in the dispute with King John in 1215, which led to Magna Carta—itself characteristically a contractual document, like a treaty of the present day. Provided allegiance had been renounced, it was not treason to attack the king. The deposition of Edward II in 1327 thus would not have been perceived by contemporaries as problematic in anything like the way in which the deposition of James II was. This reflected the greater charismatic authority accorded to the Crown in the seventeenth century than in the Middle Ages. To quote Maitland:

"The mediaeval king was every inch a king, but just for this reason he was every inch a man and you did not talk nonsense about him. You did not ascribe to him immortality or ubiquity, or such powers as no mortal can wield. If you said that he was Christ's Vicar, you meant what you said, and you might add that he would become the servant of the devil if he decline towards tyranny . . . In all the Year Books I have seen very little said of him that was not meant to be strictly and literally true of a man, of an Edward or a Henry". (Maitland, 1901)

Under the Tudors, the office of king became personified. Whereas in the Middle Ages it was not possible to separate the king as a man from his attributes as a king, under Tudor theory the king was a corporation sole, a body having a legal existence and rights and duties separate from the individuals who succeeded to the office. This body was immortal, omnipresent, infallible, and by virtue of becoming sovereign, the occupant of the throne was invested with these qualities. As a counterbalance to these views, however, there remained the precedents from the Middle Ages under which the king was regarded simply as a man like all others, who by virtue of the law was the head of state, but not the sovereign power within the state.

The peculiarity of the subsequent development of the prerogative of the Crown was that it was to become the executive authority of the United Kingdom. But the anomaly was, compared to Continental theory of the time, that it was subject to the law, as a result of the constitutional struggles of the seventeenth century. The Parliamentary party was able to support its case by deploying medieval precedents, whose complexion was coloured by a view of kingship very different from that of the Stuarts.

The development of the law of treason is interesting in highlighting changing ideas of sovereignty. The Crown had an economic incentive to expand the scope of treason as far as possible: the lands of a convicted traitor were forfeit to the Crown. A statute of 1352 placed important limitations on this expansion. The statute is a curious mixture of Christian and feudal notions with other emerging ideas of kingship which were to come to the fore dramatically in the seventeenth century. The statute provided that it was treason:

(1) to compass or imagine the death of the king, queen or the king's eldest son and heir;
(2) to violate the queen or the queen's eldest unmarried daughter, or the wife of the king's eldest son;
(3) to levy war against the king in his realms or to be an adherent of the king's enemies in his realms;
(4) to counterfeit the king's seal or money;
(5) knowingly to bring counterfeit money into England;
(6) to slay the chancellor or any of the judges while performing their offices.

The first basis of the crime was, as the name implies, treachery: the sin of Judas Iscariot. This wrong could be committed not merely against the king, but by a servant killing his master, a wife her husband or by anyone who killed a member of the clergy. These last were grouped together under the crime of "petty treason", as opposed to "high treason" against the king. This element of the crime long predated the Conquest. The second underpinning of the crime was simply the idea of a breach of the feudal bond, the duty of allegiance owed between lord and vassal, and a petty traitor's lands escheated to his lord. This duty of allegiance could lead to labyrinthine complexities when, as frequently happened, barons owed fealty to more than one sovereign, even the king of England and the king of France simultaneously. Indeed, the sovereigns could themselves be each other's vassals in their different territories, as was the king of England of the king of France in those territories in which the king of England was Duke of Normandy. These complexities undoubtedly tended to limit the scope of treason, so that the statute makes no mention of levying war outside the king's realms as an act of treason. Finally, and of significance to future developments in political theory and the strengthening of the charistmatic aspects of kingship, the king was beginning to be perceived as representing an entity beyond his feudal titles, namely, the state. Indeed, the rise of the popular perception that Europe was evolving into a collection of nation-states was an essential concomitant to the rise in importance of the charismatic aspects of kingship, both in England and in other European countries. Significantly in this regard, the idea of *laesae majestatis* was imported. Under Roman law, falsifying Caesar's image was a kind of sacrilege (Caesar was divine). Consequently, counterfeiting the king's image on coinage was treason.

5. THE EFFECT OF THE CONSTITUTIONAL SETTLEMENT ON THE ROYAL PREROGATIVE

In order to understand the change in the role of the prerogative from an adjunct of the theory of the divine right of kings, "what the prince pleases has the force of law", to a residue of powers exercised in the name of the Crown subject to certain conventions, we need to know something of seventeenth-century political theory, in particular, the theory of the divine right of kings. Treating the king as the Lord's anointed was undoubtedly an attractive part of the "kingship package" whereby pagan chiefs were persuaded of the advantages of converting to Christianity, which in turn was an important factor in the spread of the faith in the West after the collapse of the Roman Empire (see Ullmann, 1975). An imperial theory was of course embodied in Justinian's codification of Roman Law, which in turn was to be the source which enabled Roman law to revive in the Middle Ages. It must be realised, however, that the early development of the Church itself owed much to Roman law (see Ullmann, 1975). At all events, it is sufficient to realise that the theory of divine right, which found favour with the Stuart kings, had rather a long history, and rather a close association with the Roman Church. Implicit in this theory was the hereditary principle. The fact of the Restoration itself provided affirmation of this principle.

"The kingly power is by the law of God, so it hath no inferior law to limit it." (Filmer, 1680 Ch.iii s.1) The king, according to this theory, was above the law of the state, which he could mitigate or suspend at will (id. Ch.iii ss. 6 and 7). The theory in its original form was justified by reference to biblical texts. During Charles II's reign an important change permeated divine right theory. Hobbes had been able to show that the traditional biblical texts were double-edged weapons, and Robert Filmer, the subtly differentiated new theory's leading exponent, duly based it in revised form not upon biblical authority, but upon reason. He argued that society had its origins in the patriarchal family, and that the rights of the patriarch, who in developed society becomes the monarch, are endowed by nature. Since nature is God's work, the rights are divine. Adam ruled his family therefore by divine right, and the king, as heir and representative of Adam, ruled his kingdom with an equal dispensation. Modern readers who find this theory strange do so because they do not believe that reason supports the theory at all. They are in fact heirs to the rationalist tradition which emerged in the seventeenth century. A theory which was supposedly founded on reason could be destroyed by reason in the way in which a theory founded upon some supposed revelation of the will of the deity could not be (readers might like to contemplate in this context the constitutional consequences of the Islamic revolutions in a number of countries in recent times). The "demolition job" on the theory was carried out by John Locke, the greatest English political theorist of the Revolution (and one of the greatest of all time). He attacked the theory both on historical grounds, and on the basis of its reasoning. He pointed out that there was as much evidence for the right of subjects to resist tyranny, as for kings to tyrannise their subjects, and that the former right was more conducive to the welfare of the state.

In Locke's view, it was the legislature, and not the king, which "gives form, life and unity to the commonwealth" (Locke, Book ii s.212). In England, the political dialogue between supporters of the theory of the divine right of kings and its opponents came therefore to be conducted in more or less entirely secular terms.

Under Locke's theory, in a state of nature there is not much security for the observance of the laws of nature. Men must agree with each other "to join and unite one amongst another, in a secure enjoyment of their properties, and a greater security against any that are not of it" (Locke, Book ii s.131). By submitting to the state, men debar themselves from taking what measures they please for self-preservation, and enforcement of their rights. They do not, however, deprive themselves of those other natural rights which belong inalienably to all men. The state must govern in accordance with the laws which secure the natural rights of life, liberty, and property. These powers are conferred upon the government by the agreement of the community. If a government act in breach of the community's trust, it needs must be *ipso facto* dissolved (id. 221). Absolute monarchy is thus inconsistent with the objectives of society, for there is no concomitant security that the monarch will not violate all the natural rights which it is precisely the object of the state to maintain.

The state must therefore be governed according to certain fundamental principles:

(1) It is to govern by promulgated, established laws, which are not to be varied in particular cases, one rule must obtain for rich and poor alike;

(2) These laws ought to be designed for no other end ultimately but the good of the people;

(3) Taxes must not be raised on the property of the people without the consent of the people given by themselves or their deputies;

(4) The legislature cannot transfer the power of making laws to anybody else, or place it anywhere but where the people have chosen to do so (id. 142).

These ideas provided a theoretical justification for the Revolution, and reflected the political ideas of the Whigs (see below). Thus the Marquis of Halifax (1633–95) wrote that the government of England had attained the happy mesne between a monarchy "that leaveth men no liberty" and a commonwealth that "alloweth them no quiet".

Whilst there are many obvious criticisms to be made of Locke's views, they have proved enormously influential down to the present day, when the social contract which underpins them has been given, a new lease of life in the writings of John Rawls (pp.282–284).

Although Filmer's rationalist version of the "divine right" theory did not survive Locke, the legacy of "divine right" theory remains to this day. It helped the Church of England to assert a claim to divinity: the Protestants turned to the Bible for justification for their ideas, and found that the theory could be developed to justify the position of the Crown and Protestant Church of

England (one of James' mistakes was to try to use the theory to attack a Church whose position was justified by the same theory). In a residual form, it also underlies the theory of sovereignty in modern English Public Law. The theory naturally tends towards the conservation of the existing order, and in this sense, the eighteenth-century Tories with their support of Church and king, and their reverence for the existing order of things, were its practitioners. The reaction in this country to the French Revolution was to produce in Burke an emblematic and theoretically coherent exposition of this set of attitudes, wherein he attacked Locke's theory of natural rights based on a social contract. But the underpinning of Burke's ideas was utility. His particular combination—support for the existing order coupled with an appeal to principles of utility—meant that his work had features which separately attracted both Whigs and Tories (as to which see pp.71–74). Nevertheless, it is the conservative aspect of Burke's thinking which has persistently captivated his Tory disciples down to the present day.

6. PARLIAMENT AS A LEGISLATIVE BODY

The laws enacted by the Saxon kings in England were essentially recordals of the customary rules of their kingdoms. The idea that laws can be changed by a legislative act grew up quite slowly. Only within strict limits might feudal magnates legislate within their dominions, and the king as a feudal magnate legislate in his. Moreover, the king could only legislate outside his own dominions with the consent of his feudatories.

The medieval Parliament which emerged in the thirteenth century in England was an example of a phenomenon which existed throughout Europe, namely assemblies of the various orders of which society was perceived to be constituted. In England it consisted of the clergy and nobility (without whose consent it was impossible to legislate within their domains). To this extent, Parliament, like the "estates general" elsewhere, reflected feudal theory. By the thirteenth century however the towns had grown in importance and the Crown needed revenue from them by way of taxes. Consequently, an important element added to the older feudal one was the need to obtain the consent of various groups to taxation. In England the clergy withdrew from Parliament to regulate and tax themselves in their own convocation, leaving the bishops as Lords spiritual to represent them in Parliament. Thus the English Parliament became a two-part affair consisting of the Lords, which represented the magnates and higher clergy, and the Commons, which represented the towns and "notable esquires and gentlemen". The counties returned two members each, the franchise being restricted to freeholders having tenements to the annual value of forty shillings. In the boroughs (which also returned two members) the qualification for the vote differed widely—sometimes only householders had it, more usually an oligarchy of important traders held sway. This pattern of estates general was repeated throughout Europe, but the mix differed. In Sweden, for example, the Diet consisted of four estates: clergy, barons, burghers and peasants. Indeed in England additional estates were nearly added as the lawyers tended to form a distinct group (see pp.264 *et seq.*) and the Crown tended to treat with merchants as a group when needing to raise money.

The transformation of Parliament from a medieval estates into a representative body is an important part of our story. In France, by contrast, the Estates General survived until the Revolution when voting according to social order was abolished. Estates survived elsewhere for much longer (though some disappeared in 1848—the year of revolutions).

The first major programme of legislation to emerge in England came during the reign of Edward I. Indeed, in extent it remained unrivalled until the nineteenth century. It was not, however, a peculiarly English phenomenon. A fashion for legislation seems to have swept Europe at about the same time. The Church seems to have started the fashion, which is hardly surprising as, influenced as it was by Roman law, it was probably nearer to possessing a rational legal system than any secular state of the period. However, what the fashion probably evidences is that a legal profession of increasing size and importance independent of the Church had grown up in many parts of Europe. Significant as this programme was, we must not suppose that contemporaries imagined they had anything like the power to create or abrogate law that a modern legislature believes it has.

The transformation of Parliament from a feudal estates was accelerated by the events of the sixteenth century. Paradoxically, that most authoritarian of monarchs, Henry VIII, it may be argued, actually strengthened the constitutional position of Parliament when he broke with Rome. That the legislation necessary to effect the legal establishment of the Church of England, and the associated programme of radical legislation passed at the same time (including the Statute of Uses), needed the authority of

Parliament undoubtedly confirmed the centrality of Parliament in the fabric of the body politic. Thus G.R. Elton argued that the effect of the legislation was to confirm the king *in* Parliament as the sovereign legislative body, as opposed to the king *and* Parliament (see Elton, 1991). Parliament had become more than a medieval estates, a transformation which was to be crucial in the problems Charles I encountered when he tried to move towards a more absolute form of monarchy more closely aligned to that which was emerging on the Continent.

One important effect of the civil war was to enhance not merely the political importance of Parliament, but also its social importance—which proved instrumental in increasing the respect accorded to the institution. In the sixteenth and early seventeenth centuries, the Inns of Court were the focus of fashionable society. In the later seventeenth century, London society moved westwards, and in the eighteenth century, the patronage dispensed from Westminster became all-important.

In the period which led up to the civil war, the importance of the House of Commons had been increasing relative to that of the House of Lords. The House of Lords did not resist this development: indeed, under Charles II it was, on the whole, a fairly indolent body, often adjourning for days on end if no matters were sent up to them by the Commons. By the 1680s, the Lords had begun to act simply as a second chamber. During the eighteenth century, thanks to the unreformed system of representation in the Commons, the magnates of the Lords were able to exert considerable influence over the Commons. Nevertheless, the very fact that the king and nobility needed to operate in this indirect way was a reflection of the dominant position achieved by the Commons in the course of the seventeenth century. Most importantly, the control of taxation lay with the Commons. The army and the navy and other expenses of government were paid for out of sums specifically appropriated to them, and audited by Parliamentary commissioners. Inevitably, therefore, the Commons took upon themselves the decisions as to how much should be raised and how much spent for particular purposes.

In other words, the de facto position was that the government could not operate unless its ministers could command a majority in the House of Commons. Over time it became apparent that given the large powers of control assumed by the Commons, government ministers would need to be present *in* the Commons to explain and justify government policy. The emergence of the institution of the Cabinet was to solve some of the problems left unresolved by the disputes of the seventeenth century. The Cabinet was the institution by which the prerogative powers were appropriated to the disposition of the House of Commons. Informal conferences between the king and his leading ministers were a feature of William III's reign, and it was out of these that the Cabinet developed. After 1717 George I (who spoke no English) ceased to attend its meetings. George II occasionally attended, but by the middle of the eighteenth century the attendance of the king was regarded as unusual. George III only twice presided over a meeting, the last occasion being in 1781. Early Cabinets were large and loosely knit. They consisted of the heads of the major administrative departments such as the Treasury, the leading household officers and sometimes the Lord Chief Justice and the Archbishop of Canterbury. They were not cohesive ministries, being comprised rather of servants of the king. Walpole is often said to be the first Prime Minister, but his tenure of office depended on the Crown, and the Cabinet with which he worked was similarly appointed. Consequently, when Walpole fell, the Cabinet remained. Walpole did however work with a small inner Cabinet.

During George II's reign, the king's ability to form his own ministries declined. Increasingly, leaders could dictate the terms on which they were prepared to take office. The ministries working through the inner Cabinet accordingly grew more distant from the king, and closer to Parliament. In the first part of his reign, George III attempted to recover the ground lost by the Crown. Ultimately he did not succeed and after the fall of Lord North's administration in 1782 the personal share of the Crown in government declined (assisted by the king's increasing bouts of insanity). Pitt won an overwhelming victory for the Tories in 1784, and established the convention that the Cabinet must be made up of persons holding office, and of like mind with their colleagues. Former ministers could not regard themselves as still in the Cabinet, nor strictly speaking could the king take advice from persons outside the Cabinet.

As noted above, an important consequence of the revolutionary settlement was a judiciary which could not be dismissed at will. The courts could thus exercise some check on executive power. The Wilkes affair (p.72, below) led to general warrants being declared illegal (*Wilkes v Wood* (1763), also *Leach v Money* (1765)). The power of the Privy Council to commit to prison was held to be limited (if it existed at all) to high treason in *Entick v Carrington* (1765).

What emerged from the seventeenth century, then, was a rather complex series of institutions, underpinned by no tidy body of doctrine. No doubt a reason for this was the relative stability of the English state, compared to some of its Continental rivals. The condition of anarchy which reigned in France from time to time before the reign of Louis XIII is, as suggested above, an example of the instability which can occur in patrimonial government. The measures adopted by Louise XIII and Louis XIV solved these problems in a classic manner by keeping the great magnates at court for significant periods of the year. Indeed, Louis XIV's palace at Versailles was not merely a royal residence, it was an important part of the machinery of government, possessing as it did apartments designed to house the important members of the aristocracy and their servants throughout "the season". A considerable number of informers kept the king abreast of potential sources of dissent, and the prevailing pecking order was made apparent by the allocation and reallocation of the more or less desirable apartments. Elaborate rituals designed to enhance the charisma of the monarch were part of this system. For example, Louis would rise from and retire to a state bed, but actually sleep in a more comfortable (and sociable) bed elsewhere. The French Estates, as noted above, retained an essentially medieval role: it certainly did not control as the Commons did the appropriation and expenditure of state funds. The system had within it considerable rigidity, and, on the classic interpretation, it is precisely such rigidity in the face of social and economic change which leads to revolution, which was, of course, verified by the events of 1789.

7. THE EMERGENCE OF POLITICAL PARTIES

The names "Whig" and "Tory" were to be the designations of the two English parties until their evolution into the Liberal and Conservative parties respectively in the nineteenth century. The terms originated as words of abuse during the heated struggle of 1679 over the bill to exclude James II from the succession to the throne. "Whig" was a Scottish term for horse and cattle thieves. Its connotations were Presbyterianism and rebellion, hence its application to those intent on excluding James from the throne. "Tory" was an Irish term suggesting a Papist outlaw, and was applied to those who supported James' succession.

Modern political parties represent both particular programmes as set out in their manifestos, and particular interest groups either directly, or indirectly through lobbying, etc. Eighteenth-century parties fulfilled the latter function, but did not for the most part commit themselves to any particular reform programme. The Revolution of 1688 was a Whig victory, and thereafter most Tories accepted Whig ideas of constitutional monarchy, as against adherence to absolutist doctrine. In the eighteenth century, Toryism became associated with the squirearchy and Anglicanism (in Anne's reign it was mainly the country gentry who opposed religious toleration). Whiggism became associated with the aristocratic landowning families, and the financial interests of the wealthy middle classes. The Tories tended to include the supporters of the Jacobites, and to the extent that it now appears that this cause enjoyed widespread popular support, the Tories may be regarded as a popular party. However, George I came to the throne as a nominee of the Whigs, and this, together with the consequent flight of the Tory leader Bolingbroke to France, destroyed the political power of the Tories.

The Whig Party, although at the outset possessing an ideology, albeit largely Lockean, for most of the eighteenth century amounted to little more than a series of aristocratic groups, with key individuals operating in Parliament through patronage and influence. Although stratified, English society of the eighteenth century, unlike most of its Continental counterparts, permitted a fair degree of social mobility. Boys with talent from quite humble backgrounds could sometimes rise to high rank especially through a career in the law (for example, Lord Thurlow, Lord Chancellor 1778; see Simpson, ed., 1984). The system of patronage was crucial in this process: the powerful recruited the talented, rather as modern corporations try to recruit the best talents available.

In a sense, Tory sentiment proved more durable than Whig ideology. Political polarisation properly began to emerge over the Wilkes affair, and, later, the American Revolution. As noted above, an indirect consequence of the troubles of 1688 was that Britain acquired a press free from government control. John Wilkes (1727–97) founded a weekly journal, the *North Briton*, in 1762. In its forty-fifth issue it strongly criticised the contents of the king's speech at the opening of Parliament. Lord Halifax issued a general warrant for the arrest of all concerned, and Wilkes was committed to the Tower. It was then ruled by the Court that general warrants were unlawful, and Wilkes was released, recovered substantial damages and became the hero of the hour. He was subsequently declared, on four occasions, ineligible to be elected to Parliament, but in each instance was returned. In 1774 he became Lord Mayor of London and re-entered Parliament as MP for Middlesex. In 1782 the resolutions invalidating his elections to Parliament were expunged; he finally retired as an MP in 1790. Undoubtedly, the controversies surrounding Wilkes helped to politicise the two parties in a way in which they had not been politicised previously. Increasingly, from 1784 the Tory party as led by William Pitt the Younger came to represent the interests of the country gentry, merchant classes and official ministerial groups. The opposition, the Whigs as led by Charles James Fox, came to represent the interests of dissenters and industrialists, and those favouring electoral and Parliamentary reform. The desertion of many of the more moderate Whigs to the Tories in 1794 confused further the old division between the parties.

The Reform Act of 1832 was regarded by Whig historians such as Hallam and Macaulay as a sequel to the struggles of the seventeenth century. On this view, Grey's ministers were lineal descendants of the seventeenth-century Whigs, who had secured the Revolution and Constitutional Settlement. This picture, however, is largely a product of nineteenth-century ideology, and is a gross oversimplification and distortion (the reader might like to speculate as to why contemporaries needed this myth). Indeed, the Prime Minister, Earl Grey, may well have promoted the bill rather from political expediency than commitment to high principle.

The Reform Act 1832 retained for the counties the ancient forty shilling qualification for freeholders (set in 1429; 8 Hen. VI c.7), but also enfranchised copyholders, leaseholders having leases for specified periods, and tenants at will paying rent of not less than £50. In boroughs, the qualification was occupancy of property worth at least £10, the effect of which was to enfranchise portions of the middle and lower-middle classes, but not artisans generally. The Reform Act may not seem to modern eyes a very bold measure, but its psychological impact in successfully changing an institution which had remained (like many English institutions including the legal system) formally unchanged since the Middle Ages, cannot be exaggerated. The Duke of Wellington was not alone in considering the old order the most perfect which could be devised. The Act was the first ever to deal comprehensively with the system of Parliamentary representation. It was entitled "an Act to change the representation of the people", a revolutionary concept in itself, since Parliamentary representation had previously been regarded as being of communities and interest groups, rather than of the people generally.

The Representation of the People Act of 1918 effectively completed a process which had begun with the 1832 Act. It introduced adult male suffrage and gave the vote to women above the age of 30 (reduced to 21 in 1928 and 18 for both sexes in 1969).

Undoubtedly the greatest constitutional development since that time has been the accession to the Treaty of Rome, which has conceded, though it is not universally acknowledged, recognition of a legal authority superior to the Crown in Parliament.

8. THE EUROPEAN UNION

On January 1, 1973 the United Kingdom became a member of the European Community. The Treaty of Rome was implemented by the European Communities Act 1972, section 2(1) of which gives effect to Community law without further enactment. Provisions of Community law which create rights and duties in individuals in member states are said to be "directly applicable". Other provisions impose obligations on the member states, but confer no rights upon individuals as such. Some Community laws take effect automatically: they are "self-executing". Others require implementation by specific enactment in the member states. In the United Kingdom this can either be by statutory instrument under section 2(2) of the Act, or by Act of Parliament. Although the Treaty only concerns those matters with a European element, those that affect citizens of member states, where such matters are concerned "[it] is like an incoming tide. It flows into the estuaries and up the rivers. It cannot be held back." (*HP Bulmer v J. Bollinger SA* (1974), *per* Lord Denning MR at 418) If there is a conflict between national law and EC law, the latter prevails.

EC law increasingly impinges on our lives, and in the context of this chapter it is interesting as an example of bureaucracy prevailing over older forms of domination. At the present stage of development, even direct democratic processes have only a limited part to play. The legislative powers under the Treaty lie with the Council of Ministers, the European Commission, and the European Parliament. The final judicial authority is the European Court of Justice. In pursuance of the economic goal of a single market, therefore, it is bureaucratic government which has been chosen, and any authority it possesses must derive from a perception of the rationality of its methods, and the goal it is pursuing.

The growing movement within the European Community for closer union, culminated in the Maastricht Treaty of 1992, which came into force on November 1, 1993. The first part of that Treaty makes substantial amendments to the original EEC Treaty, and renames it the European Community Treaty. The second part represents a declaration of political intent, and covers such matters as co-operation in the fields of foreign policy and security, and defence. The two parts, together with the European Communities Treaties (as to which see below) are referred to as the three "pillars of the Union".

The European Communities were established under three basic treaties. The first was the European Coal and Steel Community (the Treaty of Paris 1951). To this were added the two Treaties of Rome: that establishing the European Atomic Energy Community (Euratom); and that establishing the European Economic Community which came into operation in 1958. These three treaties are the primary sources of Community law, along with their various Annexes and Protocols. For readers of this work, it is the Treaty of Rome establishing the EEC which will be of most interest. Significant changes were made to this both by the Maastricht Treaty of 1992 and by the Treaty of Amsterdam 1997. The numbering of the Articles referred to in the text below is taken from the Treaty of Amsterdam.

The law of the EEC (now the European Community), consists of Regulations, Directives and decisions in particular cases. A Regulation has general application, and is directly applicable in all Member States (Art.249). Directives are binding on the States to which they are addressed (Art.249). Regulations and Directives now all appear in the *Official Journal* in the "L" series. The "C" series of the Official Journal contains non-normative communications and information. A decision is a decision in a particular case, and is "binding upon those to which it is addressed" (Art.249). A decision can be addressed to a state, or to a group of states, or to an individual (natural or legal).

The institutions of the European Communities from which EU law emanates, fall into two main categories. There are those institutions vested with political, legislative, executive and administrative functions. These are the Commission, the Council of the European Union (formerly the Council of Ministers) and the European Parliament, on the one hand, and the judicial organs of the Communities, namely, the Court of First Instance and the European Court of Justice, on the other.

The Commission consists of 25 members (Art.213 as amended by the Protocol on enlargement). The President and other members of the Commission are nominated by national governments subject to the approval of the European Parliament (Art.214). Commissioners must be nationals of Member States, and no Member State may have more than two of its nationals as Commissioners. The practice at the moment is for the larger Member States to have two Commissioners, and the smaller ones, one. They hold office for renewable periods of five years (Art.214). In the UK the current convention is to nominate the two Commissioners to represent the two dominant political parties (*The Times*, October 15, 1980). Commissioners must not seek instructions from, or be instructed by, individual Member States, and Member States for their part must respect the independence of the Commissioners. On appointment, Commissioners must give an undertaking to the Court of Justice that they accept the obligations of their office. The European Parliament has power to compel the whole Commission to resign by passing a motion of censure, which requires a two-thirds majority (Art.201). This power has not been invoked to date (the resignation of the Commission in the late 1990s was precipitated by a damning independent report see Szyszczak and Cygan (2005) 29 et seq).

The Commission functions as a collegiate body, in that it bears collective responsibility. However, there is inevitably a certain amount of subject specialisation so far as individual Commissioners are concerned.

Obviously, if every decision had to be collectively discussed, very little would get done. A great deal of use is made, therefore, of a written procedure whereby drafts are circulated amongst the Commissioners, and if no objection is taken within a fixed period, the draft is deemed to have been approved. Any objections or amendments will be considered at a full meeting of the Commissioners. Each Commissioner has a private office or staff, who tend to be of the same nationality as the relevant Commissioner. Each has a *chef de cabinet* or principal private secretary, who may deputise for his or her Commissioner at Commission meetings. In addition, the Commission has a large administrative staff divided between the Directorates-General (of which there are more than 20) responsible for the different areas of Community activity. Each of these has a Director-General responsible to the Commissioner whose "portfolio" includes that particular subject-area. Inevitably, there is a certain degree of overlap in the functions of these Directorates-General, and it is not unknown, at a micro-level, for inconsistent policies to be pursued simultaneously by different Directorates-General. This can result in a certain amount of friction. Because communication between the Directorates-General is imperfect, it is possible to be well advanced down a particular line of policy before the fact that another Directorate-General is pursuing a different course comes to light. Equally, it is possible for two Directorate-Generals to pursue the same goal each in ignorance of the other's activities thus wasting resources. These are problems known to national bureaucracies, of course, but perhaps the EU bureaucracies are more prone to them because of the problems created by different national traditions. It may also be the case that there are structural problems which need to be addressed if the occurrence of this sort of problem is to be reduced (it would be unrealistic to suppose that it can ever be eliminated altogether). Because of its much greater opportunity to master detail (each Directorate-General having specialised staff), the Commission tends to be at an advantage over both the Council and Parliament. In the UK the job of keeping an eye on the more technical aspects of legislation being proposed by the Departments of Government is largely performed by the House of Lords, especially through its specialised committees, though the House of Commons also monitors European legislation. The European Parliament, being an entirely elected affair, may or may not have expertise available in the more difficult and technical areas, and it can on occasion be somewhat capricious.

The Council consists of one representative of the government of each Member State. A distinction is drawn between general Council meetings, and specialised Council meetings. The former are attended by Foreign Ministers and discuss both external affairs, and matters of general Community concern. The specialised meetings are attended by the members of national governments whose portfolios include the particular subject on the agenda, for example agriculture, transport, and so on. Presidency of the Council rotates between the Member States for terms of six months. Under the EC Treaty (as amended), the power of decision lies largely with the Council acting on proposals from the Commission (unless the Council request the Commission to study an area). The Commission plays a key role in initiating and formulating policy, subject to the final decision of the Council. For decision making, normally qualified majority voting is used. This procedure can be used for legislation in all areas except those set out in Article 95 (see below). Qualified majority voting is a system of weighted voting under which the largest four states each have ten votes (the smallest, Luxembourg, has two) and the votes of other States reflect their respective sizes (Art.205). Unanimity, and therefore the consent of all member governments is not required. Under this system, as under simple majority voting, a party can find itself put under an obligation under the Treaty which represents a policy of which it does not approve. It thus represents a significant erosion of national sovereignty, and it is controversial for this reason. If a proposal is rejected, it goes back to the Commission for reconsideration. The result is that proposals can go through many drafts before an acceptable position is reached. Once a decision has been taken to adopt a policy, implementation will be left to the Commission.

The Maastricht Treaty made an important innovation to the legislative process when it introduced the "co-decision procedure" involving the European Parliament. Although the latter is the only institution of the Union which (since 1979) is democratically elected, it is not itself a law-making body. Its original role was purely consultative, and whilst the Council was required to consult it on some important matters (e.g. under Arts 54, 87 and 235 of the original Treaty), it was not obliged to follow its wishes. Later, the consultation process was extended (1977), but the Maastricht Treaty effected the major change. Under the so-called "co-decision" procedure, Parliament may veto legislation by an absolute majority of its members. Originally, under Article 100 (now Art.94) of the Treaty, the Council was required to act unanimously on a proposal for the Commission before issuing directives, regulations or taking administrative action. Article 100a introduced by Maastricht introduced a new procedure, which is further improved as a result of the Treaty of Amsterdam. Article 95 (which replaces Art.100a introduced by Maastricht) provides:

"(1) By way of derogation from Article 94 . . . The Council shall, acting in accordance with the procedure referred to in Article 251 and after consulting with the Economic and Social Committee, adopt the measures for the approximation of the provisions laid down by law, regulation or administrative action in Member States which have as their object the establishment and functioning of the internal market.

(2) Paragraph 1 shall not apply to fiscal provisions, to those relating to the free movement of persons nor to those relating to the rights and interests of employed persons."

Article 251 provides that the Commission must submit its proposals to the European Parliament and the Council. If Parliament does not propose any amendments, the Council acting by qualified majority voting may adopt the measure. If Parliament proposes amendments, the Council, if it approves *all* the amendments contained in Parliament's opinion, can adopt the proposed act (again by qualified majority voting). Otherwise, it must adopt a common position and communicate this, with reasons, to Parliament. The Commission must also inform Parliament of its position. Parliament then has three months to reject the common position by an absolute majority (it can, of course, accept it). If Parliament proposes amendments to the measure, it goes back to the Council, which may vote by qualified majority to adopt all the amendements, but if the Commission objects to any of them, it must act unanimously. If the Council does not approve the amendments, a Conciliation Committee is convened by the President of the Council in agreement with the President of the Parliament. The Conciliation Committee consists in equal part of representatives of the Council and of the Parliament. They must attempt to reach a joint text which can be approved by the Parliament by an absolute majority and by the Council by a qualified majority. If the joint text is not approved, the proposed act is deemed not to have been adopted.

Legislation promulgated in breach of the Treaty procedures can be declared void by the Court of Justice (see e.g. Case C295/90, *European Parliament v Council* in which the Students' Rights of Residence Directive was annulled).

In the interests of establishing the single European market, the Commission has embarked on a massive programme of legislation with the purpose of harmonising national laws which can provide an inhibition to the free movement of goods and services. As explained above, this legislation starts out in one or other of the Directorates-General. Hardly any branch of public or private law is unaffected by it. Regulations establishing EU institutions, such as the Office for the Harmonisation of the Internal Market in Alicante take effect without further national legislation. Directives, so far as the UK is concerned, must either be implemented under section 2(2) of the 1972 Act by statutory instrument, or be implemented by special Act of Parliament, as was done in the case of the Trade Marks Directive (the Trade Marks Act 1994). National legislation must, as far as possible, be construed in accordance with Directives even though unimplemented (*Marleasing SA v La Comercial Internacional de Alimentacien SA*, Case 106/89), and states can become liable to an individual adversely affected by failure to implement a Directive (*Francovich v Italy*, Cases 6 and 9/90).

In addition to EC law, there are a number of separate treaties which are important, affecting the UK's relationship with other European countries, such as the European Convention on Human Rights, the Brussels and Lugano Conventions on Jurisdiction and Enforcement (now the subject of Reg. 44/2001 for EU member states), and the European Patent Convention. The membership of these treaties may be wider than the Member States of the EU. The decisions of the European Court of Human Rights, and those of the European Patent Office tribunals, are important sources of law in their respective areas.

9. THE CHANGING CONSTITUTION

As we have intimated, the closer political and legal integration of the United Kingdom with mainland Europe has deep implications for the British Constitution, particularly for the cornerstone doctrines of the supremacy of the Crown in Parliament and Parliamentary sovereignty.

In the post-War years, Europe began a dual process of politico-cultural and economic renewal. The rallying point for politico-cultural consensus was the European Convention on Human Rights 1950. The Convention, closely modelled on the United Nations' Universal Declaration of Human Rights 1948, set out a framework for governance in Europe that sought to respect the ideals of freedom, democracy, and the Rule of Law. Although much of the drafting work on the Convention was carried out by the British, and although the Convention was rapidly signed and ratified by he UK, it was not until the enactment of the Human Rights Act in 1998 that the principal Convention rights were formally introduced into English law. Even then, the Act does not, strictly speaking, directly implement or incorporate the Convention. Rather, it is a UK statute which must be construed in its own terms as well as in the light of the Convention. In practice, the result of this delay in giving effect to the Convention rights was that, for many years, alleged breaches were brought to the European Court of Human Rights rather than being resolved in domestic courts—and, ironically, the UK government, having taken the lead in cultivating a modern culture of respect for human rights in Europe, found itself all too often being summoned to Strasbourg to defend its human rights record.

The foundations for economic co-operation in Europe were also laid in the 1950s, with the Treaty of Rome establishing the framework for the European Economic Community. By the time that the UK joined the Community in the early 1970s, the European Court of Justice (ECJ) had developed two fundamental principles of Community law. In *Costa v ENEL* (1964) the ECJ asserted the supremacy of Community law over inconsistent national law; and, in the *Van Gend en Loos* case (1963), the Court articulated the concept of direct effect, according to which citizens of Member States would be entitled in some circumstances to enforce their Community law rights in national courts (see Weatherill and Beaumont (1999), Ch.11). Hence, when the UK joined the Community, it was necessary for the accession statute to make it clear that Community law was both directly applicable and supreme. What might not have been anticipated at the time of accession was that the ECJ would take further steps to ensure the practical effectiveness of Community law. However, in *Von Colson* (1984), the Court articulated the principle of indirect effect, according to which (stated broadly) national law is to be interpreted in the light of the wording and purpose of Community law (particularly where national law is specifically concerned with the implementation of, say, an EC Directive); and, in *Francovich* (1992), the Court re-inforced the doctrine of direct effect by ruling that, in principle, a citizen might recover compensation from its government where the Member State in question had failed to take steps to implement Community law (see Szyszczak, 1992; and section 8 above). Not surprisingly, it has taken the English courts some time to adjust to these fundamental changes. Yet, there is no doubting the supremacy of Community law (see, in particular, the *Factortame* (1991) litigation), "European" arguments are increasingly pleaded (see the *ITF* case: and Barnard and Hare (1997)) and there are clear signs of an evolving purposive style of interpretation (see Ch.4).

As we have said, these important constitutional developments flag up the need to reconsider the traditional doctrine of Parliamentary sovereignty (*cf.* Hunt, 1997). Perhaps the most measured statement of the doctrine is that, while Parliament retains the ultimate authority to decree whether the UK is a Member of the European Community and is committed to the principles of the European Convention on Human Rights, *so long as we are "in"*—and, in both cases, we are now "in" with legislative backing—then sovereignty cannot operate as an occasional veto and domestic law must be interpreted accordingly. This is not to suggest, however, that the "Europeanisation" of domestic law has yet attained a plateau of constitutional stability.

For example, there are serious concerns about both the centralisation of powers and the democratic deficit in the European Community. And, the future of the comparatively recently incorporated European Convention on Human Rights is no more certain, for one of the dominant themes accompanying the promotion of the Human Rights Act was that the integrity of Parliamentary sovereignty should be maintained. As the Government White Paper (Home Office, 1997) stated:

"[T]he courts should not have the power to set aside primary legislation, past or future, on the ground of incompatibility with the Convention. This conclusion arises from the importance which the Government attaches to Parliamentary sovereignty . . . To make provision . . . for the courts to set aside Acts of Parliament would confer on the judiciary a general power over the decisions of Parliament which under our present constitutional arrangements they do not possess, and would be likely on occasions to draw the judiciary into serious conflict with Parliament." (para.2.13)

In line with this position, the Human Rights Act 1998 seeks to accommodate respect for human rights with Parliamentary sovereignty by, on the one hand, authorising the Courts to issue a so-called "declaration of incompatibility" (s.4(2)) while, on the other hand, providing that such a declaration does not "affect the validity, continuing operation or enforcement of the provision in respect of which it is given" (s.4(6)(a)) as well as stipulating that such a declaration "is not binding on the parties to the proceedings in which it is made" (s.4(6)(b)). Whether the logic of Parliamentary sovereignty can survive alongside the logic of a commitment to human rights (which is precisely that there should be limits to legislative competence) remains to be seen (*cf.* Mullender, 1998). A week, as many have remarked, might be a long time in politics; but peaceful constitutional evolution usually takes a little longer and it will be some time before the relationship between Parliament and the Courts, together with the place of the Convention in English law, can be treated as settled (and see further Ch.8 below).

If there are problems about the evolution of national constitutions within a larger regional legal order, this applies *a fortiori* to the evolution of a regional constitution. The Constitutional Treaty for the EU, which was formally signed in 2004, needs the ratification of all Member States by the end of 2006. Following the French

"No" vote in 2005, the prospects for the Constitution look poor. If the Constitution fails, this also casts doubt on the extent to which the EU can serve as a model for the integration of human rights into a community that is bound by its commitment to free trade (see Williams (2004) and Berry (2004)). As Szyszczak and Cygan (2005) remark, while the Charter of Fundamental Rights (the "Nice Charter") has "symbolic value", "the expression that the EU is founded on the principles of 'human dignity, freedom, equality, democracy and the rule of law' does not [suffice to] form a unified political, social or even legal culture" (p 234). It is one thing to legislate a covering framework for a single European market, quite another to constitutionalise a single European politico-legal order.

10. GLOBALISATION

The development of the European Union in conjunction with the politico-legal commitment in Europe to human rights is one example of an emerging form of regional governance. It is by no means the only such example worldwide; but, even more significantly perhaps, such forms of regional governance are themselves building blocks in the evolving phenomenon of global governance. Against this backcloth of governance at local, regional, and international level, the modern pressure towards (and counter-pressure away from) "globalisation" is taking place. Of course, as one of the buzz-words of our time, "globalisation" is a term that can be over-used to the point where, as some sceptics would have it, it becomes a mere theme in search of a focus. In the present context, however, we can take "globalisation" to refer to processes that (a) effect a closer integration of national economies, cultures, and legal systems, and (b) remove barriers to trade and transaction, interaction and communication (for a narrower, economist's, rendition of this, see Stiglitz, 2001). Sometimes these processes will work in such a way that the local is able to shape the regional and the global; at other times, it will be the global or the regional that shapes the local; and, at all times, it will be where these various spheres of governance meet that the conflicts of interest will be most acute (see de Sousa Santos, 2002).

While commentators heatedly contest the meaning and nature of globalisation (many economic historians pointing out that the world economy was actually more globalised up to 1914), debating whether it is a new form of colonialism or a step towards an international commonwealth, whether economic liberalism is compatible with respect for human rights, and so on, there is broad agreement that it is a development of major significance for the local sovereign nation state. As David Held and Anthony McGrew (2002) have put it:

"[I]t is important to explore the way in which the sovereign state now lies at the intersection of a vast array of international regimes and organizations that have been established to manage whole areas of transnational activity (trade, financial flows, crime and so on) and collective policy problems. The rapid growth of transnational issues and problems has involved a spread of layers of political regulation both within and across political boundaries. It has been marked by the transformation of aspects of territorially based political decision-making, the development of regional and global organizations and institutions, and the emergence of regional and global law." (p.6)

Not only does this "vast array of international regimes and organizations" comprise the visible formal agencies of governance (such as the familiar law-making institutions of the EC and the international organs associated with the UN), it includes, too, a myriad of non-governmental organisations. Moreover, any map of global governance would have to account for the activities of transnational corporations. For the United Kingdom, where local concerns about the retention of sovereignty continue to bulk large in the nation's relationship with the larger European community, as well as shape the reception of human rights, it scarcely needs saying that the questions posed by globalisation are highly pertinent. In particular, is *formal* power slipping away from local nation states to be taken over by regional and international agencies; and to what extent are *informal* processes and players ruling the world?

Generally speaking, lawyers have not taken the lead in raising, and then addressing, the many questions presented by globalisation. However, the very inter-connectedness of the threads of the modern world surely means that law will not escape the globalising processes. According to Lawrence Friedman (2002):

"If there is a globalised world, and globalising processes, if there is a globalisation of business and trade, and a globalised culture of production and consumption, then it follows that there must also be a globalised sector of law. In the modern world, law is dense, ubiquitous and pervasive. It is logical, then, to expect some kind of legal order or legal culture on the global level, and on a global scale. The question is what does this global legal order consist of?" (p.28)

With English as the formal lingua franca of the evolving legal order, with London law firms running international practices, and with English law governing many international commercial transactions, we can say that local influence in general, and English influence in particular, is not entirely a thing of the past. Moreover, within the sophisticated legal framework that has evolved in post-War Europe, a measure of local control and difference is retained through such flexible doctrines as subsidiarity (in the case of the EC) and the margin of appreciation (in the case of the ECHR). Nevertheless, if governance is to move to regional and global centres of power, or if a particular field (such as domain names on the Internet or the environment) is to be regulated in a co-ordinated way under the aegis of international compacts, the logic of these processes must be that there is some diminution of local sovereignty—or, to put this more aspirationally, the logic is that a practice of "enlightened sovereignty" should be cultivated (see Hobe, 2002), easing the friction between local and larger interests, and on the basis of which the global legal order comes to represent a truly international community.

As we move on, therefore, to develop an understanding of the features of the English legal system and its common law style of reasoning, we should guard against being over-parochial. Beyond national legal systems, regional and global law is rapidly taking shape; and, if we are to understand law in a globalised world of economic and cultural connection, where there is an ongoing need for co-ordination, compromise and concession, we need to be alert to these developments. No more than we can treat law as a closed discipline (see Ch.2), so we cannot treat local law as an autonomous system. For, in a globalised world, an understanding of local law implies some appreciation of the larger regulatory arenas in which local legal systems are now situated (Edgeworth, 2003; Lewis, 2006).

4
JUDGE-MADE LAW

I: Statutory Interpretation

Benjamin Cardozo, the celebrated American judge and jurist, once confessed that he had grown to see that, in its higher reaches, the judicial process was not one of discovery, but of creation (1921). Some fifty years later, Lord Reid, echoing these sentiments, argued that we must come to terms with the fact that judges make law:

"There was a time when it was thought almost indecent to suggest that judges make law—they only declare it. Those with a taste for fairy tales seem to have thought that in some Aladdin's cave there is hidden the Common Law in all its splendour and that on a judge's appointment there descends on him knowledge of the magic words Open Sesame. Bad decisions are given when the judge has muddled the pass word and the wrong door opens. But we do not believe in fairy tales any more.

So we must accept the fact that for better or worse judges do make law, and tackle the question how do they approach their task and how should they approach it." (1972, p.22).

Whilst it has been contended (see Dworkin, 1978) that we do progressive judges a disservice by conceiving of them as "making law", the descriptions offered by Cardozo and Reid at least have the virtue of signalling that the judicial process is not entirely mechanical. In this, and the following, chapter, we will examine adjudication in the appellate courts, considering both how judges do, and how they should, approach the business of adjudication. The interpretation of statutes provides the focus for this chapter, and the development of case law (and the doctrine of precedent) the focus for the next.

1. INTERPRETING STATUTES: THE SOURCES OF DIFFICULTY

Vast areas of law are nowadays located within a statutory framework. Hence, if a question of law has to be resolved in relation to some matter concerning, say, town and country planning, companies, taxation, immigration, social security, race relations, road traffic, and so on, the chances are that the starting point will be a provision in a statute or a statutory instrument. Of course, where such a question is at issue, it will not necessarily be taken to court, let alone to the appellate courts (see Chs 6–8). However, where the courts are brought into the matter, judges may stamp their interpretive authority at two levels. At one level, judges may simply give an authoritative ruling on the specific question posed, binding the parties to the dispute, and settling the specific issue should it arise again in the future (*cf.* Ch.5). However, at another level, judicial interpretations may, on occasion, effectively supersede the statutory provisions themselves. For instance, section 2(1) of the Race Relations Act 1968, provided that it was unlawful for suppliers of goods, facilities, and services, to exercise racial discrimination where such supply was "to the public or a section of the public". One question to which this gave rise was whether the members of a club constituted "a section of the public". In *Charter v Race Relations Bard* (1973), the House of Lords said that the thrust of section 2(1) was to distinguish between "public" and "private" situations (the Act applying only to the former). The significance of this was twofold: first, the *Charter* dichotomy between public and private situations became the framework for the application of section 2(1); and, secondly, this framework enabled the courts to apply the Act to colour bars in clubs pretty much as they wished. Thus, in *Charter* itself, the House indicated that a key reason for holding that the East Ham Conservative Club fell into the private category was the fact that members of the club were subjected to a genuine selection test. Yet, in *Dockers' Labour Club and Institute Ltd v Race Relations Board* (1976), the selection test was effectively abandoned, the House ruling unanimously, but controversially, that a working men's club in Preston was on the private side of the line because it was open only to members (even though such "members" were not subjected to a selection procedure as contemplated in *Charter*).

Where a statute is unclear on some matter, it is ripe for interpretation. But, given that Parliamentary draftsmen strive for precise expression, what is it about statutes that makes them unclear? The standard answer to this points to (i) the inevitable "open-texture" of language (*cf.* Hart, 1961, esp. pp.124–32) and (ii) the relative indeterminacy of legislative intention. In this section, we will consider these two elements of text and intent before suggesting that a third factor, judicial values, must be brought into the reckoning.

(i) The traditional account

According to the traditional account, it is in the nature of language that it is open to interpretation. In ordinary conversation, we can, if we so wish, clear up any uncertainty about a person's meaning as and when that uncertainty arises. However, this is not so with statutes. We do not (and, sometimes, of course, we could not) go back to the authors or drafters of unclear provisions for clarification; instead, if we want an authoritative ruling, we refer the matter to the courts. Where the uncertainty hinges on the language of the text, legal argument tends to focus on some alleged ambiguity or vagueness.

Where it is argued that a provision is ambiguous, the contention is that it can plausibly be interpreted in more than one way. For instance, in *Ealing London Borough Council v Race Relations Board* (1972), legal argument revolved around section 1 of the Race Relations Act 1968, which provided that, in specified situations, it was unlawful to discriminate against another on grounds of "colour, race, ethnic, or national origins". The question was whether "national origins" referred only to a person's place of birth (which would remain unchanged through a person's life), or whether it referred also to a person's nationality (which might change during a person's life). In the case itself, the specific point to be tested was whether it was lawful for Ealing LBC to refuse to put one Mr Zesko (who was born in Poland) on the waiting list for council housing, on the ground that he did not (at the time of his application) have British nationality. The Law Lords found in favour of Ealing, ruling by four to one that "national origins" did not include "nationality". Whilst the traditional account tends to present cases of this kind in terms of the relevant statute "being ambiguous", it would be more accurate to talk about statutes "being argued to be ambiguous". The point is that, while some statutory provisions are patently ambiguous, often it is a matter of an ambiguity being prised out of the text by counsel or the judge (*cf.* Miers and Page, 1990, esp. pp.157–62). A striking illustration of this can be found in the case of *Smith v Hughes* (1960). There, the question was whether some prostitutes who were soliciting passers-by from inside buildings overlooking Curzon Street in London, had committed an offence under the Street Offences Act 1959. This hinged on section 1(1) of the Act, which provided that it was an offence for a prostitute "to loiter or solicit in a street or public place for the purpose of prostitution". On the face of it, there was no ambiguity in this provision. Quite clearly, the offence of "loitering" could only be committed if the prostitutes were actually in a street or public place; and, on a natural reading of section 1(1), it seemed equally clear that the offence of "soliciting" could only be committed if the prostitutes were physically in a street or public place (*cf.* Williams, 1981). Nevertheless, on appeal from the Bow Street magistrates, the Divisional Court found the provision to be less than clear. Having recited section 1(1), Lord Parker C.J. said:

"Observe that it does not say there specifically that the person who is doing the soliciting must be in the street. Equally it does not say that it is enough if the person who receives the solicitation or to whom it is addressed is in the street". (861)

Accordingly, in Lord Parker's view, section 1(1) could be read as requiring (a) the soliciting prostitute to be in the street, or (b) the person solicited to be in the street, or (c) both the soliciting prostitute and the person solicited to be in the street. Having excavated these ambiguities, the Divisional Court compounded the surprise by holding that the prostitutes had committed the offence (an outcome consistent only with interpretation "b").

If the submission is that a statutory provision is vague, rather than ambiguous, argument will tend to proceed within a threefold framework comprising: (i) clear cases falling within the provision, (ii) clear cases falling outside the provision, and (iii) borderline cases in between. For instance, in the town and country planning legislation, planning permission is required for any activity which counts as a "development". This is defined as covering inter alia any "material change in the use" of land. But, what makes a particular change of use "material"? Whereas we might judge that there would be no material change of use should a farmer grow cabbages instead of potatoes in a field, and that (equally clearly) there would be a material change of use should the farmer turn his field into a caravan park, we might be unsure about the materiality of the change if the farmer were simply to allow a few people to leave their caravans in his field during the winter.

The stock example of a vague provision is one which incorporates the concept of a "vehicle" (*cf.* Bell and Engle, 1987, pp.75–6). For instance, would it be appropriate to classify as a "vehicle" such items as roller-skates, prams, bicycles, horses, skate-boards, and so on? This very question arose in the American case of *McBoyle v US* (1930), where the petitioner had been convicted of transporting a stolen vehicle across state lines in contravention of the National Motor Vehicle Theft Act 1919. Section 2 of the Act defined a motor vehicle as including "an automobile, automobile truck, automobile wagon, motorcycle, or any other self-propelled vehicle not designed for running on rails . . ." The short point was whether an aircraft fell within the statutory definition of a vehicle. On its natural reading, the definition seemed to contemplate that a vehicle ran on the land; and, whilst the phrase "any other self-propelled vehicle not designed for running on rails" might have been seized upon to widen the definition, the court declined to take this opening. The offence, therefore, had not been committed.

Apart from the open-texture of language, the other ingredient in the traditional account of statutory interpretation is the idea of legislative intent. Where the statutory text is unclear, judges may sometimes fall back on what they perceive to be the underlying purpose or intention of the provision. For example, in the *Ealing* case, one argument relied upon was that Parliament could not have intended to have legislated against discrimination on the grounds of nationality. For, when racial discrimination arrived on the political agenda, the main targets for such discrimination were immigrants from the West Indies who, as Commonwealth citizens, already had British nationality. Similarly, in *Smith v Hughes*, Lord Parker C.J., having found the text unclear, recurred to what he saw as the purpose of the legislation:

"Everybody knows that this was an Act intended to clean up the streets, to enable people to walk along the streets without being molested or solicited by common prostitutes. Viewed in that way, it can matter little whether the prostitute is soliciting while in the street or is standing in a doorway or on a balcony, or at a window, or whether the window is shut or open . . ." (at 861).

Again, in *McBoyle*, the question asked was what Congress had intended, but, in contrast with *Smith v Hughes*, the court reached a restrictive answer. For, in *McBoyle*, the point taken was that, at the time of the enactment of the statute in 1919, aeroplanes were well known, from which it followed that it would have been simple enough for the legislature to have signalled its intention to include aeroplanes within the Act, had it so wished.

If legislative intent was always to be understood in only a strictly historical sense, the older the statute the less likely that recourse to such intent would assist with problems of interpretation. Not only would evidence of original intent be less reliable, the world might have changed out of all recognition. For example, in *R. v Ireland* (conjoined with *R. v Burstow*) (1997), the question was whether the offence of assault occasioning actual bodily harm, contrary to section 47 of the Offences Against the Person Act 1861, could be made out where the defendant harassed women by making silent telephone calls to them (thereby causing them to suffer neurotic disorders). Clearly, the Victorian framers of section 47 would not have had psychiatric illness in contemplation, let alone neuroses induced by (not yet invented) telephone calls. However, the House of Lords treated the legislation as being of what Lord Steyn called "the 'always speaking' type" (at 233), so that the relevant inquiry was not as to the subjective intentions of the draftsmen but "as to the sense of the words in the context in which they are used" (at 233). Putting the question in these terms, the House—assisted by the earlier decision in *R. v Chan-Fook* (1994), that psychiatric injury may amount to bodily harm under section 47—decided that, in principle, the offence could be so committed.

Although there are obvious attractions in reading and applying statutes in a counter-factual (or hypothetical contextual) spirit, asking what the draftsmen would have said if they had been asked to provide for a particular situation, such an approach is scarcely free from difficulty. No doubt, there will be cases where, no matter how we position ourselves, it is clear that the legislators would have taken a particular view on a particular unanticipated issue. Yet, is this so in *Ireland* itself? How confident are we that the decision handed down by the House of Lords is the only plausible accommodation of a legislative scheme originating in the nineteenth century with a late twentieth-century mind-set? Similarly, what might we say about a case such as *DPP v Luft* (1976), in which the question was whether the Representation of the People Act 1949 (or its predecessor in 1918) regulated election publicity and expenses where the campaign was of a purely negative character (namely, "Do not vote for the National Front candidate")? It is one thing to believe that the Offences Against the Person Act at least implies a negative attitude towards menacing telephone calls, but it is not immediately obvious whether negative publicity is incompatible with fair play during election periods (see further Brownsword, 1977).

Quite apart from the speculation involved in seeking to match historic legislative intention to contested current applications, there is the question of how far it is constitutionally proper for courts to engage in this kind of exercise. In *Royal College of Nursing of the United Kingdom v Department of Health and Social Security* (1981), Lord Wilberforce sought to lay down the relevant limits. According to his Lordship, it is perfectly proper for legislation to be interpreted broadly and flexibly where new developments "fall within the same genus of facts as those to which the expressed policy has been formulated . . . [or] if there can be detected a clear purpose in the legislation which can only be fulfilled if the extension is made" (p.822). What judges are not authorised to do is to gap-fill and second-guess Parliament's intention. Unfortunately, this tends to replace one interpretive problem (concerning the intent underlying the original legislation) with another (namely, how to read Lord Wilberforce's guidance and its application to the particular piece of legislation). So, for example, when the recent Pro-Life Alliance litigation (*R. (Quintavalle) v Secretary of State for Health* (2002 CA; 2003 HL)) was before the Court of Appeal, the Alliance clearly believed that Lord Wilberforce's guidance favoured its narrow interpretation of the Human Fertilisation and Embryology Act, 1990 (such that an "embryo" produced by electrically stimulating an egg—the egg having itself been engineered by a process of cell nuclear replacement—rather than by traditional sperm fertilisation would not count as an "embryo" for the purposes of the Act). However, the Court turned the Alliance's argument on its head, relying on Lord Wilberforce's guidance to authorise a broad and inclusive reading of the Act; and, on further appeal, the House of Lords took much the same approach, Lord Steyn saying that, because there was no good reason "why an embryo produced otherwise than by fertilisation should not have the same status as an embryo created by fertilisation . . . [this was] a classic case where the new scientific development [fell] within what Lord Wilberforce called 'the same genus of facts'" (para.26).

In a number of these cases, the question mark about the legislature's intention arises because a new technology is in play (see further, Brownsword, 2005b). This is so, for instance, in *Ireland*

and the Pro-Life Alliance case; and, indeed, the dispute in the RCN case, in which Lord Wilberforce set out his guidance, centred on a new technique for carrying out abortions. The pace at which new technologies, particularly information and bio-technologies, have come on stream is, of course, one of the themes associated with "globalisation" (see pp.83–85 above); and, because larger regulatory frameworks are needed for these global developments, it will come as no surprise to find that the problems that we have been discussing in relation to domestic legislation are replicated in relation to international legal instruments. A nice illustration is Art.11*bis* of the Berne Convention, which dates back to 1928 and which was intended to give the authors of literary and artistic works the exclusive right of authorising the broadcasting of their works. For many years, the exercise of this right was unproblematic: the various collecting societies, acting on behalf of authors, negotiated with the broadcasting organisations in their own countries. However, with the development, first, of satellite broadcasting (where the signal is sent up to the satellite before being sent down to the viewer) and, more recently, the Internet, it is unclear whether negotiation on behalf of authors should be in the country of transmission or the country of reception. The language of Art.11b is open-ended enough to comprehend both a transmission and a reception theory; satellite and Internet broadcasting were scarcely in the contemplation of the drafters; and, given that considerable amounts of money are at stake here, a pragmatic solution is likely to prevail, quite possibly with the same wording in Art.11*bis* being applied differently according to the particular broadcasting medium.

Open-textured language and unanticipated situations do not quite exhaust the difficulties. A further possibility is that a legislature may have anticipated the point, but may then have deliberately fudged the issue (Laird, 1992). For example, Parliament may have realized that the application of the race relations legislation to clubs was highly contentious, and thus framed the legislation in such a way that the issue was left unclear—thereby leaving the matter to be settled in the courts (*cf.* Dworkin, 1986(a), Ch.1). And, of course, if it sometimes suits domestic legislatures to leave matters a shade unclear, this applies a fortiori to regional and international law-making bodies where agreement may require a certain greyness in the final text.

Summing up the traditional view, the principal problem with statutes is that they suffer from the limitations of language as a means of communication; and, while an inquiry into the legislative intent may sometimes settle the point, there can be no guarantee that legislative intent will be complete or decisive on all issues. From this, it seems reasonable to infer that a "progressive" style of judging involves going behind textual unclarity to investigate legislative intent (*cf.* Law Commission, 1969). However, a number of questions are prompted by this account. For example, why do some judges stick to the text while others base themselves on legislative intent? How do the former resolve the issue where the language is unclear? Conversely, how do the latter resolve the issue where the intent is unclear? Moreover, where judges declare that such and such is the legislative intent, to whose intent precisely are they referring? Are they talking about actual or hypothetical intent (i.e. what the legislature would have intended had it addressed the particular question)? And, does intent relate to the meaning of the text or to the purpose of the legislation (*cf.* MacCallum, 1966)? Finally, drawing on the examples cited in our discussion, it may be wondered whether the traditional account can explain the restrictive approach adopted in *McBoyle* and *Ealing* as against the broad approach evident in *Smith v Hughes*. To begin to answer these various questions, we need to bring judicial values into the picture and develop a "three-dimensional" account of statutory interpretation.

(ii) Towards a three-dimensional account

The basic premiss of the three-dimensional account is that we cannot make sense of statutory interpretation unless we take judicial values seriously. Judges, it must be appreciated, have their own ideas about what is "right" and "wrong", "good" and "bad", "just" and "unjust", and so on, such views reflecting a judge's background values (or ideology).

Whilst some of these values specifically concern the appropriate role for a judge when called upon to interpret statutes, others are of a more general nature. We can start by considering the former.

In a fascinating article, Lon Fuller (1948–9) sets out the facts and Appeal Court judgments in the hypothetical case of the Speluncean Explorers. The factual situation is a variation on the theme of *Dudley and Stephens* (see Ch.2). Briefly, a group of five potholers, trapped in a cave, decide that one of their number will have to die if the remainder are to have any chance of being rescued. To select the victim, dice are thrown. The leader of the group, one Roger Whetmore, is duly selected and killed. However, when the four surviving potholers are rescued, they are charged with the murder of Whetmore, the relevant statute providing: "Whoever shall wilfully take the life of another shall be punished by death". What makes Fuller's construction of this case particularly intriguing, is that the statute seems to offer only two options: *either* the defendants must be acquitted (e.g. by saying that the killing was not really "wilful", or that, given the throw of the dice and some semblance of consent by Whetmore, they did not actually "take the life of another"; or that a defence of necessity must be implied into the statute); *or* that the defendants must be convicted, in which case they face the death penalty. Commonly, it is felt that the former option is too lenient while the latter is too severe. Is there no way out of this dilemma? One of Fuller's hypothetical judges, Tatting J., gets out of this by withdrawing from the case on the grounds that he cannot make up his mind. Law students, however, are not usually let off the hook quite so easily. Another strategy would be to argue that the phrase "shall be punished by death" is merely permissive. However, given the general understanding that "may" (not "shall") signals a permission, it would take a bold judge to argue for this interpretation (at least, in this crude fashion). Significantly, none of Fuller's judges presents this line of argument, for it surely would be condemned, not simply as a bad argument, but as an argument unworthy of a judge.

Although Fuller's judges eschew the crude tactic outlined above, they display very different understandings about the constraints upon judges. At one extreme, Keen J. argues that judges should not manipulate statutory materials. Accordingly, he objects strongly to the style of judging practised by another judge, Foster J.:

"We are all familiar with the process by which the judicial reform of disfavored legislative enactments is accomplished. Anyone who has followed the written opinions of Mr. Justice Foster will have had an opportunity to see it at work in every branch of the law . . .

The process of judicial reform requires three steps. The first of these is to divine some single 'purpose' which the statute serves. This is done although not one statute in a hundred has any such single purpose, and although the objectives of nearly every statute are differently interpreted by the different classes of its sponsors. The second step is to discover that a mythical being called the 'legislator', in the pursuit of this imagined 'purpose', overlooked something or left some gap or imperfection in his work. Then comes the final and most refreshing part of the task, which is, of course, to fill in the blank thus created. _Quod erat faciendum_.

My brother Foster's penchant for finding holes in statutes reminds one of the story told by an ancient author about the man who ate a pair of shoes. Asked how he liked them, he replied that the part he liked best was the holes. That is the way my brother feels about statutes; the more holes they have in them the better he likes them. In short, he doesn't like statutes." (at 634)

Yet, even Foster J, does not represent the opposite extreme from Keen J. For, one judge, Handy J., takes the dictates of public opinion and common sense to be guiding and resolves the issue quite independently of the statute. In other words, whilst Foster J. at least pays lip-service to the legislation, Handy J. proceeds as though the statutory provision were irrelevant. In addition to having different ideas about what is appropriate for judges _qua_ judges when confronted by a statutory text, Fuller's judges presuppose different views about their relationship with the legislature. For Keen J., the principle of legislative supremacy is axiomatic, from which it follows that judges have an obligation to keep faith with statutes, interpreting them in accordance with their plain meaning without allowing one's own conceptions of justice to intrude upon this process. The position of Foster J. is more complex. Having held that it was no part of the legislature's purpose to apply the statute to a killing such as that carried out by the explorers, he anticipates the kind of charge which Keen J. might level against his approach:

"There are those who raise the cry of judicial usurpation whenever a court, after analyzing the purpose of a statute, gives to its words a meaning that is not at once apparent to the casual reader who has not studied the statute closely or examined the objectives it seeks to attain. Let me say emphatically that I accept without reservation the proposition that this Court is bound by the statutes of our Commonwealth and that it exercises its powers in subservience to the duly expressed will of the [legislature]. The line of reasoning I have applied above raises no question of fidelity to enacted law, though it may possibly raise a question of the distinction between intelligent and unintelligent fidelity . . . The correction of obvious legislative erorrs or oversights is not to supplant the legislative will, but to make that will effective." (at 625–6)

Taken at face value, Foster J. shares Keen J.'s general principle of fidelity to the legislature, but argues for an intelligent application of this axiom. One suspects, however, that Keen J. takes Foster J.'s professions with a pinch of salt, believing that the latter regularly traverses the boundary between intelligent fidelity and downright infidelity.

It should not be thought that the differences between Fuller's judges, being merely hypothetical, have no real-world correlates. Lord Denning, for example, could well be cast in Foster J.'s role for it was a regular theme in his judgments that the courts should fill in the gaps left by the legislature. Thus, in *Nothman v London Borough of Barnet* (1978), he proclaimed:

"Faced with glaring injustice, the judges are, it is said, impotent, incapable and sterile. Not so with us in this court . . . Whenever the strict interpretation of a statute gives rise to an absurd and unjust situation, the judges can and should use their good sense to remedy it—by reading words in, if necessary—so as to do what Parliament would have done had they had the situation in mind." (at 1246).

Not surprisingly, comments of this kind sometimes elicited a reaction worthy of Keen J., most famously in *Magor and St Mellons RDC v Newport Corporation* (1952), where Lord Simonds deplored the "naked usurpation of the legislative function under the thin disguise of interpretation" (at 191). However, for a more measured articulation of the principle of judicial restraint in the face of legislation, we could scarcely improve upon Lord Diplock's comments in *Duport Steels Ltd v Sirs* (1980):

"[At] a time when more and more cases [involve] the application of legislation which gives effect to policies that are the subject of bitter public and Parliamentary controversy, it cannot be too strongly emphasised that the British Constitution . . . is firmly based on the separation of powers: Parliament makes the laws, the judiciary interprets them . . . Where the meaning of the statutory words is plain and unambiguous it is not for the judges to invent fancied ambiguities as an excuse for failing to give effect to its plain meaning because they themselves consider that the consequences of doing so would be inexpedient, or even unjust or immoral. In controversial matters such as are involved in industrial relations there is room for differences of opinion as to what is expedient, what is just and what is morally justifiable. Under our Constitution it is Parliament's opinion on these matters that is paramount." (at 541)

Accordingly, in *Duport Steels*, the House of Lords, reversing the Court of Appeal, held that secondary industrial action (undesirable though some judges undoubtedly must have regarded it) was immune from suit as "an act done by a person in contemplation or furtherance of a trade dispute" (within the meaning of s.13(1) of the Trade Union and Labour Relations Act 1974).

Before we draw general underlying values into our discussion, we should take stock. Essentially, two sets of tensions are emerging. First, there is a tension between those sets of values which argue for and against judicial restraint. On the one hand, it is argued that judges must operate within the bounds of the statutory text (that it is improper, as it were, to take a scalpel to the text); and that, on controversial political issues, the clear decisions of elected legislative assemblies must be applied. Against this, however, it is argued that where a statute, however clear, is glaringly unjust, then it is wrong for judges to operate as agents of injustice. Secondly, there is a tension between two conceptions of what is involved in keeping faith with the principle of legislative supremacy. One conception argues for a strict observance of the text, whereas the rival conception argues for an intelligent reconstruction of the statutory scheme, thereby drawing out its purpose and intent in the particular case (*cf.* Dworkin, 1986 (b), Ch.1). In this pair of tensions, we have the beginnings of an ideal-typical scheme of judicial approaches to the interpretation of statutes. However, before we develop this idea (in the next section), we must examine the way in which general background values impinge on this process.

We can start by returning to *McBoyle v US*. There, it will be recalled, it was held that the stolen aircraft was not a vehicle within the meaning of the statute, with the result that the offence had not been committed. The key to this decision lay in the so-called "fair warning" principle, which Holmes J. articulated as follows:

"Although it is not likely that a criminal will carefully consider the text of the law before he murders or steals, it is reasonable that a fair warning should be given to the world in language that the common world will understand, of what the law intends to do if a certain line is passed. To make the warning fair, so far as possible the line should be clear. When a rule of conduct is laid down in words that evoke in the common mind only the picture of vehicles moving on land, the statute should not be extended to aircraft simply because it may seem to us that a similar policy applies, or upon the speculation that if the legislature had thought of it, very likely broader words would have been used." (at 27)

This, it will be appreciated, reflects very closely the Fullerian version of the Rule of Law (see Ch.1), according to which it is incumbent on government to promulgate clear rules, and stick to them—especially where we are dealing with the criminal law and the possible imposition of punishment. Indeed, in the *Ealing* case, Lord Donovan carried this principle beyond the criminal law, arguing that the council should not be stigmatised (albeit in civil proceedings) as having practised unlawful discrimination where the statute failed to give fair warning that it covered discrimination on the grounds of nationality. In sharp contrast with the restrictive interpretations in *McBoyle* and *Ealing*, the decision in *Smith v Hughes* seems to reflect a very different philosophy. For, there, not only was the fair warning principle ignored, it was violated in circumstances where the defendant prostitutes may have genuinely believed that, by retiring into buildings (rather than accosting men in the street), they were keeping on the right side of the line which marked the boundary between lawful and unlawful solicitation.

The tensions evident in these cases crystallised explicitly in *Wills v Bowley* (1983). There, following an incident outside a nightclub in Cardiff, Wills was charged with using obscene language to the annoyance of passers-by contrary to section 28 of the Town Police Clauses Act 1847, and with assaulting three police officers in the execution of their duty. The magistrates dismissed the charge under section 28 (apparently on the ground that there were actually no passers-by to be annoyed), but they convicted Wills on the assault charge. However, the dismissal of the charge under section 28 opened up a tricky point of law. Under section 28, a police officer has a duty to arrest any person who, within his sight, "commits" any of a number of listed offences (including not only using obscene language to the annoyance of passers-by, but also such matters as flying kites, beating carpets, and furiously driving cattle through streets). Given that the magistrates had found that Wills had not "committed" an offence under section 28, did this invalidate the arrest? If so, the police officers were no longer acting in the execution of their duty, and Wills could not be convicted on the assault charge—moreover, Wills would also have had a civil law claim against the policemen for false imprisonment. By three to two, the House of Lords held that, under section 28, there must be an implied power to arrest provided that the arresting officer has an honest and reasonable belief that one of the listed offences has been committed. As Lord Bridge (one of the majority) put it:

"The persisting conflict [in the authorities and amongst the judges] may disappoint but need surprise no one, since it does no more than reflect on a small scale a wider conflict which touches many social, political and legal problems, between two equally important aims of public policy, respect for the liberty of the subject on the one hand and the maintenance of law and order on the other." (at 92)

Since it would undermine crime control objectives if police officers were unable to act on their honest and reasonable suspicions (without fear of civil counter-claims), the majority felt that "law and order" values must outweigh "liberty of the subject" values. Against this, the minority Law Lords struck the balance the other way. Thus, Lord Elwyn-Jones said:

"Where the liberty of the subject is concerned, the court should not go beyond the natural construction of the statute and the strict terms of the grant of the power to arrest without warrant." (at 72)

In other words, in terms reminiscent of the majority view in the Birmingham sex discrimination case (see Ch.2), the minority in *Wills v Bowley* argued that individuals have rights (here, to their liberty) which must take priority over considerations of inconvenience, unworkability, practical difficulty, and the like. Clearly, whereas the minority philosophy in *Wills* is in line with the thinking in *McBoyle*, the majority philosophy has more in common with the thinking in *Smith v Hughes*.

We could give many more examples (from different areas of law) of the impingement of general background values—evidence of the kind famously highlighted by John Griffith concerning such matters as the judiciary's "tenderness towards private property and dislike of trade unions, strong adherence to the maintenance of order, distaste for minority opinions, demonstrations and protests, indifference to the promotion of better race relations, support of governmental secrecy, concern for the preservation of the moral and social behaviour to which it is accustomed [and so on]". (1985, pp.225–6)

No doubt, we could also find examples in which background values inclining in the opposite direction have prevailed. For instance, although the offence of aggravated trespass in section 68 of the Criminal Justice and Public Order Act 1994 was created to deal with environmentalists who intimidated, obstructed or disrupted any "lawful activity" on the land (principally, the activities of road contractors building new highways), the section has not been uniformly interpreted against the interests of protesters and demonstrators. In at least one case, crop destroyers (protesting at the trial planting of genetically modified crops) have escaped conviction on the ground that, because no one was working in the fields at the relevant time, no "activity" was taking place (see Brown, 2001) For obvious reasons, this restrictive interpretation assists the protesters in every possible way.

Although cataloguing the impact of background values would reveal quite a lot about the "politics" of the judiciary (see Waldron, 1990, Ch.6), our immediate task is to develop a framework within which we can organise both our materials and our thoughts about the handling of legislation. Accordingly, it is to the elaboration of such framework that we must now turn.

2. THE THREE-DIMENSIONAL VIEW: A THEORETICAL FRAMEWORK

In this section, we will construct a theoretical framework within which we can structure our thinking about statutory interpretation. This framework will have two components, a typology of kinds of cases, and a typology of judicial approaches.

(i) A typology of kinds of cases

There are a number of ways of classifying the kinds of cases in which judges are called upon to interpret statutes. An obvious strategy would be to classify according to content. For instance, criminal law statutes might form one category, tax statutes another, perhaps welfare statutes another, and so on (cf. Willis,

1938). However, cutting across substantive divisions of this kind, we propose a threefold typology comprising "clear cases", "difficult cases", and "hard cases". The basis of this typology is the way in which the statute, and its application, is viewed by the interpreting judge. By a "clear case", we mean a case in which the judge (i) believes that the meaning of the statute is plain (whether this is because of the text or the underlying intent), and (ii) has no reservations about the application of the statute so interpreted (i.e. the judge does not regard the application as unjust, inconvenient, or in any way problematic). By a "difficult case", we mean a case in which the judge believes that the meaning of the statute (however regarded) is not plain. And, by a "hard case", we mean a case in which the judge (i) believes that the meaning of the statute is plain (whether this is because of the text or the underlying intent), and (ii) has significant reservations about the application of the statute so interpreted. Adopting (and adapting) Twining and Miers' (1991) terminology, we can say that the judge in a clear case is in the position of a "happy interpreter", the judge in a difficult case in the position of a "puzzled interpreter", and the judge in a hard case in the position of an "unhappy interpreter".

This typology clarifies where, and how, background values might enter into the interpretation of statutes. In *clear* cases, the judge's background values and the perceived meaning of the statute push in the same direction; thus, a routine application of the statute is to be expected. In a *difficult* case, the judge perceives no clear meaning, but his background values may offer a way of resolving the issue—the "fair warning" principle and its analogues (see *McBoyle* and *Wills v Bowley*), for example, might play just this function. Similarly, suppose that in *Charter* and *Dockers* the judges genuinely were unsure whether the race relations legislation was intended to apply to clubs. In these circumstances, their decisions might have reflected their underlying values, believing that, in cases of doubt, the interests of club members (in their freedom of (non)-association) should take priority over the interests of those excluded from clubs. In *hard* cases, the judge's underlying values offer some resistance to a routine application of the statute. What a particular judge will do in a case of this kind depends upon whether he holds to a principle of fidelity to legislative enactment, and, if so, how much weight he attaches to the principle in the instant case. Some judges (e.g. Fuller's Keen J.) will apply the plain meaning of the statute, injustice notwithstanding; other judges (e.g. Fuller's Handy J.) will follow the dictates of intuitive justice, the plain meaning of the statute notwithstanding; and other judges will apply the plain meaning on some occasions (for example when, as Lord Diplock says in *Duport Steels*, the issue is politically controversial) but follow their sense of justice on other occasions. These possibilities, however, need to be placed within a typology of judicial approaches, which is the second component in our theoretical framework.

(ii) A typology of judicial approaches

In the previous section, we noted that there were tensions between those judicial approaches which called for restraint and those which did not, and between text-based and intention-based conceptions of the principle of legislative supremacy (or fidelity to legislative enactment). From these tensions, we can draw four ideal-typical judicial approaches to the interpretation of statutes, which we can call "textual formalist", "purposive formalist", "weak realist" and "strong realist".

We can start with the two formalist approaches. For a judge following a "textual formalist" approach, statutes are to be interpreted by focusing on the language of the relevant provisions. This does not mean that there can be no reference to legislative intent; but the sole object of referring to such intent is to determine in what sense the legislators meant the words to be read. By contrast, for a judge following a "purposive formalist" approach, statutes are to be interpreted with a view to implementing the purposive scheme and decisions made by the legislature. Where such an approach is employed, the statutory language is relevant to determining the legislative purpose, but it is simply one piece of evidence. Despite their respective emphases on text and intent, both these approaches are "formalist". What this signifies is that fidelity to legislative enactment (whether understood in terms of textual meaning or legislative purpose) overrides all other underlying values. Accordingly, while formalist approaches may bring residual values into play in difficult cases (*cf. McBoyle, Wills v Bowley, Charter, Ealing*), they are not brought into play in hard cases (*cf. Duport Steels*).

In contrast to both kinds of formalist approach, both kinds of realist approach are result-orientated. Crucially, this means that neither kind of realist approach treats fidelity to legislative enactment as an overriding value. In the case of a "weak realist" approach, fidelity to legislative enactment is recognised as having some value (or utility), but it does not hold a privileged position in a regime of underlying values—it is simply one item to be weighed in calculating the right result, all things considered. In the case of a "strong realist" approach, fidelity to legislative enactment is not recognised as having any value whatsoever. Accordingly, whereas a weak realist approach involves an inquiry into what the legislature said or intended (but without any guarantee that the statute will be applied), a strong realist approach proceeds quite independently of any inquiry into what the legislature said or intended. It follows that, whilst the perception of cases as clear, difficult, or hard, has some significance for judges adopting a weak realist approach, for judges adopting a strong realist approach such perceptions are immaterial (at least, for the purposes of determining the outcome of the case).

Finally, there is the question of whether, in employing this typology, we can rely on what we read in the published opinions of judges. Where legal culture strongly supports fidelity to legislative enactment, there is little reason for formalist judges to operate covertly. Of course, in difficult cases, some formalists may be reluctant to make too open a showing of their underlying values. By and large, however, judgments written by formalists should be pretty transparent. Judgments written by realists, on the other hand, may well be much less open. In particular, in hard cases, realist judges might be tempted to cover their tracks by presenting the issue as though it were a difficult or clear case (*cf.* Brownsword, 1979; Adams and Brownsword, 1991). For example, suppose that in *Smith v Hughes* Lord Parker C.J. actually viewed the case as a hard case, the statute plainly pointing to an acquittal while his underlying "law and order" values demanded a conviction. Openly to set up the case in these terms, however, would be to provide a hostage to fortune. Accordingly, the case is first presented as "difficult" (the statute not actually saying whether the prostitutes have to be in the street), and then as "clear" (the purpose of the statute being well-known and plainly covering the situation). It follows that, while formalists will present cases as clear, difficult, or hard, according to how they actually view them, realists will tend to steer clear of hard case presentations. A pressing interpretive difficulty, therefore, is knowing whether cases presented as clear or as difficult really are seen that way, or whether realism is at work with judges employing what Lord Radcliffe has called a "facade" approach (see Paterson, 1982, pp.140–3).

3. THE RULES OF STATUTORY INTERPRETATION

Traditionally, a good deal is made of the so-called rules of statutory interpretation: the "literal", the "golden", and the "mischief" rules. It is not entirely clear whether these rules are to be understood as descriptions-cum-explanations of how judges interpret statutes (it is commonly said, for instance, that the literal rule is most widely followed), or as prescriptions of how judges ought to interpret statutes; nor is it clear whether the rules complement, or compete with, one another. In this section, we will employ our typological framework to see what sense we can make of the rules.

(i) The literal rule

According to Lord Atkinson, in *Vacher v London Society of Compositors* (1913):

"If the language of a statute be plain, admitting of only one meaning, the Legislature must be taken to have meant and intended what it has plainly expressed, and whatever it has in clear terms enacted must be enforced though it should lead to absurd or mischievous results." (at 121)

In *Vacher*, the plain meaning arose under section 4(1) of the Trade Disputes Act 1906, which purported to confer immunity on trade unions in respect of any alleged tortious acts (irrespective of whether such acts were performed in the furtherance of a trade dispute). The perceived absurdity of this was that trade unions were put beyond the reach of the civil law, allowing the union in *Vacher* to issue an alleged libel with impunity. Nevertheless, as Lord Macnaghten emphasised, it was not for the courts to deviate from the plain meaning:

"Some people may think the policy of the Act unwise and even dangerous to the community. Some may think it at variance with principles which have long been held sacred. But a judicial tribunal has nothing to do with the policy of any Act which it may be called upon to interpret". (at 118)

The parallel between *Vacher* and *Duport Steels* is striking. In both cases, the House was confronted with legislation illegitimately conferring (as the House would see it) immunity on trade unions. Yet, in both cases, restraint was advocated. In the light of our typology of cases, it will be appreciated that the literal rule applies primarily to hard case situations. Its central contentions are:

(1) that, in hard cases, judges apply the plain meaning of the statute (as revealed by the language of the text);
(2) that they do this because they treat fidelity to legislative enactment as an overriding value; and,
(3) that this is how judges ought to interpret statutes in hard cases.

In short, the literal rule maintains that judges do, and should, approach hard cases as textual formalists. As such, it is open to two lines of criticism.

First, the literal rule is incomplete. If we expect the rules of statutory interpretation to *describe* how judges operate across the full range of cases, the literal rule has one glaring deficiency. It purports to describe decision-making in hard cases (and, by implication, in clear cases); but, it says nothing about difficult cases. Precisely the same deficiency appears if we consider the *prescriptive* aspect of the literal rule: it tells us how judges ought to tackle hard cases (and, by implication, clear cases), but offers no prescription for difficult cases. Although we can begin to cover this gap by drawing on the underlying presupposition that judges do and should act like textual formalists, this does not specify which underlying values judges do and should employ in difficult cases. Secondly, even if the literal rule's description of decision-making in hard cases is sometimes correct, it mispre-scribes judicial deference to legislative enactment. Why, as Lord Denning asked in *Nothman*, should judges remain impotent in the face of glaring injustice? If, for instance, Parliament decreed in the plainest terms that all blue-eyed law students should be put to death, the literal rule would apparently prescribe that judges should enforce the rule. If so, critics (not least, blue-eyed law students) might conclude, so much the worse for the literal rule.

(ii) The golden rule

In *River Wear Commissioners v Adamson* (1877), the defendant own-ers of a steam vessel, the *Natalian*, were caught in a storm near the mouth of the Wear. The crew escaped, but the unattended vessel was carried by the storm into Sunderland docks where it struck and damaged the plaintiffs' pier. The plaintiffs sought compensation under section 74 of the Harbour, Docks, and Piers Act 1847, which provided that the owners of vessels were to be "answerable . . . for any damage done by [their vessels] . . . to the harbour, dock, or pier . . ." On the face of it, the defendants were liable under section 74, even though, in the circumstances, they were blameless and would not be liable under the common law. After some considerable agonising, the majority of the House of Lords ruled that the defendants were not liable. According to Lord Blackburn:

"[The] golden rule is . . . that we are to take the whole statute together, and construe it all together, giving the words their ordinary signification, unless when so applied they produce an inconsistency, or an absurdity or inconvenience so great as to convince the Court that the intention could not have been to use them in their ordinary signification, and to justify the Court in putting on them some other signification, which, though less proper, is one which the Court thinks the words will bear." (at 764–5)

The majority, in other words, considered that, where neither the pier owners nor the shipowners were blameworthy, it would be absurd to read section 74 as shifting the risk of storm damage to the latter (thereby creating a form of strict liability, i.e. liability without fault).

Whilst the golden rule can be read as enjoining a purposive formalist approach, in *River Wear Commissioners* itself, it seems to be promoting a realist approach to hard cases. Read in this latter way, the golden rule flatly contradicts the literal rule, its equivalent theses being:

(1) in hard cases, judges reject the plain meaning of the statute in favour of a construction which is in line with underlying values of justice and convenience;
(2) they do this because they reject fidelity to legislative enactment as an overriding value; and
(3) this is how judges ought to interpret statutes in hard cases.

Like the literal rule, the golden rule (as a script for realism) is vulnerable to two lines of criticism. First, as with the literal rule, its narrow focus on hard cases leaves it descriptively and prescriptively incomplete in relation to difficult cases. Of course, we can extrapolate from the golden rule's hard case statements, that in difficult cases judges do and should follow a realist approach. However, this says nothing about which underlying values judges do and should bring to bear upon the resolution of difficult cases. Secondly, the golden rule may be criticised as offering only a limited description of what judges do in hard cases and, more importantly, as misprescribing for such cases. Indeed, *River Wear Commissioners* nicely illustrates the latter aspect of this line of criticism. On the one hand, Lord Blackburn defended his adoption of the golden rule as follows:

"There is a legal proverb that hard cases make bad law; but I think there is truth in the retort that it is a bad law which makes hard cases. And I think that before deciding that the construction of the statute is such as to work this hardship [i.e. on the shipowners], we ought to be sure that such is the construction, more especially when the hardship affects not only one individual but a whole class." (at 770)

Against this, however, Lord Gordon (dissenting) relied on multiple citations of the literal rule, together with the usual accompanying rhetoric that it is not for the judges to set themselves above the legislature. In short, the arguments in favour of the golden rule are restatements of the arguments against the literal rule, and vice versa.

As we have said, the golden rule may be read alternatively, not as a script for realism, but in terms of a purposive formalist approach: namely, as the view that judges do and should follow the general legislative purpose, treating fidelity to the legislature as overriding. As such, the golden rule moves more into line with the literal rule, albeit relying on an intent-based conception of fidelity to legislative enactment. The upshot of this is that, as in the case of the literal rule, it is both descriptively and prescriptively inadequate in relation to difficult case situations, as well as being open to the charge that, in hard cases, its rigid deference to legislative intent sets up judges as agents of injustice.

(iii) The mischief rule

The so-called mischief rule, which emanates from *Heydon's* case (1584), presupposes that legislation is aimed at providing a remedy for some "mischief" (i.e. problem). From this it follows that the task for the judges is to interpret the legislation in such a way as to "suppress the mischief, and advance the remedy". This injunction can be interpreted both narrowly (by emphasising the mischief to be suppressed) and broadly (by emphasising the facilitation of the remedy). Thus, in the *Ealing* case, whereas the majority favoured the narrow approach (it being emphasised that discrimination on the grounds of nationality was not one of the mischiefs at which the race relations legislation aimed), Lord Kilbrandon (who dissented) took a broader approach (arguing that, if a defence of discrimination on the grounds of nationality were to be recognised, it would be even more difficult in practice for claimants to establish real cases of racial discrimination). In this light, what do we make of the mischief approach?

Essentially, the mischief approach is in line with a purposive formalist approach, with its narrow and broad applications being variations on the purposive formalist theme. Thus, it is open to precisely the same kinds of criticisms which we have just outlined in connection with the golden rule read as a purposive formalist approach. In other words, it is both descriptively and prescriptively inadequate in relation to difficult case situations; and, in hard cases, its rigid deference to legislative intent sets up judges as agents of injustice.

(iv) The New Purposivism: Pepper v Hart

As the mischief rule most explicitly recognises, the text of a statute is the product of a process that often starts with the articulation of an issue (the mischief) and the formulation of a response to that issue (the remedy). The source of a particular statute might be traced, for example, to the report of an official committee or commission (including, since the mid-1960s, reports regularly produced by the Law Commission); or it might be found in a Government White Paper; or, increasingly, the genesis of a statute might lie in a directive or decision emanating from the European Union. For anyone attempting to interpret a statute in the light of either its purpose or the mischief at which it is aimed, the background history of the legislation looks like an obvious resource. Yet, the traditional approach in the English legal system (encouraged, no doubt, by a preference for literalism) has been to take a restrictive line on the use of materials—especially materials drawing on parliamentary debates—other than the *ipsissima verba* of the statute.

Throughout the twentieth century, however, a less restrictive approach—so to speak, a new purposivism—gained ground, it being generally accepted that the reports of official committees and commissions may be relied on to identify the mischief (see e.g. Lord Diplock in *Fothergill v Monarch Airlines Ltd* (1981)). Such an approach is nicely illustrated by *DPP v Bull* (1994), where the Divisional Court was asked to rule on whether section 1(1) of the Street Offences Act 1959 covered solicitation by a male prostitute (*cf. Smith v Hughes* above). In holding that the Act applied only to female prostitutes, the Court relied on the Report of the Wolfenden Committee (1957), the recommendations of which led to the 1959 Act, and in which it is apparent that the Committee was concerned only with the mischief of female prostitution. Predictably, there are also clear indications of a more permissive approach to the use of background materials where legislation is designed to bring domestic law into line with the requirements of EU law. So, for instance, in *Pickstone v Freemans plc* (1989), where the House of Lords was called upon to interpret regulations that were intended to give effect to a decision of the ECJ, Lord Keith said that he considered it "to be entirely legitimate for the purpose of ascertaining the intention of Parliament to take into account the terms in which the draft [regulation] was presented by the responsible minister and which formed the basis of its acceptance" (at 112).

Without doubt, the decision that above all symbolises the new purposivism is that of the seven-member House of Lords in *Pepper (Inspector of Taxes) v Hart* (1993) (on which, generally, see Miers, 1993). Stated simply, the substantive point of law at issue in *Pepper v Hart* was whether an employee's "perks" (for example, flight discounts for employees of airline companies) should be valued for tax purposes at the standard market rate or at the (potentially lower) real cost to the employer. This was a matter of considerable importance to the taxpayers in *Pepper v Hart*. For they were schoolmasters at Malvern College who, for many years, had been able to educate their sons at the College at a concessionary rate (20 per cent of the full fee). Was this taxable benefit to be assessed at the full fee rate or at the level of (variable) cost actually incurred by the College? In the event, the House unanimously ruled that the latter valuation applied; and, for five of the seven Law Lords, the clinching factor was that the parliamentary history made it clear that the intention was to tax the benefit on the basis of a marginal cost valuation. Indeed, *Hansard* revealed that, during the passage of the relevant Bill, a specific assurance had been given on the very question of concessionary education for the children of teachers.

On the question of whether it was legitimate for the court to rely on the Parliamentary record, the House (with the exception

of the Lord Chancellor) took the view that, in certain circumstances, the traditional exclusionary principle should be relaxed.
Lord Browne-Wilkinson laid down the new guidelines in the
following terms:

"I therefore reach the conclusion . . . that the exclusionary rule
should be relaxed so as to permit reference to Parliamentary
materials where: (a) legislation is ambiguous or obscure, or leads
to an absurdity; (b) the material relied upon consists of one or
more statements by a Minister or other promoter of the Bill
together if necessary with such other Parliamentary material as is
necessary to understand such statements and their effect; (c) the
statements relied upon are clear." (at 640)

Given even this limited invitation to turn to the parliamentary
record, counsel (and courts) have since made frequent use of the
ruling in *Pepper v Hart*. Indeed, immediately after *Pepper v Hart*,
counsel invited the House to rely on the parliamentary record in
Warwickshire County Council v Johnson (1993). Briefly, the question
in this case was whether an employee, such as a store manager,
could be held criminally accountable under the Consumer
Protection Act 1987—which question turned on whether, within
the meaning of section 20(1) of the Act, such a person was "acting
in the course of a business of his". Although the House was
already minded to give a negative answer to the question, its
view was re-inforced by the parliamentary record which showed
quite clearly that the words "of his" had been included precisely
to ensure that individual employees were not prosecuted.

Although many regard *Pepper v Hart* as a move in the right
direction, it does give rise to predictable practical concerns but
also to an important constitutional concern about the empowerment of the executive.

First, there is the practical concern that there will be a drift
away from the strict guidelines laid down in *Pepper v Hart*, leading to more and more time being spent scanning the parliamentary record. Indeed, Lord Browne-Wilkinson himself was
one of the first to caution against counsel engaging in fishing
expeditions (trawling through parliamentary debates in the hope
of finding support for their preferred interpretation)—as his
Lordship emphasised in *Melluish (Inspector of Taxes) v BMI (No.3)
Ltd* (1995) at 468, the parlimentary record should be introduced
only where it gives a clear and direct answer to the very point at
issue. However, as Lord Steyn has remarked (Steyn, 2001), in the

real world of litigation, it is not so easy "to decline *in limine* to receive [a Ministerial statement] on the ground that the requirements of ambiguity or absurdity are not satisfied" (p.66).

This leads to a related concern. Court time and lawyers' time is money. One of the attractions of keeping interpretation close to the text is that it keeps legal argument within a tight compass. If we extend the compass for interpretative argument, we need to be aware of the costs implications—hence the concern that we have just sketched about any relaxation in the *Pepper v Hart* requirements. However, relaxation also signals greater flexibility as to the materials that can be brought to bear on legal argument and this may engender uncertainty as to both process and outcomes. In this light, one might be troubled by *R v Human Fertilisation and Embryology Authority Ex p. DB* (1997) In this historic litigation, Diane Blood argued that the Authority was acting unlawfully in denying her access to her deceased husband's frozen sperm. At first instance, Sir Stephen Brown P. rejected Mrs Blood's application after hearing arguments drawing not only on the text of the Report of the Committee of Inquiry into Human Fertilisation and Embryology (1984) (which led to the Act in 1990) and (under a broad reading of *Pepper v Hart*) statements made by the Lord Chancellor while the Bill was passing through Parliament, but also on a statement made by Dame Mary Warnock (who chaired the Committee of Inquiry) in which she speculated that, had the Committee considered such a case, it would have seen no ethical or public policy objections to allowing the woman to have access to the frozen sperm. Although Mrs Blood lost this round of the litigation, she returned to triumph before the Court of Appeal, aided not so much by a new purposivism (to the contrary, the Court took a literal approach) but by a pragmatism that recognised that the case was strictly a one-off (see Morgan and Lee, 1997).

Secondly, Lord Steyn (2001), writing extra-judicially, has voiced the following constitutional concern about *Pepper v Hart*:

"To give the exectuive, which promotes a Bill, the right to put its own gloss on the Bill is a substantial inroad on a constitutional principle, shifting legislative power from Parliment to the executive ... It is in constitutional terms a retrograde step: it enables the executive to make law." (p.68)

Ministers, as Lord Steyn points out, speak for the government, not for Parliament (not for the legislature). It follows that *Pepper v Hart* not only has the wrong focus in looking to the *executive* for evidence of _legislative_ intention, it adds legal weight to the de facto power of the former at the expense of the latter; and, what is more, the values of the Rule of Law are threatened if the executive is able to make law by strategic Ministerial statement not evident on the face of the legislation (see, too, Kavanagh, 2005). This does not mean, however, that there is no place in our jurisprudence for _Pepper v Hart_, but its role should be limited to the matter of fair dealing by the executive. In this way, _Pepper v Hart_ would make a distinctive contribution to the Rule of Law by ensuring that the executive cannot "get away with saying in a parlimentary debate that the proposed legislation means one thing in order to ensure the passage of the legislation and then to argue in court that the legislation has the opposite meaning" (p.67). In a judicial capacity, Lord Steyn has recently applied the spirit of these remarks to the use of Explanatory Notes now prepared by the government department responsible for the particular piece of legislation. Thus, in _Westminster City Council v National Asylum Support Service_ (2002), his Lordship said:

"If exceptionally there is found in Explanatory Notes a clear assurance by the executive to Parliament about the meaning of a clause, or the circumstances in which a power will or will not be used, that assurance may in principle be admitted against the executive in proceedings in which the executive places a contrary contention before a court. This reflects the actual decision in _Pepper (Inspector of Taxes) v Hart_ ... What is impermissible is to treat the wishes and desires of the Government about the scope of the statutory language as reflecting the will of Parliament." (para.6)

On this cautionary note we can return to the new purposivism which, like _Pepper v Hart_, has its limits and proper function.

Whilst the new purposivism may reflect a shift in the way that the majority of judges approach the task of interpreting statutes, the fact of the matter is that each judge will have his or her own sense of how far ordinary language can be strained in order to implement the spirit of the legislation, as indeed they will have their own ideas about how far a purposive approach can be relied on to respond to the merits in hard cases—judicial approaches, as we have said, are cut from different cloths, some formalist (whether textualist or purposivist), others realist (weak or strong). Two relatively recent cases, _Cutter v Eagle Star Insurance Co Ltd_ (1998) and _Bellinger v Bellinger_ (2003) serve to illustrate that even in the House of Lords, where interpretive freedom is at its high point, there are limits to purposivism.

Cutter involved two appeals, arising from two separate incidents in which the plaintiffs had been injured by the negligence of car drivers. In one case, the accident took place in an open car park in Grimsby; in the other case, the accident occurred in a multi-storey car park in Tunbridge Wells. In neither case was there any practical prospect of recovering compensation from the negligent driver. In both cases, insurance companies stood as the defendants under provisions contained in the Road Traffic Act 1988. The liability of the defendant insurers hinged on the interpretation of section 145(3) of the Act, the effect of which was that the insurers would be liable if the plaintiffs' injuries arose out of the use of a vehicle "on a road". The short point, in other words, was whether a car park should be treated for the purposes of the Act as a road. In both cases, the Court of Appeal ruled in favour of the plaintiffs, but the House of Lords took a different view. As a matter of ordinary language, the plaintiffs' case was relatively weak. However, they argued that the statute should be interpreted in the light of its general purpose, which (they contended) was not simply to protect the public against the use of vehicles *on roads*, but more generally against *the use of vehicles*. To this, Lord Clyde, giving the principal judgment, said:

"It may be perfectly proper to adopt even a strained construction to enable the object and purpose of legislation to be fulfilled. But it cannot be taken to the length of applying unnatural meanings to familiar words or of so stretching the language that its former shape is transformed into something which is not only significantly different but has a name of its own. This must particularly be so where the language has no evident ambiguity or uncertainty about it". (at 425)

Even allowing for the European licence, according to which it is "proper to strain to give effect to the design and purpose behind the legislation, and to give weight to the spirit rather than letter" (at 426), there are limits to purposivism: cats cannot be turned into dogs (nor dogs into cats, see Lord Bingham in the Pro-Life Alliance case (2003) at para.9), and no more can car parks be turned into roads. Of course, the House sympathised with the plaintiffs (see 431), but straining the language was not the only argument against them. In particular, if car parks were treated as roads, this might extend the scope of road traffic and vehicular offences without giving parties fair warning (for example, by requiring cars to be lit even when parked in car parks); it might afford statutory authorities greater opportunities to interfere with private property; and it might impinge on the powers of local authorities to charge for parking in off-street car parks. The consequences of bending the legislation to meet the needs of the plaintiffs, in other words, would be far-reaching and complex. In such circumstances, not only does purposivism reach its limits, the courts too cannot tackle such matters—if change is necessary, if car parks are sometimes to be roads, it is for the legislature to redraw the map.

The story in *Bellinger*, albeit arising in a very different context, is much the same. The question, there, was whether Mrs Bellinger, who was a male-to-female transsexual, should be treated as a "female" for the purpose of contracting a valid marriage. This hinged on the interpretation of section 11(c) of the Matrimonial Causes Act 1973 according to which a marriage is void unless the parties are "respectively male and female". Gender re-assignment can go so far; but, even after hormonal treatment and surgery, Mrs Bellinger lacked a uterus and ovaries and she still had the standard 46XY male pattern of chromosomes. As Lord Hope observed: "The body can be altered to produce all the characteristics that the individual needs to feel comfortable. . . . But medical science is unable, in its present state, to complete the process. It cannot turn a man into a woman or turn a woman into a man" (para 57). Nevertheless, as Lord Hope also remarked, the key legislative words "male" and "female" are "not technical terms and . . . they must be given their ordinary, everyday meaning in the English language" (para 62). In principle, the conventions of the English language might change such that a person is to be treated as "male" or "female", regardless of their biological characteristics and simply by reference to the way they dress or comport themselves. However, as Lord Nicholls saw it, to treat Mrs Bellinger as "female" would involve giving the legislative terms "a novel, extended meaning" (para 36). Crucially:

"This would represent a major change in the law, having far reaching ramifications. It raises issues whose solution calls for extensive enquiry and the widest possible consultation and discussion. Questions of social policy and administrative feasibility arise at several points, and their interaction has to be evaluated and balanced. These issues are altogether ill-suited for determination by courts and court procedures. They are pre-eminently a matter for Parliament. . . ." (para 37).

Moreover, even though the European Court of Human Rights, in *Goodwin v United Kingdom* (2002), had only very recently ruled that the treatment of transsexuals in English law was out of line with Convention requirements, the House in *Bellinger*—echoing the approach in *Cutter*—acted on a sense of the limits of its institutional competence. Hence, while the House was prepared to issue a declaration of incompatibility under the Human Rights Act (recording that the legislative provisions are inconsistent with respect for Convention rights), it was not prepared to revise the statutory distinction between male and female; if those who are born with the biological characteristics of a male of the species are to be sometimes treated as having become a female, this is another map that has to be redrawn by the legislature.

(v) Synthesis

Our discussion of the rules of statutory interpretation highlights a number of shortcomings in our understanding of how judges do approach, and how they should approach, the interpretation of statutes. In both respects, our problems centre on difficult and hard case situations.

First, in relation to difficult cases, where *ex hypothesi* fidelity to legislative enactment (however regarded) cannot be straightforwardly fulfilled, the rules of statutory interpretation are of no descriptive or explanatory assistance. What need to be investigated here are the values upon which judges characteristically rely in such cases. We also need to think about how judges ought to decide difficult cases. For example, in a case like *Wills v Bowley*, where the statute was open to interpretation, should the judges have favoured "law and order" values (as the majority held) or should they have favoured the liberty of the subject (as the minority held)? Or, again, in the race relations cases, faced with doubts about the scope of the legislation, were the judges right to adopt a restrictive approach, or should they have taken a bolder line in applying the statute to the problem of racial discrimination?

Secondly, in relation to hard cases, we can surmise that judges of a formalist predilection will favour the literal rule (which prescribes deference to the plain meaning of a statute) whereas judges of a realist persuasion will favour the golden rule (interpreted as a licence to decide in accordance with the perceived justice of cases).

However, we should not always take citations of these rules at face value. In particular, where a realist approach is in play, we cannot discount the possibility that the various rules of interpretation might be cited in an opportunistic way. Consider, for example, a case like *Smith v Hughes*, where the language of the statute points pretty clearly towards an acquittal. Here, a realist judge seeking a *conviction* might appeal either to the golden rule or to the mischief rule (broadly applied) (in fact, just the kind of presentation found in Lord Parker C.J.'s opinion); whereas the obvious move for a realist judge seeking an *acquittal* would be to appeal to the literal rule. It should also be noted that the tension between the literal and golden rules (as hard case prescriptions) does not square in any simple way with the tension between utilitarian and right-and-duty approaches (*cf.* Ch.2). For a utilitarian, if a general rule is to be adopted, there may be some sense in deferring to legislative enactment (i.e. following the literal rule). In its classical form, though, the whole point of utilitarianism is to eschew any general principles or rules, each case being determined on its specific utilities. Viewed in this way, a utilitarian would think it right to decide each hard case as it arose, sometimes deferring to legislative enactment but, at other times, following the merits of the case (i.e. operate as a utilitarian weak realist). From a right-and-duty perspective, the literal rule is unacceptable because it advocates that judges should enforce rules which plainly violate subjects' rights. But, equally, the golden rule is unacceptable if it permits judges to ignore legislation whenever the fancy takes them. What this perspective seems to require, therefore, is that judges should keep faith with legislative enactments where individual rights are not violated, but should intervene to protect such rights where legislation involves a violation. In other words, from a right-and-duty standpoint, irrespective of whether there is a formal Bill of Rights, statutes should be interpreted in such a way that they do not infringe individual rights.

To be sure, in the light of *Bellinger* (2003), it has to be conceded that this is sometimes easier said than done. It is one thing to accept that the rigidity of the law of marriage compromises the rights of transsexuals, quite another for a *court* to attempt to rectify the situation either by reading the legislation in a wholly alien way or by creating a new policy on the hoof.

4. TAKING STOCK

If we are to understand how judges approach the interpretation of statutes, two points must be underlined: first, that judges are presented with considerable interpretive leeway (arising, as the traditional account explains, from the open texture of language and the relative indeterminacy of legislative intent); and, secondly, that underlying judicial values impinge on the process of interpretation. Such values impinge at a number of levels: they predispose judges to a particular (formalist or realist) interpretive approach; in difficult cases, they may be called upon to break the deadlock between rival interpretations; and, they determine whether a judge sees a case as a hard case, and how he responds in such a situation. To advance our understanding, the pattern and origination of these values needs to be analysed and explained.

In relation to the question of how judges *ought to* approach the interpretation of statutes, the standard progressive view is that judges should incline towards purpose rather than text (i.e. should adopt a purposive formalist approach rather than a textual formalist approach). However, this offers no prescription for difficult cases (where the statutory purpose is unclear), and it implies a questionably rigid deference to legislative purpose in hard cases. On the other hand, both kinds of realist approach threaten to license judges to do what they want, and, without some considerable qualification, they do not seem to be the answer. In the next chapter, we will return to these questions when we consider a further set of difficult and hard cases.

5

JUDGE-MADE LAW

II: Case Law Development

In this chapter, our interest remains in appellate court adjudication, but our specific focus is upon judicial development of the law through the cases. Our discussion has four parts. First, by sketching the expansion and contraction of the modern law of negligence, we consider some of the leeways built into the development of the case law. Secondly, we examine the doctrine of precedent. Thirdly, in the light of our discussion of case law materials, we further elaborate our typology of judicial approaches. And, fourthly, we return to the question of how judges ought to decide cases on points of law.

With our sights set so firmly on the appellate courts, it may be objected that we suffer from what Jerome Frank called "appeal-courtitis". Frank (1949; 1950) argued that, instead of endlessly investigating the work of the higher courts, jurists should spend more time examining fact-finding operations in the trial courts. It should be emphasised, therefore, that appellate court adjudication represents only a tiny fraction of the overall amount of adjudicative business conducted in courts and tribunals; that any attempt to understand what is going on in the courts must investigate all facets of adjudication (including judicial approaches to fact-finding); and that it may well be, as Frank maintained, both that a psychological understanding of decision-making would enhance our appreciation of judicial fact-finding, and that the so-called adversarial approach to fact-finding is profoundly unsatisfactory (*cf*. Chs 6–7).

1. THE DEVELOPMENT OF CASE LAW

It is commonly thought that, if anything, the leeways in case law are even more extensive than those found in statutory materials. Whereas exercises in statutory interpretation are tied to a particular form of words, this constraint does not apply where the issue is the legal significance of a particular case. The point is that appellate court cases do not necessarily speak with one voice: there are often dissenting judgments; even if there is unanimity as to the result of a case, the judgments do not necessarily rely on identical reasoning; and, even if a particular judgment is agreed to be the relevant text, it will not necessarily lay down a canonical form of words to set the bounds of future legal argument. We need not agonise about this, for it is clear that the leeways in case law are at least as extensive as those in statutes. To illustrate this, we can trace some key developments in the modern law of negligence (*cf.* Harlow, 1987).

The law of negligence is entirely the creation of the judges. In order to recover compensation, the claimant must establish that the defendant acted in a way which fell below a standard of reasonable care; that the defendant actually caused the claimant's loss; that the damage suffered by the claimant was a reasonably foreseeable result of the defendant's carelessness; and that, in principle, it would be reasonable for the defendant to be held accountable to the claimant (the so-called "duty of care" question).

In the recent case-law, the requirement of a causal link between the defendant's carelessness and the claimant's injury has proved particularly tricky (see Hoffmann, 2005). For example, in *Fairchild v Glenhaven Funeral Services Ltd* (2002), the question was whether causation was established where the claimant, C, could establish that two distinct defendants, A and B, had each been careless in exposing C to asbestos but could not identify which party's carelessness had actually caused C's asbestos-related illness. Lord Bingham summarised the dilemma facing the court in the following terms:

"It can properly be said to be unjust to impose liability on a party who has not been shown, even on a balance of probabilities, to have caused the damage complained of. On the other hand, there is a strong policy argument in favour of compensating those who have suffered grave harm, at the expense of their employers who owed them a duty to protect them against that very harm and failed to do so, when the harm can only have been caused by breach of that duty and when science does not permit the victim accurately to attribute, as between several employers, the precise responsibility for the harm he has suffered." (para 33)

The House, judging it more unjust that a victim be denied redress than that liability be imposed on a careless employer, ruled that C is entitled to recover against both A and B. This is by no means the end of the difficulties occasioned by causation (see, in particular, *Gregg v Scott* (2005)). However, putting such matters to one side, we can say that the law of negligence hinges on three questions, the answer to each depending upon the elusive concept of reasonableness. It would not be entirely a caricature of the law, then, to say that a claimant can recover in negligence if, in all the circumstances, it is reasonable for him to do so. In what follows, we focus solely on the critical duty of care question.

The story of the modern law of negligence begins with *Donoghue v Stevenson* (1932), the case of the alleged snail in the opaque ginger beer bottle (see Ch.2). There, it will be recalled, the House of Lords decided by three to two that the manufacturers owed the pursuer, the consumer of the product, a duty of care. In the immediate aftermath of *Donoghue*, however, it was not clear how wide an application the decision had. Taking Lord Atkin's majority speech as one's guide, *Donoghue* could have been interpreted rather narrowly as a case specifically concerned with: (i) a manufacturer's liability for defective products; (ii) products which pass from manufacturer to consumer without any reasonable possibility of intermediate inspection; and (iii) foreseeable risk of injury to the consumer. Indeed, given that *Donoghue* involved (allegedly) defective ginger beer, it must have been arguable that the case was limited to liability for products (like food and drinks) which were manufactured for human consumption. On the other hand, some parts of Lord Atkin's speech suggested a much broader principle:

"At present I content myself with pointing out that in English law there must be, and is, some general conception of relations giving rise to a duty of care, of which the particular cases found in the books are but instances . . . [R]ules of law arise which limit the range of complainants and the extent of their remedy. The rule that you are to love your neighbour becomes in law, you must not injure your neighbour; and the lawyer's question, Who is my neighbour? receives a restricted reply. You must take reasonable care to avoid acts or omissions which you can reasonably foresee would be likely to injure your neighbour. Who, then, in law is my neighbour? The answer seems to be—persons who are so closely and directly affected by my act that I ought reasonably to have them in contemplation as being so affected when I am directing my mind to the acts or omissions which are called in question . . ." (at 580)

What, then, was the significance of *Donoghue*? Was it a narrow decision on product liability, or a decision advancing a general principle, the neighbour principle, as providing an answer to the duty of care question across the full range of negligence situations?

By the time of *Home Office v Dorset Yacht Co Ltd* (1970), it was clear that *Donoghue* was an authority of central significance, the neighbour principle setting the framework for the answer to duty of care questions and moving negligence away from rigid situation-based categories of liability. Accordingly, in *Dorset Yacht*, the House of Lords ruled that, in principle, the Home Office could be held liable for negligently supervising borstal boys (who, having escaped from the control of their supervising officers, damaged some yachts in Poole harbour), despite the fact that there was scant authority for imposing a duty of care in such circumstances. The point about *Donoghue* was that the law of negligence was now open to imaginative extension (rather than modest incremental expansion). Impelled by this generalising spirit, in *Anns v Merton London Borough* (1978), Lord Wilberforce formulated a "two-stage" test for the existence of a duty of care:

"[T]he position has now been reached that in order to establish that a duty of care arises in a particular situation, it is not necessary to bring the facts of that situation within those of previous situations in which a duty of care has been held to exist. Rather the question has to be approached in two stages. First one has to ask whether, as between the alleged wrongdoer and the person who has suffered damage there is a sufficient relationship of proximity or neighbourhood such that, in the reasonable contemplation of the former, carelessness on his part may be likely to cause damage to the latter—in which case a prima facie duty of care arises. Secondly, if the first question is answered affirmatively, it is necessary to consider whether there are any considerations which ought to negative, or to reduce or limit the scope of the duty or the class of person to whom it is owed or the damages to which a breach of it may give rise." (at 751–2)

Although this may seem merely to have consolidated the existing position, the two-stage test was perceived to imply a presumption in favour of finding a duty of care. Moreover, applying this bold approach, the House in *Anns* (as in *Dorset Yacht*) found that, in principle, a public authority (here, a local authority administering the building regulations) must answer for its negligence.

Cases like *Donoghue, Dorset Yacht* and *Anns* involve negligent acts or omissions, rather than negligent statements. Although negligent statements, like negligent acts, turn on negligence, English law has treated these heads of liability as related but distinct. By the middle of the twentieth century, an emerging issue was whether a duty of care would be recognised in respect of negligent statements leading to financial loss. In *Hedley Byrne and Co Ltd v Heller and Partners Ltd* (1964), the House of Lords decided that, in principle, a duty of care would lie where there was a special relationship between the parties. Although *Donoghue* could not directly settle this issue, its general conception of proximity (the neighbour test) remained the key to answering the duty question. There remained, however, an important difference between liability for negligent acts and negligent statements. With regard to the former, the standard heads of recovery were physical injury (as in *Donoghue* itself) or damage to property (as in *Dorset Yacht*). However, purely financial loss was not normally recoverable. In respect of negligent misstatements, however, the significance of *Hedley Byrne* was that it opened the way to recovery for purely financial loss, the plaintiff advertising agents in that case simply incurring financial loss as a result of relying on negligent advice from the defendant merchant bankers (the advice concerning the creditworthiness of one of the plaintiff's clients). Whilst the precise scope of *Hedley Byrne* liability remained contentious, by the time of *Anns*, it was firmly established as an important feature of the modern law of negligence.

Some fifty years on from *Donoghue*, in *Junior Books Ltd v Veitchi Co Ltd* (1983), the House of Lords seemed ready to draw the progressive strands of the intervening years into an even more extensive law of negligence. The question in *Junior Books* was whether the plaintiff building owners ("A"), who were in contract with a firm of building contractors ("B"), could use *the law of negligence* to recover the costs associated with relaying a defective floor from the defendant sub-contractors ("C") who had negligently laid the floor in the first place. (It should be explained that, because A had no direct contract with C, it was not open to A to use *the law of contract* to recover the costs from C; see Adams and Brownsword, 1990.) To sharpen the issue, the House treated A's loss (the defective floor) as a case of purely financial loss rather than damage to property. Developing the indications given in *Dorset Yacht* and *Anns* (i.e. that the law must proceed on the basis of the general principle of proximity) and *Hedley Byrne* (i.e. that in special circumstances purely economic loss may be recoverable in negligence), the House decided by four to one that, in principle, the plaintiffs were entitled to be compensated (via the law of negligence) for their purely financial losses. But, what precisely was the scope of *Junior Books*? At its narrowest, it could be read as limited to situations where building owners and sub-contractors have some exceptionally proximate relationship (the House emphasised that the relationship between the parties was almost equivalent to contract, that the defendants knew who was to be the ultimate customer for the flooring work, and that the plaintiffs relied on the defendants' skill and care). At its broadest, *Junior Books* could be interpreted as a synthesis of the *Donoghue* and *Hedley Byrne* lines of authority, allowing recovery in negligence for purely economic loss provided that there was sufficient proximity between the parties, and notwithstanding that the plaintiff would have been unable to have recovered in contract. The radical implication of this broad reading would be that, in a product liability case such as *Donoghue*, the plaintiff consumer might have a claim in negligence against the product manufacturer if the defective product, without causing physical injury, *simply fell short of the expected standard of quality or fitness* (e.g. if the ginger beer in *Donoghue* had simply been flat). On this reading, the law of negligence threatened to supersede the law of contract.

Predictably, the decision in *Junior Books* encouraged a wave of litigation, so much so that the English courts (although not the Privy Council nor the courts in the Commonwealth at large: see Hoyano, 1995; and Martin, 1996 and 1997) rapidly began to beat a retreat. This involved presenting (and thereby marginalising) *Junior Books* as a one-off decision (a case, as lawyers euphemistically put it, decided "on its own special facts"); casting doubt on the wisdom of Lord Wilberforce's two-stage test in *Anns* (insisting, in particular, that a duty of care could arise only where it would be "fair, just, and reasonable"—potentially a two-edged sword, but one tending to cut in only the one direction during the decade following *Junior Books*); overruling the decision in *Anns* itself (see *Murphy v Brentwood District Council* (1990), where seven Law Lords (rather than the usual five) convened to pronounce that local authorities were not answerable in negligence for purely economic losses arising from their administration of the building regulations); and, generally, treating claims for purely economic loss as essentially contractual rather than tortious.

For a while, even *Hedley Byrne* was caught up in this retrenchment, the courts restricting liability for professional negligence to the circle of persons for whom advice (by accountants and the like) had been directly prepared, and inclining towards an "incremental" approach in which liability obtained only in well-recognised specific situations (see e.g. *Caparo Industries plc v Dickman*, 1990). However, more recently, the courts have been willing to revert to a broad reading of *Hedley Byrne* in order to create a cause of action in negligence for meritorious plaintiffs. *White v Jones* (1995) is an instructive case in point. The story there was one that is familiar in the jurisprudence of a number of legal systems. In the English version, the story centres on one Mr Barratt who instructed his solicitors to revise his will so that his house in Birmingham was left to his two married daughters, Carole and Pauline. Unfortunately, the solicitors failed to act on Mr Barratt's instructions with due diligence and he died before the will was revised. Under the unrevised will (which was the one that counted for the purposes of inheritance), the daughters did not get the house. The question was whether the daughters, the intended beneficiaries, were entitled to compensation for the solicitors' professional negligence. As third parties to the contract between their father and the solicitors, the daughters were not assisted by the law of contract; and their claim for purely financial loss was problematic in negligence. Such doctrinal obstacles notwithstanding, the majority of the House of Lords, emulating the realist approach of the majority in *Donoghue*, ruled that practical justice favoured the daughters. As Lord Goff put it:

"[I]t is open to your Lordships' House . . . to fashion a remedy to fill a lacuna in the law and so prevent the injustice which would otherwise occur on the facts of cases such as the present." (at 268)

However, to extend the *Hedley Byrne* principle to cover a case such as this was quite a stretch: in what sense was there a special relationship between the daughters and the solicitors; had the daughters relied on the solicitors; had the solicitors assumed a responsibility towards the daughters? For the minority, there were too many negatives; and echoing the concern of the minority in *Donoghue* that there must be doctrinal integrity, this was seen as a stretch too far.

The period from *Junior Books* onwards has also been particularly instructive in relation to the so-called "nervous shock" cases (i.e. claims based in negligence but where the plaintiff has suffered a recognised form of psychiatric illness, particularly post-traumatic stress disorder). Briefly, in the early years of the twentieth century, the courts were suspicious of nervous shock claims and, initially, it was only claims by plaintiffs who were the direct victims of the defendant's negligence that had any prospect of succeeding. However, in *Hambrook v Stokes Bros* (1925), the majority of the Court of Appeal (with Lord Atkin again in the vanguard) ruled that, in principle, a plaintiff (mother) who was not a direct victim (indeed, who was not herself at risk of physical injury) could recover for nervous shock arising from a defendant's negligence—or, at any rate, recovery was possible provided that the plaintiff was the parent or spouse of the primary victim (in *Hambrook*, the primary victim was one of the plaintiff mother's children) and was at the scene of the incident (or came upon its "immediate aftermath"). *Hambrook* having set out the parameters of nervous shock liability, the law was reasonably well settled through the mid-century years. However, at much the same time that *Junior Books* fell for decision, the House heard *McLoughlin v O'Brian* (1983), a nervous shock case but again a case inviting an expansion of the sphere of liability. The question in *McLoughlin* was whether a mother who did not witness a motor accident involving members of her family, and who did not come upon the scene of the accident, but who went straight to the hospital where the survivors were being treated, could recover for nervous shock. The House held unanimously in favour of the plaintiff. At its narrowest, *McLoughlin* extended the idea of the "immediate aftermath"; at its broadest, however, the case decided (very much after the fashion of *Junior Books*) that the principle of reasonable foreseeability governed— so, if it was reasonably foreseeable that the plaintiff would suffer nervous shock, a duty of care was owed. Once again, the floodgates threatened to open and, just as the House subsequently acted to restrict liability for purely economic loss, so it acted to restrict liability for nervous shock.

In the case of nervous shock, the opportunity for cutting back on claims by secondary victims came with *Alcock v Chief Constable of the South Yorkshire Police* (1992). The claims in *Alcock* arose out of the disaster at the Hillsborough football stadium in April 1989 (on the occasion of an FA Cup semi-final between Liverpool and Nottingham Forest), where the negligence of the police in controlling access to the stadium resulted in many deaths and injuries to Liverpool supporters who were on the lower terraces at one end of the ground. Sixteen test cases went to trial in *Alcock* (with many more pending). Four of the plaintiffs witnessed the events first-hand at the stadium; the others saw the tragedy unfold on television or heard the radio transmission, or learnt about it later through conversation and the media. Fifteen of the plaintiffs were related to primary victims; the other was a fiancée. By the time that the appeals reached the House, ten cases remained—all were rejected. Setting out a revised legal framework for dealing with claims of this kind, the House emphasised that reasonable foreseeability was not sufficient and that the secondary victim had to be the right kind of person in the right place at the right time. Thus, in two of the most compelling of the appeals, a plaintiff who was in the seated upper part of the stand immediately above the terraces where the tragedy occurred and who lost two brothers, failed because (supposedly) the ties of love and affection between brothers are not normally particularly strong; and plaintiff parents who lost their son and who saw the scenes on live television, failed because scenes transmitted live on television could not normally be equated with direct sensory experience.

Understandably, the decision in *Alcock* attracted the obvious criticism that the lines of liability were drawn in an arbitrary and unduly restrictive way (see, e.g., Conaghan and Mansell, 1998). As the Law Commission (1995) asked in a post-*Alcock* review of the law in this area, is there any good reason why secondary victim plaintiffs who have a close tie of love and affection with a primary victim should also have to satisfy requirements of proximity in time and space (and perception through their own unaided senses)? Moreover, the restrictiveness of *Alcock* subsequently came to look extremely questionable in the light of decisions, first (by the Court of Appeal), allowing members of the police who were traumatised after Hillsborough to recover compensation (either as rescuers, albeit professional rescuers, rather than mere bystanders; or as employees who were exposed by their employer's negligence "to excessively horrific events such as were likely to cause psychiatric illness even in a police officer," *per* Rose L.J. in *Frost v Chief Constable of the South Yorkshire Police* (1997) at 551) and, secondly (by a split House of Lords), in *Page v Smith* (1995), allowing a plaintiff primary victim who was involved in a minor road traffic accident to recover where physical injury did *not* result (even though it was reasonably foreseeable) and psychiatric illness did result (even though it was *not* reasonably foreseeable). With the Law Commission (1998) recommending that the most serious defects in the present law (particularly the *Alcock* requirements of proximity in time and space, but also the narrowness of the recognised relationships of love and affection) should be cured by legislation, and with the House of Lords narrowly reversing *Frost* (see *White v Chief Constable of the South Yorkshire Police* (1999)) the story of nervous shock, like that of economic loss, will surely continue to run.

Gathering together the strands of this discussion, it is apparent that in relation to the duty of care question (which, it must be remembered, is just one ingredient of negligence liability) judges have considerable room for manoeuvre. General doctrinal concepts (e.g. "proximity", "reasonable foresight or contemplation", "special relationship", and *par excellence* the idea of what is "fair, just, and reasonable") are vague and open to interpretation; specific concepts (e.g. the "immediate aftermath" in the nervous shock cases) are flexible; and key distinctions (e.g. between negligent acts and negligent statements, physical injury and purely economic loss, rescuers and mere bystanders, and so on) are open to manipulation in the way that they are applied to particular cases. It is apparent, too, that earlier decisions can be confined narrowly to their particular facts (as has been the fate of *Junior Books*) or read more broadly (as, for a time, was the case with *McLoughlin v O'Brian*, and as was the destiny of the neighbour principle in *Donoghue*); and that, if a decision is seriously regretted, it can in certain circumstances (see Section 2 below) be overruled (as *Murphy* overruled *Anns*). In short, the duty of care question is a valve which judges may open or close pretty much as they wish—and the evolution of negligence liability in the modern period is very much a story of expansion and contraction with the spectre of the floodgates never far from sight.

2. THE DOCTRINE OF PRECEDENT

According to the doctrine of precedent (or stare decisis), if a particular question of law, X, is settled in case A, then the decision in case A should be applied by later courts required to rule on question X. In other words, case A sets a binding precedent in relation to question X. For example, given that *Murphy* has overruled *Anns*, future courts should reject claims based on the *Anns* principle. The doctrine of precedent does not, however, license judges to settle every point of law which may occur to them. For, within the doctrine, a distinction is drawn between the so-called "ratio decidendi" of a case (which binds future courts) and mere "obiter dicta" (which may have persuasive force, but are not binding). The idea is that, whilst an earlier court has authority to bind future courts by settling any point of law directly at issue in the proceedings (its settlement of such a point constituting the *ratio* of the decision), it may not settle any other points of law so as to bind later courts. Thus, in *Murphy*, for instance, any reservations expressed about local authorities being liable where their negligence resulted in personal injury were merely *obiter*, for this was not directly at issue in the case. It should not be thought, however, that precedent operates in a mechanical fashion. The *ratio* of a decision is not printed in red ink or anything of that kind. Rather, it is up to later judges to interpret the scope of an earlier decision and to specify its *ratio* accordingly. Whilst this does not render the very idea of *ratio* a nonsense, it does mean—as, indeed, we have seen already—that later courts have considerable freedom in determining the significance of earlier decisions (see Goodhart, 1930; Stone, 1959). For example, in *Stilk v Myrick* (1809), two sailors having deserted ship, the master promised to divide the wages of the deserting seamen among the remaining crew if they completed the voyage in accordance with their contractual obligations. The crew completed the voyage; but the master refused to pay the bonus as promised. It was held that the master's promise was unenforceable. But, what was the *ratio* of *Stilk*? Whilst one report of the case suggested that the decision turned on "policy" (that sailors should not be encouraged to bargain for additional payments when emergencies arose), another report indicated that the claim failed for "want of consideration" (the sailors, as modern writers would put it, incurring no fresh detriment in return for the promise of a bonus). Either way, did the decision apply equally to cases where the promise of additional payment was made by a third party? By the late nineteenth century, whereas the textbook writers (who were now in full swing) regarded *Stilk* as a leading case on consideration, the developing case law (somewhat inconveniently for the textbook writers) suggested that third-party promises were enforceable (even though the promisee incurred no obvious detriment). In the latter part of the twentieth century, with the development of a doctrine of economic duress, the interpretation of *Stilk* has changed once more, the Court of Appeal holding in *Williams v Roffey and Nicholls (Contractors) Ltd* (1990) that "policy" was after all the reason for denying recovery to the sailors. As Glidewell L.J. observed:

"It is not in my view surprising that a principle enunciated in relation to the rigours of seafaring life during the Napoleonic wars should be subjected during the succeeding 180 years to a process of refinement and limitation in its application in the present day." (at 520)

Subject to such refinement of *ratio*, the authority of a precedent depends upon the standing of the court that decided it in the hierarchy.

Basically, the hierarchy of courts in England and Wales comprises three tiers (see Figure 1).

At the first tier, there are courts of first instance (or trial courts). On the criminal side, these are the magistrates' courts and the Crown Courts (see Ch.6); while, on the civil side, they are the county courts and the High Court (see Ch.7.). These courts deal with a wide range of matters: making findings of fact, deciding points of law, ruling on questions of evidence during a trial, determining sentences, making awards of damages, and so on. Generally speaking, the decisions of these first-tier courts are not open to appeal. However, in certain circumstances, appeals on points of law may be permitted. The first line of appeal is to one of the second-tier courts (the Divisional Court, or more commonly, the Court of Appeal, which has both civil and criminal divisions). From these courts, a further appeal may be permitted to the third-tier court, the House of Lords. (For present purposes, we can ignore the possibility of points of law being taken to the Court of Justice of the European Community, or to the European Court of Human Rights). Within this hierarchy, precedent may have both "vertical" and "horizontal" effect. The idea of "vertical" effect is that the precedents set by superior courts bind inferior courts. In other words, the decisions of the House of Lords bind all other courts, and the decisions of the second-tier courts bind first-tier courts. The idea of "horizontal" effect is that precedents set at a particular level bind future courts in the same tier. Here, the peculiarity of the English rules is that precedent has horizontal binding effect at the second tier, but not at either the first or third tiers. In fact, for much of the twentieth century, the practice of the House of Lords was to follow its own previous decisions. However, it changed its practice rules in 1966, leaving itself free to disregard its own previous decisions (see e.g. the overruling of *Anns* in *Murphy*). As events have proved, the House has been extremely cautious about using the 1966 rules to reject one of its earlier decisions as mistaken. However, the fact that the House was at least prepared to make occasional exceptions to the general rule of precedent raised the question of

Hierarchy of Principal Domestic Courts

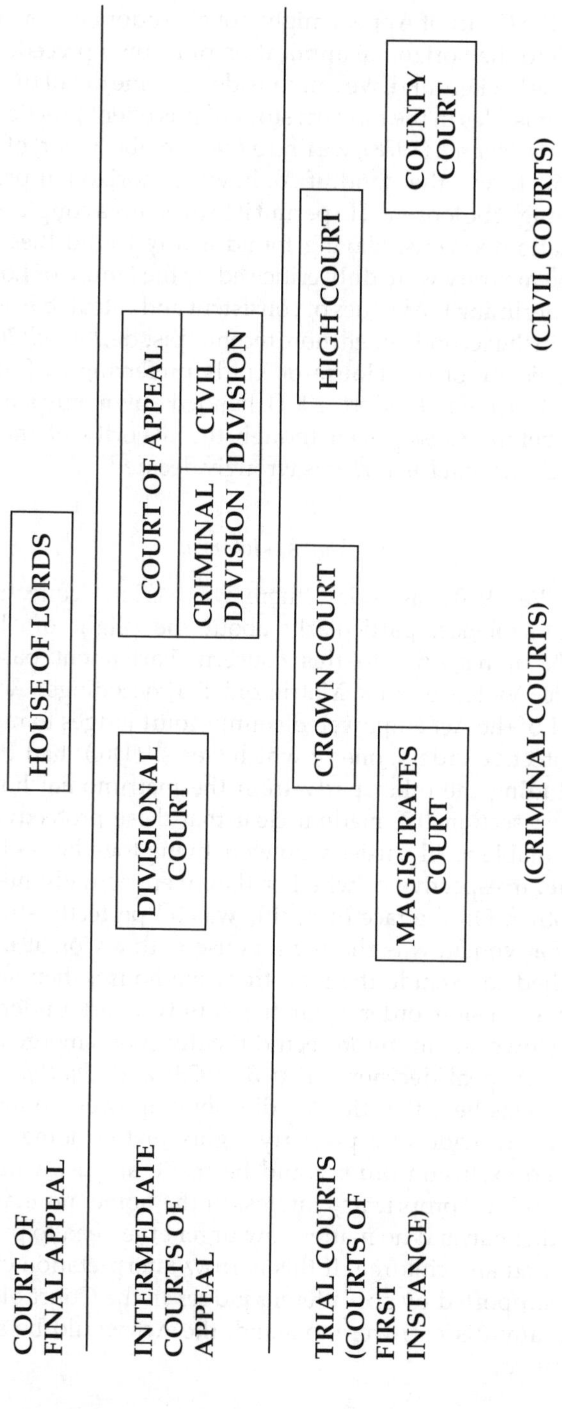

COURT OF FINAL APPEAL

HOUSE OF LORDS

INTERMEDIATE COURTS OF APPEAL

DIVISIONAL COURT

COURT OF APPEAL

| CRIMINAL DIVISION | CIVIL DIVISION |

TRIAL COURTS (COURTS OF FIRST INSTANCE)

CROWN COURT

HIGH COURT

MAGISTRATES COURT

COUNTY COURT

(CRIMINAL COURTS)　　　　(CIVIL COURTS)

Figure 1

whether the Court of Appeal might not also adopt a more relaxed approach to the horizontal application of its own precedents. With this background, we can consider in some detail two much-debated episodes in the modern story of precedent practice. In the first, *Davis v Johnson* (1978), we find a five-member Court of Appeal divided as to whether (and, if so, how) its horizontal precedent practice might be loosened to permit it to overrule a couple of recent problematic decisions. Having found a way round these precedents, the majority were duly criticised by the House of Lords, the latter underlining the virtues of consistent and calculable decision-making. In the second, much more recent, episode, *Kansal* (2001), we find a majority of the House of Lords preferring to follow the House's decision in *Lambert* (2001), handed down only a matter of months before *Kansal*, even though the majority of the House openly admits that *Lambert* was wrongly decided.

(i) Davis v Johnson

During the 1970s, as today, there was serious concern about domestic violence, particularly about the plight of "battered women". In response to this concern, Parliament passed the Domestic Violence and Matrimonial Proceedings Act 1976. Section 1 of the Act empowered county court judges to make various protective orders, one of which (see s.1(1)(c)) had the effect of "excluding the other party from the matrimonial home . . ." Moreover, section 1(2) made it clear that these protective orders were available to all parties who were living together as husband and wife, irrespective of whether they were actually married to one another. On the face of it, this was all perfectly straightforward. If a woman was sharing a house with a violent man, and she wished to exclude the man from the house, then she could seek an exclusion order from the county court under section 1(1)(c). However, an unforeseen difficulty soon emerged. In two Court of Appeal decisions, *B v B* (1978) and *Cantliff v Jenkins* (1978), it was held that the Act did not empower County Court judges to override any property rights in the home. In other words, no exclusion order could be made against a man (or a woman) with a proprietary interest in the home, no matter how violent the man and no matter how urgent the need to protect the woman and any children. If this narrow interpretation of section 1(1)(c) (supported by six different judges in the Court of Appeal, without any dissent) were to stand, the Act would be seriously undermined.

One month after *B v B* and *Cantliff v Jenkins* were heard, a five-member Court of Appeal was specially convened to hear an appeal on the same point of law in *Davis v Johnson*. There, the parties lived together in a council flat in Hackney, the tenancy being in their joint names. However, Johnson was a violent man—it was said, for example, that he kept an axe under the bed and that, on one occasion, he threatened to chop up Davis and put her into the freezer. Davis, having left the flat (taking her young daughter with her), applied to the County Court for an exclusion order under section 1(1)(c), so that she could return in safety to the flat. Although the order was granted intially, it was withdrawn in the light of *Cantliff*. On appeal to the Court of Appeal in *Davis v Johnson*, the first question was whether the narrow interpretation of the 1976 Act in *B v B* and *Cantliff* was correct. If it were, Davis' appeal would fail. However, if the narrow interpretation of the Act were judged to be mistaken (so that exclusion orders could be issued, proprietary interests notwithstanding), then a second question would arise: namely, could the court legitimately depart from its own previous interpretation of the Act? In other words, could the court ignore the horizontal application of the precedent doctrine? If not, Davis' appeal again would have to be dismissed, leaving her to make a final appeal to the House of Lords (where, of course, the decisions in *B v B* and *Cantliff* would not be binding). In a split three to two decision, the Court of Appeal allowed Davis' appeal.

As we have said, the first question for the court was purely one of statutory interpretation. The narrow interpretation of the Act was underpinned by two arguments. One argument drew on the presumption that, in the absence of the most explicit language to the contrary, Parliament must be presumed not to have intended to interfere with property rights. The second argument was more complex, focusing on the relationship between section 1(1)(c) and section 3 of the Act (the latter section reversing the effect of a (proprty-protecting) decision of the House of Lords in *Tarr v Tarr* (1973), by providing that exclusion orders could be made in favour of married spouses, proprietary interests notwithstanding). Basically, the argument was that, unless section 1(1)(c) were interpreted narrowly, section 3 would be redundant. Against these arguments, the case in favour of the broad interpretation was fairly obvious. In general terms, it was recognised that the Act addressed the mischief of battered women; empowering county court judges to make exclusion orders for the protection of such women was not a complete answer, but at least it was a move in the right direction; and the broad interpretation of section 1(1)(c) was essential if this remedy were to be advanced. More specifically, the presumption against interference with property rights must yield where legislation was concerned with the security of persons. In Lord Denning MR's words:

"It is true that in the nineteenth century the law paid quite high regard to rights of property. But this gave rise to such misgivings that in modern times the law has changed course. Social justice requires that personal rights should, in a proper case, be given priority over rights of property." (at 849)

As for the desire to spare the draftsmen's blushes should section 3 prove redundant, this was no match for the need to spare women and children the beatings dished out by violent men. Confronted with these arguments, four members of the Court of Appeal preferred the broad interpretation.

Of these four judges, however, only three were prepared to flout the court's precedent practice. At one extreme, Lord Denning MR had no difficulty about turning a blind eye to *B v B* and *Cantliff*:

"On principle, it seems to me that, whilst this court should regard itself as normally bound by a previous decision of the court, nevertheless it should be at liberty to depart from it if it is convinced that the previous decision was wrong." (at 852)

Whilst Sir George Baker P. and Shaw L.J. were equally convinced that *B v B* and *Cantliff* were wrong, they were not as willing as Lord Denning to abandon entirely the court's existing precedent practice. Accordingly, Shaw L.J. proposed that, in the truly exceptional circumstances of the case, the horizontal application of precedent should be relaxed where a previous decision of the court

"would have the effect of depriving actual and potential victims of violence of a vital protection which an Act of Parliament was plainly designed to afford to them, especially where, as in the context of domestic violence, that deprivation must inevitably give rise to an irremediable detriment to such victims and create in regard to them an injustice irreversible by a later decision of the House of Lords." (at 878)

As Lord Diplock was to observe when *Davis v Johnson* was heard in the House of Lords, Shaw L.J. had relied on a one-off exception such that "it [would be] difficult to think of any other statute to which it would apply" (at 1139). Of the four who favoured the broad interpretation of the Act, Goff L.J. stood alone in refusing to depart from the narrow interpretation applied in *B v B* and *Cantliff*. For Goff L.J., even where the previous decisions seemed incorrect, respect for the doctrine of precedent was an overriding consideration.

Although, on appeal in *Davis v Johnson*, the House of Lords unanimously affirmed the decision of the Court of Appeal (in favour of the broad interpretation of the Act), there was strong disapproval of the court's disregard for precedent. In their Lordships' view, it was the two dissenting judges in the Court of Appeal (Goff L.J. and Cumming-Bruce L.J.) who acted correctly on the precedent question. Of course, for Cumming-Bruce L.J. who favoured the narrow interpretation of the Act, there was no problem whatsoever about following *B v B* and *Cantliff*. As their Lordships saw it, therefore, the real hero was Goff L.J. who followed the previous decisions despite judging them to be mistaken. But, why should the Court of Appeal stick so rigidly to its previous decisions, even where absolutely convinced that they were wrong? Lord Salmon outlined one response to this question:

"I fear that if *stare decisis* disappears from [the Court of Appeal] there is a real risk that there might be a plethora of conflicting decisions which would create a state of irremediable confusion and uncertainty in the law. This would do far more harm than the occasional unjust result which *stare decisis* sometimes produces but which can be remedied by an appeal to your Lordships' House." (at 1153)

This smacks somewhat of utilitarian thinking: the occasional hard case creates some disutility but far less than would result from the abandonment of the precedent doctrine (particularly so, it might be thought, in contexts where morality is seriously divided—the legal response to the abortion debate being an obvious example, see Laird, 1994). Alternatively, one might attempt to defend a rigid precedent doctrine on the grounds of consistency and respect for rights. The specific issue raised by *Davis v Johnson*, however, concerned the need for having a (horizontal) precedent doctrine in the Court of Appeal. Here, in addition to the underlying arguments in favour of a precedent doctrine, it is often emphasised that the court occupies an intermediate position (i.e.

it is a second-tier court in a three-tier structure). This implies that the three-tier structure of courts in England has some grand rationale, within which it makes sense for the Court of Appeal to stick to its own previous decisions. For example, it might be argued that the function of the second-tier courts is not to change the law, but simply to ensure that trial courts apply the law as generally understood (be it good or bad law). By contrast, the function of the House of Lords is broader, encompassing responsibility for keeping the law itself (not simply trial court judges) on the right track. Provided that such a grand design were explicitly recognized, the strictures against the majority members of the Court of Appeal in *Davis v Johnson* might make some sense. However, the fact is that such a design is not explicitly recognised; and, even if it were, one might wonder whether it were the best design available. At all events, wherever the merits ultimately lie in this debate, and regardless of lectures from above, it is clear that judges will pursue their own precedent philosophies (ranging from Lord Denning's approach at one extreme to Goff L.J.'s approach at the other).

(ii) R v Lambert and R v Kansal

In *Lambert* (2001), the police observed the appellant arriving by train at Runcorn railway station, meeting two men, first in the booking hall and then in a car at the station car park, before accepting from them a duffle bag. When the police intercepted the appellant they found that the bag contained two kilogrammes of cocaine worth some £140,000. The appellant was charged with being in possession of a controlled drug, with intent to supply, contrary to section 5 of the Misuse of Drugs Act 1971. At his trial, the appellant relied on section 28 of the Act to assert that he was innocently in possession, that is, that he had no reason to suspect that the duffle bag contained cocaine (his story was that he often travelled to Liverpool to collect tee shirts for a man named John; that he set off thinking that this was a similar job; but that, on this occasion, John phoned him en route with an instruction to get off the train at Runcorn where the men that he met told him that the bag contained scrap jewellery). The trial judge directed the jury that to establish this defence, the defendant had to prove on the balance of probabilities that he did not know that the bag contained a controlled drug. In other words, whereas the burden of proof usually lies on the prosecution to prove its case beyond all reasonable doubt, in this case the burden of proof was reversed—

not only that, the burden placed on the defendant went beyond raising the possibility of innocent possession (the so-called evidential burden), it called on the defendant to establish his innocence on the balance of probabilities (the so-called legal burden). The defendant was duly convicted and sentenced to seven years imprisonment.

Now, following the enactment of the Human Rights Act, 1998, court procedures must be compatible with the right to a fair trial (as protected by Art.6 of the European Convention on Human Rights). Under the jurisprudence of the ECHR, any deviation from the general rule that it is for the prosecution to prove its case beyond reasonable doubt (a central pillar of the ideology of due process) is questionable. Accordingly, where the burden of proof is reversed, especially when it is reversed so strongly as per the direction in *Lambert*, it invites challenge under the Human Rights Act; and this is precisely what the appellant sought to do in his appeal against conviction. However, there was an important threshold question to be settled before the appellant could invoke the protective fair trial provisions of the Act. Quite simply, the trial in *Lambert* took place in 1999, after the Act went through Parliament but before its commencement in 2000. The threshold question, therefore, was whether in Lambert's appeal to the House of Lords, which was heard in 2001 (when the Act was in force), the appellant could rely on the Act to challenge the fairness of the trial which had taken place before the Act was in force. In other words, the first question for the House was to decide whether the Human Rights Act has any retrospective application.

This question took the House into a complex set of provisions in the Act, the interpretation of which is deeply contested (see e.g. Beyleveld, Kirkham and Townend, 2002) and which, at best, deal only obliquely with the issue of retrospective effect. The most explicit provision concerning retrospectivity is found in section 22(4) of the Act. Putting matters as simply as possible, section 22(4) seems to have a dual intention. First, it seems to be designed to shield public authorities against proceedings brought by parties whose complaint is that the public authority has breached Convention rights where the alleged breach took place before the Act came into force. To this extent, the Act blocks retrospective (offensive) application. Secondly, however, where a public authority has itself instigated proceedings against a party then the latter can respond by relying on the Act even if the alleged breaches took place before the Act came into force. To this extent (as it were, where the public authority lifts the shield by instigating proceedings), the Act has (defensive) retrospective effect. Whilst this makes some sense, it does not, alas, offer explicit guidance on the particular question presented by the appellant in *Lambert*. To answer that question, we need to decide whether the appeal (or the trial and the appeal) counts as a case of a public authority instigating proceedings against a party who now claims to be a victim of a breach of Convention rights. On this crucial point, the majority of the House of Lords in *Lambert* ruled against the appellant. As the majority read the provisions of the Act (in s.7) setting out the way in which alleged violations of Convention rights might be raised in legal proceedings, they noted that section 7(6) states that "legal proceedings" includes both (a) proceedings brought by or at the instigation of a public authority and (b) an appeal against a decision of a court or tribunal. From this, they deduced: (i) that there is a material distinction between proceedings instigated by a public authority and appeals; and (ii) that, because section 22(4) expressly lifts the barrier against retrospective application only in relation to proceedings instigated by a public authority, it follows that the barrier is not lifted for appeals. Reading between the lines of this contestable interpretation (which it must be appreciated denied the appellant the opportunity of arguing that he had not had a fair trial), we can sense that the majority think that, as a matter of policy, it is not a good idea to encourage appeals against convictions which were the outcome of trials conducted entirely in accordance with English law as it then stood (as was the case in *Lambert*).

Although the point at issue in *Lambert* was of limited application, because it affected only those cases that straddled the commencement of the Human Rights Act, it was nevertheless an important precedent, apparently closing off retrospective reliance on the Convention rights by appellants in the criminal process. Shortly after handing down its decision in *Lambert*, four of the same Law Lords were invited to revisit the question in *Kansal*. The alleged unfairness in *Kansal* was that statements made under compulsion by the respondent when he was examined in bankruptcy proceedings were then admitted in evidence at a subsequent criminal trial following which he was convicted of various offences under the Theft Act 1968 and the Insolvency Act 1986. On the face of it, this was a case of self-incrimination which was incompatible with the Convention right to a fair trial. Although the material facts of *Kansal* were not quite identical to those in *Lambert*, the precedent set in *Lambert* seemed to bar any challenge based on the Human Rights Act. And, so far as our discussion of *Kansal* is concerned, we need not re-enter the labyrinth of the statutory provisions as to retrospectivity; our interest now is in the attitudes of their Lordships to the precedent set by *Lambert*.

As we have said, for four of their Lordships in *Kansal*, this was a re-run of the arguments in *Lambert*. For two of their Lordships, Lords Slynn and Hutton, the case was an easy one. They believed that the *Lambert* interpretation of the Human Rights Act was either correct or, as Lord Hutton put it, "an eminently possible one" (para.111), and hence there was no reason to overrule the decision. For the other two of the original four, Lords Steyn and Hope, the position was more tricky. In *Lambert*, Lord Steyn had no doubt that the majority misinterpreted the Act and he dissented; in *Kansal*, his Lordship continued to regard *Lambert* as incorrect; but, surprisingly perhaps, he chose to follow it. By contrast, Lord Hope, who was with the majority in *Lambert*, was converted by the further arguments in *Kansal* to the view that *Lambert* was mistaken; and his view was that the precedent should be overruled. This left Lord Lloyd who, coming to the question for the first time, judged that *Lambert* was plainly wrong. His Lordship would have liked to have seen a seven member panel convened to reconsider the point (as happened, for example, in *Murphy* (above 124), *Pepper v Hart* (above 110) and, recently, in *Hall v Simons* (2000) where the House departed from its previous precedents concerning the immunity of advocates for negligent conduct of a case); but, without that being possible, he joined the majority in agreeing to follow the precedent set by *Lambert*. The tally in *Kansal*, therefore, was that two Law Lords thought that *Lambert* was correct and should be followed; three thought that it was wrong; but only one, Lord Hope, was prepared to use the 1966 guidance to overrule the precedent (at any rate, with a five-member panel).

Of these positions, those of Lord Steyn and Lord Hope stand out as most interesting. Lord Steyn remarked that he found himself in much the same position as Lord Reid in *R v Knuller (Publishing, Printing and Promotions Ltd)* (1973), one of the early test cases on the application of the 1966 guidance. In *Knuller*, the question was whether the House should depart from its notorious decision in *Shaw v DPP* (1962), in which the offence of conspiracy to corrupt public morals was questionably added to the English criminal code and in which Lord Reid dissented. Nevertheless, in *Knuller*, Lord Reid set out his reasons for exercising restraint:

"I dissented in *Shaw's* case. On reconsideration I still think that the decision was wrong. . . . But it does not follow that I should now support a motion to reconsider the decision. . . . [O]ur change of practice in no longer regarding previous decisions of this House as absolutely binding does not mean that whenever we think that a previous decision was wrong we should reverse it. In the general interest of certainty in the law we must be sure that there is some very good reason before we so act. . . ." (p.455)

Taking a similar approach, Lord Steyn concluded shortly that, even if *Lambert* gave the wrong answer to the question, it did not bear on the future prospects of the Human Rights Act, but only on a transitional issue. By contrast, Lord Hope was anxious to put the record straight. His view was that the House should not distort the early jurisprudence of the Human Rights Act by tolerating mistaken interpretations (even concerning transitional provisions) and that, in this context, "correction is more desirable than consistency" (para.53).

In *Kansal*, Lord Lloyd mentioned in passing the approach of the US Supreme Court in *Planned Parenthood of Southeastern Pennsylvania v Casey* (1992). In that case, it was widely expected that the court would overturn the permissive framework for abortion law famously set out twenty years earlier in *Roe v Wade* (1973). To the surprise of commentators, however, the swing votes in the court favoured keeping the law consistent with *Roe*. As O'Connor, Kennedy and Souter JJ put it:

"[N]o judicial system could do society's work if it eyed each issue afresh in every case that raised it . . . Indeed, the very concept of the rule of law underlying our own Constitution requires such continuity over time that a respect for precedent is, by definition, indispensable." (p.854)

On the strength of *Casey* and *Kansal*, we can say that the prevailing attitude, on both sides of the Atlantic, seems to be that, where an earlier decision is thought to be mistaken (whether as a matter of case-law development or statutory interpretation, or because of the underlying values that it seeks to advance), but still within the band of reasonable disagreement, then judges—even judges in the highest appeal courts—should exercise considerable restraint before rejecting such a (horizontally binding) precedent. In support of this restraint, we can point to the particular role and responsibilities of judges in the politico-legal order, the damage that judicial u-turns do to confidence in the courts as well as the way in which they invite further litigation, the need for calculability and consistency, and the importance of confining judicial idiosyncrasy. If only there were not hard cases and decisions that lie beyond the bounds of tolerance, everything would be straightforward.

It is time to take stock. One of the central features of our account is that judges have very considerable room for manoeuvre in handling both statutes and case law materials. Do we need to revise this picture in the light of the supposedly constraining effect of the doctrine of precedent? In relation to the interpretation of statutes, the doctrine is sometimes presented as having limited significance, for the interpretation of phrase P in statute X is not normally treated as binding where the same phrase, P, falls to be interpreted in a different statute, Y. However, the interpretation of phrase P in statute X may bind later courts called upon to interpret the same phrase in the same statutory section. For example, in *Davis v Johnson*, the county court applied the narrow interpretation of section 1(1)(c) in accordance with the decision of the Court of Appeal. Similarly, once the Divisional Court in *Smith v Hughes* had ruled on the meaning of section 1 of the Street Offences Act, it was accepted in later cases that the physical presence of the soliciting prostitutes in the street was no longer an essential ingredient of the offence (see e.g. *Behrendt v Burridge*, 1976). The point is that, where an earlier court rules specifically upon the meaning of a particular statutory provision, and where the material facts are identical, the doctrine of precedent will limit the room for manoeuvre. Where this happens, as *Davis v Johnson* illustrates so vividly, some judges will toe the line but others will try to wriggle out of the difficulty. And as *Kansal* indicates, if the court has the authority to address the difficulty head-on and remove it, even though the culture tends towards restraint, the possibility of overruling remains a real one. When we turn to the development of case law, it is unusual for the doctrine of precedent to exert quite such a strong pressure. Judges have a whole repertoire of techniques for avoiding or deflecting the impact of precedent (*cf.* Llewellyn, 1960). In particular, it is open to later courts to interpret the *ratio* of earlier cases narrowly or broadly; to distinguish earlier cases on their facts (i.e. to hold that the "material facts"—notice the slipperiness of this idea— are not identical in the cases); and to read in qualifications and exceptions which are taken to be implicit in earlier decisions.

Above all, however, where we are dealing with an area of law such as negligence, in which the substantive legal principles are themselves riddled with leeways (*cf.* s.1 of this chapter), the courts can happily respect the doctrine of precedent, because the earlier decisions can be largely applied as the later court wishes. Overall, then, the constraining force of the doctrine of precedent must be seen as having only limited significance in shaping judicial decisions.

3. JUDICIAL IDEOLOGIES

In the previous chapter, we outlined a fourfold typology of judicial approaches to statutory interpretation. We can now extend and elaborate this typology in three ways: first, by specifying it in a form which is appropriate for interpreting judicial approaches to case law; secondly, by drawing attention to the existence of (and distinction between) both *general* adjudicative ideologies (formalist and realist) and *particular* judicial ideologies (which vary from one area of law to another, and which are crucial for understanding the direction of realist decision-making); and, thirdly, by reformulating the typology as an over-arching framework of judicial ideologies (applicable to both the interpretation of statutes and the handling of case law).

First, there is the question of whether, and how, our typology can be brought to bear on judicial approaches to case law. The answer to this is very simple. Although our typology involves four kinds of approach, the central distinction is between the formalist and the realist approaches. In relation to statutory interpretation, whereas a formalist approach treats fidelity to legislative enactment as overriding, a realist approach does not. To apply this model to case law, we need only substitute "fidelity to precedent" for "fideltity to legislative enactment." In other words, in relation to case law, judges either treat the principle of fidelity to precedents as overriding (in which event they are formalists) or they do not (in which case they are realists). So, for example, in both *Donoghue v Stevenson* and *White v Jones*, we might interpret the majority's quest for a just result as textbook realism to be contrasted with the formalist approach of the minority, for whom the integrity of the precedents is a critical consideration. Moreover, the subdivisions between, on the one hand, textual formalists and purposive formalists, and, on the other hand, weak realists and strong realists, are equally applicable. Thus, while textual formalists stick closely to the language of previous decisions, purposive formalists look for the underlying intent of the case law (treating the language used by earlier judges as simply one clue to the spirit of the precedents). Similarly, while weak realists accord limited value to respect for previous decisions, strong realists proceed quite independently of any concern for the precedents.

Since realists are not primarily guided by the case law, the key to the pattern of realist decision-making is to be found in the underlying judicial values, or ideologies. In *Understanding Contract Law* (Adams and Brownsword, 2004), we suggested that realist decision-making in contract cases was dictated by two competing ideologies, which we termed "market-individualism" and "consumer-welfarism". Market-individualism has both "market" and "individualistic" characteristics. Whilst the former emphasises the perceived needs of the market-place (e.g. for security of transactions, some degree of flexibility in longer-term commercial relationships, and so on), the latter embodies the principles of "freedom of contract" and "sanctity of contract". Guided by this ideology, judges see their task as one of facilitating commerce and enforcing respect for bargains freely struck in the market-place. The rival ideology, consumer-welfarism, is more paternalistic (being especially protective of consumers and other vulnerable parties), and is generally concerned that contracting procedures and outcomes should be fair and reasonable. Quite possibly, these two ideologies have some application in areas adjacent to the field of contract. For example, in the law of negligence, decisions like *Donoghue* and *Anns* fit pretty well with a consumer-welfarist approach as, indeed, do *Hedley Byrne* and *White v Jones* (in both of which in line with welfarist thinking, responsibility towards others is intensified); and some of the thinking in the retreat from *Junior Books* fits with a market-individualist philosophy. However, these ideologies were derived specifically from contract, not negligence, cases; so a simple correspondence at this level should not be expected.

McFarlane v Tayside Health Board (2000) is an example of a rather different kind of negligence action drawing out a further layer of ideological considerations. There, the House of Lords reviewed the legal position where a perfectly healthy, but unplanned, child is born following negligent execution of a vasectomy or sterilisation. In some legal systems, the parents are fully compensated; in others, there is limited recovery (for the pain, discomfort and inconvenience of the pregnancy but not for the cost of rearing the child); and in others the damages are reduced by the benefits of having a child. As Lord Steyn (2002) has subsequently conceded, a one-dimensional commitment to corrective justice would point to full recovery in cases of this kind; but the law also takes account of distributive considerations (i.e. judgments are made about which kind of claims should be prioritised for compensation) and, on this basis, the majority of the House in *McFarlane* ruled that limited damages only were recoverable. Further, in the case itself, his Lordship remarked:

"[T]o explain decisions denying a remedy for the cost of bringing up an unwanted child by saying that there is no loss, no foreseeable loss, no causative link or no ground for reasonable restitution is to resort to unrealistic and formalistic propositions which mask the real reasons for the decisions. And judges ought to strive to give the real reasons for their decision. It is my firm conviction that where courts of law have denied a remedy for the cost of bringing up an unwanted child the real reasons have been grounds of distributive justice. That is of course, a moral theory. It may be objected that the House must act like a court of law not like a court of morals. That would only be partly right. The court must apply positive law. But judges' sense of the moral answer to a question, or the justice of the case, has been one of the great shaping forces of the common law." (89)

It scarcely needs to be said that these comments are very much in line with the view advanced in this chapter that, if we are to understand the dynamics of case-law development, we must look behind formal doctrine to identify the real reasons for decision—that is, we must seek out and map the governing ideologies (complex and varied though they might be).

As if to underline the complexity of such an exercise, the jurisprudence of *McFarlane* was soon afterwards supplemented by *Rees v Darlington Memorial Hospital NHS Trust* (2003), where a seven-member panel of the House of Lords split 4 to 3 in determining a question that involved a twist on the story in *McFarlane*. Briefly, Ms Karina Rees, a severely visually handicapped woman, was concerned that her eyesight would prevent her from giving a baby (or young child) proper care and attention. Accordingly, to prevent a pregnancy arising, she underwent a sterilisation operation. However, the procedure was not carried out as it should have been and, about a year later, Ms Rees became pregnant, duly giving birth to a baby boy, Anthony, who was a healthy and normal child. The question for the House was whether *Rees* was distinguishable from *McFarlane*. In other words, is it material for legal purposes that an unplanned-for healthy child is born to a *disabled* parent (*Rees*) rather than to a parent who is free of disability (*McFarlane*)? Even if, following *McFarlane*, there is to be no compensation for the costs of rearing an unplanned-for healthy child, should there be compensation to cover the *additional* costs incurred by a disabled parent? In *Rees*, at least three ideological strands are in play, two relating to general adjudicative considerations, with a third relating more specifically to the objectives and shape of the law of negligence. First, all seven Law Lords are agreed that this is not an occasion to re-consider the core ruling in *McFarlane*—indeed, mindful of the recent decision of the Australian High Court in *Cattanach v Melchior* (2003), where a bare majority departed from the *McFarlane* view, their Lordships present a united front in emphasising the importance of sticking with contestable precedents in order to achieve some settlement in the law. Secondly, however, their Lordships are divided as to the limits of judicial creativity and innovation. In *McFarlane*, Lord Millett suggested that, even if the claimants should receive no compensation for the costs of rearing an unplanned-for child, they might nevertheless be awarded a conventional sum of £5,000, or so, to reflect their loss of control over their family planning. In *Rees*, the majority embrace this option, proposing that an award of £15,000 might be appropriate. Against this, however, the minority reject such a strategem as stepping over the limits that regulate judicial creativity (see especially Lord Steyn at para 46). Thirdly, their Lordships are again divided as to the priority between the claimed fairness, justice and reasonableness of singling out disabled mothers, such as Ms Rees, for the kind of compensatory treatment claimed and the importance of drawing defensible lines in the sand. While the minority prioritise compensation for Ms Rees (which they assume will be significantly higher than the conventional award proposed by the majority), the majority doubt the feasibility (either as a matter of fairness or coherent legal policy) of drawing a line between such exceptional claimants and claimants who for other reasons (e.g. depression or impoverished circumstances) experience unusual difficulty or expense in raising an unplanned-for child.

Accordingly, if we are to understand case law adjudication, we need to combine our *general* typology of judicial approaches (formalist and realist) with the many *particular* ideologies discernible in the various areas of law. Now, whereas the basic fourfold typology of judicial approaches is of general application (irrespective of the area of law under investigation), the particular ideologies must be specified (and respecified) as we move from one area of law to another. Thus, as we move away from contract (and the market-place) the specifically contractual ideologies of market-individualism and consumer-welfarism must be replaced altogether. For example, if we were to examine the particular ideologies at work in the law concerning the admissibility in criminal proceedings of illegally obtained evidence, we might start with the quite different contrast between the ideology of crime control (which would tend to admit such evidence) and that of due process (which would tend to exclude such evidence). Similarly, as *Davis v Johnson* highlights, if we were to explore the particular ideologies prevalent in matrimonial disputes, we might find a patriarchal ideology (favouring men, marriage, and property) in competition with a liberal ideology (favouring the interests of physical integrity, women, and children). Of course, at a higher level of generality, these particular ideologies (as indeed the general judicial approaches) should be reducible, in principle, to utilitarian or right-and-duty frameworks. For present purposes, however, the important point to grasp is that each substantive area of law has, so to speak, its own local ideological field with its own special characteristics.

Finally, we can convert these ideas into an over-arching framework of judicial ideologies. Quite simply, whether judges are dealing with the interpretation of statutes or cases, their basic approach must be of either a formalist or a realist nature. For formalists, fidelity to "law" (in the sense that legal positivists would understand this, see Ch.1) is overriding; for realists, it is not. For formalists, where the law is clear (whether in statutes or precedents), it must be applied; for realists, there is no question of the law being routinely applied in hard cases. Where judges adopt a formalist approach, their emphasis may be either textual or purposive. For a textual formalist, the law is to be found in the language actually contained in statutes and judicial opinions. For a purposive formalist, whilst the language found in statutes and judicial opinions offers a clue as to the legislative intent and the spirit of the case law, there is no question of being a slave to the language of the law. Either way, of course, formalists will respect the doctrine of precedent (sometimes—*cf.* Goff L.J. in *Davis v Johnson*—to the letter). By contrast, realists (whether weak or strong) do not regard themselves as slaves to either the language or the purpose of the extant materials, nor to the doctrine of precedent (*cf.* Lord Denning MR in *Davis v Johnson*). Judges of a realist persuasion are guided by their own background values; and, as disputes scan from one area of law to another (irrespective of whether such disputes ostensibly centre on statutory provisions or on case law), so different particular ideologies come into play. Accordingly, the key to understanding appellate court decision-making lies in exploring the tensions between the general ideologies of adjudication (i.e. the range of formalist and realist approaches) together with the operation of particular ideologies in each area of substantive law. (Moreover, as John Merrills (1988, Ch.10) has persuasively argued, such an ideological framework is equally relevant to understanding the practice of international courts, such as (in his study) the European Court of Human Rights.)

4. HERCULES AND THE HARD QUESTION

In the final section of this chapter, we can return to the perplexing question of how judges should decide cases in the appellate courts. The choice seems to lie between the four fundamental approaches to adjudication, textual formalist, purposive formalist, weak realist and strong realist. After sketching the obvious arguments for and against each of these approaches, we can consider two sophisticated models of adjudication, Ronald Dworkin's (1978, 1986b) "rights thesis" (which is a variation on the purposive formalist theme) and Richard Wasserstrom's (1961) "two-level" procedure for adjudication (which is a variation on the strong realist theme).

Whilst textual formalism may attract some support on the ground that it keeps faith with the law, it would be more accurate to say that the approach involves a blind adherence to the formal texts. This leaves it open to two lines of objection. First, it fails to come to terms with the textual limitations of legal materials, not only leaving it ill-equipped to deal with difficult cases but, more significantly, leaving its adherents with too many difficult cases. Secondly, by blindly applying the rules, textual formalists may become agents of injustice. Faced with these objections, it is natural to turn to one or other of the realist approaches. The attraction of realism (when contrasted with textual formalism) is that judges concentrate on the merits of cases and do not get cornered into deciding against their consciences. However, on reflection, in addition to the obvious anxieties that we may have about both the consistency and calculability of realist decision-making, we must be concerned that realist judges follow their own lights rather than the values enshrined in the statutes and precedents. If judges were philosopher-kings, being omniscient in all matters pertaining to values, a realist approach would be fine (at least, provided that due allowance were made for good faith reliance on the formal rules); but, in the absence of such omniscience, realism seems to be as hard to defend as textual formalism. As so often happens, the deficiencies in outlying positions encourage the search for a middle-way solution, in this instance, purposive formalism. On the one hand, purposive formalism seems better equipped than textual formalism to deal with cases where the text is unclear. For, by treating legal materials simply as evidence of an underlying intention or principle, purposive formalism promises to reduce the number of intractable difficult cases. On the other hand, there is no question of purposive formalists simply following their own lights after the fashion of the realists. Nevertheless, it may be objected that, in difficult cases, purposive formalism becomes a crypto-realist approach as judges ultimately follow their own lights, while, in hard cases, the formalist base of the approach entails that judges may become agents of injustice and find themselves deciding against their consciences. We seem to be going round in circles. Our next move, therefore, is to consider whether Ronald Dworkin's elaboration of a purposive formalist approach advances the arguments in its favour.

Dworkin's theory of adjudication, the "rights thesis", focuses on those kinds of cases, typically "grey" appellate court cases, where the settled rules do not give decisive guidance. (Dworkin calls such cases "hard cases", but he is clearly referring to "difficult cases", as we would term them). The leading actor of the rights thesis is Hercules, an ideal-typical judge, whose adjudicative practice reflects Dworkin's view of how judges should proceed. First, Hercules examines the extant formal legal materials which are relevant to the case (e.g. in a negligence suit, he considers the precedents dealing with negligence liability). This, however, is no mechanical exploration of the materials. Nor is it simply a matter of seizing on this or that precedent. Hercules attempts to reconstruct the full set of materials in a way which fits smoothly with the law as articulated. To underline the nature of this part of Hercules' work, Dworkin employs the evocative metaphor of a chain-novel. If novelist A writes chapter one of a book, and then passes the manuscript on to novelist B to write chapter two before passing the manuscript on to novelist C, and so on, the resulting book will only retain a narrative coherence if each writer works within the framework set by those who have preceded him. According to Dworkin, Hercules is akin to a chain-writer who is well down the chain; thus if he is to maintain narrative coherence he cannot simply ignore landmark decisions in the court's record. So far so good (although *cf.* Fish, 1987). However, the problem with complex legal systems is that their materials are tremendously rich and varied. Just imagine Hercules' predicament had he been called upon to decide an economic loss case in negligence in England at a time when the retrenchment from *Junior Books* was underway but by no means complete. At this juncture, even Hercules would be unable to articulate the legal position in such a way as to square every circle. Here, a more modest target would have to be set. Instead of reconstructing the law in an entirely harmonious and coherent way, Hercules would have to settle for identifying those statements of the legal position which had an adequate anchorage in the materials. In other words, instead of demanding a perfect fit at the first stage, the rights thesis demands that Hercules relies only upon those articulations of the law which pass a minimum threshold of coherence.

Faced with a range of possible statements of the legal position, each of which has survived the filtering process represented by the first step, Hercules proceeds to the second stage of his task. Here, he tests each of the statements against the background moral principles of his community. Let us suppose, therefore, that Hercules had been called upon to decide the question in *Donoghue v Stevenson*. Having surveyed the case law, he might have judged, at the first stage, that two articulations of the law passed the threshold requirement of fit. On the one hand, the authorities generally implied that negligent manufacturers were answerable only to those who purchased directly from them, and not to third parties (such as the pursuer in *Donoghue*). On the other hand, some exceptions were recognised, and these could be reconstructed into the principle that manufacturers should be liable to third parties where a test of relational proximity was satisfied. At the second stage, therefore, the question for Hercules would be whether prevailing moral principles were for or against the pursuer. Generally, if a person was injured as a result of the negligence of another, it would probably have been accepted that the latter should compensate the former. The sticking point in *Donoghue*, however, was that the manufacturer's activities were undertaken in pursuance of various contracts to which the pursuer was not a party. Hercules would have to ask himself, therefore, whether this was morally relevant given the community's standards. If, all things considered, he judged that background moral principles were in favour of a decision for the pursuer, then Hercules (like Lord Atkin) would find for the pursuer on the basis of that reconstruction of the case law which licensed such an outcome.

The rights thesis promises to improve the argument in favour of purposive formalism in two ways. First, it underlines the extent of the resources available to judges who apply this approach to difficult cases; and, secondly, far from setting up their own values against those enshrined in the legal materials, purposive formalists who emulate Hercules will apply their best interpretation of the community's background morality. On reflection, however, these supposed gains may seem more apparent than real. The problem is that Hercules is, if anything, too resourceful. Where the legal materials are complex, it seems altogether too easy for Hercules to articulate the law in more than one way, each such statement of the law satisfying the requirement of fit. If this simply led Hercules back to a consensual unequivocal background morality, purposive formalism would seem to be acceptable as a conduit leading to agreed community standards. However, where a community's morality is complex and divided, Hercules can reconstruct this pretty much as he wants, and his best interpretation of the materials becomes *his* preferred view. In other words, purposive formalism as elaborated in the form of the rights thesis arguably is tantamount to a realist licence.

Whereas Dworkin starts from a right-and-duty base, Richard Wasserstrom advances an out-and-out utilitarian theory of adjudication. For Wasserstrom, the object of adjudication, as of any other action, is to maximise utility. What he proposes, therefore, is a particular kind of utilitarian (strong) realist approach—a two-level procedure—for judges. According to this procedure, judges should first determine what would be the "best rule" to govern the question at issue (i.e. that rule which, if generally followed, would best promote utility). For example, in a case like *Donoghue*, a judge should review all possible rules for manufacturers' product liability, ranging, at one extreme, from no liability at all (i.e. consumers use products entirely at their own risk) to, at the other extreme, strict liability for producers (i.e. producers must compensate those injured by their products, irrespective of whether they—producers—were in any sense at fault). In so reviewing the options, Wasserstrom's judge would not be constrained in any way by the existing rules. However, in determining the best rule, the judge should not focus narrowly on short-term considerations; the longer term effects of the rule should also be taken into account. For instance, if a judge hearing *Donoghue* were to be attracted by a rule imposing strict liability on producers, he should not adopt it before taking into the reckoning any counter-productive features of the rule in the longer run (e.g. certain producers withdrawing from the market). Having identified the best rule, judges should then simply apply that rule to the case at hand.

Wasserstrom's proposal takes the sting out of a number of standard objections to a strong realist approach. In particular, assuming that all judges observe the two-level procedure, and calculate utility in a similar way, decision-making should be reasonably consistent and predictable. On the minus side, however, the proposal can only appeal to committed utilitarians (and, even then, some utilitarians doubt the wisdom of Wasserstrom's theory, see Hodgson, 1967). Also, it should be noted that Wasserstrom promotes his theory on the basis of the bizarre stipulation that he is prescribing an adjudicative model for a legal system in which there is no legislature. In contrasting Wasserstrom with Dworkin, this is a matter of some importance; for it is central to Dworkin's overall view that collective goals (like utility) should be set by the legislature, whereas judges should eschew all such policy decisions sticking strictly to right-and-duty questions of principle. In other words, Dworkin's view presupposes a specific division of labour as between legislative and judicial institutions which cannot be fitted directly onto Wasserstrom's model where the judges seem to have both legislative and judicial functions. Even so, in relation to case law adjudication, it is clear that Dworkin and Wasserstrom are directly at odds over the respect to be accorded to (and the materiality of) previous decisions.

Many years ago, the American jurist Roscoe Pound (1908) identified three demands to be made of adjudicators:

"the demand for full justice, that is for solutions that go to the root of controversies; the demand for equal justice, that is a like adjustment of like relations under like conditions; and the demand for exact justice, that is for a justice whose operations, within reasonable limits, may be predicted in advance of action." (p.605)

For Pound, this meant that judges should not apply the law with a logic oblivious to common sense and experience, but nor should judges simply follow the perceived equities of a case.

Ideally, judges should strive to apply the law intelligently, producing a workable and just result in the concrete case at issue. A century later, the prospect of achieving a satisfactory accommodation of these demands seems as elusive as ever. To progress we surely need to follow the lead provided by Dworkin and Wasserstrom, clarifying both our moral starting point (whether we are with the utilitarians or the right-and-duty theorists) and how we view the general responsibilities of the judiciary in the broader constitutional scheme of things. To reflect upon such matters will not produce instant answers, but at least it promises to put us on the right track.

5. SUMMARY

In response to Lord Reid's challenge, what can we say about how judges do, and how they should, operate in the Appeal Courts? Judges, we have suggested, approach their task in various ways. At the level of general adjudicative ideology, in relation to both statutes and precedents, the basic approaches are either formalist (textual or purposive) or realist (weak or strong); and, within specific substantive areas of law, a range of particular ideologies is apparent. To improve our understanding of these matters, however, we need to consider whether there is any pattern to these ideologies. Could it be, for example, as John Griffith has famously argued (1991), and as Lord Devlin has effectively conceded (1978), that English judges tend to be conservative, typically being protective of the interests of capital and property, and supportive of established institutions of authority? If so, how do we account for this? If not, is there some different pattern, or no pattern, and how do we account for that? As for the vexed question of how judges *should* decide cases, there is a danger that, faced with the usual platitudes about the need for certainty, consistency, and justice, we either tread water or, *faute de mieux*, put our faith in a middle-way position (probably purposive formalism). If we are to break out of this mould, we must return to first principles, political and moral, seeking an understanding of where judges fit into the broader constitutional scheme of things (see further Ch.8 and Conclusion).

6

LEGAL PROCESS

I: The Criminal Justice System

What is crime? The answer is by no means as easy as we might suppose. For present purposes probably the best, though by no means very helpful definition is that of Glanville Williams (Williams, 1955):

"an act that is capable of being followed by criminal proceedings, having one of the types of outcome (punishment etc.) known to follow these proceedings."

Certainly when courts have needed to decide whether a particular proceeding is a criminal cause, or not, they have tended to use the practical test as to whether the proceedings may result in the punishment of the offender. If they could do so, then the proceeding is criminal (see e.g. *Armand v Home Secretary and Minister of Defence of the Royal Netherlands Government* (1943)). The crucial difference between crimes and civil wrongs then is the element of punishment. Although there is the possibility of a court awarding punitive damages to a claimant in a tort action, the circumstances in which it might do so are very limited (see p.215). In general the rule applied in civil cases is that damages are compensatory only (the odd aberrant award in defamation cases is largely attributable to the anomalous survival in those cases of the civil jury (see p.199)). Of course, it must be remembered that the same act can give rise both to a liability to compensate the victim, and to punishment. A car dealer who sells a car with the odometer turned back is liable both in civil law for breach of the warranty of correspondence with description under section 13 of the Sale of Goods Act 1979, and to criminal prosecution under the Trade Descriptions Act 1968. The distinction we draw between crime and civil wrongs is not universal. It was not sharply drawn in Imperial China, for example, where civil disputes could lead to the losing party being punished (see Allee, 1994).

The essence of a crime then is its potential to lead to punishment (we will not broach for the time being the exact meaning of "punishment" nor the reasons for inflicting it; see pp.188 *et seq.*). Punishments in modern Western societies are imposed by the state, and it must be realised that, in less developed societies, the concept of punishment for deeds we would regard as criminal may be virtually or entirely absent. If we look, for example, at the various codes of the Anglo-Saxon kings in England, we will find that they consist largely of tariffs of the amounts payable to a person or his relatives for such things as causing injury or death (see Attenborough, 1922; Plucknett, 1960, Ch.1. For example 3s compensation for a punch on the nose—Laws of Aethelbert, AD *c*.602, cap.57). In fact, these tariffs probably principally comprised an attempt to regulate the blood feud which might otherwise follow, for example, the death of an individual. The blood feud survived in parts of southern Europe into modern times, but in northern Europe it tended to disappear as the state appropriated the task of maintaining "law and order".

One of the key implications of the state assuming responsibility for maintaining order is that it thereby acquires an important monopoly: the modern criminal justice system testifies to the state's exclusive right to determine what counts as a "crime", to decide who has offended, and to set and administer appropriate punishments. For victims, the state's monopoly means that there is no longer a legitimate avenue of private redress and retribution: but, in return, the modern criminal justice system promises a fairer and more efficient regime for dealing with crime. Such promises, however, are easier to make than to deliver; and public confidence cannot be taken for granted.

Consider, for example, that most serious of crimes, murder. If ever there is a case of the law needing to command public confidence, it is here. Yet, according to the Law Commission (2005), the law of murder in England and Wales is "a mess", the law of homicide operating with a blunt distinction between murder and manslaughter. However, because unlawful killings come in all shades of culpability, the crude portmanteau approach fails to do justice to the varieties of offence. For example, the category of murder

"encompasses both the 'contract' killer who commits a premeditated killing for gain and the person who, suddenly involved in an argument, instinctively picks up a knife and inflicts a wound that he or she did not intend to be, which proves, fatal. Each is guilty of murder and subject to the mandatory life sentence." (*ibid* at 1.29)

As for manslaughter, it applies alike to a person who sets fire to a house, intending to frighten but not to kill the occupier, and one who, losing his temper in an argument with a neighbour, throws a punch which, quite unexpectedly, proves fatal (*ibid* at 1.30). And, then, there are cases such as infanticide and mercy killing, not to mention the liability of accessories. With a view to bringing the law closer into alignment with public expectation, the Commission is consulting on the possibility of adopting a three-way distinction between first degree murder, second degree murder, and manslaughter.

On the one hand, victims (and potential victims) demand that their interests are properly protected: crime prevention should be accorded high priority and punishments should be commensurate with the expectations of victims. On the other hand, civilised societies draw the line at intrusive enforcement and draconian punishments, and jib at wrongful convictions. In consequence, as we foreshadowed in Chapter Two, we find in modern criminal justice systems a constant see-saw between, on the one hand, the ideals of utility and efficient control of crime (including the ideal of a workable system for those, especially the police, who actually have to operate it) and, on the other hand, the ideals of due process and respect for the rights of individuals.

So far as the criminal justice system in England and Wales is concerned, the last decade has seen important developments in relation to both sets of ideals. On the one hand, the enactment of the Human Rights Act 1998, which inter alia incorporates the Convention right to a fair trial (see our earlier commentary on *Lambert* and *Kansal*, at 136 *et seq*), suggests that the rights of suspects and defendants are to be given a high priority; but, on the other hand, the restriction on the right of silence in 1994 (see below at 157) coupled with a penal policy that has led to a rocketing prison population seem to speak more to what Andrew Ashworth has described as a "repressive turn in the politics of criminal justice" (Ashworth, 2002, p.1). In the latest round of this "clash between ... two sets of ideologies, the promotion of human rights and the struggle against serious crime" (*ibid*), it seems that the latter is again dominant; for the government's plans for the modernisation of the criminal justice system represent a further turn away from the ideals of due process (see below at 174)

In this chapter, our concern is with the task of maintaining "law and order" (and the tensions associated with this task). We will first of all give a basic account of modern criminal procedure in

England and Wales, before looking a little more closely at the concepts of crime and punishment.

1. A SKETCH OF CRIMINAL PROCEDURE

Today, the basic division of crimes lies between "arrestable" and "non-arrestable" offences. Arrestable offences are those serious enough to warrant a sentence fixed by law, namely murder, treason and piracy with violence, those for which a person, not previously convicted, may be sentenced to a term of five years (or might be but for the restrictions imposed by section 33, Magistrates Courts Act 1980), and attempts to commit such offences (Police and Criminal Evidence Act 1984, s.24) or other offences Parliament has made arrestable, e.g. taking a motor vehicle without consent. Non-arrestable offences are all other offences. For procedural purposes, a second division of crimes is between those triable by magistrates' courts—"summary offences"—and those triable "on indictment" before a judge and jury in the Crown Court. Indictable offences are divided into four classes. Class 1 are serious offences (e.g. murder) which must be tried by a High Court judge. Class 2 are serious offences (e.g. rape) which must generally be tried by a High Court judge unless the presiding judge of the Circuit orders otherwise (the presiding judge of each Circuit is a High Court judge). Class 4 are the large number of offences normally to be tried by a Circuit judge or Recorder or Assistant Recorder (though they can be tried by a High Court judge). Class 3 is a residual category consisting of offences not falling into any of the other Classes, for example causing death by reckless driving. They are normally tried by a High Court judge. Some minor offences, for instance most motoring infringements, are triable only summarily; some serious offences, such as murder or causing death by reckless driving, are triable only on indictment. But many offences can be tried either way—summarily or on indictment (see Magistrate's Courts Act 1980, Schedule I for a list of such offences, and other enactments may specify trial either way—*ibid*, s.17). In the first instance it is for the magistrates' court to decide, having heard representations from the prosecution and defence, what mode of trial is appropriate (*ibid*, s.19 *et seq*.). If it decides on summary trial, it must inform the accused of his right to trial by jury, and the accused must then consent to summary trial. The accused must also be warned that if he consents to summary trial, he may, if convicted, be committed to the Crown Court for sentence (because the limited sentencing powers of the magistrates are thought to be insufficient) *ibid* s.20.

A prosecution for an offence is in general begun either with a formal complaint to the appropriate magistrates' court (an "information is laid") resulting in a summons being issued by the court, or by charging the accused, in which case the charge sheet serves as the information. After being charged, the accused will either be released on bail, or kept in custody. The duties of the police in the latter case are described later. If the accused fails to show up in court after being summoned or charged, the magistrates can issue a warrant for his arrest. The vast majority of offences are of a minor nature, for example many motoring offences, and the result of the information will be a summons to the accused. In theory, anyone can lay an information, but in practice, of course, it is usually the police, or some other official body such as the Customs and Excise, who do so. Usually, in the case of minor offences, the accused will have been caught "red handed"—speeding, for example. More serious offences may also come to court in this way, but many will be the result of a police investigation.

The principal investigative powers of the police (to stop and search; to seize evidence; to arrest and search suspects; to detain and to question suspects; to take fingerprints and bodily samples, and so on), together with the correlative safeguards for suspects, are largely regulated by the Police and Criminal Evidence Act 1984 (PACE) and the Codes of Practice setting out its detailed implementation (and also to a lesser extent by the Criminal Justice and Public Order Act 1994). Whereas the former Act (PACE) closely followed the recommendations of the Royal Commission on Criminal Procedure (Philips Commission, 1981), the Criminal Justice and Public Order Act was preceded by the Royal Commission on Criminal Justice (Runciman Commission, 1993) but it does not straightforwardly implement the Runciman recommendations—indeed, the Government proceeded to amend the law concerning the inferences to be drawn from a suspect's exercise of the right to silence (see ss.34–38 of the 1994 Act) despite the fact that the Commission had recommended that no such amendment should be made. A common strand in the background to the setting up of both Commissions was a concern that the criminal justice system was producing too many miscarriages of justice (in particular, too many high profile convictions that were subsequently quashed as unsafe). At the time of the Philips

Commission, the cause célèbre was the *Maxwell Confait* case, which raised questions about the adequacy of the safeguards against false confessions (see Philips, 1981, pp.2–3). However, by the time of the Runciman Commission, a string of miscarriages of justice had come to light, most famously the cases of the "Guildford Four", the "Birmingham Six", Judith Ward, and the "Maguire Seven", each of which involved alleged terrorist offences, but also the cases of the "Tottenham Three" and the "Cardiff Three", neither of which involved terrorist offences. Reflecting on such cases, Andrew Ashworth (1994) summarises the recurrent problems as follows:

"The most common *pre-trial* faults lay in the concoction or falsification of evidence by police officers, in non-disclosure by forensic scientists, and more generally in non-disclosure by the prosecution to the defence. In some cases there was oppressive conduct by the police during questioning, with or without actual violence . . . The most common *post-trial* faults lay in the slow and cumbersome procedures for referring cases to the Court of Appeal, and in that Court's reluctance (at least until recently) to overturn jury verdicts, especially if such a decision would imply that the police had not told the truth." (p.13, emphasis added)

Such recurrent problems, however, are not easily rectified. Quite apart from resource limitations and resistance within the police to interventions that cut across the culture of law enforcement, reformers must be careful not to trade one kind of miscarriage of justice (the conviction of the innocent) for another (the acquittal of the guilty). For, from the point of view of maintaining public confidence in the criminal justice system, there is little to choose between wrongful convictions and wrongful acquittals.

Although the legal framework instituted by PACE might not have stemmed the flow of miscarriages of justice, there is no doubt that it represented an important watershed in the evolution of the criminal justice system. For the first time, the scattered, uneven, and sometimes inadequate provision for police powers (deriving from a mixture of statute, common law, and local bye-laws) was rationalised in a single statute. And, what is more, PACE made a serious and systematic attempt to balance police powers (and the interests of crime control) with safeguards for suspects (and the interests of due process). This historic accommodation was guided by the three ideals of "workability" (on the crime control side) and "fairness" and "openness" (on the due process side). So, for example, in the sensitive area of police powers to stop and search, there are provisions for reasonable steps to be taken to notify persons who are to be searched of various matters including the object of the proposed search and the grounds for making it; and, after a search has been carried out, a written record is to be made unless it is not practicable to do so. Similarly, PACE attempts to strike a balance between the needs of the police in relation to the detention of suspects for questioning and the interests of suspects in having access to legal advice. Accordingly, in the interests of fairness and openness, section 58 of PACE provides:

"A person arrested and held in custody in a police station or other premises shall be entitled, if he so requests, to consult a solicitor at any time."

Section 58(8), however, reflecting the need for workability, provides that an officer may authorise delaying the provision of such a facility in certain circumstances, such as when the consultation will lead to the alerting of other suspects. In *Samuel* (1988) the accused was arrested on suspicion of robbery and burglary. His request to see his solicitor was denied, inter alia, because it was believed that access to a solicitor might result in other suspects being inadvertently warned. The Court of Appeal decided that in order to prevent access to a solicitor the officer must believe, and have reasonable grounds for so believing, that it is very probable that the solicitor will, if allowed to consult with the detained person, commit the offence of interfering with the course of justice or inadvertently do something which will have such effect. Since solicitors are officers of the court, Hodgson J. observed that it would be very rare for the police to be able to form such a view. It appeared that the real reason why access had been refused in *Samuel* was that the police believed a solicitor would counsel silence, and thereby hinder them in their efforts to question the prisoner and recover certain firearms. However, Annex B of the Code of Practice expressly provides that access to a solicitor may not be delayed on the grounds that he may counsel silence (on the inferences to be drawn from a suspect's silence see ss.34–38 of the 1994 Act). The court therefore excluded a confession made by the accused during the period when he was wrongfully denied his rights under section 58.

Potentially, the power of the courts to exclude evidence (including confession evidence) that has been improperly obtained is an important guarantee of due process. In *Samuel*, the court invoked its powers under section 78 of PACE, according to which evidence may be ruled inadmissible where it would have "an adverse effect on the fairness of the proceedings". In principle, it might also have applied its powers under section 76 of PACE, which provides specifically for the exclusion of confession evidence where it has been obtained by oppression, or the like, such as to render it unreliable. In fact, however, it was not argued in *Samuel* that the circumstances in which the confession was obtained amounted to oppression. Although *Samuel* struck "a notable symbolic blow in favour of the right to legal advice" (Ashworth, 1994, p.103), it gives a somewhat misleading picture of the general approach taken by the English courts to questions of this kind. Thus, shortly after the decision in *Samuel*, the Court of Appeal emphasised in *R v Alladice* (1988) that, in the absence of bad faith by the police, exclusion of evidence under section 78 depended on whether a fair trial would be possible. It followed that a breach of section 58 would not automatically lead to exclusion—and, indeed, in *Alladice* itself, the court took the view that the denial of access to a solicitor was not prejudicial to the defendant because he was already aware of his rights (especially his right to silence). Moreover, once we move away from confession evidence, the tilt towards workability is even more pronounced, the basic principle being that courts are not concerned with how evidence that is relevant and reliable has been obtained (see e.g. *R v Sang* (1980)). The force of this approach can be seen quite clearly in two later cases, *R v Bailey* (1993) and *R v Khan* (1996).

In *Bailey*, two youths were arrested and charged with being involved in robberies. However, the youths had exercised their right to silence when interviewed, and the police really needed more evidence. Accordingly, hoping that the youths might incriminate themselves when off-guard, the police secretly bugged a cell and duped the youths into believing that they were being put together in the (bugged) cell only because of an uncooperative custody officer at the police station. Not realising that the police were taping their conversation, the youths made damaging admissions while they were together in the cell. Although the police were guilty of deception, there was no reason to doubt the reliability of the admissions and the Court of Appeal duly held that the evidence should not be excluded. Similarly, in *Khan*, the police obtained evidence of the appellant's involvement in the importation of drugs by placing a listening device on the outside of a house (without the knowledge or consent of the house-holder). Various objections were raised against the admissibility of the evidence thus obtained, particularly that the Home Office guidelines for the use of listening devices were not sufficiently accessible to the public (simply being placed in the library of the House of Commons) and that there was a violation of the right of privacy (as recognised, for example, by Art.8(1) of the European Convention on Human Rights—represented, but not directly implemented, in the UK by the Human Rights Act 1998, s.1 and Sch.1). The objections, however, were decisively (and willingly) rejected. As Lord Nolan confessed:

"I have reached this conclusion not only quite firmly as a matter of law, but also with relief. It would be a strange reflection on our law if a man who has admitted his participation in the illegal importation of a large quantity of heroin should have his convic-tion set aside on the grounds that his privacy has been invaded." (at 302)

If *Samuel* suggests a growing concern for due process, decisions such as *Alladice*, *Bailey*, and *Khan* suggest a clear tendency in the opposite direction.

As we mentioned in our introductory remarks, it is a little sur-prising that there should be signs of a drift away from due process values at just the time that the government has pro-claimed the importance of human rights by incorporating the European Convention on Human Rights. Article 6 of the Convention, as we have noted previously, provides for the right to a fair trial. In principle, such a right should be treated as dynamic and capable of development, reflecting our best under-standing of what due process and the Rule of Law requires. Andrew Ashworth (2002, p.13 *et seq.*) has identified ten specific procedural rights (or safeguards) that might be argued for under the general right to a fair trial. These are: (1) the right to be pre-sumed innocent; (2) the privilege against self-incrimination; (3) the right of silence; (4) the right to legal aid and assistance; (5) the right to be brought promptly before a court; (6) the right to release pending trial; (7) the right to disclosure of documents (against the prosecution); (8) the right to confront witnesses; (9) the right to be tried on evidence not obtained by violation of fundamental rights; and (10) the right not to be placed in double jeopardy. To some extent these rights are expressly protected by the Convention—for instance, Article 6.2 declares that "everyone charged with a criminal offence shall be presumed innocent until proved guilty according to law" and Article 6(3)(d) provides for the defendant's right "to examine or have examined witnesses against him"—and, with one exception, support for the other rights can be derived from the jurisprudence of the European Court of Human Rights. The one exception is the ninth right in the list: here, although Article 3 of the Convention expressly prohibits torture or inhuman or degrading treatment, the right to a fair trial has not been connected as such to observance of background fundamental rights (such as the right to privacy). Although, as we have seen (above, 18), English law has adopted a doctrine of abuse of process that does connect the right to a fair trial to procedural propriety at the pre-trial stage, *Khan* reminds us that this is not quite the same as connecting this right to respect for the Convention rights. And, if we were to judge the tendency of English law relative to Ashworth's check-list, we would find that it is away from rather than towards these due process benchmarks.

Before we return to our sketch of the criminal process, it is worth saying that any judgment as to the tendency of a particular criminal justice system needs to be sensitive to more than one level of evidence. For example, political rhetoric may highlight one set of values (human rights, or victims' rights, or whatever) but the terms of the relevant legislation may not be fully consistent with these values; within the legislation itself, such as in PACE, we may find that due process values are qualified by workability clauses—likewise with common law doctrines (*cf.* McBarnet, 1981); and, of course, the way in which the courts interpret and apply the legislation will reflect a complex interplay of ideological values of the kind that we have discussed already. At the level of practical policing, where legal doctrine encounters a culture of crime prevention and detection, then the stresses and strains may force a rift between the law in the books and the law in action, yet again showing the trajectory of the law in a rather different light (see Dixon *et al*, 1991).

As a result of their investigations the police may conclude that a particular individual has committed an offence. In what circumstances may they arrest him or her? The police may obviously arrest a person if the magistrates have issued a warrant for his or her arrest; they may also arrest if they have reasonable grounds for suspecting that he or she has committed an arrestable offence. They may arrest in certain other cases where no arrestable offence has been committed—for example, where a person impedes their enquiries, by refusing to give his or her name and address, or by giving one which is manifestly false or by some other such failure. In other cases the suspect will merely be summoned. If he or she fails to obey the summons, a warrant may be issued for his arrest.

Following arrest, the suspect must be taken as soon as possible to a "designated police station", which is one where there will be a "custody officer", who must be a sergeant or higher ranking officer. The custody officer decides whether there is sufficient evidence to charge the suspect. If there is not, the suspect must be released:

"unless the custody officer has reasonable grounds for believing that his detention without being charged is necessary to secure or preserve evidence relating to an offence for which he is under arrest or to obtain such evidence by questioning him." (PACE, s.37(2))

Under PACE, the general rule was that a suspect may be held for up to 24 hours at a police station at the end of which period he or she must either be charged or released (s.41(1)); but, where the suspect is detained in connection with a "serious arrestable offence" (s.116), this period could be extended to 36 hours (s.42(1)). However, the position has been modified by section 7 of the Criminal Justice Act 2003 such that, in relation to any arrestable offence (whether serious or not), the initial period for detention without charge may now be extended to 36 hours. The extension must be granted by a superintendent or a magistrate, who must be satisfied that the investigation is being conducted diligently and expeditiously. The grounds for granting such an extension are that it is necessary in order to secure or preserve evidence or to obtain evidence through questioning (this being the most common ground for extended detention). In some cases, it may be possible for the police to obtain authorisation to hold a suspect beyond the 36 hour limit. However, in two respects, the rules become more restrictive at this stage: first, a warrant for further detention must be obtained from the magistrates (s.43); and, secondly, the offence in connection with which the suspect has been arrested must be within the "serious arrestable" category. This can extend the period in custody, but the period cannot end later than 96 hours after the "relevant time" (this being defined by s.41(2) ordinarily as the time of a person's arrival at the police station or twenty-four hours after his arrest, whichever is earlier). At the end of this period the suspect must be released or charged (s.44). An exception to the 96 hour limit for detaining a suspect is under the Terrorism Act 2000, which has its own machinery granting detention without trial (changes to this are currently being debated in Parliament). If charged, the suspect may not be questioned further (Code of Practice for the Detention, Treatment and Questioning of Persons by Police Officers, para.17.5 as laid down by the Home Office under the powers conferred by s.60, and see Practice Direction [1989] 2 All E.R. 415).

The questioning of suspects at police stations (though not elsewhere, such as in police cars) is tape recorded. Two copies are made, and the suspect is given one copy. The effect of this practice has been to reduce the tendency of suspects to challenge confessions on the basis that, for example, they were forced out of them. Suspects are not obliged to answer the questions put to them by the police, and, as noted above, they must be informed of their right to consult a solicitor (*ibid*, s.58).

Obviously, the right to have a solicitor present would be of academic interest to many suspects, since they could not afford to pay for one, unless some provision were made for subsidy from public funds. In order to try to deal with this problem the system of a rota of "duty solicitors", which was originally intended to ensure that the accused needing the services of a solicitor in court could get one, was extended to attendance on suspects at police stations. Unfortunately, notwithstanding that those wishing to be duty solicitors at magistrates' courts must make themselves available for police station duties, so poor are the rates of pay that many solicitors dropped out of the scheme and it is encountering difficulties in meeting its obligations. The Access to Justice Act 1999 provided for the setting up of a Criminal Defence Service (as part of the Community Legal Service (CLS)), but the duty solicitor schedule is still in operation though now funded by the Criminal Defence Service. The Criminal Defence Service (CDS) helps people who are under investigation or facing criminal charges. By ensuring that people accused of crimes have access to legal advice and representation, the CDS also helps the police and courts to operate fairly and efficiently. The General Criminal Contract is the means through which all criminal defence work is funded, up to disposal in the magistrates' courts, by the CDS. We will return to this shortly. In addition, there is the Public Defender Service (PDS). PDS Offices are served by solicitors and accredited representatives who are directly employed by the Legal Service Commission but provide independent advice, assistance and representation. The first four Public Defender Service offices opened in Birmingham, Liverpool, Middlesborough and Swansea in 2001. Further offices have since been added in Cheltenham, Chester, Darlington and Pontypridd. In Australia, Canada and the United States salaried state lawyers act as "public defenders". The Scottish Law Commission recommended in 1980 the introduction of this scheme in Scotland on a limited experimental basis (Hughes Commission, 1980: 110–12). No action, however, was taken to implement it. The problem with this system, at least as it operates in the US, according to American research is that it tends to reduce the adversarial element in the trial process and to promote "plea bargaining" (i.e. a bargain between the prosecution and the defence in which, for instance, the latter agrees to plead guilty to a less serious charge in return for the former agreeing to drop more serious charges—see pp.42–43). Thus, the participating lawyers on both sides tend to see greater advantage in co-operation with each other than in conflict (see Skolnick, 1967).

On 9 February 2006, a committee chaired by Lord Carter of Coles, reported on the urgent need for whole-system reform of criminal legal aid, the cost of which had risen from £1.5 billion in 1997 to £2.1 billion at the time of the report. It concluded that many of the inefficiencies in the current system are outside the control of the solicitors and barristers who provide defence services. The committee sought to promote a market-based solution. The object would be by 2009 to have a smaller number of larger, more efficient, good quality suppliers of legal services profiting from increased volumes of work at lower cost. These suppliers would work under new contracting arrangements to deliver police station and associated court work. The contracts would cover a group of police stations, and their associated magistrates and Crown Courts. The Legal Services Commission's preferred supplier approach will provide the basis, and payment will be by block grant for the duration of the contract. High cost cases will be paid for under individual case contracts with defence teams working to strict cost and case management rules. A key part of the thinking behind these reforms is that payment by hours worked does not provide incentives for suppliers to be efficient. Accordingly, the new system must reward efficiency. The committee also recognises the need to reduce the complexity and bureaucracy of the current system. It remains to be seen how the government will deal with these proposals.

Our system, under which the principal interrogation of the accused is conducted by the police, is radically different from the system obtaining in most European countries, where the interrogation is often carried out by magistrates (for an account of the French procedure see Cooper, 1991). This was formerly the position in England and Wales. Under a statute of 1555 the justices were required to question suspects and witnesses, and record their answers in writing. The material thus gathered would then be used in the trial court as the basis of the case against the accused. With the organisation of police forces in the nineteenth century, however, the police took over the function of interrogating suspects. The first step in committing an accused charged with one of the more serious offences to be tried before a jury then became the preliminary examination. In the preliminary examination the police case was presented to the magistrates who recorded the evidence and decided whether or not there was a prima facie case against the accused—whether there was sufficient evidence against the accused to justify sending him for trial (the court was not concerned at this stage with questions of guilt or innocence). Since 1967 instead of calling witnesses and recording their evidence, witness statements have been used. It was still possible for the defence to ask witnesses to attend court. However, under the Criminal Procedure and Investigations Act 1996 (s.47 and Sch.1) no witnesses are called. All prosecution evidence must be handed to the court in written form, and if the defence wants to challenge whether there is sufficient evidence for the case to be sent to the Crown Court, this evidence is read out. The defence and prosecution then have the right to make representations as to whether the case should be sent to the Crown Court or the defendant discharged.

Once a suspect is actually charged, he or she can apply to the magistrates' court for legal aid. The readiness to grant this varied considerably from court to court around the country, notwithstanding attempts to obviate these variations (see pp.261 *et seq.*). Since the grant of legal aid before the Crown Court was fairly invariable, there was thus an incentive for defendants to opt for trial on indictment where this was possible, because they would almost certainly get legal representation in the Crown Court. Given the necessity for an accused to be advised properly in an accusatorial system if it is to operate fairly, the many imperfections of the system were regrettable. A system which ensured that any defence there might be was adequately presented, and on conviction all relevant information placed before the court, was clearly what should be aimed at. As noted above under the Access to Justice Act 1999 a Public Defender Service (PDS) is being established under the auspices of the Legal Services Commission (see below, 261). The other prong of the strategy, as we said, is for the Commission to develop contracts for various kinds of criminal defence work. The target was to have all criminal services contracted out to solicitors by 2003, but at the time of writing the process is still continuing (see Ch.7).

In criminal proceedings, the accused can simply plead "not guilty" i.e. plead the general issue, requiring the prosecution case to be proved in all respects in law and fact. In civil cases the possibility of pleading the general issue was cut down and finally abolished in the nineteenth century by various Common Law Procedure Acts. The object of this was to force parties to try to clarify the issues between them before a case came to court. The Criminal Procedure and Investigations Act 1996 attempts to modify the situation under which the prosecution remained in ignorance of the basis of the defence case (with the exception of an alibi defence) until the hearing itself. Under section 5 before committal for trial the defence must give the prosecution a defence statement setting out in general terms the nature of the defence, including the name and address of any alibi witnesses. It may be that if the criminal courts themselves took a more active role in the preparation of cases for court, trials could be shortened, focusing specifically on the disputes of law or fact which still remained between the parties. In civil suits the interlocutory process could include asking the other side to answer questions of fact (interrogatories), which in general they had to do. Under the new procedure this has been replaced by a right to obtain "Further Information" (see pp.196–197). There must also be a pre-trial exchange of witness statements. A similar procedure might have its place in criminal cases (only the defence, at present, has copies of the prosecution witness statements). However, to operate it, defendants would need proper representation. Nevertheless, some moves in this direction in the Crown Court might result in a more efficient process. Certainly an acquittal rate of around forty-three per cent on not-guilty pleas in the Crown Court suggests either that far too many innocent people are being prosecuted, or that too many prosecution cases are badly prepared. By contrast, the conviction rate in civil law countries is usually much higher, and there is no evidence that more innocent people are being convicted.

If the offence is merely a summary one, or is one triable on indictment but the accused has not opted for trial on indictment, the ensuing procedure before the magistrates is the trial itself. The prosecution "opens" by summarising its case, then presents its evidence, thereafter the defence either submits "no case to answer" (that the prosecution have failed to establish a key ingredient of the offence or that the evidence is so weak the court could not reasonably convict) or presents its evidence and sums up its case. The defence has the right to make an opening or a closing speech, but in practice invariably opts for the latter (so as to have the last word). The prosecution may, at the discretion of the court, be permitted to make a second speech. If this is allowed, it will be made before the defence's closing speech. The court then considers the evidence (adjourning for this purpose in difficult cases), and in the case of lay justices may call in the clerk at this stage for advice on points of law or evidence. It then reaches its decision, and either convicts or acquits the accused. If it convicts, it will, after considering probation officers' reports and other such relevant information and any observations by the defence upon these matters, pass sentence. It is to be noted that unless the accused has put his character in issue, it is only after conviction that the accused's previous convictions will be read to the court, to be taken into account in sentencing. Appeal on points of law raised by the facts, or on the grounds of procedural irregularity, is to a Divisional Court. Otherwise appeal is to the Crown Court.

The order of events in a trial before the Crown Court is broadly similar, except that generally both the prosecution and the defence sum up their cases to the jury at the end of the evidence, the defence having the last word—see *R. v Bryant* (1978) at 692 *et seq.* for a history of the practice on closing speeches. The judge then sums up for the jury, who then retire and determine their verdict. The summing up will both advise the jury on the law applicable to the case and the issues of fact which they must decide, and will, having regard to the applicable law, result in a conviction or acquittal of the accused. Obviously, the way in which the judge sums up can influence the outcome of the case (judges in the United States for this reason are not permitted to sum up), but it does not always do so in the obvious way. It is not unknown for impatient judges who have summed up too favourably for the prosecution, and too dismissively of the defence, to find that juries acquit (on the basis that the accused has not had a fair trial).

Appeal from the Crown Court is to the Court of Appeal Criminal Division (see fig.1, p.131). As in the case of the magistrates' courts, there is also the possibility of judicial review (Supreme Court Act 1981, s.29(3)).

The right to jury trial is perceived to be one of the foundations of civil liberties; for this reason, it is enshrined in the US Constitution; and for this reason, too, it is stoutly defended by proponents of the due process perspective (see e.g. Harman and Griffith, 1979). Whether or not the jury's performance over the centuries actually supports this perception is debatable (see Cornish, 1968, Ch.5); and, in recent times, even if we can make our excuses, the presence of a jury has not prevented some spectacular miscarriages of justice. Nevertheless, it is arguable that, by bringing lay citizens into the courtroom to act as impartial decision-makers, the institution of the jury represents a safeguard against case-hardened professionals and generally inspires public confidence in the integrity of the system (*cf.* Chamblis and Seidman, 1971). However, from the 1960s onwards the jury has been under sustained attack on several fronts. First, there has been a concern that professional criminals are able to manipulate jury trial, most egregiously by "nobbling" or intimidating the jurors themselves. This led to the introduction, by the Criminal Justice Act 1967 (now the Juries Act 1974, s.17), of majority verdicts, putting an end to the centuries-old tradition that the jury had to be unanimous. It should be said that majority verdicts are not routinely accepted: it is only where a jury has failed to achieve unanimity and has gone back to the court to obtain leave that a majority verdict (of at least ten in a full panel of twelve jurors) may be brought in. Nevertheless, given that the prosecution must prove its case beyond reasonable doubt, one might wonder how well this sits with acceptance of majority verdicts. Secondly, there has been a concern that jurors do not always follow more complex cases—hence, the Roskill Committee's (1986) proposal to try fraud cases without a jury. Thirdly, because juries need to have things explained to them in simple terms, there is a concern about the length and expense of jury trials. For governments intent on saving money for legal aid (see below 259), this is a cost to be trimmed (with knock-on effects, it should be said, for the Criminal Bar; see e.g. Grant, 2000). Following recommendations made by the Auld Committee (2001), the government and the legal profession again found themselves at loggerheads with regard to the importance of jury trial. And, although the profession headed off the most threatening of Auld's recommendations (namely, for a unified three-division Criminal Court, with much of the Crown Court's business being sent to a jury-less middle division), the government's latest plans for the criminal justice system do include further restrictions on the involvement of juries (see below 174).

One of the strengths of the jury is supposed to be that it is a randomly selected body chosen from across society. Viewed in this light, the removal of jurors' occupations from the jury list (to prevent challenges on this ground) may seem laudable. On the other hand, it became apparent in 1978 that the police had for some years been "vetting" jury panels in major cases. In 1980 the Attorney-General published guidelines. Guideline Three provides "there are certain exceptional types of case of public importance where it is in the interests both of justice and the public that there should be further safeguards against the possibility of bias"; and Guideline Four defines the classes of case broadly as: (a) cases in which national security is involved and part of the evidence is likely to be heard in camera; (b) terrorist cases. Whilst the first category does raise special considerations, because few would argue that it was undesirable to exclude from the jury panel persons known to spy for foreign powers for example, the latter category gives cause for disquiet, especially in view of the several wrongful convictions of supposed IRA terrorists in recent years.

A further erosion of the traditional role of the jury has been the tendency in modern times to try to limit the offences for which the accused can opt for trial by jury (see e.g. Auld, 2001). The right to trial by jury was, for example, removed in the case of a number of public order offences by the Criminal Law Act 1977. That Act also cut down from seven to three the defence's right to challenge jurors, and, in fact, the defence's right of peremptory challenge was abolished altogether by the Criminal Justice Act 1988 (s.118). Although the prosecution cannot technically challenge without cause at all, because it can require any juror to "stand by" (i.e. to go back into the panel to be called on to serve only as a last resort), in effect, it has more or less an unlimited possibility of peremptory challenge.

As we will see in Chapter 7, the civil jury has virtually ceased to exist in this country. Moreover, in coroners' courts the coroner's power to dispense with juries was much widened by the Criminal Law Act 1977 (now the Coroners Act 1988, s.8), and even where such juries are used they cannot now cast the blame upon someone (Coroners Rules 1984, r.42).

It is highly unlikely that the jury will ever recover the ground it has lost, and the main question is whether it is likely to lose yet more ground. There is little concrete evidence to support the views of those who argue that juries are poor judges of fact (*cf*. Baldwin and McConville, 1979, and Freeman, 1981). Indeed, researching the reliability of jury decisions is by no means straightforward and intuitively we may suppose twelve heads to be better than one (even an experienced one). Equally, technology is available which can help a jury to understand even complicated frauds, using computer-generated graphics. Given that attacks on the jury in modern times have tended to come from senior police officers (notoriously, see Mark, 1973) and the executive, we should perhaps be cautious about permitting the further erosion of an institution which, for all its faults, does appear to enjoy public confidence, partly no doubt because it consists of the public.

Any system is likely to produce a number of wrongful acquittals and convictions, but, especially in relation to the latter, those who attack the jury might reflect how much more damaging to the perceived legitimacy of the system it would be if it were a judge alone who had got it wrong. Nevertheless, juries *do* get it wrong from time to time, and there obviously needs to be some sort of review procedure. Unfortunately, the Criminal Appeal Act 1968 provided only three grounds upon which a first instance Crown Court decision could be upset: that the conviction was unsafe and unsatisfactory; that the court was wrong on a question of law; or that there was a material irregularity in the course of the trial. On too many occasions it had become apparent that persons whose appeals had failed before the Court of Appeal Criminal Division were in fact innocent. This led to calls for a review of the present system and, following recommendations made by the Runciman Commission, the Criminal Cases Review Commission (CCRC) was established under the Criminal Appeal Act 1995 to investigate suspected miscarriages of justice. Already, however, the tension between due process and workability is manifesting itself with the CCRC building up a growing backlog of cases and delays of three or four years.

In addition to the CCRC, the Criminal Appeals Act 1995 has simplified the grounds on which the Court can allow an appeal. The Court must allow an appeal against conviction if they think the conviction is unsafe. A conviction can be judged "unsafe", for example, where the defendant has been denied a fair trial.

A feature of our trial process is that the role of the judge is supposed to be entirely passive. He or she sits as referee, impartial between the prosecution and the defence. In practice, some judges are given to intervening to a considerable extent, interrupting counsel while they are speaking, and asking their own questions of witnesses (carried to excess this can be a ground of appeal). By contrast, the role of the judge in many European countries is active—his or her official duty is not merely to "referee the match", as it were; he or she is specifically entrusted with the task of trying to establish what happened (see Merryman, 1969). Generally speaking, English procedure is quicker, especially given the possibility of entering a guilty plea at various stages thereby curtailing the trial. Indeed, as noted in Chapter 2, the system actually puts a certain amount of pressure on an accused to plead guilty, and undoubtedly as a result, some people plead guilty to offences they have not committed (see pp.42–43). Recently the Auld Committee has suggested a system of sentencing discounts so that the earlier a plea of guilty is tendered, the greater the discount. It also recommended that the defence be able to request the judge to indicate the maximum sentence in the event of a plea of guilty at that stage (Auld (2001) p.443). Whether it is better for a few people to be convicted of offences they did not commit than to have prisoners waiting months, even years, for trial as happens in some European countries is a difficult question. Obviously, we would all subscribe to the proposition that a just legal system should not convict the innocent. We would also, however, subscribe to the proposition that the innocent should not languish in prison for long periods awaiting trial. It is yet another illustration of the tension between due process and workability.

Up to this point we have said little or nothing about either the judges, or the prosecutors. The bulk of Crown Court work is done by Circuit Judges, Recorders and Assistant Recorders. Recorders and Assistant Recorders today are usually barristers paid on a part-time basis for sitting as Crown Court judges (they can, however, be solicitors). Until recently, unlike our European counterparts, we had no judicial career structure. In recent times, however, the Lord Chancellor's Department (upon whose advice the Crown appoints judges) has made it clear that Recorders are expected to have proved themselves as Assistant Recorders, and Circuit Judges as Recorders. A number of Circuit and county court judges are now being appointed to the High Court. It seems that the Lord Chancellor is moving towards a settled career structure for judges such as we have for civil servants.

Magistrates are of two sorts: ordinary men and women generally possessing no legal training, and District Judges (Magistrates Courts) who have to be qualified barristers or solicitors. Lay justices have to have a qualified clerk present to advise them on points of law and admissibility of evidence. Obviously, in the nature of things, many clerks acquire considerable influence over the lay benches they service and sometimes effectively "run the court". Both lay magistrates and District Judges act as judge and jury in the cases they hear. In both cases the conviction rate tends to be higher than in the Crown Court, and this cannot entirely be explained away on the basis that defendants with weak cases may prefer to have their cases heard before the magistrates than to run the risk of going down before a Crown Court judge and getting a more severe sentence. Juries may often err too far in favour of the accused, but undoubtedly there is a danger that some magistrates may become biased in favour of the prosecution.

The prosecution case is prepared by the Crown Prosecution Service. This body was set up by the Prosecution of Offences Act 1985 to take over the prosecution of offences from the Local Authority Prosecutions Departments and the police. Under the former system, either solicitors or barristers employed by Local Authorities, or the police themselves, prosecuted cases. Where the police themselves prosecuted, they would either send a senior officer with experience of appearing in court to conduct the case in the magistrates' court, or employ a solicitor to do it for them. In the higher courts, the prosecutors' departments would instruct the barrister directly, but the police had to do so through a local solicitor. One of the problems with this system was that it tended to produce biased prosecutors. Even where there were Local Authority Prosecutions Departments, they were often in the same building as the police. When they were not, the fact that they worked closely with the police meant that those employed in them tended to become "prosecution-minded". For this reason they sometimes failed in their duty to present the prosecution case with fairness to the defence. The Crown Prosecution Service is an independent body, whose titular head is the Attorney-General, but whose real head is the Director of Public Prosecutions. It is broadly equivalent to the Scottish Procurator Fiscal system. In each area there is a Chief Crown Prosecutor, and below him Branch Prosecutors who run the offices in the larger towns. These offices are manned by a number of Crown Prosecutors who conduct the prosecutions in court, and office staff. The principal function of the Service is "to take over the conduct of all criminal proceedings, other than specified proceedings, instituted on behalf of a police force." The decision to prosecute in the first instance is still taken by the police, but once the decision has been taken the Service takes over, and has power to take in the name of the DPP any steps the DPP might take.

The Service's internal rules require sensitive cases, however, to be referred to a higher level. Crown Prosecutors are solicitors or barristers. The system is national and centralised, and is part of the Civil Service. It is not what was envisaged by the Royal Commission on Criminal Procedure, which recommended a local service. There is some evidence that the Commission's fears that a national service would be bureaucratic and out of touch with local feeling were justified.

Following the Auld Committee's recommendations (2001) (mentioned above) and the Halliday review of sentencing (2001), the Government published a White Paper, *Justice for All* (2002), outlining its plans for overhauling the criminal justice system. These plans found substantial expression in the Criminal Justice Act 2003. An object of the changes made by the Act was to ensure that more guilty defendants are convicted. According to the government's Executive Summary to achieve this [the government] will:

- improve defence and prosecution disclosure by increasing incentives and sanctions to ensure compliance;
- allow the use of reported evidence ('hearsay') where there is good reason, such as where a witness cannot appear personally;
- allow for trial by judge alone in serious and complex fraud trials, some other complex and lengthy trials or where a jury is at risk of intimidation;
- extend the availability of preparatory hearings to ensure that serious cases such as drug trafficking as well as complex ones can be properly prepared.

At the trial [the government] will:

- allow the court to be informed of a defendant's previous convictions where appropriate;
- remove the double jeopardy rule for serious cases if compelling new evidence comes to light;
- give witnesses greater access to their original statements at trial;
- give the prosecution the right of appeal against rulings which terminate the prosecution case before the jury decides; and
- increase the proportion of the population eligible for jury service.

All the above are the subject of the provisions of the 2003 Act.

Several of these proposals attack some of the most stoutly defended features of the due process model of criminal justice—for example, the defendant's right to be tried on the facts of the instant case and not on his or her previous record; the exposure of acquitted persons to the risk of a second prosecution; and further incursion on jury trial. At a time when the right to a fair trial has been squarely incorporated into English law by the Human Rights Act 1998, this might seem a strange stance for the government to take.

2. ELEMENTS OF CRIME

"It is a fundamental principle of criminal law that a person may not be convicted of a crime unless the prosecution have proved beyond reasonable doubt both (a) that [the defendant] has caused a certain event (in a result crime) or that responsibility is to be attributed to him for the existence of a certain state of affairs (in a conduct crime), which is forbidden by criminal law, and (b) that [the defendant] had a defined state of mind in relation to the causing of the event or the existence of the state of affairs." (Smith & Hogan, 2005, p.34)

The event or state of affairs is called the *"actus reus"*, the state of mind the *"mens rea"* of the crime. A crime generally requires both *actus reus* and *mens rea*.

An interesting illustration of the need for both of these elements to be present is *Fagan v Metropolitan Police Commissioner* (1969). The defendant motorist accidentally drove his car on to a policeman's foot. The policeman requested him to move off his foot, but he refused to do so and was prosecuted for assault. The majority of the Divisional Court held that an offence had been committed, but Bridge J. dissented on the cogent argument that mounting the policeman's foot was accidental, and consequently since no *mens rea* was present no offence had been committed. When the defendant refused to drive off again, there was simply an omission, so that no *actus reus* for assault existed (for a discussion of an entertaining series of cases where people have been charged with offences they intended to commit, but failed to do so, for example because the consignment of heroin they thought they had acquired was harmless vegetable matter, see Clarkson (1987)).

Many societies have not had a concept of *mens rea*. The codes of the Anglo-Saxon kings, for example, generally list only acts on the occurrence of which compensation must be paid to the victim or his kin. In later codes a distinction between deliberate and accidental acts is starting to appear, however. Thus the laws of Aethelred II (968–1016) contain a passage stating that the case of involuntary or unintentional killing is different from that of one who offends of his own free will. Undoubtedly, one of the principal reasons why this element came to be required was the influence of Christianity, which required some sort of moral blameworthiness on the part of an accused person (Plucknett, 1960, p.64). Other advanced non-Christian societies might never develop this element, or develop it to a much lesser extent, however. Imperial Chinese law in the eighteenth and nineteenth centuries, for example, differed from European notions in this respect. Although in theory it distinguished between murder (punishable by death) and accidental killing or manslaughter (for which compensation had to be paid), in practice it operated with rather different notions of culpability (though it may be noted that it had far fewer capital offences than English law in the late eighteenth and early nineteenth centuries). For example, in 1784, when a salute fired by a British ship accidentally killed a Chinese bystander, the Chinese authorities insisted that a gunner be surrendered to them for execution, although it was impossible to determine which gunner had fired the shot, and the killing was clearly accidental. To them, the act was more important than the motive. The ethical balance of a just reign had to be restored by exchanging the victim's injured spirit for a life, and a gunner chosen more or less randomly was eventually executed by them. One of the incidents which led up to the first "Opium War" was the result of a Chinese civilian being killed by some drunken British sailors, possibly accidentally. Again, it was impossible to establish who was responsible. Nevertheless, the Chinese authorities insisted that someone be surrendered to them for execution "For if the principle that a life is not to be paid for with a life is once admitted, what is it going to lead to?" (see *Cambridge History of China*, Vol. 10, pp.189–90). The views of the Chinese authorities in these cases outraged the British at the time, outrage which may well be shared by the reader. The reader should pause, however, and contemplate further the element of individual blame which is at the heart of Western views as to what conduct, and who, should be punished. The underpinning of it seems to be the Christian view that an individual voluntarily chooses to sin. But does he? To the extent that such a choice necessarily posits the existence of ultimate free will, there is a serious philosophical difficulty. Although this has been much debated, there is nevertheless an argument which is difficult to counter that the existence or otherwise of free will is something which in the nature of things we cannot know: it is inherently beyond knowledge. On this view ultimately we cannot know whether or not our actions are predetermined. Calvin, it will be recalled, came to the view that since God is omniscient, our destinies are predetermined. Many rationalists would argue that it is impossible to know whether or not that is the case.

At a less lofty level, we are happy to convict a prisoner, then to hear all sorts of evidence about impoverished home circumstances, sickness, marital stress, etc., which might have predisposed the prisoner to commit the crime and to take such matters into account in reducing the sentence. At this point the reader may well say "Ah! but an important function of sentencing is to cure the offender of his propensity to do mischief". A prisoner who has suffered a temporary aberration as a result of exceptional difficulties will be easier to "cure" than a hardened or dangerous criminal (who may need to be locked up simply for the protection of society). Now we are off to the races, however, because if "cure" really were the name of the game, and society generally accepted this, there would not be screams of outrage when the perpetrator of a rape was put on probation. This outrage is based on two ideas which appear in different mixes in different cases, but are usually running in tandem: deterrence and retribution (*cf.* Cavadino & Dignan (2002), esp. Ch.2).

Of these two, deterrence is the more problematic. In the first place, there is the ultimate problem of predetermination. To the extent that the actions of a person are predetermined, it is meaningless to talk of deterrence. At a more humdrum level, assuming that potential criminals are rational economic beings, as other members of the political economy are supposed to be, they will make their decision whether or not to commit a crime by much the same thought processes as are employed when they decide whether or not to buy an electric toaster, and which model to buy. They will weigh the probable benefit to themselves resulting from the crime, against the costs (including opportunity costs) of committing it or not committing it. In the cost side of the equation, they will weigh the seriousness of the penalty likely to be inflicted, against the probability of its being inflicted. It is on this last count especially that deterrence through ever more severe penalties tends to founder. Essentially, the problem is that even an enormous increase in the numbers of police would not necessarily raise the number of convictions very much, simply because a large number of crimes *cannot be* solved. For example, a large number of burglaries are cleared up because having been caught for something else the accused confesses to them, asking for them to be taken into consideration to clear the slate. A further problem is that the more swingeing the penalty, the more sure courts tend to need to be before they will convict. This may be a partial explanation of the paradox that whilst the number of offences for which criminals could be hanged was increased dramatically in the late eighteenth and early nineteenth centuries, the number of persons actually executed declined (Hay, 1975, Essay 1). Deterrence is for these reasons not necessarily a particularly effective way of reducing crime. Strategies of crime prevention such as "traffic calming" measures, brighter street lighting, and possibly CCTV, may well be both more efficient and cost-effective. This suggests that another element is perhaps behind the rhetoric of "stiffer penalties", and that element is of course retribution.

Retribution is clearly a response of primitive societies to acts of which they disapprove. To a large extent, it is concerned with satisfying the human desire for vengeance, but it is not necessarily confined to vengeance against an individual, it can be exacted from a group. The blood feud represents retribution in a fairly pure form, but it tends to involve the family of the wrongdoer collectively (and we will also recall the case of what was in effect collective responsibility imposed by the Chinese authorities in the incidents described above). Liability imposed on a group can represent pure retribution: it can also, however, have a deterrent function. Collective responsibility, as we saw in Chapter 3, was used from later Saxon times as a way of controlling crime. Where social groupings are small and tightly knit (as in the traditional family), it is probably quite an effective strategy, as those closely connected with a person are best likely to know his or her weaknesses and propensities, and to take steps to neutralise them if they could result in harm to the group as a whole. This was the principle underlying, for example, the collective fines mandated under the Norman system of frankpledge. However, what works in small relatively homogeneous groups will not work in loosely knit modern societies. This point should perhaps be borne in mind in evaluating the arguments that the parents of young malefactors should be made to bear a greater share of liability for their actions.

This is a convenient cue to introduce another facet of the "law and order" problem. The French sociologist Emile Durkheim drew attention to an important difference between primitive groups and advanced societies. Primitive groups tend to be relatively small, and individuals tend to be subordinated to the shared values of the group. Such groups usually have a low level of tolerance for individuals who do not hold the same values. Durkheim used the term "mechanical solidarity" to describe the social cohesion of such groups. As society develops, and the division of labour between its members grows, individuals increasingly cease to share a common set of values. One reason for this is that the very tasks performed by individuals will to an extent influence their outlook on the world: a bank manager does not view the world in quite the same way as a professional gambler, and at a less trivial level there is obviously much truth in the view that the way you earn your money (or even do not earn it) will colour your view of the world. This idea reaches its most comprehensive expression in the Marxist idea of ideology (see Ch.10). For the present, however, we are concerned only with Durkheim's analysis. He suggested that in advanced societies there is necessarily a wider toleration of different values, but there will inevitably be conflicts of interest, so that the constraints represented by the law administered by the courts become necessary. He described the cohesion of advanced industrial societies as "organic solidarity", as opposed to the "mechanical" solidarity of primitive societies. Durkheim's characterisations are "ideal types" (see Ch.2), and any given society may have elements of mechanical solidarity present, though the predominant solidarity is organic. (In this light, readers may sense that the Criminal Justice Act, by declaring that the purposes of sentencing are punishment, public protection, crime reduction and reparation, tells us something about the basis of social solidarity in England and Wales at the start of the 21st century).

Clearly calls for "a return to Victorian values", reflect (somewhat naively because the historical evidence simply does not support the view that all or even most parts of Victorian society shared the same set of values) the truth that in societies with a high level of shared values, crime in the sense of deviance from the shared values, will not be a major problem.

3. WHY ARE CERTAIN ACTS "CRIMINAL"?

This takes us to the thorny question as to why certain acts are labelled as "criminal" in modern societies. Not all societies after all would designate even wanton killing as murder in our sense.

For example, the early nineteenth-century Zulu king Shaka was routinely attended by a retinue of executioners who dispatched those he chose on the spur of the moment. It would appear that he did not act in this way out of a desire to inflict pain but rather because he regarded his subjects as being roughly on a par with ants. So far as his subjects were concerned, it was conduct which if not liked, was at least expected of a king and was part of the charisma attaching to the office (Morris, 1973, p.67). Indeed, in societies where the king is clothed with divinity, the concept of the king as the "lord of life and death" may be at the heart of the religion (see Gale, 1956 on the Kubaka of Buganda, Mutesa).

Obviously, some crimes are introduced purely as a response to the necessities of technological developments. You do not need road traffic laws if you have no road traffic, but as soon as you do you have to have at the minimum a rule as to which side of the road you keep to, thereby automatically treating as deviant those who do not obey the rule of the road. Other changes in what is regarded as deviant behaviour, however, are obviously products of social mores which may shift. For example, the minimum age for marriage was classically fourteen for a boy, and twelve for a girl (we will recall that Juliet in Shakespeare's *Romeo and Juliet* was thirteen). All that was required for a valid marriage by the Canon Law was the mutual consent of the parties followed by consummation. At the present day in England and Wales, an eighteen year-old boy and a thirteen year-old girl getting into bed together with the intention of sealing their eternal devotion one to another would quite likely find themselves subsequently in the hands of social workers, and the boy might well end up in front of a juvenile court.

Other crimes on the other hand have a more apparently economic base. Whilst Proudhon's statement "all property is theft" is a self-evident tautology, nevertheless, the particular concept a particular society has of property will determine what amounts to theft (see Ch.1). Thus, in our society, borrowing someone's bicycle to get home after missing the last bus is an offence, even though the borrower intends to return it the next day (Theft Act 1968, s.12(5)). By contrast, in a primitive society with a high level of shared property, borrowing the one available boat without consent might not be regarded as wrong. On the other hand, although the primitive society may regard the boat as communal property, no doubt it is not envisaged that one member will deprive everyone else of their fishing by hogging it all the time. Such conduct, if it occurred, would no doubt be regarded as deviant.

Another way of looking at the problem in relation to modern rational societies is in terms of goals. What is regarded as criminal in a society which has reached the point of thinking in terms of making laws for itself (see Ch.3) will be a reflection of the goals of those who make the laws. These laws can be judged objectively at two levels: the rationality of the goals themselves, and the rationality of the means chosen to achieve them. To give an example of an apparently irrational goal, certain American states purported to regulate the permissible way in which husbands and wives could have sexual intercourse: basically they must have it front to front. But if the purpose of marriage is procreation, it ought not in principle to matter how they copulate if, as it were, it delivers the goods. The goal appears to be irrational, and the means to achieve it, a law, even more so because it is inherently unenforceable. If the law has any rationale, it seems to be in terms of the strand of Puritanism which regards natural disasters as a visitation from the Almighty amounting to a punishment for wickedness. By putting on the statute book an unenforceable law, these societies, we may suppose, intended to offer the Almighty a public declaration of their morality. An example nearer to home was the curious custom in the British Isles of requiring pubs to close at certain times. In an advanced industrial society, reducing the amount of drunkenness is a rational goal because drunkenness reduces productivity, causes accidents, etc. But given that the amount of any product consumed is primarily a function of demand and money available, the only effect of reducing public house hours is likely to be to speed up drinking. This of course was precisely what happened. When combined with the custom of drinking in rounds (itself it would appear promoted accidentally by a Victorian law requiring drinks to be paid for "on the nail") the result was to promote drunkenness, precisely the opposite intent of the law. In fact the law had two origins: the desire of the Puritans to drive the public out of the taverns into the churches caused them to close the taverns during the hours of divine worship on Sundays. The other source was a measure of 1915 intended to prevent munition workers going on shift drunk. Although this measure appeared to be successful at the time in reducing drunkenness, it is more likely that the apparent amelioration was due to the simultaneous removal into the armed forces of a large part of the male drinking population (and their subsequent slaughter on the Somme and other battlefields). Indeed, this seems to be a good example of the sort of false statistical correlation which bedevils criminological analyses. At all events, if we were to rationalise the law in present-day terms, it seemed mainly to be concerned with limiting the working hours of bar staff, albeit at the expense of increased drunkenness. It is no accident that the relevant unions over the years were vigorous opponents of change as they were to deregulation of the opening hours of shops. The analysis given above seems to be borne out with the coming into force of the Licensing Act 2003 in 2005. So far, there does not appear to be evidence of increased drunkenness, and there is a certain amount of anecdotal evidence that the abolition of compulsory 11.00pm closing is have a civilising effect.

This leads us to a concluding point. The necessities of maintaining advanced industrialisation will lead to much behaviour being regarded as criminal which in a primitive society would not be. It is probable for example that a large part of Tudor England was drunk for quite a large part of the time (see Hoskins, 1956, p.109). A modern society could not tolerate this, because it is much too dangerous at the present level of technological development. However, the low levels of drunkenness, comparatively, in modern industrial societies are as much a product of people being obliged to modify their behaviour in order to perform their tasks, as they are a product of legislation. Legislation, whilst as explained above in some ways promoting drunkenness, has, on the other hand, been successful in discouraging specific types of act now thought to be anti-social such as drunken driving. But, we will recall our analysis of deterrence above, in which we pointed out that the probability of detection and conviction was part of the equation. When the Road Safety Act 1967 first made conviction more likely by introducing an absolute standard of permissible blood alcohol, there was indeed a sharp drop in road accidents in which the fall in the amount consumed by drivers seemed to play a part. However, enforcement was not at first very rigorous, and gradually the accident statistics came to look more and more as they had done before the Act. Only more recently, when the police were encouraged to raise the likelihood of being stopped and tested, did the statistics again begin to indicate a downturn.

Like the motor car, many new technologies have resulted in crimes undreamt of by our ancestors. Thus, recently, we have seen a number of computer-related crimes develop. No doubt when so-called "thinking" robots appear, we will need to create yet more crimes.

We have up to now focused mainly on the relationship between the changing catalogue of crimes and industrialisation. Marxists, by contrast, would focus on the economic infrastructure, the transition from feudalism to capitalism, and changes within capitalism. We have already seen in Chapter 3 how feudalism entailed its own specific concept of treason. Similarly, Marxists would view changes in the criminal law in modern times in terms of the development of capitalism. For example the criminalisation of trespassing by the Criminal Justice and Public Order Act 1994 (s.61—strengthening earlier legislation which it replaces) (previously of itself simply the civil wrong of trespass), might be viewed (disapprovingly) as an aspect of bourgeois property values triumphing over communal entitlement to share the land. Views such as this necessarily entail a criterion of how things ought to be distributed which is either in terms of needs, or deserts, and it is by no means clear which side these criteria would favour on the issue of trespassing by squatters or the like (or indeed many other similar issues). Certainly, it is improbable that they would prescribe any universal rule on the matter. In fact the evaluation of legal rules against criteria of distributive justice raises some very complex problems. We attempt to introduce the reader to these in Chapter 10.

4. THE LIMITS OF THE CRIMINAL LAW

Although it may seem from the previous section that the goals to be pursued by a modern rational society identify themselves as society develops (as road traffic law became a necessity after the invention of the motor car), at the margins there will be fundamental disagreements both about the goals to be pursued and about the means to pursue them. Nowhere is this more striking than in the debate about the making and enforcement of "victimless crimes".

In *R. v Wilson* (1996), the defendant, having used a hot knife to brand his initials on his wife's buttocks, was charged with an assault occasioning actual bodily harm under section 47 of the Offences Against the Person Act 1861. The branding, however, was not aggressive, being carried out at the wife's instigation (she wanted to bear a physical mark of her love and affection for the defendant), with her full consent, and in the privacy of the matrimonial home. Reluctantly, the trial judge (treating himself as bound by the House of Lords' decision in *R. v Brown* (1993)—see below) ruled that the offence had been committed. On appeal, however, the Court of Appeal held that consensual branding was really no different from consensual tattooing (thus distinguishing *Brown*, which concerned consensual sado-masochism), and that no offence had been committed. According to Russell L.J.:

"Consensual activity between husband and wife, in the privacy of the matrimonial home, is not, in our judgment, normally a proper matter for criminal investigation, let alone criminal prosecution." (at 128)

In these remarks, Russell L.J. echoed a point that we touched on in the previous section, namely that a rational criminal justice system will not commit resources to making and enforcing "victimless" crimes. There is, however, an important question of principle at stake in *Wilson*. This is the question of the legitimate limits of the criminal law and, in particular, the question of whether it is permissible for legislatures or courts to penalise conduct in which the participants freely engage and which harms no third party.

As we have said, in *Wilson*, one of the difficulties was that the point was arguably covered by *R. v Brown* (1993). There, in a 3/2 decision, the majority of the House of Lords held that the consent of the participants was no defence where the defendant sado-masochists were charged with wounding and assault under respectively sections 20 and 47 of the Offences Against the Person Act 1861. Although each of the opinions given in *Brown* adopts its own distinctive approach, the underlying question of principle is most clearly an issue for Lords Templeman (majority) and Mustill (minority). Put shortly, Lord Templeman's view is that the criminal law is for the protection of society, including the protection of society's basic values. So, for example, even if taking drugs results in no direct harm to others, it is rightly criminalised because it is "a practice which ... if allowed and extended is harmful to society generally" (at 82). As for sado-masochism:

"Society is entitled and bound to protect itself against a cult of violence. Pleasure derived from the infliction of pain is an evil thing. Cruelty is uncivilised." (at 84)

Lord Mustill, by contrast, founds his dissenting view on two considerations: first, that respect for the Rule of Law demands that the offences created by the 1861 Act should not be taken beyond their intended range (see further Ch.8); and, secondly, "that the state should interfere with the rights of an individual to live his or her life as he or she may choose no more than is necessary to ensure a proper balance between the special interests of the individual and the general interests of the individuals who together comprise the populace at large" (at 116).

Lord Mustill's support for individual choice as to life-style is an idea that, in the modern debates, is often traced back to John Stuart Mill's classic essay "On Liberty" (1859). Mill famously argued that coercion should not be exercised against mature individuals if their conduct was merely self-regarding (i.e. if it caused no tangible harm to others—or, if it did cause harm to others, then it was harm to which the latter freely consented). According to Mill, respect for individual freedom entails that coercion should not be exercised moralistically or paternalistically to save individuals from harming themselves (physically or spiritually)—over their own bodies and minds, as Mill put it, individuals must be treated as sovereign. A century later, the Wolfenden Committee (1957), whose remit was to make recommendations with regard to the regulation of homosexuality and prostitution, took up the Millian script, saying that it was not the function of the criminal law "to intervene in the private lives of citizens" (para.13) and insisting that "there must remain a realm of private morality and immorality which is, in brief and crude terms, not the law's business" (para.62). The Committee's approach prompted a celebrated debate between Lord Devlin (1965) and HLA Hart (1963). On the one side, Devlin argued that Wolfenden had made a fundamental error in thinking that the function of the criminal law was to protect individuals. To the contrary, the criminal law was primarily for the protection of society; there was no realm of conduct that could be safely put beyond the reach of legal regulation; and, in the final analysis, if ordinary people found the private lives of a minority intolerable, then the criminal law rightly intervened. On the other side, Hart sprang to the defence of Wolfenden. In Hart's view, even if Mill had taken his onslaught against physical paternalism to extreme lengths, the line drawn by Wolfenden between the public and private sphere was essentially correct. For Hart, the critical point was that, if a society takes individual freedom seriously, then it cannot reserve the right to abridge such freedom whenever it takes offence at the way in which non-conforming individuals choose to conduct their private lives.

Although questions of sexual mores bulk large in debates about the legitimate scope of the criminal law, the robust individualism advocated by Mill invites a broader application, contending for a legal immunity wherever conduct is entirely self-regarding or where participation in a particular activity is backed by consent (and has no injurious effect on any third parties). Such a broad principle has an obvious application to participation in contact sports (especially boxing: generally, see Law Commission (1994)) as it does to the increasingly controversial question of euthanasia. To take up this latter point, many legal systems make it a criminal offence for a person to aid or abet a suicide—and, in principle, such an offence covers situations where physicians participate in assisted suicides at the behest of their patients. Yet, there is a growing body of opinion that argues that respect for the autonomous decisions of individuals (including life terminating decisions) dictates that mercy killings of this kind should be exempt from the criminal law. Such an opinion prevailed some years ago in the Netherlands; more recently, it was adopted in the Northern Territories in Australia (where the law in question survived for some nine months, and four terminations, before being overturned by the Australian Parliament); and, in the United States, it has been popularised by the widely-reported activities of Dr Jack Kevorkian. In opposition to this view, it might be argued that respect for autonomy actually weighs against decriminalisation; for, without the protection of the criminal law, there is a risk that vulnerable people may request terminations to which they have not properly consented (*cf.* the reasoning of the Canadian Supreme Court in the case of *Sue Rodriguez* (1993)). Or, it might be argued that, over time, decriminalisation would so change the culture of respect for life that (as Lords Devlin and Templeman might put it) society has the right to defend itself against such an insidious threat (and, see Devlin (1986) for his Lordship's reflections on the famous trial of Dr John Bodkin Adams, where the critical question was whether lethal doses of heroin were administered to ease the patient's suffering or simply to accelerate her death).

With the enactment of the Human Rights Act 1998, these questions concerning life and death and the limits of the criminal law were brought before the House of Lords in *R. (Pretty) v DPP* (2002). Mrs Pretty, who suffered from motor neurone disease, sought to establish legal immunity for her husband (who was not a physician) should he assist with her suicide. Without this immunity, Mr Pretty would be liable to be prosecuted under section 2(1) of the Suicide Act 1961 for aiding and abetting his wife's suicide. When the DPP refused to give such advance immunity, Mrs Pretty applied for a judicial review designed to establish whether the restrictive position taken by English law is compatible with the Convention, specifically with reference to the right to life (Art.2), the right not to be subjected to torture, or to inhuman or degrading treatment or punishment (Art.3), the right to respect for private and family life (Art.8), the right to freedom of thought, conscience and religion (Art.9), and the general right against discrimination in the enjoyment of the Convention rights (Art.14). The gist of Mrs Pretty's case was that these Convention rights enshrine a right to self-determination (encompassing a right to choose when and how to die) and that the State was either obstructing the exercise of this right or not doing sufficient to assist its exercise. The House of Lords rejected this application, doubting that any of the Convention rights was engaged in the way that Mrs Pretty contended and, mindful of the need to protect the vulnerable (as in the *Sue Rodriguez* case), regarding the restrictions retained by English law as justifiable—tellingly, Lord Bingham remarked (at para.28) that, even in the Netherlands, there would be no advance immunity for Mr Pretty. Undeterred, Mrs Pretty took her case on to the European Court of Human Rights (2002). There, she repeated her argument that "the right to self-determination [runs] like a thread through the Convention as a whole" (para.58). As in the House of Lords, this argument failed. However, in relation to Article 8, the Strasbourg Court went some way towards meeting Mrs Pretty's claim, saying that, where the law prevents a person from exercising their choice to avoid what they consider to be an undignified and distressing end to their life, the right to private life is at least engaged; accordingly, the burden lies on the State to justify this encroachment on the citizen's right. Where the State's case is that the restriction is imposed by law for the protection of the rights and freedoms of the vulnerable, the only question (under Art. 8(2)) is whether the interference is necessary and proportionate. The Court was satisfied that the State could justify section 2(1) of the Suicide Act by reference to these standards. Sadly, Mrs Pretty died shortly after the Court ruled against her and the legacy of her litigation (as of the *Rodriguez* case) is a reminder that, even if rights are the only arguments that count, a tragic choice may have to be made where recognised rights stand opposed against one another.

The law, as we have emphasised, is riven with ideological tension; and the questions raised by Mill and Wolfenden, debated by Hart and Devlin, and acted on in cases such as *Brown* and *Wilson* set up at least two layers of tensions. At one level, we have competing views as to the legitimate function of the criminal law, with the libertarian ideology articulated by Mill, Wolfenden, Hart, and Lord Mustill in _Brown_ coming into conflict with the social (and community moral) defence ideology relied on by Lord Devlin and, most recently, by Lord Templeman in _Brown_ (and, generally, _cf_. George, 1988). At another level, however, we have potential tensions relating specifically to the responsibilities of the courts in a community committed to the ideals of the Rule of Law, democracy and freedom. In such a community, if the courts are the custodians of public morality, do the judges discharge their responsibilities by backing the judgments of the majority, by backing the minority, or by testing out both majority and minority views against the moral ideals that define the community as the particular culture that it is (_cf_. Dworkin, 1978; Leader, 1990)? Ten years on from _Brown_, with the defendants finally losing their appeal before the European Court of Human Rights (see _Laskey, Jaggard and Brown v United Kingdom_ (1997)) (where they argued unsuccessfully that the decision violated Art.8(1) of the Convention, according to which "Everyone has the right to respect for his private and family life . . ."), a famous chapter in the law has come to a close. However, the fundamental issues concerning the legitimate scope of the criminal law remain as contested and as controversial as ever.

5. PUNISHMENT

We have hinted at some of the philosophical difficulties involved in holding a person criminally "responsible" and thus deserving of punishment. However, up to this point we have treated the concept of punishment which is central either to deterrence theory, or to retribution, as unproblematic. Roughly, it is something unpleasant which a person would rather not have happen to them. This is a reasonable enough working definition, though in implementation it usually operates on some sort of objective criteria—what people _generally_ would prefer not to happen to them, for some people might actually consciously or unconsciously seek some sort of punishment. There is, for example, evidence that many boys at Eton and other nineteenth-century public schools, actually enjoyed being flogged (see Chandos, 1984, p.234). These days there is the well-known phenomenon of the dosser who throws a brick through a shop window in the hope of spending Christmas in prison. Obviously, the concept of "punishment" in either of these cases is problematic. At a less obvious level, there appear to be a significant number of crimes committed with the subconscious hope of arrest and punishment. Shoplifting, which is often committed by well-heeled, middle-aged, middle-class ladies appears sometimes to be explicable on these grounds. It may, for example, be a way of indirectly punishing a husband, or simply reflect a desire to atone for a life of comparative luxury. The other side of this coin is the evidence that certain individuals are predisposed to becoming victims (see Mawby and Gill, 1987, pp.11–12; Miers, 1978, pp.15 *et seq.*).

We have also touched only briefly on *who* we punish. In our society it is a sentient being whose conduct caused the prohibited act; we require some blame to attach to the offender. We generally do not punish insane persons, and do not impose collective liability. To this latter rule there are, however, exceptions. Thus corporations may be fined for the actions of their employees, for example in failing to comply with health and safety regulations, and recently the concept of corporate manslaughter has been much discussed in the context of some serious accidents involving public transport in which many people were killed or injured. In more primitive societies, where the elements of charisma and tradition are predominant features of the law (see Ch.1), the distinction between secular law and God's law may not be very clearly drawn, and thus the law may be perceived as extending to non-sentient beings, which after all were held to be God's creatures. In medieval Europe for example, it was not uncommon for animals to be tried for crimes as though they were human beings (with counsel to plead on their behalf), and if convicted they were punished as human beings. The explanation for this apparently bizarre practice seems to be that the animal that, say, killed its master was in some way a creature offending against God's law, and stirring deep-seated fears of lawlessness (see Evans, 1987) which seems also to be an element in the present day desire to create "victimless crimes" (see above). Similarly, in such primitive societies the trial process itself may be a mystical method of trying to ascertain God's will, as in the case of trial by ordeal—by fire or water or burning coals—which was common all over Europe until the Church banned it in 1215. Weber characterised such irrational decision-making as "Kadi" justice (Weber, 1978, pp.976 *et seq.*, from "kadi"—a magistrate in some Islamic countries). He juxtaposed Kadi justice to reasoned decisions taken on the basis of formally rational rules. Elements of Kadi justice survive, however, even in modern societies. There is an element of it present in the decisions of magistrates and juries in our own legal system, for neither have to justify their findings of fact in formally rational terms.

CONCLUSION

Richard Danzig has made the following biting remark about the American criminal justice systems (Danzig, 1973):

"Perhaps no institutions in urban America offer so much evidence of their shortcomings and so little of their successes as those bureaucracies which compose our municipal criminal justice systems ... a strong case can be made that America's criminal justice systems neither control, nor consider, nor correct criminality." (pp.1–2)

This criticism could with some fairness be levelled at our own system. We hope perhaps that some of the problems and contradictions we have outlined in this chapter will go some way towards explaining why this is so. Thus, even to the extent a law can deter, its effectiveness will be undermined if the police cannot secure the conviction of offenders. They cannot secure the conviction of all offenders, simply because, as we suggested, many crimes are inherently insoluble. No doubt solubility would be enhanced by universal compulsory DNA-testing and fingerprinting, random powers of search of person and property, and a general right to arrest and question, but to what extent would the public at large be prepared to see such an erosion of their liberties (as opposed to the liberties of those they label "criminal")? No doubt too, the present system of trial acquits many guilty people, especially where juries are involved. Would we be prepared to dispense with juries though? If individually we were charged with an offence of which we were innocent, would we prefer to be tried by magistrates, a single professional judge, or a judge sitting with a jury? Conversely, the system of guilty pleas undoubtedly results in the conviction of innocent persons. Yet would we be prepared for the delays which abolition of the guilty plea would cause? Could the government afford the money necessary to obviate those delays by appointing many more magistrates and judges, and if it could, would there be sufficient suitable people? Again, therefore, we come up against the tension between due process and workability which has been one of the main themes of this chapter.

Finally, if, as is the case, the present range of punishments do not prevent further offences by convicted criminals, should we consider rendering such persons mentally or physically incapable of committing again the offences for which they have been convicted? For example, should rapists be castrated, or violent people be treated with aversion therapy (see Anthony Burgess' novel *A Clockwork Orange*)? Given our ideas of human dignity, which are part of our inheritance from the Enlightenment, would we be prepared to stomach this (and see further on human dignity, below at p.299 *et seq.*)?

7

LEGAL PROCESS

II: The Civil Justice System

In 1985, a major review of the civil justice system was launched, the intention being that proposals would be brought forward to reduce the delay, cost and complexity involved in civil litigation. The final report of the review having been published in 1988 (*Report of the Review Body on Civil Justice*), its principal recommendations were enacted in the Courts and Legal Services Act 1990.

Without doubt, the 1990 Act was something of a watershed in the history of the English legal system, representing the most extensive changes since the Judicature Acts swept away the remnants of the mediaeval system of courts in 1875. The Act (as amended by the Access to Justice Act 1999) grants full rights of audience to solicitors, and empowers the Lord Chancellor to extend rights of audience to other professions (for example, Fellows of the Chartered Institute of Patent Agents or of the Institute of Legal Executives can acquire rights of audience though restricted to particular types of proceedings). It is a moot point whether the so-called "cab rank" principles should apply to advocates other than barristers (the Lord Chancellor's Advisory Committee rejected the proposal that the principle should apply to solicitor advocates). According to this principle, a barrister cannot refuse to accept a brief on behalf of a client, provided he can pay the fee, or is legally aided or the case is being done on a conditional fee basis. There is no guarantee, however, that clients will get their chosen barristers (especially those with heavy caseloads), prompting some cynics to remark that like cabs, counsel are never available when they are wanted! At all events, if the cab-rank principle were to be applied to solicitor advocates, this would surely make rights of audience less attractive to those who wished to act as advocates only occasionally and on a selective basis.

Two key ideas underpin the 1990 Act. First, the market for legal services must be made more open and competitive—hence the onslaught on restrictive practices in the legal profession (see

Ch.9). Secondly, the most sophisticated judicial resources should be reserved for the most demanding kinds of cases; thus, there should be much more flexibility about the distribution of cases between the High Court and the county court. In this chapter, it is this second idea which is of particular interest to us. For, in assessing the changing nature of the English legal system, we must remember that it aspires to afford citizens a resource for resolving their disputes which functions in *both an efficient and a just manner*. In other words, the civil justice system, like the criminal justice system, is constantly faced with the challenge of how best to secure a satisfactory balance between the demands of workability and due process.

More recently, a further round of reforms aimed at reducing the cost, complexity and delay associated with the civil justice system was generated by Lord Woolf's review (Woolf, 1996). Stated boldly, the Woolf reforms aimed to improve the efficiency of the system by changing a culture that is geared to adversarial dealing and days in court. In its place, Woolf sought to promote more co-operation between the disputants (for example, in relation to the use of experts), the attitude that settlement is the norm and litigation a last resort, and management of cases so that resources invested in disputes are not disproportionate to the disputed sums involved (see below p.195 *et seq.*). As a result, relatively low value cases will now be fast tracked, the Woolf ideology supporting practical arrangements whereby such cases are handled, as some commentators have put it, in "in a cheap and cheerful way" (Goriely *et al*, xviii).

The Woolf review led to the Civil Procedure Act 1997 under which the Civil Justice Council was established. The main role of the Council is to promote the needs of civil justice and advise the Lord Chancellor about the modernisation of the system. For example, the Council helped to put in place a scheme of fixed costs in road traffic claims. This was achieved through a mediation between personal injury lawyers and insurers. Procedurally, the significance of this mediation is that it suggests that policy can sometimes be more satisfactorily set by direct negotiation between the parties involved rather than by top-down ministerial decree. Substantively, the mediation needs to be read against the background of the failure of the Woolf reforms to cut costs (see below p.200), of the "no win no fee" scheme now being used to finance personal injury cases (see below p.210), and of the increased costs placed on the insurance industry by the Access to Justice Act 1999 (see below 210–211).

Finally, in this context of modernisation, the Civil Procedure Rule Committee was set up following the 1997 Act. The Committee has promulgated one set of procedural rules for the High Court, the Court of Appeal and county courts. We start our discussion of the civil justice system by reviewing these rules.

1. HOW CIVIL DISPUTES ARE PROCESSED

It is easy for a law student to form the view that legal practice involves a daily struggle with statutory interpretation and law reports (which is what academic law consists of). Although a few specialists are frequently concerned with these matters, the day to day life of most lawyers is concerned with procedure, or perhaps, we should say procedures. In the case of litigation lawyers, their stock-in-trade is a mastery of the complex bureaucracy of the courts with which they deal. Focusing exclusively on the substantive law in fact leads to a distorted view of the legal system, for substantive law and procedure are intimately related. Sir Henry Maine made the famous observation "So great is the ascendancy of the Law of Actions in the infancy of Courts of Justice, that substantive law has at first the look of being gradually secreted in the interstices of procedure" (Maine, 1883, p.389). Even today, we would suggest that procedure has an indirect influence on the development of some areas of substantive law. For example, it may well be that the reluctance of the common law to develop the law of passing off into a general tort of unfair competition, is connected with the need of the parties to have battle lines clearly drawn at the commencement of the trial in an adversarial process (see e.g. the *Pub Squash* case (1981)). Limiting the tort to a misrepresentation calculated to damage the plaintiff's goodwill in this country (see *Reckitt and Coleman Products v Borden* (1990) at 406, *per* Lord Oliver), defines fairly clearly the territory to be fought over. An example of passing off would be where the defendant is alleged to have sold goods bearing the claimant's trade mark, as in *Arsenal FC v Reed* (2002) where the defendant sold scarves and other Arsenal football memorabilia unauthorised by the claimant. The claimants failed in passing off because the defendant made it clear to his customers that this was unauthorised merchandise. A general tort of unfair competition comprehends the proposition that it is unlawful to reap what another has sown, which is a much less clearly defined form of action (see dissent of Brandeis J. in *International News Service v Associated*

Press (1918) for the undesirability of creating vague and uncertain monopolies). Conversely, the substantive law can affect procedure. For example, the Lord Chancellor drew attention to the way in which the fragmented state of the law governing the care and upbringing of children has led to a fragmentation of proceedings and remedies. To remedy this, the Children Act 1989 created a single body of substantive law, and an opportunity to provide consistent procedures.

Accordingly, we believe that it is important that readers should at least have some idea of basic court procedure in civil matters.

(i) High Court and County Court

Until fairly recently, the procedure for starting an action varied according to whether the case was begun in the county court or the High Court. This was changed as a result of the recommendations of the Woolf Committee and the Civil Procedure Rules 1998. We will focus on the new procedure which came into force on April 26, 1999. The new Rules apply *both* in the High Court and in the county court. By far the most important innovation introduced by the Rules is "Case Management": the court not merely lays down the rules by which the litigants must play, it assumes the role of *manager* of the litigation brought before it. At the heart of "Case Management" is the concept of the "Management Track". There are three tracks:

- **The Small Claims Track** for cases with a financial value of not more than £5,000. Also, cases that do not require a substantial amount of pre-hearing preparation or cases that should not incur large legal costs. No expert evidence may be given without permission, the court may give summary judgment, strike out a statement of case (a pleading) and even deal with a case without a hearing.
- **The Fast Track** for cases (other than personal injury claims) with a financial value of not more than £15,000. Also, cases that require some, but not substantial, pre-hearing preparation, cases that can be tried in one day or less, a case in which oral expert advice will be limited to one per party in any field and expert evidence in no more than two fields. Different monetary limits apply to the allocation of personal injury claims. On allocation the court gives directions for the management of a case, and sets a timetable including a date of trial or a trial period. The standard time between allocation and

trial is 30 weeks. A listing questionnaire is filed 8 weeks before the hearing and the parties can expect 3 weeks' notice of the trial date.

- **The Multi-Track** is the category which embraces all other cases. On allocation the court gives directions for the management of the case and sets a timetable or fixes a case management conference and/or pre-trial review which a party's legal representative must attend. A trial date or trial period is fixed as soon as practicable. Dates for conferences, pre-trial review, and trials can only be varied by the court.

After service of the defence, or at an earlier stage if the court so orders, one or more of the parties may ask for a stay to enable negotiations or alternative dispute resolution (ADR—see pp.202 *et seq.*) to take place. The court may order a stay on its own initiative.

In managing litigation the court must have regard to the "overriding objective" which is to deal with cases *justly*. This includes, so far as practicable, ensuring that parties are on an equal footing, saving of expense, and dealing with a case in ways which are proportionate to the amount of the claim, the importance of the claim, the complexity of the issues and the financial position of the parties.

In line with the policy of harmonising High Court and county court procedure, a number of more minor changes were made. The principal ones are as follows.

- Proceedings are initiated by only one form of document, a "Claim Form", not different forms as formerly. The party initiating proceedings is known as the "claimant", but it remains correct to use the term "plaintiff" for all cases where that was the way in which the party starting the proceedings was decribed.
- "Statements of Case" are the formal documents in which the parties set out their respective cases. They are served between the parties as well as being filed in Court. The claimant's first statement of case after the claim form is called the "particulars of claim". The defendant's statement of case is called a "defence" and this can include a counterclaim against the claimant.
- Either party to the action can ask the other to give further information about its case and the court itself can order this. In the first place, however, a party should serve a request for further information on the other.

- Defence: the mechanics of pleading a defence are now regulated more fully. A defendant may no longer simply deny an allegation: reasons must be given, and if what is disputed is the facts, i.e. the version of events given by the claimant, the defendant must state his or her version.

- All "statements of case" (including "further information") must be verified by a "Statement of Truth". This can be signed by the party concerned or by their legal representatives. The absence of such a statement will be treated as a procedural irregularity preventing the use of the "Statement of Case" in evidence.

- The use of affidavits (sworn statements of evidence) is now largely unnecessary. Instead signed written statements are used, verified by a statement of truth. Cases where affidavits are still necessary include applications for freezing injunctions and search orders.

- The procedure in relation to judgment in default of giving notice of intention to defend, and judgment in default of defence are now combined. If the defendant fails to return the acknowledgement of service or to file a defence, the claimant can obtain judgment in default against the defendant. The claimant thereby obtains judgment without there being a trial. In certain cases, however, judgment in default is not available, e.g. in claims for delivery of goods under agreements regulated by the Consumer Credit Act 1974. If it is irregular, such a default judgment must be *set aside regardless of the merits* (case law of the Court of Appeal to the contrary is thus abrogated). If the judgment is regular, it will still be set aside if the defendant can establish "a real prospect of success".

- "Summary judgment" against a claimant or defendant may be given on the ground that "the defendant has no real prospect of success" (see *Saudi Eagle* (1986)) or that the defendant has no real prospect of successfully defending the claim or issue, thus bringing the summary judgment test into line with the test for setting aside a default judgment.

- Costs: the general rule is that the losing party must pay the winner's costs, but the court *must* have regard to the conduct of the parties not only during but before the proceedings including whether "pre-action protocols" (which are laid down) have been followed, and whether the value of the claim was exaggerated. The court may order a payment on account where the assessment of costs may be delayed. The court may also order the production of privileged documents, e.g. correspondence between solicitor and client.

The obvious intention behind the last provision, as indeed it is the thrust of the new Rules, will be to change the climate of litigation from a game in which you follow the rules, but use them to the best advantage of your client at the expense of the other party's interests, to achievement of the objective of justice. The former county court's procedure was, in principle, much more "user friendly" than the High Court's. However, solicitors involved in the system tended to find the High Court system more satisfactory, largely because under it they had control over the procedures, whereas in the county court they did not. No doubt personal litigants found the county court easier to deal with, but for professionals and their clients, the High Court system worked more smoothly. Here again then, we find a tension between the needs of different groups, and indeed an illustration of the age old problem of matching supply and demand through a centralised bureaucracy. How well the new Rules have resolved these tensions is still debatable. Their radically innovative nature gave cause for concern, because they are less than clear on a number of important points. The former Rules of the Supreme Court had developed an encrustation of case law since the Judicature Act 1875, and this case law settled many uncertain points. Similarly the County Court Rules had a great deal of case law to elucidate them. Certainly, there have been more decisions reported on points of procedure than at any time since the misconceived Hilary Rules of 1834 came into force (see below at p.200 *et seq.*). Litigants have had to bear the cost of clearing up the uncertainties in the new Rules, and it may be that in commercial cases, if the Rules are not seen to function well, we will see a transfer of work into other jurisdictions. This is possible because they exist in the context of the present tendency to "forum shop" around the courts of the member states of the Brussels and Lugano Conventions on Jurisdiction and Enforcement, and the Civil Judgments and Enforcement Act 1982 which implements them in the UK. These Conventions are now implemented by Reg.44/2001 in EU member states. These unsatisfactory Conventions, enable litigation to be played as a game in which the advantage is with the party initiating the proceedings (and can be used both to achieve a cheap and speedy result, and to prevent a result from being reached where a party thinks it is in the wrong). Having regard to this, litigants with the resources to play this game will still be at an advantage when compared with more poorly endowed litigants. However, for non-commercial disputes, and those where the Conventions do not give scope for forum shopping, litigants will have to live with the Rules.

The county court's jurisdiction was limited historically. From July 1, 1999, however, the Lord Chancellor abolished the £5,000 ceiling for actions in contract and tort. If the value of the case is £15,000 or below it *must* be started in the County Court. If the value exceeds that sum it can be started in the High Court. All but the largest personal injury cases, where the damages claimed exceed £50,000 are required to be commenced in the county court, and all general cases are allocated for trial by having regard to their importance, substance and complexity. The High Court is reserved for public law and other specialist cases, and for general cases of unusual importance, substance and complexity.

Most High Court and county court trials are by judge alone. Juries are met with only where there is an allegation of fraud, malicious prosecution, false imprisonment, or in defamation actions. Under section 69(3) of the Supreme Court Act 1981 there is discretion to allow jury trial in other cases, but it is rarely exercised (See *H v Minister of Defence* (1991)).

The order of proceeding is as follows. If allowed by the judge, the claimant opens and presents his case, the defendant then presents his case, the defendant sums up, then the claimant sums up, finally the judge gives his decision which will in the first place be a finding of fact, secondly it will be an application of law to those facts, and finally an order will be made: that the action be dismissed, or that the claimant be awarded damages or other relief such as an injunction. The final part of the judge's order will be as to costs. As noted above, in this country the basic rule is that the losing party pays the other's costs—"costs follow the event". This does not mean that the losing party must reimburse the other for everything he or she has spent. In both the county court and the High Court there are scales of payments which the losing party must make, and the losing party is entitled to dispute the winning party's bill at the "Taxation" which is a hearing specifically to determine the amount of costs to be paid to the winning party. The judgment given in court, must next be formally entered and sealed by the court—"pronouncing judgment is not entering judgment; something has to be done which will be a record" (*Holtby v Hodgson* (1889)).

Any of the matters in the judgment may be the subject of an appeal which, whether from the county court or the High Court, is to the Court of Appeal. However, only rarely will the Court of Appeal interfere with the findings of fact, or permit fresh evidence to be adduced which may contradict earlier evidence.

Whilst what was set out above is an account of the ordinary county court and High Court procedure, there are other procedures. An important category for example is the without notice application. For instance, where it is feared that a defendant might destroy evidence a search order may be sought or where the defendant may remove assets from the jurisdiction if it knew it was being sued a freezing injunction may be applied for, or in any case where urgent action is required—for example, to prevent the unlawful eviction of a person from his or her home. Usually these applications are made to a judge of the Chancery Division. Without notice applications are also used in the case of search orders. It would defeat the object of the exercise to give notice to a person who it is felt is likely to destroy evidence that an application is about to be made to stop him or her from doing so. The first the defendant will know about it in such cases, therefore, is when a solicitor and his assistants descend with their order. The defendant must comply with the order, or be in contempt of court. Because such a procedure is draconian and could be open to abuse (as a way of gaining access to a competitor's premises to carry out industrial espionage, for example), the circumstances in which such orders may be made are very strictly controlled. Moreover, the claimant must generally give an undertaking to pay (and satisfy the court that it will be able to pay) the defendant's damages and costs if at the end of the day the claimant loses.

There are other courts with civil jurisdiction. District Judges of the county court have a trial jurisdiction in small claims and fast track cases. Magistrates courts have limited civil jurisdiction notably in family matters. It should also be noted that the procedure in family cases in the county court and High Court has certain special features.

(ii) Evaluating the Woolf Reforms

The changes outlined above represent the most fundamental overhaul of civil procedure in England and Wales since the Judicature Acts. The object of the reforms, as we have said, was to cut costs and delays. In the first, they seem to have failed (Gibb, 2003); for, whilst they encourage more cases to settle without a trial, this is at the price of "front-loading" the costs to try to identify at an early stage the real issues in the dispute between the parties (see, too, Goriely, *et al*, 2002). What went wrong?

In 1964, the first major reform of High Court procedure since the Judicature Acts was implemented. The authors of the 81st edition of the White Book, which contained the new rules, wrote:

"The amendments made in [the Rules] since 1883 have been numerous—increasingly numerous—and during recent years the Rules have usually been amended several times a year. On the whole, the changes have not been fundamental, and in several cases, indeed, *have represented experiments made and abandoned, sometimes without apparent knowledge of the history of similar experiments in the past.*" [emphasis supplied]

Woolf's attempt to make the parties spell out their cases more clearly finds an historical echo in the notorious Hilary Rules of 1834. It is worth dwelling *en passant* on these Rules because they anticipate to a remarkable extent the shallow thinking that underlay the Woolf reforms. In the first part of the nineteenth century, there were still only fifteen common law judges, the same number as in the Middle Ages. These fifteen judges were required to deal with the vastly increasing case-load which reflected the growth of the economy and population, consequent on the industrial revolution. One solution would have been to increase the number of judges, but by a piece of lateral thinking of which our modern bureaucrats would be proud, they sought to cut down the length of trials and possibly promote more settlements by reforming the rules of pleading. So, as a result of the proposals of the Second Report of the Common Law Procedure Commissioners, the Hilary Rules tightened the rules of pleading by reducing the possibility of defendants pleading the "general issue" which was the equivalent of "not guilty" in a criminal case. Instead, most issues had to be specially pleaded. The Rules remained in force for only about twenty years but, during that time, cases were marked by their extreme technicality due to arguments as to whether or not a case was properly pleaded (Holdsworth, 1923). The experiment was largely abandoned in the Common Law Procedure Act 1852. So it has gone on, as the editors of the White Book observed (above)—experiments have been made and abandoned, sometimes without apparent knowledge of the history of such experiments in the past. Nothing has worked very well, because the problem actually lies elsewhere.

At this point, it may be asked why litigation in common law jurisdictions is generally more expensive than is the case in civil law jurisdictions. The fundamental difference between the common law and civilian inquisitorial systems is not, as many suppose, in the *extent* to which resources are devoted to these tasks; whilst the differences in this regard must not be minimised, the really important difference lies in *whose* resources are devoted to carrying out these tasks. In civil law systems, they are usually those of the state. In common law systems, leaving aside legal aid, they are usually those of the parties. To put it another way, in common law systems, the parties' legal advisers carry out many of the tasks carried out by court officials in civil law systems. It has, of course, to be said that the common law system leads to a certain duplication of tasks, but that is the price paid for the parties remaining substantially in charge of steering their own cases, rather than having them steered by a judge. The real question, therefore, is whether or not the price is worth paying.

Of all litigation, that involving patents tends to be in a league of its own for expense. Accordingly, in the early 1990s, a Patents County Court was set up, in the expectation that this would provide a forum for low cost litigation. In that, it largely failed, though it is nevertheless a useful adjunct today to the Patents Court which is part of the Chancery Division of the High Court. Impecunious litigants do not necessarily have simple non-complex cases and, if justice is to be done, the same bureaucratic procedures (in the technical sense used at p.252) need to be gone through as in cases involving rich litigants. Necessarily, some cases will involve one rich party and one poor party. Obviously, the court has a role in preventing those processes from being used abusively by the former to the prejudice of the latter— but the fundamental question remains: who pays? This is the key question, and failure to acknowledge this is likely to result in pointless tinkering, of which there has been rather too much in our legal history.

The Woolf reforms embodied in the CPRs have probably cost litigants a great deal more money than they have saved. Certainly, as we have said, since the CPRs came into force, there have been more cases reported involving points of procedure than at any time since the ill-conceived Hilary Rules.

(iii) Alternative Dispute Resolution ("ADR"): Arbitration and Conciliation

With few exceptions judges, in the nature of things, tend to be "jacks of all trades". In technical commercial cases the parties may well prefer to entrust the settlement of their dispute to experts in the field. For this reason, as well as for privacy (court hearings are generally open to the public), and also because it is thought to be cheaper (though this is often illusory), parties in commercial disputes frequently prefer to have their dispute resolved by an arbitrator. This has the further advantage in the case of litigants from different countries that an arbitrator can be chosen who can speak the language of each party, and who is familiar with the law and practice of each party. The agreement to go to arbitration is contractual. The arbitration award when it is made also has contractual effect, and can be sued on as a contract. The arbitration itself must, of course, observe the rules of due process in the same way as a court hearing. Indeed, apart from the relative informality, the two types of procedure are quite similar.

International arbitrations are lucrative, and most advanced countries, are keen to attract this business. The Arbitration Act 1979 (now consolidated in the Arbitration Act 1996) was passed mainly because the United Kingdom procedure offered too many ways for the loser to dispute an award, and therefore undermined one of the more desirable features of arbitration—that the arbitrator's decision be final. The Act severely restricted the possibilities of challenging an award (though of course the courts continue to have a supervisory role in ensuring that due process is observed).

For some kinds of local dispute there is the Chartered Institute of Arbitrators' Standard Consumer Arbitration Scheme, approved by the Office of Fair Trading and providing an alternative to litigation in cases involving the Law Society, the Royal Institute of Chartered Surveyors, insurance companies, the Association of British Travel Agents, British Rail, the Post Office and British Telecom. Appeals from these arbitrations go to the Commercial Court. As well as private arbitrations, there are court, and court-annexed, arbitrations.

An arbitration, like a court action, is an adversarial procedure. An arbitrator acts in more or less the same way as a judge, refereeing the dispute between the parties. A conciliator by contrast tries to assist the parties to settle their differences amicably. Like an arbitration, the procedure depends upon agreement between the parties to submit to conciliation. They will agree to include a conciliation clause in their contracts when relations between them are sufficiently friendly to hold out the prospect of amicable settlement. Primitive societies often resolve disputes routinely by conciliation (see Llewellyn and Hoebel, 1941). As "mechanical solidarity" (see Ch.6) gives way to "organic solidarity", proceedings tend to become more adversarial. The popularity of conciliation in modern commercial disputes is an indication, however, that specific groups in modern societies may possess a high degree of shared values. This is borne out by those studies of various areas of commerce which have shown that the ultimate sanction of court proceedings plays a relatively minor part in either ensuring that parties perform their contracts, or in resolving disputes between them when one party asserts the other has not done what it promised (see Beale and Dugdale, 1975). In the nature of things, conciliations are relatively informal affairs compared to arbitrations. This is not to say that a conciliation is not conducted according to certain rules. The parties may for example agree to adopt the United Nations Commission on International Trade Law Rules of 1980. The conciliation commences when one party accepts the other's invitation to conciliate under the Rules. There may be up to three conciliators. If the parties cannot agree about who is to do the conciliation, they must approach an appropriate institution to help them, but unlike arbitration, there is no compulsory procedure for appointing conciliators. The parties are barred from instituting either judicial or arbitration proceedings during the conciliation. If it fails, the conciliator cannot then sit as arbitrator (though the parties could agree that he or she should).

Under the Industrial Tribunals Act 1996 (ss 18 and 19) the Advisory, Conciliation and Arbitration Service (ACAS) is given a role in settling matters which are, or could be, the subject of proceedings before an industrial tribunal, for example a claim for equal pay or complaint of sexual discrimination.

(iv) Other Forms of ADR

Disenchantment with the delays, expense, complexity and frustration caused by the civil litigation procedure in this country has led to a proliferation of alternatives, some of an experimental nature (see Mackie, 1991). Thus we have mediation, mini-trials, and the ombudsmen (as to the latter see Ch.8). The CPRs allow judges to "stay" court proceedings, i.e. stay the proceedings temporarily, so that the parties can try mediation or other forms of ADR. The problem with most of these ADRs is that they depend upon the consent and goodwill of the parties involved. Only judicial proceedings and arbitrations result in legally enforceable judgments and awards. On the other hand, the adversarial nature of these procedures does tend to increase the hostility between the parties. In addition, the very fact that costs are mounting may be a disincentive to concede, especially in a winner-takes-all system such as ours. Thus it is not unknown for disputes which on any rational basis should have been settled at an early stage to become a fight to the death because neither party can afford to give up the chance of winning.

Mediation is a procedure which has been developed to attempt to deal with the problems endemic in adversarial procedure. Sometimes "mediation" is called "conciliation", but it is better to confine the use of this latter term to the alternative to arbitration discussed above. A mediator is a third party who attempts to help parties reach their own solutions to their problems. He or she is specially skilled in this, but a mediator cannot force the parties to do what he or she counsels. As with conciliation, it tends to work best where the parties enjoy fairly good relations—for instance, it may help to settle a dispute between partners as to the proper interpretation of their partnership agreement. The Family Law Act 1996 (Part II) provided for mediation in matrimonial disputes, adversarial procedure being seen as accentuating grievances and inhibiting constructive dissolution of marriages. This procedure was never brought into force, however. In January 2001 the then Lord Chancellor issued a press release which indicated that Part II did not meet Government objectives of saving marriages or helping divorce problems with a minimum of acrimony, and intended to repeal it. At the time of writing this has not been done, however.

Mini-trials involve the presentation of the parties' cases by their lawyers before nominated executives and an independent advisor (e.g. a senior solicitor or barrister or judge). A mini-trial is private, and cheaper, than court proceedings, but again the award cannot be enforced. On the other hand, if litigation does ensue, the issues in dispute should have been narrowed, so that the proceedings will be shorter.

However, so long as the parties are in a state of hostility, litigation will be the only solution which is not to say on the other hand that all litigation is hostile, for example, executors or trustees may seek the court's guidance on the meaning of a clause in a will with the support of the beneficiaries under it.

2. ARE THE COURTS OPEN TO ALL?

Civil litigation, even in the county court, is expensive (and it can be financially ruinous, especially where the usual "costs follow the event" rule is applied). Economic rationality will often dictate keeping a dispute well away from lawyers and, for those who cannot afford to litigate, there is anyway no option. It was to deal with the latter that the modern legal aid scheme was introduced. The scheme has evolved through three principal stages. As first established under the Legal Aid and Advice Act 1949, the scheme was administered by the Law Society. Eligibility was means-tested and support was further limited by a merits test. However, despite constant tinkering with the eligibility criteria, successive governments had difficulty in keeping the costs of the scheme under control. If there was concern about the efficiency of the scheme, there was concern, too, about its effectiveness in securing access to justice—it was a standard complaint that provision of legal services was rather patchy across the country and that, in practice, it was only the very poor (supported by legal aid) and the very rich (who were self-financing) who could afford to litigate (in Ch.9 we consider the provisions which have been made over the years for the representation of poor persons before the courts, and the background to those provisions). Thus, the scheme entered its second phase when, in 1988, the Legal Aid Board, set up by the Legal Aid Act 1988, took over the administration of the scheme. The Board operated for about a dozen years during which time the government's general philosophy in relation to public service provision—value for money, quality assurance, targeted funding, contractualisation, and the like—began to make its impact on the commitment of public finances to legal advice and assistance. For instance, it was during this period that solicitors' firms began to be franchised for legal aid work and that contracts were piloted. It was also during this period that moves were made to set priorities for funding and to co-ordinate the various providers of legal services. Despite all this, expenditure on legal aid continued to rise relentlessly through the 1990s. It was against this background that the legal aid scheme entered its third, and current, phase with the enactment of the Access to Justice Act, 1999. Under the Act, a Legal Services Commission replaces the Board with responsibility for funding both civil and criminal cases—the former as part of the Community Legal Service ("CLS") and the latter as the Criminal Defence Service—as well as co-ordinating the various providers of civil legal services.

In this latter (co-ordinating) capacity, the CLS brings together into local networks organisations offering legal and advice services. These include solicitors, Citizens' Advice Bureaux, Law Centres, local authority services (including libraries), community centres and various other organisations. These networks are supported by Community Service Partnerships made up of representatives of the Legal Services Commission, local authorities, and other funders and providers of advice. Many of the organisations in the Partnerships offer all or some of their services free, but some charge for their services. To help people who cannot afford to pay for legal services, the Community Legal Services Fund exists, and replaces the old civil legal aid scheme. The Commission administer this Fund with eligibility being determined by using the Financial Eligibility Calculator (available on line via the Legal Services Commission's home page). The user simply enters figures in the boxes provided, and the results appear and can be printed out. If the user is ineligible, he or she can use the print-out when applying for Pro Bono help under the scheme established by the Bar and solicitors under the auspices of the Legal Services Commission.

In contrast to the open-ended (demand led) way in which the legal aid fund has previously operated, the Lord Chancellor will set an annual budget for the CLS; and, in line with the government's new public management ideology, the Commission is placed under a statutory duty to secure best value in its use of the funds allocated for this purpose. The effect of these changes in conjunction with the Woolf reforms is to put more support into advice and assistance rather than litigation, to encourage mediation (in family disputes) and settlement, and to channel claimants towards lawyers who are more specialised in the relevant area of work, whose work is framed by its own particular procedures and protocols, and who are working within contracted organisations meeting the quality standards set for the CLS.

In all three phases, the core of the legal aid scheme has been to fund advice, assistance, and representation (although, under the 1999 Act, the remit of the Legal Services Commission is rather broader) with a considerable portion of legal aid expenditure being applied to family proceedings. In all phases, there have been restrictions on the kind of matters that can be supported by legal aid—actions for defamation, for example, are a well-known exclusion (the fear being that, otherwise, there would be a flood of unmeritorious applications, see Matthews and Oulton, 1971, p.48, n.14) as are conveyancing and the making of wills. With the introduction of conditional fee agreements (see below at 210) legal aid has been withdrawn from personal injury cases (although not from actions for medical negligence) and the Access to Justice Act further excludes legal aid (other than the provision of general information) for claims concerning malicious falsehood, disputed boundaries, trusts, companies and partnerships (legal aid is not available anyway to firms or companies), or for other matters arising out of the carrying on of a business. In place of the former merits test, a Funding Code (see above) now sets the priorities for determining the grant of civil legal aid. Finally, although legal aid is available for proceedings in civil courts, it is not generally available for representation before tribunals (a much criticised restriction given the volume of cases that flow through tribunals) and the 1999 Act withdraws funding for advocacy before the Lands Tribunal or Commons Commissioners.

One of the problems endemic in civil matters is that of the vexatious litigant: the litigant who becomes obsessed with a grievance against someone, or frequently some institution. The grievance may be real or imagined, but in any event under no circumstances could it lead to a successful action against anyone. Clearly, defendants can find even worthless claims against them frightening and oppressive. Although the court has inherent jurisdiction to strike out proceedings which are obviously frivolous, vexatious or an abuse of its process (*Marchioness of Huntly v Gaskell* (1905)), the defendant must make application to the court. The court also has power, on application by the Attorney-General, to order that no proceedings may be instituted by a person without leave of the High Court. It will make such an order if it is satisfied that a person has habitually and persistently and without reasonable ground instituted legal proceedings, whether against a particular person, or against different persons. In certain specific cases, where groundless threats of proceedings could be especially oppressive, special provision has been made. Thus such threats in patent proceedings can result in damages being awarded against the threatener (Patents Act 1977, s.70), and there is the tort of abuse of process which is capable of applying to all kinds of proceedings. Nevertheless, those with the means to do so frequently pursue weak claims against persons about whom they feel aggrieved. Defamation actions against newspapers are an obvious example. Apart from the possibility of the proceedings being struck out as vexatious, the principal sanction against such litigants is the possibility of having, at the end of the day, to pay the defendant's costs, which can be considerable.

Costs cannot, in general, be awarded against legally aided lit-igants, and this consideration was possibly another reason why defamation actions cannot be funded from the Community Legal Servies Fund. This exclusion has the result, however, that the reputations of persons of substance are in this sense better protected than those of persons of no substance. As Scarman L.J. said in *Goldsmith v Sperring* (1977) at 501, in discussing critical references to the plaintiff's wealth:

"Wealth may have afforded him the chance of invoking the law to protect his reputation in a way in which, alas, a poorer man could not. If so, the inference is that this branch of the law is not, as it should be, available to poor men".

If it were, would it signify much? A statement is defamatory if it is calculated to hold up the plaintiff to "hatred, contempt or ridicule" (*Parmiter v Coupland* (1840) at 108, *per* Parke B.). But, in applying this test, the law operates with a concept of "right think-ing members of society generally" (*Sim v Stretch* (1936) at 671, *per* Lord Atkin). This has the effect of excluding hatred, contempt or ridicule amongst your peer group, if that group's mores are not shared by society generally (see *Mawe v Piggott* (1869) where the plaintiff was said to have denounced Irish nationalist conspira-tors). Whilst this might be seen as bias in favour of the dominant group built into the law of defamation itself, it is bias, as it were, working towards the centre. As Pollock CB asked rhetorically in *Clay v Roberts* (1863) at 398:

"Would it be libellous to write of a lady of fashion that she had been seen on the top of an omnibus, or of a nobleman that he was in the habit of burning tallow candles?"

Of course a bias is built into the law of damages, for a poor per-son's reputation is likely to be worth less economically than that of, say, a well-known actor or pop star. This, perhaps, was another reason for excluding defamation from the legal aid scheme.

The exclusion of matters of company and partnership law, and other matters arising out of the carrying on of a business has a further effect in significantly reducing the availability of legal aid. In the recession of the early 1990s many small businessmen in litigation against, for example, dishonest franchisors, became nearly insolvent, but under the old legal aid scheme could con-tinue their actions with legal aid. This will no longer be possible, and they must look to the conditional fee scheme to continue their actions.

As noted above, whereas the old legal aid scheme was demand led, the Community Legal Services Fund is set by the Lord Chancellor, with a sub-budget for ordinary civil cases and another for family matters. Under the old scheme, the Legal Aid Committee had to be satisfied that the case was a "runner" and the prospects of success remain a consideration under the current scheme. This tended to have the effect, however, that marginal cases were pursued much less frequently in this country than in the United States for example. Lawyers there have always been permitted to take cases on the basis that if they win, they will keep a percentage of the damages recovered (usually a third). The merits of this system are that it does ensure a much wider accessibility to the court system for ordinary people, but (as explained in Ch.9) it was prohibited in this country in 1853. Such "contingency fees" have certainly been a factor in the much more rapid development of American law than English law in fields such as product liability. It has also had some undesirable effects, however, notably in relation to allegations of medical malpractice where insurances have been driven to a very high level as a result. Indeed, it is the case that surgeons have become wary of carrying out treatment at all in certain cases. The problem has been exacerbated by the fact that damages in the United States are fixed by juries, who add on to the global amount they award the cut they think the successful party's attorney will take. For these reasons there has been opposition to the suggestion that such a practice might be introduced in this country. There is in addition the problem of the "costs follow the event" rule. This rule is not generally applied in the US, where parties usually pay their own costs. In Scotland the so-called "speculative system" has always operated in which the lawyer is entitled to his fees in the case of a win, but nothing otherwise. This system differs from that described below in that no increase in fees is recoverable. Under the 1990 Act, a "conditional fee" system could be introduced in England and Wales (s.58) and this was done by statutory instrument in 1995. It could also be introduced in Scotland (Law Reform (Miscellaneous Provisions) (Scotland) Act 1990, s.36) and this was done by statutory instrument in 1992. Under this system the lawyer is entitled to an *increased* fee for a win. The client has to agree in writing the normal fee and the "success fee", that is to say the percentage by which, in the event of a win, the fee is to be increased up to the amount permitted (the Law Society has advised solicitors that success fees should be voluntarily capped at 25 per cent of the damages actually recovered—so, for example, if a normal fee is £2,000 and the success fee £1,000, then (i) if the client recovers £50,000 damages, the fee payable out of damages will be £3,000 but (ii) if the client recovers only £2,000, the fee payable will be £2,500 (£2,000 plus only £500 of the agreed success fee, this reflecting the 25 per cent cap where damages are £2,000)). If the claimant loses, he or she will pay nothing in respect of their own legal costs; and it is possible to insure against the risk of having to cover the costs of the winning party. Under the 1995 Order, conditional fee agreements (CFAs) were limited to personal injury, insolvency and human rights cases; but, even after some extension in 1998, CFAs are not available for criminal cases and matrimonial causes. The scheme was amended by the Access to Justice Act 1999, most importantly making the winning party's success fee and insurance premium (covering the risk of loss) potentially recoverable from the losing party.

In what is rapidly becoming a mixed economy for the funding of litigation, CFAs are being used to finance personal injury claims that once would have been supported by the legal aid scheme (see Fenn *et al*, 2002)—there is also some use of CFAs to finance claims, such as actions for defamation, that never were supported by legal aid (see Dyer, 2002a). However, particularly with regard to the former, it is unclear whether CFAs are an adequate substitute. Undoubtedly, some solicitors will welcome being released from the bureaucracy and delays associated with obtaining and then running a case under a legal aid certificate (one of the factors, of course, which also prompts some solicitors to desert the legal aid scheme in favour of private work: see e.g. Dyer, 2002b). And, it seems that the payouts recovered from defendants (both by way of settlement and in relation to costs) are broadly comparable irrespective of whether the claim is financed by a CFA, legal aid or standard hourly fees (Fenn *et al*, p.49). However, there are obvious drawbacks with CFAs: in particular, solicitors worry about the complexity of CFA financing and the cash-flow problems to which such agreements can give rise. Above all, though, the perceived disadvantage of CFAs is that there is an element of financial risk and the more risky the case the greater the financial risk involved in taking it on. This suggests that claimants with high risk personal injury claims may have difficulty in finding a firm willing to take the case on a CFA basis; conversely, "CFAs work most smoothly and profitably for 'bulk work'—that is small, quickly resolved, easy cases handled in bulk" (Goriely *et al*, 2002, p.37). From the point of view of legal practitioners, however, the market for bulk work has been compromised by the operation of claims intermediaries who, as readers will be aware, advertise heavily and maintain a high profile. In favour of such intermediaries, it can be said that they proactively attempt to improve access to claimants; however, the costs incurred by claimants who enter the civil justice system via intermediaries is a countervailing cause for concern (see Fenn *et al*, p.50; Goriely *et al*, p.21–23). We will have occasion to comment again on the success (or failure) of the CFA scheme in Chapter 9 (below at 260).

The "costs follow the event" rule, like the limited provision for financial assistance, is one of the discouragements to the average person to litigate in this country. These discouragements may be haphazard in that they are not part of a scheme rationally thought out, but neither are they altogether accidental. The courts simply do not want the large amount of work that much wider access to the system would entail, because they could not cope with it— and, indeed, many disputes concerning such matters as unfair dismissal, redundancy, sexual and racial discrimination, and the like, are dealt with by tribunals rather than the court system. It is the case, therefore, that a large number of claims which might be resolved judicially are not. To some extent we might say this is quite a good thing, because there are categories of disputes, such as those between neighbours, where litigation is simply "war carried on by other means". On the other hand, how many people have been fobbed off when a small consumer durable has proved defective because the shop has refused to accept its basic liability under the Sale of Goods Act? It was to attempt to deal with these types of case that the County Court Small Claims Procedure (now the Small Claims Track—see p.195) was introduced.

3. WHAT IS THE OBJECT OF COMPENSATION?

As noted in Chapter 6 the object of civil proceedings is to compensate the claimant (or defendant in the case of a counter-claim). The normal award is damages, though injunctions are also common to stop a defendant committing a continuing tort, or carrying out an intention to commit one. Unlike civil law systems, specific performance is awarded only in quite limited instances, namely in the case of contracts for the sale of land, and occasionally in the case of "specific goods" ("goods identified and agreed upon at the time the contract is made"—Sale of Goods Act 1979, ss.52 and 62). The reason usually given for the general award of specific performance for contracts for the sale of land is that each piece of land is in the nature of things unique. The same used to be said of contracts for the sale of ships, but it is now clear that this is not so (*CN Marine Inc. v Stena Line* (1982)). In fact the rule that specific performance will not be awarded if damages are an adequate remedy means that the award of specific performance in contracts for the sale of goods is very rare indeed (see *Société des Industries Metallurgiques SA v Bronx Engineering Co. Ltd* (1975)). In *Sky Petroleum Ltd v VIP Petroleum Ltd* (1974), however, the plaintiffs obtained an interlocutory injunction to restrain the defendant from breaking a contract to supply them with all the petrol they should require over a 10-year period. The injunction in this case was in effect a decree of specific performance, and the case, which occurred against the background of the first oil crisis, was unusual in that if the defendants broke their contract, the plaintiffs would be forced out of business. In other words, damages would not have been an adequate remedy. In the case of contracts involving an element of personal services, specific performance is not awarded because it would be impossible to supervise such an order effectively, and even if it were possible to do so would in effect amount to judicial slavery (*Francis v Municipal Councillors of Kuala Lumpur* (1962)). Specific performance might be awarded in the case of sales of unique goods such as antiques, and this would be a rare instance of what economists call the "consumer surplus" being protected in English law (see Harris, Ogus and Phillips, 1978).

As noted above, the common law's reluctance to award specific performance of contracts is in sharp contrast to the position in most civil law systems where specific performance is a normal remedy and, of course, this presents problems for those who would wish to see a greater harmonisation of legal regimes within Europe (see above 79). It can be argued however that the common law's view is more consonant with economic efficiency. Suppose A contracts to sell to B a truck worth £11,000 for £10,000. Before it has been delivered, X comes along and offers A £12,000 for it. A then tells B that he is prepared to break his contract with him unless B offers more than £12,000. B refuses to pay more and A sells and delivers the truck to X. Presumably X can make greater profits out of the truck than B, otherwise B would have upped his offer. B can claim damages for the loss of his bargain (i.e. £11,000 − £10,000 = £1000). A is then £1000 better off as a result of selling to X. We have achieved "Pareto optimality": we have managed to make someone better off without making anyone else worse off, and have thereby allocated resources efficiently (see Posner, 1992, p.119). Whether or not A's failure to honour his contract with B works an injustice on B is, however, another matter.

Injunctions are used fairly extensively to protect intellectual property on the other hand, though again it is the rule that they should not be granted if damages are an adequate remedy. But, for example, in the case of pirated goods infringing the plaintiff's trade mark, if an injunction were not granted, the public could be deceived into buying the counterfeit goods thinking they were the claimant's. Consequently, in such situations injunctions are usual, almost invariably on an interlocutory application by the claimant. Where on the other hand there is no likelihood of public deception, but for example a genuine issue between two reputable companies as to whether the defendant's product infringes the claimant's patent, then at the end of the day if it is held that there is infringement, the defendant can be ordered to compensate the claimant for the working of his patent, generally on a notional royalty basis (i.e. what the defendant would have had to pay the claimant if he had negotiated a licence—see *Catnic v Hill and Smith (No. 2)* (1983)).

Injunctions formerly called *"quia timet"* are also granted to prevent a threatened infringement of the claimant's property right, for example if the defendant threatens to put up a high building which would block the claimant's right to light.

One of the most problematic aspects of awards of damages used to be the need to assess them at the time of the case. A court might for example assess the damages of a road accident victim at £10,000 on the basis of the medical evidence in front of it. Some years later, it might become apparent that the claimant had suffered a more serious injury than had been suspected. Had this been known at the time, the award would have taken into account the considerable expenses of extra nursing help etc. needed by the claimant. Other typical cases where these problems used to arise were those involving asbestos-related diseases, post-traumatic neurosis and arthritis. Even where the risk was known, and taken into account in assessing the damages, the amount might be seriously eroded by inflation when the condition in fact developed (see *Hubert v Gill* (1981)). Conversely, it is not unknown for claimants to require much less compensation than they were awarded, perhaps because unforeseen progress in treatment cures them. These problems have partly been dealt with since July 1 1985 by allowing claimants to claim provisional damages in High Court actions. The county court has similar powers, which were implemented after the increase in the court's personal injury jurisdiction in 1991 (under the County Courts Act 1984, s.51—CCR O.22, r.6A operates by applying the relevant provisions of the RSC to county court proceedings). These provisions supplement two earlier devices, namely the claimant accepting an interim payment (rather than a final payment), and split trials whereby the issue of liability is determined first, and then if the defendant is found liable, an interim payment is made, and the issue of the final damages left to be resolved when the situation has become clearer. Since in such cases the interim award is not final, the device of a payment into court is not in itself appropriate. Payment in (now "Part 36 payment") is a strategy by which a defendant hopes to reduce its liability. If, after a payment in, the claimant presses on and at the end of the day recovers the same, or a lesser, sum than the payment in (the trial judge has no knowledge that a payment in has been made), the claimant will generally lose his costs from the payment in, and conversely, have to pay the defendant's. Payment in is a strategy which requires rather a nice calculation on the part of the defendant. In cases of an interim award, the sum offered by the defendant will be a sum offered on the basis that the condition which it is feared the claimant may develop in the future will not materialise, and an agreement that the claimant is entitled to provisional damages. Thus, the offer must include a submission to the award of provisional damages, so that the claimant may get an additional amount if things turn out for the worst. Obviously, the value of provisional awards to claimants depends upon the likelihood of defendants being able to pay at a future time. When therefore the defendant is not backed by insurance, it may be a safer strategy to go for a final award at the trial.

Exemplary (or punitive) damages are awarded only in rare cases; for example, where there is oppressive or unconstitutional conduct on the part of servants of the State (including the police); and in those cases where the defendant has calculated that it is economically more advantageous to commit the tort than to pay compensation to the claimant, such as a newspaper publishing a story it has reason to believe is untrue (see *Rookes v Barnard* (1964); *Cassell v Broome* (1972); and *A B v South West Water Services* (1993), on which see Pipe (1994)). There is also provision allowing the court in copyright infringement actions to award additional damages for flagrancy (Copyright Designs and Patents Act 1988, s.97(2)).

A claimant awarded damages has a variety of weapons at his disposal to ensure that they are paid. In the county court where an individual defendant is involved, attachment of earnings orders are very common. The judgment creditor in a High Court action can request his judgment be registered in the county court in order that he can get such an order. The claimant in either a High Court action or a county court action can also get an order to seize the defendant's goods and sell them up to an amount sufficient to satisfy the judgment debt, and it can charge the defendant's land and garnish (have assigned to it) the defendant's bank accounts. It has not been possible since 1868 to seize the debtor's person, but in revenue and matrimonial cases a court can order a defendant (whom it believes has the means) to pay or, in default of payment, to be imprisoned. It can also imprison a judgment debtor who refuses to turn up and be examined as to his means. A surprisingly large number of civil debtors used to end up in prison in the days when imprisonment in default of payment was a general means of enforcing payment of debts in the county court (see Rock, 1973). Evidence would be given of the defendant's means, and the court would make an order of committal to prison suspended on condition the defendant paid the instalments it thought he could afford (which were usually quite small). Nowadays, attachment of earnings orders are an important means of recovering judgment debts, but these can only work if the debtor has employment.

In March 2003 the government published a White Paper on 'Effective Enforcement: improved methods of recovery for civil court debt and commercial rent and a single regulatory regime for warrant enforcement agents' (Cm 5744). At the time of writing, however, no legislative action has emerged in respect of this.

Obviously, the best way of ensuring that a creditor gets, for example, a hire purchase or credit card loan paid back, is for it to ensure that it does not lend to persons without the means to pay. The law ought not to encourage too easy giving of credit by making it easy for creditors to recover money from debtors of small means by providing draconian remedies through the courts. The present system is intended to encourage finance houses and the like to make proper enquiries about a potential customer's means *before* lending him or her money. Clearly, however, the most creditworthy debtor can suffer the misfortune of unemployment or sickness, and indeed the evidence is that such unfortunates make up by far the largest category of defaulters. One device which is often adopted to obviate this problem is to require the debtor at the outset to take out insurance cover against such contingencies.

A useful device which can be used against foreign defendants is to seize their ships and aircraft within the jurisdiction (see *Primero Congreso del Partido* (1978) where a dispute between Chile and Cuba concerning a shipment of sugar was resolved by the courts in this country with whom the case had no other connection than that a Cuban ship, the *Primero Congreso del Partido* happened to be being built in Sunderland, and this ship was seized).

CONCLUSION

As we remarked at the outset, the ideal is that a civil justice system should afford citizens an efficient means of securing a just resolution of their disputes. Although Lord Chancellors may be imbued with a reformist zeal, the way ahead is never entirely straightforward (Mackay, 1991). On the one hand, easier, cheaper, speedier access to more user-friendly courts may not only overload the system, it may also have unintended and unwelcome consequences beyond the courts—for example, a litigation explosion may precipitate an insurance crisis, pushing up costs to the customer, and driving doctors into defensive medicine. On the other hand, attempts to lighten the courts' load by experimenting with alternative forms of dispute resolution (mediation and the like) and "no fault" compensation schemes may compromise standards of justice and dilute the sense of responsibility. With governments being unwilling to commit unlimited resources to the civil justice system, and with the philosophy of "value for money" continuing to shape political thinking, it will be interesting to observe the impact of the most recent reforms—in particular, we should monitor whether changes designed to improve the efficiency and effectiveness of the system succeed in doing this and, if so, whether success is bought at the price of just resolution of disputes.

8

LEGAL PROCESS

III: The System of Administrative Justice

As noted in Chapter 3, Dicey considered government based on the Rule of Law to be the antithesis of "government based on the exercise by persons in authority of wide, arbitrary, or discretionary powers . . ." (1939, p.188). In this chapter, we consider the extent to which our system of administrative justice endeavours to keep faith with the spirit of the Rule of Law, both by confining the actions of public authorities within the bounds of their lawful powers and by checking the exercise of public discretionary powers—in short, by seeking to reduce arbitrary governance (cf. Ganz, 1987; and Craig, 2003). We can introduce this topic by considering the case of *Congreve v Home Office* (1976).

In January 1975, the Home Secretary announced that, as from April 1 1975, the colour television licence fee would be raised from £12 to £18. Many licence holders, encouraged by the press, believed that they could avoid paying the increased fee by making an early application to renew their licences. One such person was Mr Congreve, a partner in a firm of City solicitors, whose licence expired on March 31 1975. Accordingly, a few days before the expiry of his licence, Mr Congreve applied at a Post Office for a twelve-month £12 licence. The Home Office had, in fact, instructed Post Office counter clerks not to accept early renewals of this kind; but, because Mr Congreve did not disclose that he already held a licence, the counter clerk failed to apply the Home Office instruction. In the event, some 24,500 overlapping licences of this type were issued. These licence-holders duly received letters from the National TV Licence Records Office (acting as agent for the Home Office) saying that, unless an additional fee of £6 were paid, the overlapping licence would be revoked. Some paid the £6, but others, including Mr Congreve, held out. Finally, on November 11, 1975, an ultimatum was sent to the recalcitrant licence-holders: either they paid the additional £6 by December 1, or their licences would be revoked. Three days later, on November 14, Mr Congreve issued proceedings against the Home Office seeking a declaration that, if the Home Secretary were to revoke the overlapping licences, this would be unlawful and invalid—that it would be ultra vires (i.e. beyond the Minister's lawful powers).

At first instance, Phillips J. ruled that revocation of the licences would not be unlawful. Under section 1(4) of the Wireless Telegraphy Act 1949, the Home Secretary had a broad power to revoke licences, and, whilst this power was not to be exercised in bad faith, or arbitrarily, or in some wholly unreasonable way, there was no evidence to suggest that the legality of the threatened revocation was vitiated by considerations of this kind. The fact of the matter was that Mr Congreve had attempted to avoid paying the additional licence fee; the game was up and he now had the choice of either paying the proper fee or not using his television. On appeal, however, the Court of Appeal took a rather different view of the matter. Once again, the nub of the issue was whether the Home Secretary had good reasons for revocation (the licences now having been revoked in line with the ultimatum). As Lord Denning M.R. saw it:

"The real reason [for the revocation] . . . was that the department did not like people taking out overlapping licences so as to save money. But there was nothing in the Regulations to stop it. It was perfectly lawful: and the department's dislike of it cannot afford a good reason for revoking them. So far as other people (who did not have the foresight to take out overlapping licences) are concerned I doubt whether they would feel aggrieved if these licences remain valid. They might only say: 'Good luck to them. We wish we had done the same.'" (*Congreve v Home Office* (1976) at 652)

In short, enterprising licence-holders had taken advantage of the Home Office's incompetence, and it was not open to the latter to retrieve its mistake by abusing the statutory right of revocation. Accordingly, the court unanimously reversed Phillips J. and granted Mr Congreve a declaration in the terms sought.

Congreve suggests that, even in these days of government by large departmental bureaucracies (both centrally and locally, together with countless quangos), the Rule of Law is not yet dead (*cf.* Kamenka and Tay's, 1980, account of the movement from a *Gesellschaft* type of law to a "bureaucratic-administrative" model). For, the courts, on occasion, are prepared to champion the rights of the citizen against what they see as the abuse of state power. However, the double qualification in this statement—"on occasion", and "what they see"—must be emphasized. Our discussion of the administrative justice system begins, therefore, with an attempt to locate just when and where the courts are prepared to intervene in the field of public administration.

1. GCHQ AND ALL THAT

Undoubtedly, one of the landmark decisions of modern times is *Council of Civil Service Unions (CCSU) v Minister for the Civil Service* (1985) (the *GCHQ* case). Given that the case involved a challenge to the legality of the Prime Minister's action (the Prime Minister, as Minister for the Civil Service, being the defendant), the proceedings attracted considerable public interest. However, there are two quite separate, and altogether more important, reasons for looking at the GCHQ case in some detail. First, it establishes, albeit in formal terms, a framework for the operation of judicial review of public decision-making; and, secondly, in contrast with *Congreve*, it highlights one kind of occasion when the courts will not stand in the way of the administrative machine.

The dispute in the GCHQ case centred on trade union rights at the Government Communications Headquarters (GCHQ) at Cheltenham. The main function of GCHQ, which is a branch of the Foreign and Commonwealth Office, is to provide signals intelligence for the government and to ensure the security of UK military and official communications. Staff at GCHQ were encouraged to belong to trade unions and most did so, belonging to unions which were members of the Council of Civil Service Unions (CCSU). On January 25, 1984, the Foreign Secretary, to the surprise of staff and unions, announced in the House of Commons that the government had decided to ban national trade unions at GCHQ. Instead, staff at the establishment would be permitted to belong only to a departmental staff association approved by the director of GCHQ. As we have said, this announcement came as a surprise, for, contrary to the usual practice, there had been no prior consultation between management and the unions about this important alteration to the conditions of employment at GCHQ. In March 1984, the applicants (the CCSU together with various persons employed at GCHQ) obtained leave to bring proceedings for judicial review of the legality of the government's decision. It should be noted that, in 1977, following recommendations made by the Law Commission (Law Commission, 1976) the procedure for challenging the legality of action taken by public authorities was considerably simplified. Even so, the new procedure, the application for judicial review under Order 53 of the Rules of the Supreme Court, still required the applicant to obtain leave to proceed before the review might take place. Whilst the applicants succeeded before Glidewell J., both the Court of Appeal and the House of Lords rescued the Prime Minister from further embarrassment by ruling that the ban at GCHQ was lawful.

The nub of the applicants' case was not that the government had no power to ban national trade unions at GCHQ—it was fairly clear that, under article 4 of the Civil Service Order in Council, which was made in exercise of the royal prerogative (*cf.* Ch.3), the relevant power existed. Rather, the applicants complained that there had been no consultation prior to the government's decision and that, given previous practice, this defeated legitimate expectations, thereby rendering the ban invalid. Although the application was to be rejected, the House of Lords was in no doubt that the failure to consult represented a procedural irregularity capable prima facie of invalidating the decision. As Lord Fraser said:

"Legitimate, or reasonable, expectation may arise either from an express promise given on behalf of a public authority or from the existence of a regular practice which the claimant can reasonably expect to continue". (at 401)

The practice at GCHQ clearly established an expectation of consultation. Indeed, even on January 9, 1984 (which was a couple of weeks after the Prime Minister's instruction to impose the ban, but before its announcement in the House of Commons) the Cabinet Secretary intimated to the CCSU that there would have to be consultations before polygraph security screening could be introduced for staff at Cheltenham. Other things being equal, therefore, the failure to consult was a procedural impropriety which invalidated the decision.

The failure to consult, it must be appreciated, was not an oversight. It was wholly intentional. By the time that the case reached the House of Lords, the government's defence rested almost entirely on considerations of national security. Briefly, the background to the ban was that there had been various forms of industrial action at GCHQ, causing concern both to the government and, one imagines, to its partners in NATO. Most seriously, in March 1981, about 25 per cent of the staff went on a one-day strike, as a result of which parts of the operation were virtually shut down. Such industrial action did not relate specifically to a dispute at GCHQ—it was taken in pursuance of a national dispute between the government and the unions over civil service conditions. However, there was evidence that the unions were aware that GCHQ was a sensitive target and that the government would be vulnerable if pressure were to be applied there. Accordingly, the ban at GCHQ was designed both to reduce the government's vulnerability and to safeguard its intelligence operation. However, the government, fearing that consultations in relation to the proposed ban might occasion disruption at GCHQ, decided to impose the ban without consultation. The case, therefore, involved a straight choice between giving effect to the staff's right to be consulted or backing the government's concern to maintain national security. Put in these terms, the Law Lords agreed that there could be only one answer: national security was an overriding interest.

The first lesson of the GCHQ case, therefore, is that judicial review pretty well ends where national security begins. According to Lord Scarman, who represented the most liberal line on this question in the GCHQ case:

"Once the factual basis is established by evidence so that the court is satisfied that the interest of national security is a relevant factor to be considered in the determination of the case, the court will accept the opinion of the Crown or its responsible officer as to what is required to meet it, unless it is possible to show that the opinion was one which no reasonable minister advising the Crown could in the circumstances reasonably have held". (at 406)

This suggests that the courts have a serious role in assessing whether, on the facts, national security is implicated in a particular decision. However, once the court accepts that national security is involved, its reviewing role is quite perfunctory; for, even on the most liberal judicial view, the court may only upset a decision where it is prepared to hold that the government's assessment of the needs of national security is so outrageous as to fall beyond the bounds of reason (but, in the post-Human Rights Act setting, some courts might be more bold: see *A v Secretary of State for the Home Department* (2004)).

The second feature of the GCHQ case which has importance for our purposes is its setting out of a framework for judicial review.

Lord Diplock advanced the following suggestion (which was actively endorsed by Lord Roskill):

"Judicial review has I think developed to a stage today when . . . one can conveniently classify under three heads the grounds upon which administrative action is subject to control by judicial review. The first ground I would call 'illegality', the second 'irrationality', and the third 'procedural impropriety'. This is not to say that further development on a case by case basis may not in the course of time add further grounds". (at 401)

In relation to "illegality", Lord Diplock said that "the decision-maker must understand correctly the law that regulates his decision-making power and must give effect to it" (at 410). For example, in *Congreve*, if the Wireless Telegraphy Act 1949, had empowered the Minister simply to issue, but not to revoke, television licences, then revocation supposedly pursuant to the statutory power would have been a straightforward case of illegality. By "irrationality", Lord Diplock said that he basically meant so-called "*Wednesbury* unreasonableness", which he elaborated as "a decision which is so outrageous in its defiance of logic or of accepted moral standards that no sensible person who had applied his mind to the question to be decided could have arrived at it" (at 410). Although Lord Diplock's formulation of the *Wednesbury* concept, with its emphasis on defiance of "logic" or "accepted moral standards" is somewhat idiosyncratic, there is no doubt that the *Wednesbury* test is one of the central features of judicial review. In *Associated Provincial Picture Houses Ltd v Wednesbury Corporation* (1948), the plaintiff cinema owners sought a declaration that the defendant local authority had acted *ultra vires* in granting a licence for Sunday performances subject to the condition that children under the age of fifteen should not be admitted (irrespective of whether they were accompanied by an adult). The plaintiffs' contention was that this condition was unreasonable. However, in an important judgment, Lord Greene MR insisted that the court had no warrant to substitute its idea of a reasonable condition for the licensing authority's idea of a reasonable condition. In other words, even if Lord Greene and his fellow judges in the Court of Appeal would not have imposed a condition excluding children under the age of fifteen, this was not sufficient to invalidate the condition. To hold the condition *ultra vires* as unreasonable, the court would have to be satisfied that it was so unreasonable that no reasonable authority could ever have made such a decision. And this, as Lord Greene famously declared, "would require something overwhelming" (at 230). Finally, in the *GCHQ* case, Lord Diplock explained that by "procedural impropriety", he referred to cases where a public authority failed to act with procedural fairness. This would encompass violation of the classical principles of natural justice (essentially the twin principles of "*nemo judex in causa sua*" (no one should be a judge in his own cause) and of "*audi alteram partem*" (each party should be heard), respectively prohibiting bias in decision-makers, and requiring decision-makers to afford to persons affected by their decisions an opportunity to make representations); violation of the basic duty to act fairly (including breach of the principle of legitimate expectation as recognised in the *GCHQ* case); and "failure by an administrative tribunal to observe procedural rules that are expressly laid down in the legislative instrument by which its jurisdiction is conferred" (at 411).

We do not need to agonise about whether Lord Diplock's classificatory scheme is the best available. At the very least, it points to three aspects of decision-making upon which judicial review might focus. First, there is the ostensible source of authority for the decision. If the statute, or whatever, does not grant the power claimed, the decision is manifestly invalid. Secondly, there are the procedures leading up to the decision, encompassing both "external" requirements (e.g. provisions for consultation, and opportunities for a hearing), and "internal" requirements (*viz.*, the range of considerations and motivations guiding the decision-maker). Whether the procedural demands are external or internal, they may be either explicitly laid down in the authorising provisions or merely implicit. However, as both *Congreve* (which concerned internal procedural matters) and the *GCHQ* case (which concerned external procedural matters) illustrate, violation of merely implicit requirements can render a decision invalid. Finally, review might focus on the substance of a decision, the argument being that, whilst the procedural requirements appear to have been observed, the decision is flawed on the basis of the *Wednesbury* reasonableness test.

Recalling the leeway which exists in handling statutes and precedents, it will be apparent that the framework of judicial review leaves the judges with plenty of options. For example, empowering statutes may be open to interpretation; the idea of implicit procedural requirements is very open-ended; and the *Wednesbury* reasonableness test may be used both as an excuse for non-intervention (where the threshold of unreasonableness is set high—so-called "super-*Wednesbury*") as well as a reason for intervention (where the threshold of unreasonableness is lowered) (*cf.* Prosser, 1979; Hunt, 1997). What we must consider next, then, is the pattern of intervention and non-intervention.

2. INTERVENTION AND NON-INTERVENTION

In *Chief Constable of the North Wales Police v Evans* (1982), Lord Brightman expressed the orthodox view that "[j]udicial review is concerned, not with the decision, but with the decision-making process' (at 154). To put this another way, it is not for the courts to review the merits of decisions made by public authorities, but simply to ensure that such decisions are neither manifestly illegal nor taken in violation of procedural requirements. Hence, whilst in both *Congreve* and the *GCHQ* case the courts were willing to engage in review, in *Wednesbury* they declined to get involved in assessing the merits of the local licensing authority's decision. This suggests that, whereas the courts will intervene where the decision of a public authority is challenged on procedural grounds, they will not intervene where the challenge is to the merits of the decision. Whilst this pattern may have some plausibility, things are not so simple. For, in practice, the courts cannot always be relied upon to rectify clear procedural violations; nor can they be counted upon to eschew direct assessment of the merits of decisions.

As the *GCHQ* case illustrates, procedural rights are overridden by considerations of national security. However, on occasion, altogether less compelling considerations may suffice to bar redress for procedural violations. A good example is *R. v Secretary of State for the Environment, Ex p. Ostler* (1977), a case arising out of a plan to relieve traffic congestion in Boston by building an inner relief road. Objections to the plan were to be dealt with in two stages, the first stage concerning the relief road itself, the second stage the side roads feeding in to the relief road. An inquiry into the first stage plans was held in September 1973. Ostler, a corn merchant in Boston, raised no objection because there was no indication that his premises would be affected. Following the inquiry, in March and May 1974, the relevant compulsory purchase and highway orders were made. However, in July 1974, supplementary orders were made for the widening of a particular road, Craythorne Lane, which would involve demolishing part of Ostler's property. Ostler objected; his objections were considered at the second stage inquiry in December 1974; but, at the inquiry, he was not allowed to object to the proposals confirmed in the first stage orders. The inquiry inspector recommended that the widening of Craythorne Lane should be approved and, in July 1975, the Minister acted on this recommendation by making the necessary orders. Now we come to the nub of the case. In December 1975, Ostler found out that, in 1973, a secret deal had been agreed between the Department of the Environment and a local firm of wine merchants, whereby the latter withdrew their objections to the first stage proposals in return for the former guaranteeing them access to their premises by widening Craythorne Lane. In the light of this fresh evidence, Ostler sought to have the first stage orders quashed on the grounds that there had been bad faith by the Department and a breach of the rules of natural justice.

Assuming that the facts as pleaded by Ostler were true, there could be no denying that he had been treated unfairly. If the agreed plans for Craythorne Lane had been published at the first stage inquiry, Ostler would have had an opportunity to object before the plans for the relief road had already been, as it were, set in concrete. Although the Department was prepared to contest Ostler's account of the matter, it thought that this was unnecessary, arguing that it was too late for the validity of the first stage orders to be challenged. The point was that the relevant legislation provided that, within six weeks of the orders being made, an appeal against their validity could be brought before the High Court, but that, thereafter, their legality was not to be questioned. Upholding the Department's view that Ostler was out of time, the Court of Appeal ruled that the orders were no longer open to challenge. As Lord Denning M.R. explained:

"[T]he policy underlying the statute is that when a compulsory purchase order has to be made, then if it has been wrongly obtained or made, a person aggrieved should have a remedy. But he must come promptly. He must come within six weeks. If he does so, the court can and will entertain his complaint. But if the six weeks expire without any application being made, the court cannot entertain it afterwards. The reason is because, as soon as that time has elapsed, the authority will take steps to acquire property, demolish it and so forth. The public interest demands that they should be safe in doing so. Take this very case. The inquiry was held in 1973. The orders made early in

1974. Much work has already been done under them. It would be contrary to the public interest that the demolition should be held up." (at 136)

Without doubt, it would have been extremely inconvenient to have opened up the first stage orders. Pursuant to those orders, eighty per cent of the land had been acquired and ninety per cent of the buildings demolished. On the other hand, Ostler could not have acted more promptly than he did (once he became aware of the secret agreement), and it hardly lay in the mouth of the Department to complain that he should have objected sooner. Nevertheless, all things considered, the court judged that it was more important that traffic congestion in Boston should be speedily relieved than that Ostler's rights should be fully respected.

In *Ostler*, the court gave no indication that it thought that, even if Ostler had been able to challenge the first stage orders, he would have failed anyway to prevent the widening of Craythorne Lane. Had such suspicions been harboured, this, too, might have served to bar a remedy. In *Glynn v Keele University* (1971), for instance, it was held that, although the University had clearly breached the rules of natural justice when exercising its disciplinary powers against the applicant student, its decision should not be set aside. The key point was that, whilst the student had been denied a hearing, the facts were not in dispute—he was one of a number of students who had committed a University offence by appearing naked on the campus. Accordingly, if there had been a hearing, the applicant could have done no more than put forward a plea in mitigation. Whilst the court did not entirely discount the significance of such a plea, it ruled that this was not sufficient "to justify setting aside a decision *which was intrinsically a perfectly proper one*". On one reading, the applicant failed in *Glynn* because a hearing would have made no difference to the University's disciplinary decision. On another reading, he failed because the court approved of the University's decision. Either way, however, it is arguable that the court failed to take the question of procedural fairness sufficiently seriously (*cf.* the reasoning in *Alladice*, Ch.6, p.160).

At this stage, an important general restriction on the availability of judicial review should be noted. This is the doctrine of *locus standi*. As we have said already, no application for judicial review may be made unless leave has first been obtained. Additionally, section 31(3) of the Supreme Court Act 1981 (which formalises the Order 53 procedure) provides that the court shall not grant leave unless "the applicant has a sufficient interest in the matter to which the application relates." Similarly, where there is a statutory six-week appeal provision (as in *Ostler*), this is normally available only to those persons who are "aggrieved" by the decision. In other words, applicants for judicial review must have the requisite "standing" to initiate the proceedings. In principle, phrases like "sufficient interest" and "person aggrieved" are elastic enough to be interpreted restrictively or broadly—and, although the English tradition has tended to be restrictive, the cases by no means uniformly fit this pattern (see e.g. Hilson and Cram, 1996).

A good example of the restrictive approach to *locus standi* is *R. v Secretary of State for the Environment, Ex p. Rose Theatre Trust Co.* (1990). The case arose when, during the development of a site at Southwark, the remains of the Rose Theatre were unearthed. This excited considerable attention because the Rose was a theatre in which most of Marlowe's plays were performed and in which two of Shakespeare's plays received their first performance. The Rose Theatre Trust Co., comprising a number of persons well-known in archaeology and in the arts together with local residents, was formed with a view to protecting the site. Accordingly, the Trust applied to the Secretary of State to list the Rose as a scheduled monument of national importance under the Ancient Monuments and Archaeological Areas Act 1979. Once scheduled, development of the site would require special consent (i.e. over and above ordinary planning permission). However, the Secretary of State, impressed by the willingness of the developers to co-operate with the preservationists, declined to schedule the site. The Trust sought judicial review, the application being contested by the Secretary of State, the site owners, and the developers. One of the questions, raised by the latter two defendants, was whether the Trust had *locus standi*. Having dismissed the Trust's arguments on the substantive grounds of the challenge, Schiemann J. held that, in any event, the Trust did not have sufficient standing. Whilst the individuals concerned with the Trust were certainly not the proverbial "mere busybodies", and whilst they admittedly had a more-than-average interest in seeing the Rose preserved, they did not have sufficient interest, within the meaning of the law, to entitle them to have the decision reviewed.

In contrast with the restrictiveness of the *Rose Theatre* case, we can cite a trio of more recent decisions, *Equal Opportunities Commission v Secretary of State for Employment* (1994), *R. v Inspectorate of Pollution, ex parte Greenpeace Ltd (No. 2)* (1994), and *R.*

v Secretary of State for Foreign Affairs, Ex p. World Development Movement Ltd (1995), in each of which a significantly broader view of standing was taken. One of the questions in the *EOC* case was whether the Commission had sufficient interest to challenge the legality of the Employment Protection (Consolidation) Act 1978, on the ground that its provisions for part-time workers (with regard to eligibility for unfair dismissal and redundancy payments) were indirectly discriminatory and constituted a breach of the United Kingdom's obligations under EC law. Given that there had already been some recognition of the EOC's capacity to initiate judicial review proceedings (e.g. in the *Birmingham City Council* case, see Ch.2), the majority of the Law Lords accepted Lord Keith's view that "it would be a very retrograde step now to hold that the EOC has no *locus standi* to agitate in judicial review proceedings questions related to sex discrimination which are of public importance and affect a large section of the population" (at 919) (and see further Villiers and White, 1995). Similarly, in the *Greenpeace* case, Otton J. held that Greenpeace had sufficient standing to seek judicial review of the decision made by HM Inspectorate of Pollution and the Minister of Agriculture, Fisheries and Food to vary the authorisations for the emission of radioactive waste at Sellafield, Cumbria (this was in connection with the testing of British Nuclear Fuels' new thermal oxide reprocessing plant). Although Greenpeace lacked the official status of a body such as the EOC, Otton J. took the view that its expertise in environmental matters and its experience in the relevant body of law would be of assistance to the process of review; and its interest in the particular decision was secured by its 2,500 Cumbrian members. Finally, in the *World Development Movement* case, the court held that the WDM had sufficient interest to justify a challenge to the legality of the Secretary of State's purported authorisation of funding for the Pergau dam in Malaysia under the provisions of the Overseas Development and Co-operation Act 1980. Given that the WDM (with some 13,000 supporters in the UK) was acting on behalf of potential recipients of overseas aid, rather than directly to protect the interests of its own members (let alone to protect their health and safety, as in the *Greenpeace* case), it was fairly contended that the applicants were "at the outer limits of standing" (at 619). Nevertheless, detecting "an increasingly liberal approach to standing on the part of the courts during the last 12 years", and weighing "the importance of vindicating the rule of law ... the importance of the issue raised ... the likely absence of any other responsible challenger ... the nature of the breach of duty against which relief is sought . . . and the prominent role of [the WDM] in giving advice, guidance and assistance with regard to aid" (at 620, *per* Rose L.J.), the court had no difficulty in confirming its jurisdiction to hear the application.

Although the cases are not easily reconciled, it would be quite wrong to regard Schiemann J. (in the *Rose Theatre* case) as insensitive to the consequences of a denial of standing. For, writing shortly after his decision in *Rose Theatre*, he graphically underlined the implications of a restrictive approach to standing:

"[W]herever someone is . . . excluded by reason of *locus standi* rules, the law regards it as preferable that an illegality should continue than that the person excluded should have access to the courts. It is important . . . that this basic fact should be appreciated." (1990, p.342)

In the context of the case-law from *Rose Theatre* onwards, however, the arguments about standing are much more complex. No longer, can the issue be seen simply in terms of finding the right balance between the vindication of individual right (the checking of alleged illegality) and the time and resource implications (for both courts and administration) if there is to be a judicial review. As Carol Harlow (2002) has pointed out in an important article, this body of case-law concerns the standing of groups rather than individuals, some of these groups claiming to represent the interests of associational members, others to speak for the larger public interest, and some, indeed, claiming a mixture of the two. Furthermore, at the same time that the standing rules are being relaxed in a seemingly ad hoc fashion to allow for group-driven judicial review, third-party intervention by campaigning groups is being permitted almost as a matter of course. (It will be recalled that Lord Hoffmann's participation in the hearing of the Pinochet appeal proceedings was judged improper because of his connection with Amnesty International's charitable wing; but this only became an issue because Amnesty had been permitted to intervene in the extradition proceedings). What such developments amount to, claims Harlow, is "a shift away from the traditional bipolar and adversarial lawsuit familiar to common lawyers, to something more fluid, less formal and possibly less individualistic in character" (p.7); and, with this, the lines between the political process and the judicial process (the latter characterised by independence, objectivity, and finality) become blurred. The larger cautionary message from Harlow is that third-party intervention in the courts cannot compare with full-scale consultation in the political process; that groups given standing to speak to the public interest may, in fact, represent only a narrow and particular segment of that interest (the majority of campaigning groups defining their role in terms of political advocacy for a particular view); and that, although the rhetoric of participatory democracy is everywhere, the pressure to turn the legal process into a free-way could lead instead to a free-for-all. Quite simply, the courts are not equipped to act as surrogate legislators and, so long as we value the distinctive contribution made by the judicial process, we should not try to elide it with the political (similarly, see Hannett, 2003).

From matters of procedure, we can turn to questions of substance, starting with the celebrated case of *Roberts v Hopwood* (1925). There, Poplar Borough Council, being empowered under section 62 of the Metropolis Management Act 1855 to pay its employees "such salaries and wages as . . . [the council] may think fit", thought fit to pay its workers "model" wages. The district auditor, having found that wage increases paid by Poplar since 1914 exceeded cost-of-living increases by between eighty-five and two hundred per cent (and that wage levels were maintained even when the cost of living fell materially), disallowed £5,000 and surcharged the councillors in question. The councillors sought to have the auditor's decision quashed. Although the councillors succeeded before the Court of Appeal, the House of Lords ruled unanimously in favour of the auditor. The speeches suggest three grounds in support of this decision. First, the council had acted illegally by paying monies which were so generous that they could no longer be regarded as "wages" within the meaning of the statute. Secondly, the council had offended against canons of procedural propriety by taking improper considerations into account. As Lord Atkinson put it:

"The council would, in my view, fail in their duty if, in administering funds which did not belong to their members alone, they . . . allowed themselves to be guided . . . by some eccentric principles of socialistic philanthropy, or by a feminist ambition to secure the equality of the sexes in the matter of wages in the world of labour." (at 594)

Thirdly, the councillors, being bound to accord due weight to the interests of ratepayers, had exercised their discretion in a way which was beyond the bounds of reasonableness. Without doubt, though, the driving force behind their Lordships' intervention was their manifest aversion to the "eccentric" policy of the Poplar councillors.

Nearly sixty years later, in *Bromley LBC v Greater London Council* (1983), the left-wing eccentricity of another London council (this time, the now defunct GLC) again attracted the attention of the Law Lords. Having won the GLC elections in 1981, the Labour-controlled council set about implementing its election promise to cut bus and tube fares by 25 per cent. This involved raising a supplementary rate precept from the London boroughs. Bromley Borough Council sought a declaration that the GLC had acted ultra vires, exceeding its powers under the Transport (London) Act 1969. As in the Poplar case, the Law Lords unanimously ruled against the council's misguided philanthropy (at the ratepayers' expense). To appreciate the gist of their Lordships' reasoning, we need not enter far into the labyrinthine statutory provisions. Under section 1 of the 1969 Act, the GLC had a duty to "develop polices, and to encourage, organise and, where appropriate, carry out measures, which will promote the provision of integrated, efficient, and *economic* transport facilities and services for Greater London". It will be noted that the emphasis in relation to "economic" is ours, not the statute's. However, although there are many different nuances in the speeches (see Dignan, 1983; Loughlin, 1986, pp.69–75), their Lordships effectively read section 1 as though it emphasised "economic" in just this way. And, judged by the standards of entrepreneurs in the private sector, the GLC Labour group (like their earlier counterparts in Poplar) clearly failed the test. In essence, as John Griffith (1985) has remarked, the underpinning of the Law Lords' decision was primarily their "strong preference for the principles of the market economy with a dislike of heavy subsidization for social purposes" (at 212).

Hard on the heels of *Bromley*, came *Pickwell v Camden LBC* (1983), in which the district auditor thought he detected a fresh outbreak of Poplarist philanthropy, this time in Camden. Briefly, faced with severely disruptive industrial action in their borough, Camden council reached a local agreement with their manual workers. This agreement, containing a so-called "Camden supplement" (which guaranteed a minimum weekly wage of sixty pounds for a thirty-five hour week), proved to be rather more generous than the national settlement which was eventually agreed. The district auditor sought a declaration that the Camden settlement was *ultra vires*. The court, however, not only thought the circumstances in Camden vastly different from those in Poplar, but also that the decision in _Bromley_ (with its emphasis on the local authority's fiduciary duty to its ratepayers) did not comprise a licence for interfering with the exercise of discretionary powers in local government. Ormrod L.J. reasserted the orthodox view particularly strongly:

"[The] question for this court is not whether Camden made a bad bargain for the ratepayers, or were precipitate in making the offer to the strikers, or could have achieved a cheaper settlement by waiting, or made a better bargain by different tactics. These are matters for the electorate at the next election. The question for the court is whether the evidence establishes that no reasonable local authority could have made a settlement on such terms." (at 1004)

Given, then, that judicial review was seen to concern illegality rather than imprudence, the district auditor's application was dismissed.

Even from this small sample of cases, it will be apparent that the pattern of intervention and non-intervention is not entirely straightforward. As _Congreve_ illustrates, the courts will, on occasion, interfere with central government decisions, even if it causes some embarrassment and inconvenience. But we should not rejoice too readily in the survival of the Rule of Law. For, it is arguable that the courts find too many excuses for failing to deal with clear cases of procedural irregularity, and succumb too often (_Pickwell_ notwithstanding) to the temptation to substitute their own preferred policies for the policies adopted by democratically elected bodies.

3. CONTROLLING THE ADMINISTRATION

So long as the courts condone procedural irregularities, judicial review can only go so far towards controlling the administration. The effectiveness of judicial review, however, is further limited by a number of factors, in particular: the absence in English law of any general duty to give reasons for administrative decisions; the tendency to rely on individuals being prepared to apply for judicial review (bearing in mind that damages are not awarded for invalid administrative action per se); the power of the administration to correct and remake invalid decisions; and the absence of significant constitutional restraints on government.

If administration is to be fair and open, it is important that decision-makers should give reasons for their decisions. In England, the Tribunals and Inquiries Act 1958 (as consolidated in 1971) places a duty on many tribunals to furnish reasons (written or oral) for their decisions (provided that reasons are requested before the giving or notification of the decision). Similarly, where land-use planning decisions go to appeal (irrespective of whether there is an inquiry) reasons are always supplied as a matter of practice. However, in the absence of such special arrangements, public administrators in England, unlike in many other jurisdictions, are not subject to a general requirement to give reasons for their actions—the duty to give reasons is not yet recognised as a third principle of natural justice. The argument in favour of recognising such a general duty (although ultimately rejected by the High Court of Australia) was vigorously proposed by Kirby P., sitting in the Court of Appeal of New South Wales, in *Public Service Board of New South Wales v Osmond* (1984):

"The overriding duty of public officials who are donees of statutory powers is to act justly, fairly and in accordance with their statute. Normally, this will require, where they have a power to make discretionary decisions affecting others, an obligation to state the reasons for their decisions. That obligation will exist where, to do otherwise, would render nugatory a facility, however limited, to appeal against the decision. It will also exist where the absence of stated reasons would diminish a facility to have the decision otherwise tested by judicial review to ensure that it complies with the law and to ensure that matters have been taken into account which should have been taken into account or that matters have not been taken into account which ought not to have been taken into account." (at 467)

As Kirby P.'s thinking in *Osmond* indicates, the case for recognising a general duty to give reasons may be put on the ground of simple fairness as well as on the ground that it is a prerequisite for effective judicial review (see Justice, All Souls, 1988)—quite apart, of course, from any incidental advantages flowing from general reason-giving, such as improving the quality of decisions and strengthening public confidence in the administration. Although, as we have said, English law declines to recognise a general duty to give reasons for an administrative decision, in *Doody v Secretary of State for the Home Department* (1993), the

House of Lords made the significant concession that such a duty may be implied in appropriate circumstances—and rested the concession on the alternative grounds of what minimum standards of fairness require or what effective judicial review requires.

The administrative decision under scrutiny in *Doody* was that of the Home Secretary in setting the penal element (i.e. the period designed to reflect considerations of retribution and deterrence, only after the expiry of which questions of discretionary release may arise) to be served by particular mandatory life sentence prisoners. The central issues were whether such prisoners should be entitled (i) to make representations about the length of the penal element, (ii) to know the judges' advice and reasoning in relation to the penal element, and (iii) to have reasons from the Home Secretary for his decision (bearing in mind that, in a significant number of cases, the Home Secretary will depart from the judges' advice). The first entitlement having been conceded by the Secretary of State, Lord Mustill was clear that the second entitlement must follow, "for the prisoner cannot rationalise his objections to the penal element without knowing how it was rationalised by the judges themselves" (at 109). The third entitlement was more controversial. However, Lord Mustill was in no doubt that this right, too, was required, not merely as an act of "simple humanity" (at 110) but as a matter of fairness—inconvenient though it sometimes might be. Alternatively, given that it was agreed that the Home Secretary's decision on the penal element was susceptible to judicial review, Lord Mustill held that effective review of the decision presupposed that the prisoner must have access to the decision-maker's reasons—for, without such material, neither the prisoner (nor the courts) would be in a position to ascertain whether the decision-making process had gone astray.

Although the decision in *Doody* may come to represent a watershed in English administrative law (see Lindsay, 1994), it should not be thought that the adoption of a general duty to give reasons would be a panacea. For one thing, there is a danger that if administrators were subject to the duty they might resort to defensive statements, or merely recite "standard" reasons, or even observe the duty in the breach (compare, for example, the post-PACE experience in relation to the stop and search recording requirements noted in Ch.6). In this context, consider Harry Street's somewhat cynical observations about the realities of reason-giving by tribunals:

"Take the ordinary case before an administrative tribunal. The citizen is never told in his papers notifying him of the hearing of his right to ask for reasons. Neither the clerk nor the chairman tells him at the hearing. When he loses and is fobbed off by the tribunal without explanation, he then goes to a solicitor for the first time. The solicitor asks the tribunal for its reasons, to be told 'Too late—if you don't ask for them at the time, you are not entitled to them.' A former member of the Council on Tribunals wrote ... that 'most tribunals give their reasons as a matter of course.' ... My experience of tribunals generally was so contrary to his that, within the next month after reading it, I made a point of visiting several different tribunals. Not one of them gave reasons within the meaning of the Act when announcing its decision. Of course I dare say they would if a member of the Council had given a fortnight's notice of his intention to attend!" (Street, 1975, p.68)

Moreover, the duty to give reasons might prove of limited value on quite another count. Just because frustrated property developers and the like often find ammunition for appeals in reasoned decision-letters, it does not follow that the giving of reasons will be as helpful to those who are less well-advised or who cannot afford to invest in legal proceedings.

This leads to a second point. The application for judicial review, somewhat after the fashion of private law remedial techniques, relies to a large extent on proceedings being initiated by aggrieved individuals. Admittedly, test cases can be brought by pressure groups (the Child Poverty Action Group, for example, regularly initiates test case applications in relation to social security matters see Roger Smith, 1986; and see generally Prosser, 1983). Also, as the GLC "fares fair" case illustrates, local authorities can mount challenges at the expense of their ratepayers (but, often, this is a device to air local government, rather than individual, grievances concerning the impingement of central government policies). The fact remains, however, that, if judicial review (as presently constituted) is to protect the individual against illegal public administration, a good deal depends upon aggrieved individuals being willing and able to bring issues to court. The problem with this is that many individuals, unlike Mr Congreve (who, it will be recalled, was a partner in a firm of City solicitors), will not realise that an issue could be taken to court, and, even if they do appreciate this, they may judge that the expense and inconvenience simply does not warrant initiating legal proceedings. Whilst such inhibitions are not peculiar to the system of administrative justice (*cf.* Ch.7), they are exacerbated by the fact that, in English law, a successful applicant for judicial review is not awarded damages for financial loss flowing from invalid administrative action (unless a separate action in negligence or the like can be brought). This means that there are limited incentives for seeking judicial review. Moreover, where an applicant is motivated by financial considerations, the court may spring a trap by denying *locus standi*. For example, in *R. v Commissioners of Customs and Excise, Ex p. Cook* (1970), two book-makers sought judicial review against the Commissioners. The applicants wanted the Commissioners to collect off-course betting tax in accordance with the letter of the law, thereby forcing some of their competitors out of business. However, the court refused this application, partly on the ground that the applicants were motivated by an ulterior purpose. Yet the irony is that, without this ulterior purpose, the bookmakers surely would have had no incentive to challenge the legality of the Commissioners' practice. Granted there are some individuals who are prepared to seek judicial review simply for the sake of securing strict compliance with the law; but such persons are few and far between and they certainly do not conform to the role-model of the commercial entrepreneur of which the courts are so enamoured in other contexts.

If judicial review is to be a more effective mechanism of control, it cannot rely on the happenstance interventions of individual applicants. Ideally, there seems to be a need for a publicly funded body, independent of government, available to receive complaints from aggrieved individuals, and able to initiate proceedings for judicial review in appropriate cases. In England, the various Ombudsmen (in particular, for both central and local government, and the National Health Service) represent the nearest approximation to such a model. The approximation, however, is far from close. For example, the remit of the Parliamentary Commissioner for Administration (the PCA), whose office was established in 1967, is to investigate complaints made by members of the public who allege that they have suffered injustice in consequence of maladministration (basically at the hands of central government departments and a number of quangos). On the positive side, the PCA's services are free to the complainant, his (or her, as it presently is) brief—maladministration—is broader than illegality as such (the general facts pleaded in *Congreve*, for instance, were also the subject of complaints to, and a report by, the PCA), and he or she regularly succeeds in obtaining *ex gratia* payments for complainants. On the negative side, however, unlike the Ombudsmen in many other jurisdictions, there is no direct access to the PCA (complaints having to be filtered through a Member of Parliament), and the PCA cannot personally initiate an investigation. Given the traditional relationship between MPs and their constituents, together with relatively easy access to MPs through their constituency "clinics", the filter system may not seem too objectionable; and the evidence is that direct access is generally opposed amongst Parliamentarians (see Drewry and Harlow, 1990, pp.758–61). Whatever the net balance between these positive and negative features of the scheme, the fact of the matter is that the case-load of the PCA is growing, with more than 2,000 complaints received in 2001–2002 (representing an increase of 24 per cent on the previous and the highest figure on record) and with the workload being maintained at a similar level. Moreover, even if the PCA's office still has a relatively low profile, it is arguable that the heavier utilisation of the PCA's services is consistent with the growing fashion for channelling complaints to both ombudsmen (as in connection with insurance, banking and legal services) and "almost ombudsmen" (e.g. the Information Commissioner; see Birkinshaw, 1991).

A further feature of judicial review is that victory for the applicant may be of a short-term nature only. The point is that public authorities may be able to rectify the invalidated decision. For example, if the court had quashed the University's decision in *Glynn* on the grounds that there had been a breach of the rules of natural justice, the University could have reconsidered the case (duly observing the requirements of natural justice) and reached precisely the same decision. It follows that the control exercised by judicial review is simply of a corrective nature. Indeed, it is open to government to respond to judicial declarations of invalidity by issuing curative regulations with retrospective effect (i.e. reversing the actual ruling in the case in question). The existence of such power at Westminster and in Whitehall raises a further concern about the adequacy of judicial review as a means of controlling government.

The doctrine of Parliamentary Sovereignty, of which the English are so proud, can be viewed in a number of different lights. Historically, it represents the limitation of arbitrary monarchial government (see Ch.3); most recently, it represents the claim of the British to regulate their own affairs free from the meddling of the Euro-bureaucrats (as, for example, in the important *Factortame* (1991) litigation where domestic legislative attempts to protect UK fishing quotas against Spanish vessels were suspended pending determination of their compatibility with EC law). However, in the context of judicial review, the doctrine is a licence for governments to change the rules at will. Judges may review the legality of public administration, but only on terms which, in the final analysis, government itself dictates. Of course, membership of the EC has important implications for the control of national governments, because Community law prevails over national law. Nevertheless, what is conspicuously lacking in the constitutional arrangements within the United Kingdom is a set of overarching domestic restrictions on government. The doctrine of Parliamentary Sovereignty coupled with representative democracy is a licence for the majority to tyrannise the minority; but, where representative democracy becomes an elective dictatorship, Parliamentary Sovereignty becomes a licence for a minority to tyrannise the majority. These observations prompt the vexed question of whether a Bill of Rights should be adopted (see, e.g. Zander, 1979; Atiyah, 1983, pp.108–12).

It has often been argued that a Bill of Rights is unnecessary. In England, it is said, civil liberties exist to the extent that fundamental freedoms (such as freedom of speech, movement, association, conscience, and so on) are not prohibited, and it would not affect the position if such freedoms were to be declared as rights. This argument, however, misunderstands the significance of according rights to individuals. As we have seen (in Ch.2), where individuals are recognised as having rights, interference with those rights calls for special justification. Accordingly, if a Bill of Rights were to be introduced, government would not be permitted to undermine the protected interests simply on the grounds of routine political convenience. Wherever there was a derogation from rights, the onus would be on government to make out a special justifying case. The point about a Bill of Rights, therefore, is that it would be much more than a well-meaning (but strictly superfluous) declaration of intent; it would guarantee rights by confining legislative competence. Once this is understood, it becomes apparent that the courts would be called upon, as upholders of the constitutional guarantee, to play a key role. To this, a number of objections may be advanced. Some argue that English judges are likely to be too conservative to give full effect to the spirit of a Bill of Rights, others that, in practice, instruments of this kind have unintended side-effects as they are exploited by powerful interests. There is also the concern that the adoption of a Bill of Rights would cast the judges more overtly in a political role, possibly leading to a diminution in public confidence in the courts and to an ideological roller-coaster of decision-making as has been the experience with the American Supreme Court (*cf.* Woodward and Armstrong, 1979). With the incorporation of the greater part of the European Convention on Human Rights into domestic law (see Ch.3 and s.5 below), the practical credentials of something akin to a Bill of Rights are to be put to the test. For, although the Human Rights Act 1998 stops short of empowering the judges to strike down primary legislation that is found to violate the protected list of rights, there can be little doubt that the Act re-writes the groundrules according to which the administration is to be open to challenge—if not quite a Bill of Rights then the Act, as Keith Ewing has remarked, "represents an unprecedented transfer of political power from the executive and legislature to the judiciary, and a fundamental re-structuring of our 'political constitution'" (Ewing, 1999, p.79; and see Griffith, 1979).

To sum up, the debate about the Bill of Rights, whatever the merits of the rival arguments, implies that the real question is not so much about controlling government, but about laying the foundations for legitimate governance. This calls for at least three things: an effective system of (judicial) review; an appreciation of the bounds of legitimate legislative and administrative competence; and strict observance by the reviewing body of its jurisdictional limits.

4. THE QUALITY OF PUBLIC ADMINISTRATION

Necessarily, decision-makers can only be held accountable for their decisions (whether by judicial review, complaints to Ombudsmen, questions in Parliament, or whatever) *after* they have made their decisions. However, it is arguable that a system of administrative justice will be deficient if it ignores procedures for public participation *prior* to decisions being made. To some extent, this may be seen as a vehicle for controlling public authorities: requirements for consultation, the opportunity to raise objections, and to make comments, and the like, may have some preventive confining influence, as well as setting up additional grounds for judicial review after the event (as the *GCHQ* case shows). However, it is equally arguable that public participation enhances the quality of public administration (making for rational, not merely, lawful governance); and that, anyway, it is unjust and undemocratic to deny citizens the right to participate directly in public decision-making (*cf.* Macpherson, 1977).

In principle, procedures for public participation might be built into a broad sweep of administrative decision-making, and might assume a wide variety of forms (ranging from the notice-and-comment procedures associated with the American Administrative Procedure Act 1946, to trial-type procedures with presentation of evidence and cross-examination of witnesses). In England, however, procedures for public participation have not been systematically incorporated into the broad field of administrative decision-making. Rather, formal public participation has tended to be confined to the area of land-use planning, where there are well-established procedures for consultation and public inquiry. In particular, public inquiries are held where strategic plans for an area are published, where new trunk roads are proposed, and, of course, where an exceptional development (such as a new London airport or power station) is proposed. The flavour of such inquiries can be gathered from the decision of the House of Lords in *Bushell v Secretary of State for the Environment* (1981). In 1972, the Secretary of State published draft schemes for the construction of two fifteen-mile sections of the M42 and M40 to the south and south-east of Birmingham. Many objections were made and a public local inquiry was held. At the opening of the inquiry, the inspector ruled that he would not restrict the scope of the discussion to the question of the proposed lines along which the motorways would be built. Instead, it would be open to the objectors to challenge the need for the motorway, but this would not extend to reviewing the government's general transport policy (and nor would it be open to the objectors to cross-examine the DoE witnesses on the question of need). Having heard the evidence on need (in particular, the DoE traffic forecasts), the inspector recommended that the draft schemes (subject to minor modifications) should be confirmed. However, in between the close of the inquiry and the inspector making his report, the DoE adopted a revised method of projecting traffic flows, in the light of which it was apparent that the objectors' case against the need for the motorways was strengthened. Nevertheless, the Secretary of State declined to re-open the inquiry and he duly accepted the inspector's recommendations. Two of the objectors applied to have the schemes quashed on the grounds inter alia that the inspector's refusal to permit cross-examination of the DoE witnesses and the Secretary of State's refusal to re-open the inquiry constituted breaches of the rules of natural justice. The House, by a majority of four to one, dismissed the application.

Bushell captures rather nicely the pros and cons of public inquiries. Dealing with the former, Lord Diplock said:

"The purpose of the inquiry is to provide the minister with as much information about those objections as will ensure that in reaching his decision he will have weighed the harm to local interests and private persons who may be adversely affected by the scheme against the public benefit which the scheme is likely to achieve and will not have failed to take into consideration any matters which he ought to have taken into consideration." (at 94)

In other words, an effective public inquiry should be instrumental in promoting a more rational decision-making process (from which, presumably, more rational decisions would follow). Put this way, therefore, one might wonder why the inquiry was not re-opened to reconsider the crucial question of the traffic projections. After all, it was the government's own policy to determine the need for (and priority to be given to) the building of a particular stretch of motorway largely by reference to the traffic forecasts; so, if the forecasts were seriously flawed, the government's decision must have been irrational. The majority of the Law Lords in *Bushell*, however, were impressed by an important countervailing consideration. Namely, that the wheels of administration tend to grind pretty slowly, and, the more the public has to be involved, the longer it takes for final decisions to be made. As it was, the public local inquiry in *Bushell* lasted for one hundred working days, spanning a period of more than six months; the inspector took eighteen months to produce his report; and the Secretary of State took another fourteen months to consider the matter before making the authorising orders. To have permitted cross-examination would have extended the proceedings; and to have re-opened the inquiry would have further delayed matters.

Whilst there is widespread academic support for the idea of participatory rights, not all writers see this as an unqualified good. Indeed, in a passage of trenchant criticism, Sir Desmond Heap throws down the gauntlet to the proponents of public participation:

"One reason why I have always had my doubts about the principle of citizen participation is that it seems to me to strike at the very roots of an elective democracy. If we do need to have this new idea, then surely this must indicate a breakdown in the customary system of democratic government by elected representatives . . . [The] elected representatives having been elected, should . . . be allowed to get on with the job.

Another argument against citizen participation is the fact that it is nearly always negative in effect .. Whenever . . . groups of citizens do turn up at an Inquiry, it is usually to criticise, in a completely negative fashion, whatever it is the local authority seeks to do. On the law of averages the local authority can't be wrong every time!

Another reason I doubt the validity of citizen participation is that it leads increasingly to what I would call 'town planning control by the angry neighbour'. I think it better that town planning control should be left in the hands of what, I hope, can still be described as a relatively impartial body, namely, the [local planning authority] . . .

One of the worst things about citizen participation is that people participating are frequently ill-informed about what is going on . . . In the outcome, they frequently fail to get what they are advocating . . . This having occurred, participating citizens are left with a sense, and sometimes a bitter sense, of frustration and the feeling that they have not had a fair deal." (1975, pp.35–6)

Much of Sir Desmond's reasoning is guided by utilitarian considerations: participation does not lead to better decisions, it frustrates disappointed participants, and—one of Sir Desmond's favourite themes—it drastically slows down the planning process. But this is not the end of the matter: against those who argue that participation facilitates rational decision-making, Sir Desmond paints a picture of uninformed, angry, negative, discourse; and, against those who argue that participation is in line with democratic requirements, he maintains that it is actually incompatible with the concept of elective democracy. This is too complex a case to attempt to rebut within the bounds of this discussion. However, three points should be borne in mind. First, as *Bushell* highlights, decision-making in a representative democracy operates at a number of levels. In the case of motorways, there are high policy decisions concerning national transport policy, local implementation decisions concerning the precise line of a particular road, and questions concerning the need to build a particular motorway at a particular time. At none of these levels, however, is it self-evident that representative democratic politics is subverted by allowing for broader public participation (e.g. by inviting comment on Green Paper transport discussion documents at the highest level, and by holding public inquiries to focus on local issues). Secondly, the reason why citizen participation is often negative is because many public inquiries are basically opportunities for objectors to be heard. It does not follow that members of the public are incapable of playing a constructive part in inquiry proceedings. Finally, if the proponents of public participation could show that individuals have a right to participate in public decisions, this would short-circuit that very considerable part of Sir Desmond's reasoning which rests on utilitarian premises (*cf*. Ch.2). We can briefly pursue this point.

One of the most sophisticated attempts to argue for participatory rights is to be found in Ian Harden and Norman Lewis' challenging book, *The Noble Lie* (1986). Their strategy is one of immanent critique (see Ch.2), arguing that the right to participate follows from the shared assumptions that we make about our constitutional arrangements. They argue that the bedrock of the constitution, the idea of the Rule of Law, not only commits us to non-arbitrariness and accountability, but also to the idea that decision-making processes should be rational. As they put it:

"Democratic concerns and the need for learning processes to ensure the efficiency of the policy process lead ineluctably to the view that some form of participatory decision-making is required as a source of knowledge, a vehicle of information and a foundation for consent." (at 72)

But, what kind of participatory right does such an argument underwrite? Given that we are dealing with a *right* to participate, participatory opportunities must not be by administrative invitation only (*cf*. the style of the examination in public for structure plans introduced in the 1970s). Even so, the idea of a *participatory* right is open to interpretation. In particular, assuming that participants are to have an advisory rather than an executive role in the decision-making, what kind of advisory role is envisaged? On one conception of a participatory right, members of the public are entitled to state their objections, to air their grievances, and generally to address the administration in a self-interested way. On another conception, the members of the public participate as advocates for the public interest, compelling the administration to take a hard look at all the options. Whilst the former view presents participation as a one-way process (the members of the public merely saying their piece to the decision-makers), the latter conceives of participation as a vehicle for a two-way informed dialogue between members of the public and the decision-makers (compare Harlow, 2002). Clearly, serious proponents of participatory rights must presuppose a conception of this latter kind (with its radical implications for open government and freedom of information). Of course, Harden and Lewis' supporting argument (being in the nature of an immanent critique) could be sidestepped if one were to deny any commitment to democracy and the Rule of Law; but, in practice, few are likely to stand on such a denial which, anyway, would surely speak for itself.

5. BACK TO THE RULE OF LAW: OVERVIEW

To return to the point at which we started this Chapter, the Rule of Law requires governments to respect due process in the sense that established procedures are to be observed. In the most general terms, as the House of Lords reminded us in the *Bennett* case (see Ch.1), compliance with the Rule of Law entails that short-cuts on the part of the administration are not to be tolerated; and, as the Court of Appeal insisted in *Congreve*, loopholes in the law are not to be rectified by mere executive fiat. The Rule of Law, in short, is not a rule of political convenience—it is a rule of procedural integrity.

Now, if we think of a legal system as having three principal sub-systems (the criminal justice system, the civil justice system, and the administrative justice system), then a running theme of the sketch offered in this and the previous two Chapters is that of a tension between the imperatives of each sub-system and the particular way in which the demands of the Rule of Law articulate themselves in each sub-system. Or, to put this another way: the reason why we can justifiably characterise the sub-systems as respectively systems of criminal *justice*, civil *justice*, and administrative *justice*, is precisely because each system incorporates (to a greater or lesser extent) the values of due process. Such an incorporation, however, does not come without cost: in each case, respect for the Rule of Law operates as a constraint on the unbridled pursuit of the system's own particular imperatives.

In the case of the criminal justice system, the tension between crime control (the system imperative) and due process has been well-rehearsed—seminally in Herbert Packer's work (1969) and by both academics and law reform bodies from then on. The Rule of Law demands that criminal offences are clearly advertised in advance, that defendants are not penalised on an ambiguity, that offences are not stretched beyond their natural range, and so on—demands, it will be recalled, that were taken seriously inter alia by Holmes J. in *McBoyle v US* (Ch.4) and, more recently, by Lord Mustill in *Brown* (Ch.6). As Lord Diplock put it in *DPP v Withers* (1974), it surely cannot be right that a defendant is convicted "if it takes days of legal argument and historical research on appeal to [the House of Lords] to discover whether any crime has been committed even though the facts are undisputed" (at 761). The Rule of Law also demands that police powers should be clearly circumscribed (as the minority emphasised in *Wills v Bowley* (Ch.4)). And, due process argues for a wide range of safeguards at all stages of the criminal justice system—from arrest, detention, and questioning, through to trial, appeal, and review—with a view to ensuring that the innocent are not convicted.

In the case of civil justice, the tension is perhaps less well-rehearsed. However, the main pressures at work are fairly obvious. On the one hand, the system imperative is the efficient resolution of disputes. On the other hand, due process demands the vindication of rights, which in turn entails that decision-makers should be impartial, that the parties should be given every opportunity to present their cases, and that, generally, procedures should be designed to elicit the truth. Such is no more than one would expect of the mainstream court system. However, adopting these standards of due process, the Franks Committee (1957) famously recommended that the tribunal system, too, albeit designed to provide cheap and informal justice, should aspire to openness, fairness, and impartiality. Unfortunately, though, accuracy is not everything—not even for the supporters of due process. For, if the unrelenting pursuit of accuracy involves expensive and cumbersome procedures, we may find that justice is delayed for some and denied altogether to many (see Zuckerman, 1994, 1996).

When we turn to the system of administrative justice, the tensions are again fairly visible. Whether one looks at the higher or the lower levels of public governance, the imperative of the system is to administer things smoothly and efficiently. Due process, however, insists that things are administered in accordance with established conventions and procedures. So, for example, when the Government tried to change the tariff under the Criminal Injuries Compensation Scheme by publication in a White Paper, the majority of the House of Lords ruled that this must be regularised by legislation, even though the proposed scheme would then be exposed to extended scrutiny and debate in Parliament (see *R. v Secretary of State for the Home Department, Ex p. Fire Brigades Union* (1995); and Ganz (1996)). Due process also dictates that citizens should have rights to participate and to hold decision-makers accountable (seminally, in the context of the administration of planning law, see McAuslan, 1980); and, as we have seen throughout this Chapter, procedural constraints of this kind may slow down decision-making and generally operate against the demands of administrative expediency. Nevertheless, if we value due process, expedient administration must take second place. As Lord Mustill put it in *Doody*:

"The giving of reasons may be inconvenient, but I can see no ground at all why it should be against the public interest: indeed, rather the reverse. This being so, I would ask simply: is a refusal to give reasons fair? I would answer without hesitation that it is not." (at 110)

The public interest, in other words, is not to be equated with whatever procedures and practices happen to suit the administration at a particular time.

Another way of looking at the relationship between the Rule of Law, due process, and the system imperatives is to focus on the element of *imposed* decision-making that is involved in the operation of a legal system. The courts are authorised to make binding rulings; the administration is authorised to make a variety of binding determinations; and, everywhere, legal officials make decisions that may or may not be in line with our preferences and to which we may or may not have specifically consented. Given that such powers are being conferred upon the courts, the administration, and legal officials in general, the Rule of Law can be understood as setting the terms on which powers are so transferred—due process is, as Lon Fuller (1969: see Ch.1) portrayed it, part of a compact that citizens make with government. It is clear, however, that bargaining (whether real or hypothetical) is not restricted to laying down the terms of a background constitutional settlement which sets the framework for governance in accordance with the Rule of Law. On the contrary, bargained decisions (in the sense of negotiated decisions to which the parties formally consent) are very much part of the day to day functioning of a legal system. Much bargaining of this kind occurs in a channel which leads directly to imposed third-party adjudication (as is the case, for example, with plea bargains made in the criminal justice system and out of court settlements made in the civil justice system); and, in the context of administrative justice, bargains may be struck with regulators in the knowledge that sanctions may be invoked by the latter should satisfactory undertakings not be obtained. There is also bargaining, however, that is situated at some distance from imposed solutions—and, indeed, one of the strands that has contributed to the growing interest in ADR (see Ch.7) is precisely the thought that it would be a good thing if disputants regained control over their conflicts in the hope that, with or without the assistance of third-party facilitators (mediators), they might define the issues in their own way and freely arrive at an acceptable resolution (see Roberts, 1993).

Although bargaining necessarily takes place in the shadow of the law, we might suppose that the ideals of the Rule of Law (and of due process in particular) have no application to bilateral negotiation and settlement—at least, we might think that such ideals have no application provided that bargained settlements (a) satisfy a test of free and informed consent, and (b) are compatible with the legally protected interests of third parties. These provisos, however, are not to be taken lightly. First, the requirement that settlements must be genuinely consensual has a considerable critical edge, for there is not always a bright line between imposed and consensual settlements, between coercive and non-coercive processes (see Ingleby, 1993; and, generally, see below). For example, plea-bargains and out of court settlements may be made in a context in which one party might be in a very much weaker negotiating position than the other (possibly because of differential resources but also because the law might exert pressure to settle, e.g. by offering certain kinds of incentives to those who are "co-operative"). Secondly, the protected interests of third parties might set significant limits to the terms of legitimate settlement. For example, a (mediated) settlement between divorcing spouses would be unacceptable if it failed to give due weight to the interests of any children of the marriage (*cf.* Bridge, 1996); and, similarly, a deal struck between a local planning authority and a developer would be unacceptable if it licensed unreasonable interference with local residents' enjoyment of their property (*cf.* English, 1996). On analysis, however, not only are these provisos not to be taken lightly, seemingly *they reconnect bilateral negotiation with the Rule of Law*—and, in particular, the requirement of informed consent (which can be unpacked to prohibit fraud and coercion, and to require good faith and disclosure, and so on) can be seen as an important articulation of the ideal of due process.

Finally, some might argue that a conception of the Rule of Law that limits itself to questions of process and procedure is too weak. The Rule of Law, it might be said, is essentially concerned with the protection of human rights, which means that due process must operate alongside a range of substantive ideals. According to Stephen Sedley (1995), for example, if "the rule of law is to mean much, it must at least mean that it is the obligation of the courts to articulate and uphold the ground rules of ethical social existence which we dignify as fundamental human rights" (p.391). On this view, government is doubly constrained: not only must it operate in accordance with its own published procedures, it must not trench on (substantive) human rights. The force of such a double constraint was nicely illustrated in Lord Mustill's dissenting opinion in the *Brown* case. As we have seen, his Lordship was concerned that the charges put under sections 20 and 47 of the Offences Against the Person Act 1861 involved stretching those offences beyond their intended range (thus violating due process). However, Lord Mustill also expressed reservations about the very idea of penalising the defendants' conduct, the argument being that there must be a freedom-based right to engage in any activity free of criminal sanction provided that (as Mill put it) the tangible interests of (non-consenting) others are not harmed thereby. In other words, the Rule of Law can be violated both by the way in which the criminal justice system operates as well as by the substance of the criminal law.

If the courts are the custodians of the Rule of Law, it matters a great deal whether we confine the Rule of Law to matters of due process or whether we also recognise it as having a substantive dimension. Without addressing this question, the respective responsibilities of the administration and the courts will lack any clear and principled base; and, as Harden and Lewis (1986) have remarked, this has led the English courts to vacillate between:

"a helpless quietism and an active interventionism which has too often appeared to depend on the judges' views of the merits of particular policies rather than upon a view of their role in the constitutional order of things." (p.203)

And, to be sure, so it must have seemed in the 1980s. However, the 1990s saw a transformation of the constitutional landscape. First, in a flurry of extra-judicial writing, incorporation of the

European Convention on Human Rights was advocated and, more generally, it was claimed that the courts should play a leading role in the protection of human rights (see e.g. Browne-Wilkinson, 1992; Bingham, 1993; Laws, 1993; Sedley, 1995). Secondly, in the courts, the judges increasingly showed a willingness to be guided by the principles of the Convention (see Hunt, 1997) as well as to follow the lead given by Lord Bridge in *Bugdaycay v Secretary of State for the Home Department* (1987) that, where administrative decisions impinged on fundamental human rights, then they must be subjected to "anxious scrutiny" (at 531). Thirdly, the principal Convention rights were duly incorporated into domestic law by the Human Rights Act 1998 (see Ewing, 1999). With the Act still bedding in to the jurisprudence of English law, it is too early to be confident about its impact. It is important to remember, however, that there are any number of ways in which the courts can take the sting out of challenges that rely on the Act to allege a violation of Convention rights. As Dianne Pretty's case (2001) highlighted, the courts might decide that a particular Convention right is not engaged—the right to life, for instance, may be held not to include the right to die. Even if the right is engaged, it may be a right which the Convention allows to be limited in the public interest (such is the case, for example, with the Convention rights to private life and to freedom of expression); and the courts may, in the particular case, defer to Parliament's judgment concerning the requirements of the public interest (*cf.* Edwards, 2002; Ewing, 2004; and Steyn, 2005). The scheme of the Act also discourages confrontation between judges and politicians. In particular, section 3(1) places the courts under an interpretive obligation to read down legislation, "so far as it is possible to do so", in a way that is compatible with the Convention rights. In the light of our account of interpretation earlier in the book, we can take it that courts wishing to avoid a head-on challenge will find extensive possibilities for reading down legislation in this way. Even if the legislation goes beyond the bounds of possibility (or permissibility) under section 3(1), unlike in some jurisdictions, the Act does not empower the courts to "strike down" or "strike out" legislation that violates Convention rights; in the last resort, section 4 provides for the courts to issue a declaration of incompatibility. The effect of such a declaration—even though it creates some pressure for local law to be brought into line with the Convention and, indeed, invites the use of a fast-track procedure for compliance—is *not* that the offending legislation is rendered invalid. Nevertheless, despite the scope for interpretation built into and around the Convention rights, and despite the measures within the Act that are designed to maintain Parliamentary sovereignty, it would be worrying if, from time to time, judges did not rely on the Act to hand down decisions that challenge government policy. Where human rights so pinch, politicians may squeal and even threaten to further confine their impact, for example, by invoking the provisions for derogation as per Article 15 of the Convention (see Lester, 2003). Quite where this leaves the courts, and the long-term future of the Convention rights, within "the constitutional order of things" is a moot point. However, if we take the Rule of Law seriously, the commitment to human rights is an encouraging sign and the Act has to be regarded as one of the cornerstones of any constitutional settlement that will serve in the twenty-first century (*cf.* Lewis, 1996).

9

THE LEGAL PROFESSION AND LEGAL SERVICES

In this Chapter we attempt to explain the present form of the legal profession, and the role of that profession in society. Most people know that the legal profession in this country is divided into solicitors and barristers. What is less frequently realised is that these professions compete for certain kinds of legal work with other professions. Thus, accountants deal with such things as tax and company liquidations. Patent agents and trade mark attorneys handle both contentious and non-contentious intellectual property work. Insurance brokers advise on such matters as pension schemes. In fact, if we think about the entire field of legal services provided by these groups, we may begin to have some inkling of the answer to that hoary old question: why do we need lawyers?

A feature of modern states is the all-pervasiveness of bureaucracy, using that term in the non-pejorative sense in which it was used by Weber (i.e. a rule-governed administration with a specialisation of function). Inevitably we lack the time, and possibly the inclination, to instruct ourselves in every aspect of the bureaucracy with which we need to be familiar in order to maximise our opportunities. For example, a person who sets up in business as a joiner will no doubt wish to maximise his or her earnings in the trade which he or she knows and understands. He or she will work very long hours and possibly devote such free time as he or she has to securing work. He or she will need, however, to make arrangements for the keeping of accounts for the Inland Revenue, and possibly also VAT. He or she will need to know when and if he or she should incorporate. He or she will also be well advised to make provision for retirement. He or she may need to rent a workshop. All of these matters require knowledge of highly technical areas of law. It is usually more economical for the joiner to work at what he or she understands, and along with others in a similar position, to partake of the time of persons who already have expertise in the relevant fields of law, such as accountants, insurance brokers and solicitors. The real puzzle in the modern world then is not why we need people with legal expertise, but why in England and Wales the persons providing legal expertise have come to be divided up in the way they are. It should be noted that England and Wales is not alone in dividing up legal work amongst a number of professions. Indeed, some sort of division is the rule, but, largely for historical reasons, the nature of the division varies. Since the Access to Justice Act 1999, both solicitors and barristers have had equal rights of audience in all courts, and the Lord Chancellor can extend rights of audience to other professions, and has done so (see p.192).

The guild origin of the legal professions (outlined in s.3 below) was reflected in the fact that, up to the Second World War, the principal requirement for qualifying either as a solicitor or as a barrister was to serve a period of apprenticeship (known as "articles" in the case of solicitors, and "pupillage" in the case of barristers), and to pass the relevant professional body's examinations (the requirement of passing an examination was in the case of both professions a reform of the Victorian era). If would-be solicitors or barristers went to university, it was not usually to study law. A number of university law schools did exist, but all were by modern standards very small, and most tended to subsist largely by virtue of articled clerks doing a year's course required by the Law Society, and part-time students reading for a degree at the same time as doing their articles. This situation began to change in the post-war period, to the extent that by the end of the 1960s taking a law degree had become the usual first stage in qualifying either as a solicitor or as a barrister. The "three-tier" pattern which has subsisted for roughly the last forty years has been a law degree, a professional legal practice course, and a period of traineeship or pupillage. Many students also take non-law degrees and "convert" by taking a one year course and the Common Professional Examination. In some areas of practice a science degree is more-or-less a requirement.

We have noted in Chapter 7 that the Courts and Legal Services Act 1990 was something of a watershed in relation to the civil justice system. The Act could also, in principle, effect far-reaching changes in the present structure of legal education. It is likely that the first stage will remain much as it is at present, though changes may be made to the list of "core courses" a student is required to take for a degree to qualify for exemption from Part I of the professional examinations. The main change so far has been that in the second stage, some of the teaching of the College of Law has been transferred to certain universities, and similarly the course formerly taught only in the Inns of Court School of Law/City University is now taught in seven other law schools.

The Act also made it possible to extend the right of doing conveyancing to building societies and banks (s.36), but these provisions have never been brought into force. In practice, licensed conveyancers, authorised under the 1988 Act, are few in number and the solicitors' monopoly on conveyancing, in practice, remains intact. The origins of this monopoly are explained at p.267. For the present it may be noted that its existence was important in enabling solicitors to subsidise non-economic work, notably in providing legal services to those unable to afford them. The income from ordinary conveyancing is now much reduced, however, not by competition from non-solicitors, but by competition between solicitors themselves. A combination of the abolition of scale charges (fixed fees based on the value of the property conveyed) which had to be charged by all solicitors, and the abolition of the prohibition on advertising, have enabled the public to shop around for the cheapest deal. We can start by examining this problem of legal services for the poor in some detail.

1. LEGAL SERVICES FOR THE POOR

The problem of providing legal services for poor persons is an enduring one. It is a product of the growth of a formally rational legal system and the need for expert legal advisers thereby created. It has been pointed out that most people do not have the time, inclination or ability to familiarise themselves with the law. As a result, they may fail to secure their entitlements.

The problem is as old as the legal system. In the earliest period, it would appear that the clergy with whom, as we explain on p.264, the early development of the legal system was associated, would offer legal assistance. Even after 1217 when they were forbidden to plead in court, it would seem that clergy could appear for poor persons, basing this duty on Isaiah 1: 17: "Do justice for the fatherless, plead for the widow". Mediaeval kings in any event regarded it as a duty to ensure that poor persons had access to justice in the sense of being regarded as equal before the law (poverty itself being regarded as part of the natural order of things). In some parts of the country, it is possible that local courts were accessible to the poor. Coke (1552–1634) observed that it was the wisdom of the common law that men should not be troubled with suits of small value in the king's courts, but that they should be determined and heard in the country with small charge and little or no travel and loss of time (2 Inst. 311). This implies that local courts were functioning at the time. The truth is, however, that the traditional local jurisdictions had tended to decline in the later Middle Ages. This was the reason why from the sixteenth century local Courts of Requests or Good Conscience began to be established modelled upon Henry VIII's Court of Request (see below), but at the time Coke was writing few such courts would have existed. Over the ensuing period up to the organisation of the county courts in 1846, however, Courts of Requests were established in many parts of the country. Their jurisdictional limit was £5. Procedure was cheap and expeditious, but they tended to become traders' debt-collecting courts (see Winder, 1936). Eventually, they were absorbed into the county courts system.

In the Middle Ages the General Eyres on their visitations (see p.52) would hear complaints from poor persons, but such visitations were, in the nature of things, sporadic. From Henry III's reign (and probably earlier), the Common Law Courts could issue writs free to poor persons. In 1494 (2 Hen VII c.12), it was provided that indigent plaintiffs (today "claimants") (but not defendants) should have free process and representation (the "*forma pauperis*" procedure). Defendants were not included in the scheme until the nineteenth century. The endemic problem of the vexatious litigant was dealt with by the threat of flogging or the pillory for unsuccessful pauper plaintiffs (claimants) (23 Hen VIII c.15 (1531) which provided that a poor person was not to be liable for his opponent's costs but for "such other punishment as shall be thought reasonable", this being interpreted in Elizabeth's reign as meaning whipping or the pillory (see Egerton, 1945)— the rule about non-liability for costs did not apply in Chancery: *Scatchmer v Foulkard* (1701)). A more humane way of dealing with this problem was introduced in 1774 by requiring counsel's certificate as to the merits of the case, a system which however had the fundamental flaw that counsel was generally given no other statement of the facts than that of the pauper applicant. In the sixteenth century, the civil law Court of Requests and the Star Chamber (which dealt with ordinary civil business as well as the State trials for which it is notorious) offered justice to poor persons. It is also to be borne in mind that there was no formal prohibition on contingency fees (see p.210 *et seq.*) until 1853 (Rule 28 Trinity Term). It is quite possible that cases such as *Armory v*

Delamirie (1722), in which a sweep's boy successfully sued a jeweller who refused to return to him a jewel he had found in a chimney, were dealt with on this basis. If so, the boy's legal representatives would have committed the tort of champerty, and the fee would have been irrecoverable, though this would not have affected the boy's right to the jewel (see *Hilton v Wood* (1863)). In practice, the likelihood of an attorney failing to recover his fees from a successful plaintiff would probably be slight.

The *forma pauperis* procedure did not apply in the county courts (see however *Chinn v Bullen* (1849), not followed in *Cook v Imperial Tobacco* (1922)) which, like the Courts of Requests they replaced, tended to be traders' debt-collecting courts. In 1883 the *forma pauperis* procedure set up by Henry VII was modified. A new High Court procedure substituted a requirement for applicants to be worth less than £25 (for contemporary critiques see Sprigge, 1891, and *The Times* leader of December 30, 1912; as to the rather better scheme in operation in Scotland, having its origins in an Act as early as 1424, see Stoddart, 1979). The scheme covered both plaintiffs (claimants) and defendants. Unfortunately, it preserved the worst features of the former system. Counsel still advised on the merits on the basis of the applicant's statement alone. In consequence, cases received assistance which had no prospect of success in court. Moreover, no provision was made for the expense of assembling evidence, including witness expenses. The scheme covered only the lawyers' services which were provided free. When the Lawrence Committee examined the workings of the scheme in 1919 it found that out of the certificates granted under the scheme, 2215 out of 4101 applications made, 2137 were in respect of matrimonial matters (Lawrence, 1919). Many who obtained certificates were unable to file their petitions because they were unable to afford the out-of-pocket expenses. It was the fact that such a high percentage of the scheme's resources were devoted to matrimonial matters which resulted in its near collapse with the demobilisation of troops in the aftermath of the First World War. In 1923 the Law Society took over its administration. It ran the scheme up to the establishment of the Legal Aid Board by the 1988 Act. This, in turn, is now superseded by the Community Legal Service (see p.207).

In effect therefore, until the arrival of the modern Legal Aid Scheme in 1949, the representation of poor persons was largely dependent upon the charity of the legal profession (for critiques of the situation between the wars—see Gurney-Champion, 1945; *Solicitor*, 1932). To put the seemingly disproportionate amount of resources devoted to matrimonial disputes into perspective, two points need to be made. First of all, the other major cause of poor persons' litigation, namely industrial injuries, was to a large extent looked after by trade unions, and the Women and Children's Protection Societies in various parts of the country would finance litigation in their field of activity (as would certain other charities). Secondly, few other problems affecting poor people were likely to be defined as "legal", as those who gave their services to the Poor Men's Law Centres discovered (see Egerton, 1945, Ch.XIV—Egerton was Registrar of Cambridge House Free Legal Advice Centre which in 1943 dealt with 4367 new cases and recovered £5000 for clients, which was a great deal in 1943, especially for poor people). Nevertheless, to modern eyes it does appear strange that such a great proportion of scarce resources needed to be devoted to matrimonial matters, particularly the obtaining of the actual divorce itself. It must be recalled, however, that divorce at the time required proof of a matrimonial "offence" such as adultery. Nowadays, the dissolution of a marriage is a relatively cheap bureaucratic act, and most resources go on the more obviously problematic aspects of the dissolution such as financial arrangements, and arrangements for the children. However, the modern position has been reached only after a significant shift in moral climate. Those who regret this shift might reflect on the costs; not to mention hypocrisy, of the old system (for entertaining accounts of the fabrication of evidence of adultery where money was no object see A. P. Herbert's novel *Holy Deadlock*, and Evelyn Waugh's *A Handful of Dust*).

The Legal Aid and Advice Act 1949 implemented the recommendations of the wartime Rushcliffe Committee. This Act made provision for the payment of legal fees by the state, from a fund administered by the Law Society (a system which remained unchanged until the Legal Aid Act 1988 transferred administration to the Legal Aid Board—now superseded by the Community Legal Service. Nevertheless, even after the introduction of this scheme, considerable subsidies were provided by the legal profession. In the first place a ten per cent deduction was made from the fees paid from the Legal Aid Fund as the profession's contribution to it. Secondly, preliminary advice, and the work entailed in getting a legal aid certificate were done either for no charge or for a nominal fee. Even after the introduction of the so-called "pink form" scheme, and the later "green form" scheme, this sort of work was not really profitable. Consequently, while most firms would do such work as a social duty, they did not go out of their way to seek it. This, coupled with the long maintained bar on advertising legal services (now abolished see p.254), meant that there was in society quite a lot of what in the 1960s came to be referred to as "unmet legal need" (see Morris, White and Lewis, 1973).

The laws affecting poor people were becoming ever more complex, especially social security laws, but it was not worth the while of most solicitors to specialise in advising people whether or not they were getting their due. It was also felt that the middle-class image solicitors had frightened people off, so that those suffering such misfortunes as minor personal injuries for which they might claim did not do so. There was undoubtedly truth in these perceptions, though, paradoxically, those frequently in trouble in the criminal courts (where they would be legally aided), often came to regard the solicitors who acted for them in these matters as their family solicitors to whom they would turn for advice on other matters.

Nevertheless, there remained many in need of legal assistance who did not obtain it. In response, Law Centres were conceived, as an extension of the "Poor Man's Lawyer" movement, mentioned above. This had started in the 1890s as an adjunct of the Church Settlement Movement and had resulted in the establishment of such places as Cambridge House and Toynbee Hall, both in the East End of London (see Blott, 1917; Egerton, 1945, Ch.4). When the Finlay Committee (1928) examined the problem in 1928 there were about 55 Poor Men's Law Centres in London, and seventy in the provinces staffed by lawyers giving their services voluntarily. The need for such centres was felt to be diminished by the introduction of the Legal Aid scheme in 1949, and it was only when, in the 1960s it was realised that many people were not being helped by the scheme that the modern Law Centres were set up in various poor neighbourhoods of the larger industrial cities. Sometimes they were sponsored by local authorities, sometimes by charitable trusts, sometimes in other ways. They were staffed at least partly by barristers or solicitors, and would recoup some of their overheads from the Legal Aid fund. Many of their cases were referred from the Citizens Advice Bureaux, themselves set up in 1939 partly as a response to the same problems. A similar Law Centre movement had started in the United States before the British one, but it was largely as an adjunct to the clinical programmes operating in various law schools. In Britain, the teaching of professional skills is not an important part of a university law course (because they are taught at graduate level in the professional schools). Consequently, very few British law schools have been involved in such programmes.

At present, the budgetary problems of some local authorities make the future of the Centres they fund problematic (see Cunningham, 2001). Law centres are largely dependent on local authority funding (though, firms of solicitors and businesses do provide some funding as well), and at the best of times this has been patchy. The Law Centre movement has undoubtedly helped a lot of people who might not otherwise have been helped. However, a problem which the more radical members of the movement quickly came up against was that their clients shared certain problems, problems ultimately susceptible only to a political solution, problems thrown up by laws and procedures formulated by groups more politically powerful than they were (see Morris, White and Lewis, 1973, p.48: "Whose law is it that defines unmet need?"). One solution was to attempt to exert collective pressure by unionising. Thus a Claimants' Union was formed for those in receipt of social security benefits, both with a view to advising and helping claimants to get their entitlements, and to lobby on their behalf for changes in the law. A union for prisoners was also formed (Preservation of the Rights of Prisoners (PROP)), both to improve the conditions of prisoners, and to help them after discharge. Again, like the Law Centre movement, these bodies no doubt helped some people, but ultimately they succeeded only partially in their objectives. Some Law Centres have also seen their role as fostering group action, educating communities about their rights, orchestrating campaigns for or against legislative change, and selecting test cases to fight in order to gain changes in the law, or to highlight anomalies. This strategy had its limitations, however, and also had in some cases the unfortunate result of providing an excuse for the removal of local authority financial support on the ground that these activities were "political" (see e.g. Cooper, 1983, pp.268–70, for the closure of the Hillingdon law centre).

The problem is an extremely complex one, and the solution of simply putting more money into the then Legal Aid Fund would not, for the reasons explained above, have produced the results that might have been hoped for. Although the legal aid scheme was undoubtedly considered by many at its inception to be a counterpart of the National Health Service, the analogy is misleading. Apart from anything else, as the Finlay Committee observed. "It is manifestly in the interests of the State that its citizens should be healthy, not that they should be litigious" (1928, para.17—a passage worth thinking about at a number of levels). Moreover, as was pointed out above in relation to divorce, a change in the law can remove the need to litigate.

The response to the problem in the 1980s was to try to make the system cheaper to operate, by simplifying procedure, and by increasing competition (enabling legal services to be advertised for the first time). These approaches culminated in the Courts and Legal Services Act 1990 and the Civil Procedure Act 1997.

At the same time, the Legal Services Commission has been set up with a fixed budget (see p.207), and a large amount of work previously paid for under the legal aid scheme has been transferred to the conditional fees scheme. Adding to our earlier remarks concerning the success of this latter scheme, it should be noted that research at Sheffield University for the Law Society (Shapland *et al*, 1998) found the following:

- The poorest clients were not able to afford the insurance premiums which are an important feature of the scheme (see pp.210–211);
- Those with risky cases may find it difficult to find a solicitor to take them on; and
- Especially in the case of accidents at work (and this can apply in other cases as well), it is difficult for the solicitor to estimate the likely cost, and often at the end of the day, cases have cost solicitors more than the fee they are allowed to charge.

Later studies have pointed to similar conclusions. In short, there has probably been a significant reduction in the legal services the poor used to receive.

In criminal cases, historically the problem of the unrepresented poor defendant did not really exist; in serious matters, felonies, the rule was, until 1836, that the defendant could have no representation, nor could he or she give evidence. Behind this prohibition lay the theory that the judge acted as counsel for the accused, and it is evident from such judges' court notebooks as have survived from the eighteenth century that judges did in fact act in this way, some no doubt more zealously than others. There is also evidence that assize judges "bent the rules" and sometimes allowed representation (see Cockburn, 1972). The rule barring defendants from being represented was changed in 1836 (6 & 7 Wm. IV c.114 s.1); while the rule preventing the defendant from giving evidence was not abrogated until as late as 1898 (Criminal Evidence Act 61 & 62 Vict. c.36 s.1).

In cases where representation was permitted, there was the "dock brief" scheme under which the defendant could instruct any barrister in court on payment of one guinea (if he did not have this amount the judge selected counsel for him). Senior counsel tended to flee when they saw the possibility of a dock brief coming their way, and in practice the system offered an opportunity for young counsel to gain experience in advocacy.

Under the scheme originally set up by the Poor Prisoners' Defence Act 1903 and revised by subsequent Acts, the defendant was permitted to apply either to the Police Court (i.e. magistrates' court) or to the trial court for a defence certificate, if he had insufficient means and in other cases if it was desirable in the interests of justice. Local authorities funded this scheme, and the wide variations in applying it in different courts no doubt in part reflected the parsimoniousness or otherwise of particular local administrations, especially as many magistrates were also local councillors (see *Solicitor* (1932), who states that the then current Act was a dead letter in the provinces). Criminal proceedings were not brought under state funding until the Legal Aid Act 1974.

Under the present scheme which, it will be recalled, was brought into being by the Access to Justice Act 1999, the courts continue to be able to grant a defendant legal aid; but, eventually, it is intended that the Legal Services Commission should have the responsibility for granting rights of representation in criminal cases. The considerations that are relevant to deciding whether or not to grant legal aid (which are similar to those applicable before the 1999 Act came into force) are:

- whether the person concerned would, if the case were to be decided against him or her, be likely to lose his or her liberty or livelihood or suffer serious damage to his or her reputation;
- whether the case involves a substantial point of law;
- whether the person concerned may be unable to understand the proceedings or to state his or her own case;
- whether the proceedings may involve the tracing, interviewing or expert cross-examination of defence witnesses; and
- whether it is in the interests of another person that the defendant is represented.

In addition, the defendant is means tested. Those on job seekers' allowance or otherwise having low incomes get representation free; others have to pay a contribution. At present, the defendant can choose any lawyer from those having a contract with the Legal Services Commission (the Commission having signed criminal contracts with about 3,000 solicitors' offices). However, in May 2001, the Public Defender Service (PDS) was launched in Liverpool, under which scheme the Commission directly employs solicitors to provide criminal defence services. There are now a number of PDS offices in operation and this gives the Commission a further option as to the delivery of criminal defence work (see p.165 above).

This section will probably have served, amongst other things, to reinforce readers' preconceptions about the two branches of the legal profession. The ground covered in the following section will, we hope, begin to reveal some features of the legal landscape that the reader may not have thought about. It will serve as an introduction to the attempt to understand the legal profession at the present day, which we make in the third section.

2. THE DEATH OF THE BAR?

At the opposite end of the market, as it were, the last thirty years or so have seen the burgeoning of large international commercial law firms. These possess the armies of specialised lawyers needed to deal with large company flotations and mergers, large-scale construction contracts and the like. An inhibition to the further expansion of such firms is felt by many people to be the rule preventing solicitors from forming partnerships with other professions. As noted at the outset, accountants and insurance brokers handle work which in many countries is handled by lawyers. Consequently, there are provisions in the Courts and Legal Services Act enabling this rule to be relaxed. This has led the Bar to fear that it might be relaxed in favour of barristers becoming partners of solicitors, so that a whole generation of bright but struggling young barristers might be snapped up by City firms and their equivalents in the provinces. Although in the short term this would not affect the Bar much, in the longer term it could lead to the demise of the profession, because as the older generation retired, the work they had done would have to be taken over by solicitors' firms. But would the disappearance of the Bar be an unmitigated disaster?

Just as there is a great disparity between solicitors' practices, so is there between those of barristers. Whilst numerically the common law bar which handles crime and common law civil work is the greater, there are many barristers carrying on practices in the specialised fields. What these specialists offer, amongst other things, is a service to general solicitors' practices which cannot afford to employ a specialist because they have insufficient work to justify the expense of retaining them. So, for example, small businesses sometimes get involved in trade mark disputes with large companies. They go along to their local solicitors who advise them on their business generally, and they instruct a barrister specialising in trade marks. The solicitor is, in effect, time-sharing that barrister with other firms of solicitors, patent agents and trade mark attorneys who instruct him or her. Although the services of such specialist barristers do not come cheaply, they do tend to come more cheaply than those of the firms of solicitors who employ specialists in such things. The reason for this is that barristers' overheads are often as much as two-thirds lower than those of solicitors. This is partly because barristers need less office space than solicitors because they employ little in the way of secretarial help, and because they often share rooms. It is this factor of lower overheads which has been responsible for the growth of new sets of common law Chambers in various parts of the country where they have taken over the work abandoned by the local firms of solicitors because they cannot make it pay. Barristers can by contrast make a reasonable income out of it.

Economic considerations of this sort tend to be overshadowed in debates about the reform of legal services by a cloud of rhetoric about "professional standards". But, it is unlikely that removal of the Bar's monopolies will bring about its demise, though the removal of the prohibition on partnerships with solicitors might.

3. UNDERSTANDING THE LEGAL PROFESSION AT THE PRESENT DAY

In order to understand the present form of the legal profession in England and Wales, it is necessary to consider its historical development. Whilst this will tell us something about the function of the professional bodies, it will not tell us very much. To attempt a deeper analysis, we then consider various sociological explanations.

(i) Historical development

(a) The emergence of barristers

As we explained in Chapter 3, unlike most parts of the Continent, England saw the very early emergence of a centralised system of justice associated with the Royal Court. At first the judges of the Court of Common Bench (which would become the Court of Common Pleas) were civil servants, some indeed were clergy, for, as we noted in Chapter 3, there is an important link between the Church, which since its early days had run itself on rational bureaucratic lines, and the development of formally rational legal systems in the secular field. The development of the common law can be viewed as the spread of bureaucratic rationality into fields formerly the preserve of tradition and charisma. In particular, the common law courts were largely to supplant the ancient local courts, notably those of the shire and hundred. By about 1200 it is possible to say that the judicial function had become a specialisation separate from other civil service roles: we have a judicial profession, with judges being appointed from those who had served as apprentices to the previous generation of judges.

A legal profession operating in the central courts appeared in the course of the thirteenth century. Two factors must have facilitated this development: the language of the court was Norman French; and the simple problem of geography—it was impossible to make all the journeys necessary from a litigant's local estates to the Royal Court in order to conduct a case as a personal litigant. Litigants therefore required both persons who could speak for them in court, and agents or attorneys for procedural purposes who could stand in their shoes and act on their behalf and bind them in their absence, or excuse their non-appearance (see Palmer, 1976). In the early days there does not appear to have been a clear division between the persons who performed these quite distinct functions. In the later thirteenth century it seems that the Common Bench judges were deciding who they would permit to appear as advocates before them, and that these persons were beginning to form an elite which stood apart from other legal practitioners. During the fourteenth century, this elite group of pleaders in the Common Bench was organised into a guild known as the "order of serjeants at law". Admission of a person to this guild was conducted by the judges of the Common Bench. (An interesting account of the life of a serjeant, "Sir William Shareshull" who lived from *c.*1289 to 1370, during a crucial period in the development of the legal profession, can be found in Putnam, 1950.)

The order of serjeants declined in the later Middle Ages along with the Court of Common Bench, which lost business to other courts, notably the King's Bench. By the eighteenth century the Common Bench had become a shadow of its former self, but judges of the Royal courts were still required to be serjeants. From early in the sixteenth century, however, barristers other than serjeants were appointed to the bench, being formally created serjeant simply for the purpose. The need for this formality was only dropped when the High Court was created in 1875. By the 1670s the order of serjeants had been overtaken in importance by the King's Counsel, the first such patent having been granted to Francis Bacon in 1603.

As well as the serjeants there were other practitioners who might practise as advocates in the Court of King's Bench, the Chancery, the Exchequer and before the judges on circuit, as well as in the lesser courts. They might also practise as legal advisers to magnates, as attorneys and perform various of the other legal tasks required at the time. By the second part of the thirteenth century it would appear that some sort of legal education was available, for texts of lectures and disputations survive. In the 1280s there was a group of students referred to as "apprentices of the bench". They sat in a special gallery in the Court of Common Bench known as "the crib". In the fourteenth century the legal apprentices began to concentrate themselves in accommodation around the area where the four Inns of Court now stand. In a typically medieval way, the accommodation shared by these apprentices was organised along collegiate lines, as in the monasteries, collegiate churches, or the colleges at Oxford and Cambridge; and food and drink were taken communally. There were many of these collegiate establishments, but, by the early fifteenth century, the present four Inns had emerged predominant, and were henceforth known as the "four Inns of Court". There continued to be a number of lesser establishments known as the Inns of Chancery, of which by 1500 there were nine, each associated with a particular Inn of Court. These were the Inns of the attorneys and clerks. They survived into the nineteenth century, but became redundant with the organisation of the attorneys and solicitors through the Law Society (which in 1823 succeeded an earlier body known as The Society of Gentlemen Practisers, being incorporated by Royal Charter in 1832). By Tudor times, the Inns of Court and Chancery were regarded as the "Third

University of England", providing lectures and other forms of teaching for their students.

The civil lawyers, who practised as barristers in the Court of Admiralty, the Court of Requests, and certain other tribunals organised themselves in a similarly collegiate manner, the institution in their case being known as Doctors' Commons. But there was an important difference in their education: they studied their Roman law at university. As explained elsewhere (Adams and Brownsword, 2004, Ch.2), the conflicts associated with the civil war period were to result in a severe curtailment of the work of the civil law courts. The disruption caused by the war itself also effectively ended the educational function of the Inns of Court.

(b) The emergence of solicitors
Just as the Common Bench came to regulate those who could appear before it, it also came to regulate those who could carry out the procedural side of litigation on behalf of clients: issuing process, entering judgment etc. Those attorneys who were recognised by the Court were regarded as "officers" of it (solicitors at the present day are officers of the Court). In the sixteenth century, litigation in the Court of King's Bench burgeoned. Here, as in the case of all courts other than the Common Bench, it would appear that there was at first no regulation as to who could appear or act for litigants.

In the fifteenth century, another occupation appears, that of "solicitor". These were persons who "solicited causes", helped clients through the legal labyrinth, instructing on their behalf attorneys or counsel as need be. There seems to have been a view that only barristers or attorneys could act as solicitors. Indeed in the later sixteenth century an attempt was made to ensure that solicitors had to be young barristers exclusively. However, it seems that simple shortage of manpower doomed this attempt to failure, for there was sufficient advocacy work to occupy the Bar, leaving the preliminary interviews with clients and procedural matters to the solicitors and attorneys. As a result, in the seventeenth century, the division of responsibility between the newer professions of solicitor and barrister mirrored that between attorney and serjeant of an earlier period. Out of such divisions formal rules emerged preventing barristers from undertaking the work of solicitors, and excluding attorneys from the Inns of Court. During the late seventeenth and eighteenth centuries the status of solicitors increased rapidly. They, after all, acted as the legal advisers to the wealthy. The general increase in prosperity, and the proliferation of wealthy potential clients, necessarily increased the demand for the services which solicitors offered. Elaborate devices were devised, for example, to ensure that the family estate could not be frittered away through the profligacy of one particular incumbent, just as at the present day solicitors and accountants devise elaborate schemes to ensure that family wealth is not frittered away unnecessarily in taxes.

By the Napoleonic wars at the end of the century, as a group solicitors were sufficiently rich and important to be regarded as a fruitful source of revenue for the war effort. In 1804, partly in order to palliate solicitors for an increase in the stamp duty which both deeds of partnership and articles of clerkship attracted they were granted a monopoly over conveying land for a fee (44 Geo. III *c*.98 s.14). This was the end of a long battle for conveyancing work with the Scriveners' Company (chartered by James I in 1616), a battle which the solicitors profession had largely won by the early eighteenth century. In the course of the nineteenth century, solicitors were to absorb the work of their civil law equivalents the proctors, notably in probate, divorce and Admiralty work. They also acquired rights of audience in the new County Courts which were set up in 1846 (see Abel-Smith and Stevens, 1967, Ch.3).

The conveyancing monopoly may have fulfilled one of its original purposes, which was to raise standards, but it also had some undesirable consequences. Many solicitors' practices came to depend on it as their principal source of income, even subsidising other non-profitable work from it, such as assistance for poor persons. The traditional system of unregistered conveyancing is cumbersome and inefficient, but the fear of losing income under a system of registered conveyancing led solicitors to drag their feet with regard to reform. A feature of advanced market societies is that land comes to be regarded as a commodity like any other. In consequence, the public cannot see why the purchase of land should involve more formalities than the purchase of a car. In fact, it cannot be quite so simple (even though most conveyancing is now of registered land), for the obvious reason that the number of third-party interests which can affect land are inherently greater than those which can affect goods—you cannot have a right of way over a motor car for example!—but that is not something which the public tend to think about. The political response to this was the licensed conveyancer scheme introduced by Part II of the Administration of Justice Act 1985. As noted above this scheme has had little impact. However, the increased competition between solicitors firms has, as noted above (see p.254), resulted in a sharp reduction in ordinary conveyancing fees. As noted above, the money generated from conveyancing helped to subsidise non-profitable work for those who could not afford to pay market rate fees. With this income gone, no doubt the majority of the profession will concentrate on profitable work, though some individuals may provide their services to the poor "pro bono".

(ii) What is a legal profession?

The above account of the development of the modern form of the legal profession, may have suggested to the reader a number of questions about the role of the profession at various stages of its development. The following account may suggest some answers to those questions. Our focus is the role of the professions at the present day.

We will recall Durkheim's point about the fragmentation of values in advanced industrial societies (p.179). Durkheim also suggested that in such societies the collapse of traditional moral order could be rectified only by the formation of moral communities based upon occupational membership. This theme was developed by others who suggested that professions were distinguished from entities trading in the market-place by their orientation towards the provision of services to the community. According to Parsons (Parsons, 1968) the professions were orientated towards their collectivity, rather than their own individual members. Indeed, some even argued that this professional ethic would spread into industry, leading to a new moral order. Others regarded the professions, especially the legal profession, as bulwarks against the encroachment of state bureaucracy. By contrast Weber viewed the legal profession as *part of* the process of bureaucratisation—a view which, we have suggested, is informative. The growth of monopolistic practices on the part of the legal professions can thus be seen as part of the problem of bureaucracies generally. C. Wright Mills (Mills, 1956), far from regarding the spread of professionalism as an expansion of a service ethic viewed it as symptomatic of the explosion of experts and technocrats in modern societies, and narrow specialism tends to go with narrow vision.

Parsons, as noted above, considered that professions were community-orientated occupations applying a systematic body of knowledge to problems which are highly relevant to the central values of society. The legal profession, in his view, is thus a paradigm case. The problem, however, with a modern society is to identify what interests are shared equally by all sections and interests in that society. The legal profession will, inevitably, not apply values which are of equal relevance, or are even shared by all (Rueschmeyer, 1964). The Parsonian view entails that the rewards earned by the legal profession be commensurate with society's need to ensure that the right talents are available for their central role in maintaining the social fabric. A response to this is, however, that any given system of rewards is simply the result of a particular group's arrogation to itself of the power to claim those rewards, and the legitimisation of those claims.

By contrast with Parsonian "structural-functionalism", classic Marxist theory has little to say about the legal profession (see Abel, 1988, pp.5 *et seq.*). In Marxist theory the relations of production are always divided into two classes, and it is the conflict between these which provides the motor of change. Under capitalism, the two classes are the bourgeoisie, who are the owners of the means of production, and the proletariat whose labour provides the surplus value by which the bourgeoisie make their profits. In this scheme, it is unclear where professions lie. Marx did not really address this problem directly. On one view, the professions are an historic residue of the former mode of production, feudalism, and are simply part of the residue of petty bourgeois artisans, a group which Marx appeared to think would vanish as labour and capital became more polarised. On the other hand, he also appeared to think that the concentration of capital would require more functionaries. In short, Marx himself did not give the matter much thought, and later Marxists have had to address the fundamental question as to whether the legal and other professions are likely to ally themselves with capital or with labour, or to constitute a separate grouping within the class struggle (see Abel, pp.21 *et seq.*)—a question whose posing, incidentally, entails the professions' self-image as a unitary group.

What are we to make of all this? Perhaps the most instructive analysis is that of Johnson (Johnson, 1972), who analyses professions in terms of the attainment of competitive advantage in the market. Johnson accepts the view that professionalism is a product of the division of labour in modern societies (*ibid.*, p.41). In all advanced societies, the emergence of specialised occupational skills creates a situation where people are increasingly dependent on the skills of others. At the same time, the area of common experience and knowledge between the providers of the services and the consumer diminishes, so that consumers are more dependent on, and less able to make, an informed choice between the different providers of the services they wish to purchase. Professions are a mechanism which emerges to "manage" the tension inherent in this situation. They produce a body of practitioners the consumer can trust. Professionalism is a peculiar type of occupational control, rather than being something inherent in the nature of a particular occupation such as that of lawyer or doctor. A profession is thus not an occupation, but a means of controlling an occupation (*ibid.*, p.45). The conditions for professionalism according to Johnson developed in Britain as a consequence of the Industrial Revolution and the associated rise to power of an urban middle-class (*ibid.*, p.52). The need for legal services, which had been restricted largely to the upper classes, filtered downwards (rather as in modern times it has filtered down much further). The emerging middle class in Britain not only created the demand for legal services, crucially, it also provided the recruits for the growing professions. The Bar's essentially mediaeval guild structure thus underwent a subtle transformation, and the foundation of the Law Society can be viewed as part of the same process.

Professionalism in this sense is necessarily associated with a homogeneous occupational community, that by the same token is able to exercise effective colleague control. But, according to Johnson, a profession can only survive if its constituents' activities are confined to a relatively low degree of specialisation, and for so long as its recruits are drawn from similar backgrounds. As practitioners come to be drawn from more diverse backgrounds, and to specialise in particular branches of law, the profession as a control mechanism is likely to be weakened, and eventually the "college", the professional organisation itself, will begin to fall apart. Divisions are appearing in the legal profession at the present time. If a split occurred, it would not be the first time. In 1847 provincial solicitors set up the Metropolitan and Provincial Law Association upon the Law Society's failure to secure the appointment of solicitors as judges in the new county courts (see Abel-Smith and Stevens, 1967, Ch.3). At the present day, the divergence of interest between various types of practitioner is at least as great as that between London and provincial solicitors in the mid-nineteenth century. For example, a solicitor specialising in company work has very little in common in his day-to-day practice with a matrimonial specialist, a patent barrister very little with a criminal practitioner. Not only are the fields of law in which they specialise different, but the routines of their working lives will not be the same, and, of course, the way you earn your living tends to colour your view of the world. The company law specialist may indeed have more in common with members of accountancy firms, and similarly the other specialists mentioned may more naturally belong with members of other professions. We have already mentioned the relaxation of the rules prohibiting partnerships in solicitors' firms for practitioners accredited by other professional bodies. This could lead to the appearance of new professional bodies representing these newer groupings, bodies that would serve a similar function to those that exist at present. Indeed, we would modify Johnson's view that professionalism can only exist where there is a fairly low degree of specialisation by pointing out that specialisation can of itself produce the necessary homogeneity of outlook, and by the same token, the need for homogeneity of background is weakened. The Bar also exhibits stresses symptomatic of the power struggle for control of the General Council between the common law bar, and the specialists, notably the commercial bar. It may be that we will, in the foreseeable future, witness the dissolution of the present dichotomy between solicitors and barristers into more fractured, diverse new groupings and relations, which between them will absorb what at present constitute other professions. Although the medical professional bodies have survived the growth of a large number of specialisations, that may be because the common focus—the human body and its defects—and the common workplace—hospitals—provide a sufficiently unifying impetus to preserve a community of outlook (see Rueschmeyer, 1964); though the tensions between specialists and general practitioners are apparent even here.

The central predicament in deploying professionalism as a market control mechanism lies in the tension between the *esprit de corps* which is its essence and the right of the heterogeneous body of consumers it serves to make an informed choice. Indeed, the more the services of lawyers come to be regarded as commodities, the less legitimate will the exclusive right of the profession to purvey the product be seen to be. This, as noted above, is very apparent in the case of ordinary domestic conveyancing, and the relaxation of the prohibition on advertising can be viewed in this light also. The function of the ban on advertising, according to Johnson, was to minimise the threat to the homogeneity of members by limiting the degree to which wealthy and influential members could advance themselves still further to the point where the weaker would either disappear, be absorbed, or form their own pressure group which might ultimately split off.

There is therefore nothing immutable about the present organisation of the legal profession. The same market forces which called it into existence, or at least were responsible for its present form, may equally well destroy it. If the present professional organisations survive, it will be because as bodies they serve an economically useful function. It may be that the Bar's professional organisation will be under less pressure than that of solicitors, for the Bar is still fairly small. On the other hand, were the Bar to grow significantly, it is quite likely that it would begin to fragment. If a largely generalised judiciary were to be replaced by more specialised judges not necessarily drawn from the ranks of the practising Bar, the disintegration of the present organisation of the Bar would be highly likely.

4. SOME CONCLUDING THOUGHTS

The Royal Commission on Legal Services (Benson, 1979) accepted the traditional view that the legal profession, both through its collective organisation and in the practice of its individual members, is dedicated to serving the public interest. Accordingly, the professional bodies legitimately control entry into the profession, regulate conduct, and maintain responsibility for disciplining members. Restrictive practices might abound, but the presumption was that these were designed to maintain the quality and integrity of legal services, and thereby protect the public against rogue practitioners. Now, one of the significant aspects of this traditional characterisation of the legal profession is that it denies the popular perception that lawyers are no more than grasping money-makers. On the contrary, the legal profession, *as a profession*, is to be distinguished sharply from mere occupational groups such as trade unions. Lawyers are not simply traders in legal services; the profession stands above the exigencies of the market-place, being guided by the demands of the public interest rather than by the dictates of supply and demand.

However, as the Royal Commission worked on its Report, the legal profession was in the process of undergoing rapid change. In particular, the number of lawyers in practice, both solicitors and barristers, was increasing dramatically (doubling over the twenty-year period from the 1960s onwards); solicitors' firms were tending to get very much bigger (in the 1960s a firm would be counted big if it had a dozen partners or more—indeed there was a legal limit of twenty partners, whereas now there are several firms with in excess of one hundred partners); and, as we have emphasised already, lawyers on both sides of the profession were becoming very much more specialised. During this period, the public service ethic did not die: some lawyers were conspicuously committed to *pro bono* work. A number of large commercial firms began to subsidise Law Centres, and those who worked in those Centres obviously had a direct commitment to acquiring the special expertise which their services require. Nevertheless, public interest lawyering of this kind was very much at the margins of professional life, which continued to be dominated by routine criminal, matrimonial and conveyancing business, and by the growing corporate and banking business. Significantly, though, the expansion and fragmentation of the profession sowed the seeds for the idea that such business was indeed *business*. In other words, the pressures for lawyers to regard themselves in a more businesslike light were building up.

With the Courts and Legal Services Act 1990, a further wedge was driven between the profession and the public service ethic. The Act was based on the assumption that the public interest is better served by an open and competitive market for legal services (with some regulation for quality control) than by restrictive professional practices. Accordingly, the members of the legal profession are to be regarded (and, presumably, are to regard themselves) as no more than economically rational providers of particular services, chasing profits and maintaining their market position only so long as clients choose to deal with them. In some fields, such "marketisation" of the legal profession may seem to be in the public interest. For example, as noted above, when competition was increased in domestic conveyancing, conveyancing charges fell dramatically. However, it is a moot point whether, in the longer run, treating law as just another sector of the service economy will be in the public interest, particularly if the profession accepts the invitation to maximise profits and if access to legal services is dictated by the ability to pay. As we remarked at the end of Chapter 7, the effect of the reforms of the 1990s are as yet unclear, and should be watched with interest.

Coda on Clementi

In December 2004, Sir David Clementi concluded his wide-ranging review into the provision of legal services. As noted above, the Law Society is a body created and run by the solicitors' profession, and the public perception has been that in handling client complaints it is a case of lawyers looking after the interests of other lawyers. The government felt it had to do something about this, and Sir David's brief was to carry out a wholesale review of the provision of legal services in England and Wales, that is all legal services, not just those offered by solicitors, barristers and legal executives. Not only was he to look at reforming the way the legal profession is regulated, but to consider the organisation of the profession itself, and in particular legal disciplinary practices where solicitors and barristers and legal executives set up together, and multi-disciplinary practices in which solicitors and other professionals such as accountants or other non-legal professionals set up together. Following a consultation process in which three regulatory models were proposed, Sir David eventually opted for the model which would affirm the status quo, with the Law Society, Bar and the Institute of Legal Executives still dealing with regulation, representation and training, but with an additional upper tier, the Legal Services Board, created to review their actions. In addition, the professional bodies would devolve their representational from their regulatory functions. An Office of Legal Complaints would be established, under the supervision of the Legal Services Board, to deal with client complaints. Legal disciplinary practices will be permitted once a code of practice has been agreed by the Legal Services Board. Multi-disciplinary practices are not ruled out for the future.

The most important difference as and when these recommendations are implemented is that a much clearer complaints system will be put in place. In October 2005, the government published a White Paper, 'The Future of Legal Services: Putting the Consumer First'. Broadly speaking, the White Paper adopts the Clementi recommendations. Meanwhile, with effect from January 2006, the Law Society has already split its regulatory and its representational functions. It has established a Regulation Board and a Consumer Complaints Board, the latter being an interim measure until the Office of Legal Complaints is set up. The Law Society Council will be much reduced in numbers, and will lose its regulatory powers.

Meanwhile, the City of London Law Society which was established in 1969 continues to grow in strength, and this combined with the implementation of the Clementi recommendations on legal disciplinary and multi-disciplinary practices could have a profound effect on the present organisation of the legal profession, for the reasons set out in section 3(ii) above.

10

CONCLUSION

Climbing the Mountain

The thrust of our discussion has been that, if we are to understand law, we must be prepared to ask a variety of questions and draw on a range of approaches. However, from time to time, it is essential that one should take stock, that is, that one should pause to reflect on the overall theoretical position (if any) emerging in one's thinking. Quite possibly, no discernible pattern in one's thinking may be apparent, simply some tentative, apparently unconnected, answers to some of the questions one has posed. On the other hand, it may be that one can identify consistent themes in one's thinking; perhaps, for example, like Bentham, one might come to see the principle of utility as the fundamental resource for both explaining and evaluating conduct. Having thus come to identify oneself as a utilitarian, one would no longer address issues arising in the practice of law in an *ad hoc* way; instead one would systematically address such issues as a self-conscious utilitarian. The point of this concluding chapter, therefore, is not to rehearse what has gone before, but to consider the process of taking one's understanding of law to a higher level, to a level where one is able to identify a position which synthesises and crystallises that understanding.

When we talk about formulating "a position", we mean something more than an eclectic patchwork of different theories and approaches. We mean a coherent general position, the components of which comprise a harmonious whole. It may be, for instance, that one thinks that some questions are best answered by a Marxist analysis, others by Dworkin's political philosophy, others by Freudian psychology, and yet others by Posner's economic analysis of law (1972). However, if these strands are incompatible, one has a series of contradictory views rather than a coherent position. What we have in mind, therefore, is a reasoned, consistent, coherent position rather than a number of views selected either on a "pick 'n' mix" basis or as a matter of blind faith. Although a position, so characterised, must comprise a set of beliefs underpinned by a consistent scheme of reasons, this is not to say that one must regard one's fundamental axioms as "correct", "true", or "right" in any absolute sense. One may simply treat one's position as a statement of one's reasoned beliefs, or commitments, or of the views which, after due reflection, one provisionally accepts as the best currently available. Whichever way one regards it, however, to qualify as a position a set of views must satisfy minimal standards of reflectiveness, internal consistency, and coherence.

Where might we begin in our attempt to formulate a position concerning the practice of law? As we saw in Chapter 2, first-order questions about law are structured around a number of basic lines of inquiry, each with a choice of general approaches; and, in principle, our point of entry might be any one of these lines of inquiry and its concomitant approaches. For the sake of argument, therefore, let us start with explanatory inquiry and the options offered by the classical sociologists. If we were to take this path, where might it lead to?

1. FRAMEWORK BELIEFS ABOUT THE SOCIAL WORLD

At various points in this book, we have attempted to provide sociological explanations of aspects of the legal system. In doing this, we have mainly drawn on the work of the classical sociologists, Marx, Weber, and Durkheim. The question to be asked now, therefore, is whether one begins to see oneself as consistently taking a Marxist, or a Weberian (essentially "phenomenological"), or a Durkheimian (essentially "functionalist") line. For these purposes, we can begin with Marx, for the Marxist position offers a clear perspective on a number of important matters.

Although Marxism involves a number of difficult concepts, not to mention a range of possible interpretations, it is underpinned by a relatively simple and easily grasped thesis. Undoubtedly, this is one of the explanations of its enduring appeal over the years. This thesis is that class conflict, conflict between those classes who own and control the means of production and those who do not, is the cause of events, states of affairs, and transformations in the social world. It follows that class conflict is the key to understanding what is going on (and why), not only in the social world at large, but in the practice of law as part of the social world. Whilst there is ample scope for argument about the fine-tuning of this view, the basic Marxist line must be that, in the last resort, law (its doctrines, institutions, and the work of its officials) is guided by the invisible hand of class interest (as to the legal profession's role in this, see Ch.9). Class conflict, in other words, explains law, determines law, and structures law.

Now, the Marxist view has two major attractions for anyone seeking to develop a position. For one thing, it promises to yield a virtually complete understanding of law, not only laying bare the mechanics of the practice, but also adding for good measure a thoroughly negative evaluation. What is more, the Marxist interpretation of law has more than a little plausibility (see e.g. Collins, 1984; Kairys, 1982). After all, it does not strain the imagination too much to see the doctrinal defence of private property (in both the criminal and the civil law), the protection of the interests of employers (in labour law) and of landlords (in housing law), and so on, as evidence of a bias in favour of ruling class interests. Equally, there is little difficulty in viewing a legal profession that spends a great deal of its time dealing with conveyancing, probate, corporate, and tax work as largely dedicated to servicing the needs of the ruling class (see Ch.9). Even so, one might wonder whether the Marxist view is wholly adequate. Three reasons for such doubt are worth highlighting.

First, in sharp contrast with Durkheim and the functionalists, the Marxist emphasis might be seen as resting somewhat too heavily on the centrifugal rather than the centripetal tendencies in social life. Thus, Marxism might be seen as emphasising the dynamics of change at the expense of the mechanisms which make for social solidarity and stability; conflictual rather than co-operative social relationships; and action motivated by fear and coercion rather than genuine consensus and legitimacy. Secondly, Marxism, in company with the functionalists, but in contrast with the phenomenological approach, anchors its explanations in large-scale structures (viz., in classes—in their particular Marxist sense—and class conflict). This raises an obvious question about the place of the individual, particularly of individual reasons, purposes, and actions, in the grand explanatory scheme. Thus, whilst it might be thought appropriate to explain behaviour in the physical and natural worlds without attending to reasons and purposes, this might be seen as singularly inappropriate in relation to human beings in the social world (*cf.* e.g. Winch, 1958). Moreover, the Marxist account of the evolution of social orders, culminating in the fully communist order and the withering away of both the state and the law, might be seen as inviting a deterministic reading such that individuals find themselves cast (and trapped) in a drama the script of which has been written for them, rather than by them.

Thirdly, the Marxist account is extremely reductive, making all explanation hinge in some form or another upon class conflict.

If one harbours doubts of this kind about the Marxist line, the Weberian approach might seem to be a better bet. According to Weber, explanations of social phenomena must be adequate both causally and at the level of subjective meaning. It follows that, for Weber, explanatory inquiry must be rooted in the purposes and reasons which individuals have for acting, and in the way in which such individuals interpret and perceive the social world. Explanation, in other words, involves seeing situations through the reasoning and interpretations of the individuals so involved. At the heart of Weber's theory, therefore, is his typology of social action, in which he delineates four types of reasons for action: affectual, traditional, instrumental (*zweckrational*), and expressive (*wertrational*) (see Weber 1964, pp.115–18). Although Weber's own attempt to apply this typology to action and reasoning within the practice of law is less than satisfactory (see e.g. Kronman, 1983), it suggests a particular method of explanatory inquiry in relation to law. In fact, the "ideological" approach to interpreting adjudication, which we have discussed in detail elsewhere in relation to contract (see Adams and Brownsword, 2004), and which we have generalised in this book (see Chs 4 and 5), is very much in line with Weberian methodological canons. Since this part of our discussion is somewhat abstract, it may be helpful to elaborate briefly on this matter.

One of the principal items on the law student's curriculum is reading reported cases—characteristically, appellate court cases, where argument focuses on specific questions of law. Within the black-letter tradition, this is largely a matter of gutting the *ratio* of the case (which, generally speaking, is conveniently summarised in the headnote to the law reports) and moving on rapidly to the next case on the reading list. This militates against probing behind the surface of the case—in particular, against pausing to ask oneself what is really going on. In response to this restriction, we have proposed a typology of general judicial ideologies (i.e. variations on formalist and realist approaches) which we suggest may be employed for interpretive purposes. This framework is Weberian in spirit in more than one sense. First, if judicial decisions are to be understood, then the starting point for explanation is with the perceptions that judges have of their role as adjudicators (i.e. their general judicial ideologies) in conjunction with their specific values and ideals (i.e. their particular ideologies). Secondly, there is no standard interpretation of each case.

Explaining appellate court decision-making cannot be reduced to one simple idea (such as "keeping faith with the law" or "promoting the interests of the ruling class"). And, thirdly, the ideologies, as a range of ideal-types can be applied in a Weberian fashion at both macro and micro levels. In other words, they can be used to capture trends in the courts (which is perhaps how we should read Weber's own views about the dominance of a formal-rational approach in modern law) as well as to characterise the approach taken by a particular judge in a particular case (see e.g. Adams and Brownsword, 1991).

Although a Weberian approach at least seems to be rooted in the actions and reasons of distinct individuals, it, too, might be regarded as inadequate. For one thing, the use of ideal-types might be seen as stipulating *ab extra* an arbitrary interpretive scheme which is then imposed on the phenomena. More seriously, perhaps, Weberian explanation seems to treat individuals as, so to speak, free-standing constellations of reasons and purposes. There must surely be some place for the manner in which individuals are socialised. In other words, as Weber acknowledged, explanation must be causally adequate too; and we need to investigate the causes which account for individuals holding their particular views. It follows, then, that we might feel the need for a larger explanatory picture, which of course prompts the thought that background social structures and constraints after all might have to be taken into account in constructing one's position.

If one were to conclude that none of the options offered by the classical sociologists was entirely satisfactory, it might nevertheless be possible to construct a position which drew on a number of ingredients in the classical writings. It is often said, for example, that the work of the influential contemporary writer Jürgen Habermas should be seen as an attempt to synthesise Marxist and Weberian perspectives (see, too, the historical work of Fernand Braudel (1973) on the significance of the relations of production for the development of civilisations). Such an enterprise, however, must be more than an incoherent spatchcocking of diverse ideas. Despairing of, or fearing, the complexities entailed in such an approach, the reader might be tempted to seek comfort and solace by espousing a particular line as a matter of faith (*cf.* the position of the so-called structural Marxists, such as the late Louis Althusser). Whilst there is no denying that such blind dogma constitutes a line, it fails to qualify as a "position", in that it makes no attempt to come to terms with the idea of understanding as a rational enterprise.

2. THEORIES OF JUSTICE

If Marxism stands out as a candidate to constitute a virtually comprehensive position, then very much the same can be said about Utilitarianism. For, a utilitarian has a view about the psychology of human action (people generally prefer "pleasure" to "pain') as well as a theory about the appropriate ends for legal doctrines and institutions (viz., to aim to maximise utility). Whereas, in Volume I of *Capital*, Marx paid Bentham the backhanded compliment of being "a genius in the way of bourgeois stupidity", many modern liberal political philosophers have paid tribute to Bentham by treating Utilitarianism as their principal target. Accordingly, in this and the next section, we can take Bentham and Utilitarianism as our foil for discussing, first, theories of justice and, then, the idea of rights.

In considering the question of justice, we will concentrate, not on the justice of particular transactions (commutative justice), but on the fairness of the basic structure of society. Since law is located within a wider social setting, it will be appreciated that matters concerning background fairness may often be pertinent to issues arising within the legal system. For example, if resources are distributed very unevenly in a particular society, one may query whether it is legitimate to punish a pauper for stealing a loaf of bread from a person who has a surplus of loaves. More generally, this is the question of whether there can be just punishments in an unjust society. However, it would be a mistake to see the fairness of the basic social structure as relevant to law only in this indirect way. The point is that the legal system is intimately, and directly, concerned with such basic matters as the protection of political and civil liberties, equality of opportunity, the distribution of resources, and care and concern for the welfare of citizens. To put this slightly differently, a legal system is necessarily a reflection of a society's philosophy of justice.

Now, for a utilitarian, in principle at least, the right approach to such matters of basic justice is clear. Quite simply, the basic design of society should be such as will maximise utility. Accordingly, if, say, recognising political and civil liberties would be productive of disutility, then such liberties should be withdrawn. For example, if spreading the franchise, or allowing freedom of religious expression, were seen as incompatible with maximising utility, then so much the worse for the right to vote and freedom of conscience. Of course, for the utilitarian, there may be difficult judgments to be made about which particular basic design will maximise utility; but, subject to this caveat, all questions of justice are simply to be referred to the criterion of utility. To this, we should note one important reservation. Some utilitarians (so-called "rule-utilitarians", like Wasserstrom, *cf.* Ch.5) hold that the correct approach in a particular case is to apply a rule which, if it were generally followed in similar situations, would maximise utility. Such rule-utilitarians may argue that the best rule for legislators is to ensure stringent protection of various individual freedoms (freedom of speech, association, conscience, and the like); and, it is in this light, that we can perhaps best understand John Stuart Mill's impassioned defence of civil liberties in his celebrated essay "On Liberty" (1859). For our purposes, however, we can treat our utilitarian foil as a simple act-utilitarian position, in which the right action is that particular act which promises in its consequences to maximise utility.

Does Utilitarianism offer the best line on questions of basic justice? In his seminal book, *A Theory of Justice* (1972) John Rawls argues that it does not. On the contrary, Utilitarianism, Rawls contends, puts a great strain on human benevolence, for it contemplates calling upon some individuals to make great sacrifices so that aggregate utility may be maximised. To be blunt, utilitarians can approve of societies of huge inequality, and indeed of considerable misery amongst an underclass, provided that the overall result (net utility) is compatible with utilitarian criteria. Intuitively, this may seem downright unfair. Rawls, however, seeks a stronger demonstration of the unacceptability of Utilitarianism. To this end, he invites readers to enter into a thought experiment—to place themselves in the so-called "original position"—in which they, effectively, have to imagine themselves as founding members of a new society. Their task is to prescribe the basic structure of this new order. The first twist in this experiment, however, is that the founders are to approach their task in an entirely self-interested, although rational, way. In other words, they are not to concern themselves with the needs and interests of others. The second twist is that this self-interested approach is to be made behind what Rawls terms a "veil of ignorance". By this, he means that the founding members, in settling the features of the basic social structure, will be ignorant of the position which they will eventually occupy in that society. In other words, whilst founding members are fully in control of the design of their society, they have no control over their place in that society (nor, indeed, over the biological, physical, intellectual, and personal characteristics with which they will be duly endowed). That is, they have no control over whether they will join their society as male or female, white or black, strong or weak, quick or slow, paupers or millionaires, and so on. If this imaginative exercise runs as Rawls expects, then the founding members will build into the basic design of their society a number of features which will guarantee a floor of entitlements for all members; for, the rational founding member will incorporate only such features as one would find acceptable, no matter what one's ultimate social station. So, for example, the basic design would prohibit discrimination on grounds of race, sex, or religion; otherwise a founding member might find him or herself a victim of licensed prejudice (remember, founding members have no control over their race, sex, or religious propensity). Similarly, the starting point for distributive fairness must be that members are entitled prima facie to equal shares of their society's goods and resources. In fact, Rawls turns this round (in the form of the so-called "difference principle") to contend that social and economic inequalities can be justified only if they operate to the benefit of the least advantaged (i.e. if inequalities mean that everyone is better off than would be the case with an equal distribution). In practical terms, what this amounts to is that Rawls believes that modern democratic liberal welfare polities by and large fit the bill, respecting their citizens' basic political and civil liberties, and redistributing wealth across the economy (via taxation) where it is clear that the gains of the better-off no longer promote the interests of the less well-off.

Criticisms of the Rawlsian theory are legion. Many find his imaginative thought experiment either too fanciful or blatantly rigged. It is not clear, for example, why the founding members cannot adopt some form of Utilitarianism provided that it is hedged with minimal constraints (see Barry, 1973). This suggests that Rawls' view stands or falls on the merits of his substantive view of justice (see e.g. Nagel, 1975). Here, Rawls' critics on the Left (e.g. Fisk, 1975) argue that inequalities are corrosive of social relations and productive of envy; while his critics on the Right, notably Robert Nozick, argue that Rawls leans too heavily on the better-off.

According to Nozick (1974), there is something of a paradox in Rawls' argument. For, whilst Rawls lays great emphasis on the process by which his hypothetical contractors in the original position develop their social design, he seems much less interested in the processes of contract in the non-hypothetical real world. This, argues Nozick, is symptomatic of a profound error made by

Rawls (and many other writers), namely thinking that a just society is to be equated with some substantive distributive pattern (or end state). In other words, the (mistaken) premise is to believe that each just society will conform to some pattern of holdings. Against such a view, Nozick advances his own "entitlement theory of justice" ("From each as they choose, to each as they are chosen"), this being a theory which gives primacy to the processes by which goods are attained. Put simply, provided that one fairly acquires goods, then one justly holds them; and, because outcomes of fair acquisition are infinitely variable, it is wrong to equate justice with a particular end state blueprint. Nozick's challenge to Rawls is neatly captured in his famous example of Wilt Chamberlain, a basketball superstar. Here, Nozick invites us to specify the pattern of a just society as we see it, and then assume that such conditions obtain. Next, we are to assume that the fans at Wilt's club voluntarily drop money into a collection box in an attempt to keep Wilt at the club. Assuming that a substantial collection is made for Wilt, the (just) pattern of distribution will now have changed. Two questions follow from this. First, given that Wilt's gains have been fairly acquired, how can we coherently regard the resulting distribution as unjust? And, secondly, if we are to redistribute Wilt's gains, does this not presuppose a high degree of legal intervention? The sting in both questions is that Rawls takes freedom too lightly.

For obvious reasons, questions of social justice are a major bone of contention between the Right and the Left. Characteristically, protagonists on the Right emphasise ideas of traditional entitlement, desert, and (as we have seen in Nozick's case) freedom from interference, while protagonists on the Left favour ideas of equality and need (see Miller, 1976). These concepts, however, are by no means straightforward, as we can see if we reflect a little on the traditionally opposed notions of desert and need.

Formally speaking, justice is getting one's "due", and on the Right this is taken to mean that justice is getting one's deserts. This sounds plausible enough, but can we give any meaning to the idea of desert? If we say that A deserves to be paid more than B, we probably mean that A makes a higher social contribution than B, or that A makes more effort. In support of the contribution basis, Locke argued that everyone has a right to the whole product of his labour. Moreover, this view seems to be presupposed by the Marxist contention that the bourgeoisie expropriate the surplus value generated by the proletariat (i.e. the implication is that the workers are entitled to the full value of the product of their labour).

However, there are obvious problems about assessing contribution in modern productive conditions where labour is mixed with plant and machinery and where workers often operate as part of a team. If contribution is problematic, what about effort? Lawyers, for example, may argue that their rewards are deserved because of considerations of effort, both at the training stage and after qualification. However, effort alone is not enough; there has to be innate ability and some degree of luck. Since it is hard to separate out these elements, we seem to run into difficulties again.

Apart from practical problems associated with the concept of desert, there is a much deeper philosophical difficulty. The argument that desert should be rewarded assumes that the deserving are in some sense responsible for their actions and achievements. Yet if it is largely a matter of natural and social providence whether we happen to have the right qualities at the right time, it is hard to see why we deserve any credit for this. Such issues have come to a head in the United States in relation to affirmative action programmes where, for example, students from minority groups (mainly Blacks, Asians, Chicanos, and Hispanics) are admitted to universities with lower academic grades than their majority white counterparts. Rejected whites argue that this is unfair, that, given their better academic qualifications, they deserve the places reserved for minorities. In response to this, however, some defenders of affirmative action have argued that there is no reason whey the criterion for university entry should be so heavily slanted towards academic attainment, and that, anyway, academic attainment does not signal desert in any absolute sense. What they mean by this is that the concept of desert is relative to particular practices in which specific qualities are identified as relevant ("desert" thus means whatever we want it to mean) (see e.g. Dworkin, 1986(a); Sandel, 1984). Moreover, those individuals who happen to have the right qualities at the right time have no real control over the possession and development of such qualities. To this sobering thought, we can add another. If desert makes little sense in the context of rewards and opportunities, perhaps it is equally incoherent in the context of punishments (see Honderich, 1976). If so, we cannot justify punishing offenders on the grounds that they deserve to be so treated. It may be felt, therefore, that desert is a suitable slogan for the rhetoric of politicians, but a fragile idea once subjected to serious analysis.

On the political Left, the concept of need is much vaunted. Indeed, the idea bears the imprimatur of Marx's own famous declaration: "From each according to his ability, to each according to his needs." What, however, do we make of the idea of needs? In the next section, we will sketch a theory of morality advanced by the American philosopher Alan Gewirth. In anticipation of this discussion, however, we can say that Gewirth's theory treats human beings as having needs at a number of levels. Most importantly, individuals need their freedom and basic well-being if they are to be able to function as "agents" (i.e. as actors capable of voluntarily forming and pursuing purposes). The idea of a person's basic well-being connotes those essential or intrinsic needs (concerning physical and psychological integrity, food, clothing, and shelter, and the like) which must be satisfied if individuals are to function as agents. The precise nature of these needs may be open to argument, but, in general terms, we can be confident that millions of people in the Third World together with the underclasses in Europe and the United States fall below this level of basic well-being. Accordingly, a society which fails to satisfy these needs when it is in a position to do so must be condemned as unjust.

This benchmark of basic well-being assists us in making a number of judgments about responsibilities and priorities in a just society. For example, it sets a target for the treatment of the disabled. Of course, there are exceptional cases, such as the pianist Paul Wittgenstein (brother of the philosopher Ludwig) who, having lost his right arm in the First World War, became renowned subsequently for his one-handed performances (including his performances of Ravel's left-hand piano concerto which was written specially for him). Whilst we can but admire such resourcefulness, it seems a poor argument for suggesting that we have no real need for our arms or legs, or the power of movement. Similarly, the idea of basic need provides some guidance for the fair allocation of scarce resources. For instance, if a hospital has to choose between admitting a patient with lung cancer, or one with in-growing toe-nails, the needs of the former seem palpably more urgent than those of the latter. On the other hand, the concept of basic needs does not overcome the objection that the undeserving needy should not get priority. Thus, if the patient with lung cancer has been a heavy smoker despite knowing of the risks, some might think that justice demands that he should take second place to the person with in-growing toe-nails. And, of course, the issue of the undeserving needy is a perennial problem in relation to funding welfare programmes for the less well-off and the unemployed (*cf.* Clarke, Cochrane, and Smart, 1987).

Suppose, however, that we start thinking about needs which go beyond the basic set. Some caution now seems to be appropriate.

Whilst our basic needs are applicable whatever we want to do (i.e. whatever our purposes), specific wants and purposes carry with them specific needs. However, as Herbert Marcuse (1972) pointed out, in a mass consumer society saturated with advertising and dominated by materialistic values, individuals may want things which they do not really need. There are, so to speak, true and false needs, the latter being imposed upon individuals by capitalism and consumerism. The logic of this is that justice demands that we attend only to genuine, non-manipulated, needs. But, unless we stick to basic needs, it is hard to see quite how we might discriminate between genuine and false needs. Perhaps the answer is simply to distribute resources equally once basic needs are satisfied. This proposal, however, might be thought to raise further difficulties. If individuals may want things which they do not need, then they may need things which they do not want. How do we deal, for instance, with the ascetic who does not welcome his share of the resources? The short answer seems to be that the ascetic can simply waive his right to such resources, allowing them to be distributed equally amongst others. More seriously a regime of equal distribution makes no allowance for the different levels of requirement implicated in different life-plans. Some life-plans can be resourced at little cost, but others are hugely expensive. Again, there is a short answer: each individual starts with an equal (fair) share; life-plans are freely chosen; resources can be traded; but there is no guarantee that each individual will have adequate resources in relation to that individual's chosen life-plan—some individuals will be disappointed, but such is life (even in a just society) (see Ackerman, 1980). However, against this view, we can recall the Nozickean theme. Does this rigorous equalisation imply that individuals will not be free to transfer resources from one generation to another? Meeting basic needs is one thing, but flat equalisation arguably neglects the importance of individual freedom.

Our brief discussion of the concepts of desert and need should indicate that, in the quest for a position, neither of these paths offers a trouble-free option. In both cases, however, there is a further difficulty. This is that the philosophies of desert and needs are philosophies of individual (human) rights. So, whilst deserts and needs are in opposition across the political arena, they have a common enemy in the shape of those, like Bentham, who contend that human rights should not be taken seriously. This takes us to the next section of our discussion.

3. HUMAN RIGHTS

The tension between utility-based and rights-based reasoning has been one of the principal themes of this book. If rights are to be taken seriously, this shapes one's view about a legitimate constitutional settlement and the Rule of Law, the function of judges, the design of the criminal, civil, and administrative justice systems, the proper role of the legal profession, and the place of legal services—in short, rights-based reasoning (like its utilitarian rival) informs one's thinking about all aspects of law. Accordingly, if we are searching for a position, the adoption of rights-based reasoning would carry us a long way forward.

Although the idea of human rights is fashionable—indeed, the culture of human rights is firmly entrenched in Europe and elsewhere—there is a hard-nosed sceptical tradition, encapsulated in Bentham's famous aphorism that talk of natural (or human) rights is "nonsense on stilts"—or, as Alasdair MacIntyre has put the point more recently, that a belief in rights is on a par with a "belief in witches and in unicorns" (1981, p.67). This scepticism should not be misunderstood. It is not denied that positive rules, statutes, precedents, and the like, can confer rights on individuals. Sceptics, for example, would not deny that in the Birmingham sex discrimination case (see Ch.2) the girls had a right not to be treated less favourably than the boys. However, they would insist that this right rested entirely on legislative enactment. Accordingly, on this view, if the Sex Discrimination Act were to be repealed, the girls would no longer have this right; individuals simply do not have rights prior to positive enactment or recognition. Against this, advocates of human rights insist that there are rights independent of positive enforcement or acceptance. How is this view to be sustained?

In *Taking Rights Seriously* (1978), Ronald Dworkin contends that citizens have a right to be treated by their governments with equal concern and respect. Although Dworkin believes that this axiomatic right is consistent with the Rawlsian justificatory strategy of the original positiom, he does not really concern himself very much with the question of why his statement of rights should be accepted. Rather, his book is largely addressed to those who already accept this idea, in the sense that his intention is to underline the full implications of acceptance. Whilst this might seem somewhat brazen, it really does no more than return the utilitarians' denial of rights in kind. After all, if an individual accepts that humans have rights (and duties)—and there are

plenty of people who do accept this, as well as international declarations and conventions to similar effect—then it cuts little ice
for the sceptics to say that they do not accept the idea. This is just
a stalemate of acceptance and non-acceptance.

For Dworkin, the absence of any deeper foundations for his
position is not an embarrassment. His philosophical approach
requires that we should reflect on our fundamental commitments
(those values which we confidently accept and would reluctantly
surrender) and take things from there. On this view, it makes no
sense to inquire whether such commitments are "true" or "correct"; they are simply the cornerstone views which one accepts,
and no further justification is necessary or possible. To out and
out rationalists, however, this seems unsatisfactory: unless we
can give reasons for our beliefs (reasons independent of the bold
declaration that certain commitments are accepted), we have no
basis for reliance, no basis for taking a position, no basis for holding that individuals have rights, and no basis for criticising those
who deny or violate rights. In this light, we can consider briefly
the complex, but potentially critical, moral theory developed by
Alan Gewirth.

In his seminal book, *Reason and Morality* (1978), Gewirth gives
the classical Kantian approach to morality a powerful modern
expression, arguing that those who see themselves as agents
(roughly, as beings who are prospectively capable of voluntary
and purposive action) are logically committed to recognising certain rights and duties which constitute the principles of inter-
agent conduct. Gewirth's argument employs what he terms a
"dialectically necessary" method. It is "dialectical" in the sense
that it proceeds exclusively within the first-person viewpoint of
an individual agent; and it is "necessary" in the sense that it is an
argument based on agency per se, not on agency given certain
contingent features. Each step in the argument is presented as
logically required, so that Gewirth purports to present an iron
proof for the existence of rights.

Briefly, the three main steps in the argument are as follows.
First, because agents must have a positive attitude towards their
particular freely chosen purposes (they must, in this modest
sense, want to achieve their freely chosen ends), they must have
a positive attitude towards the means to those particular ends.
More generally, they must have a positive attitude towards those
means which are essential for purposive action, irrespective of the
particular ends chosen. Gewirth identifies such essential means
as an agent's freedom and basic well-being (hereafter, simply

well-being). Accordingly, the first step is completed with the agent's realisation that he needs his freedom and well-being whatever his purposes, which is to say that he must have a negative attitude towards interferences with his freedom and well-being (unless, of course, he licenses such interference in order to pursue a particular purpose). The second step is to convert this negative attitude towards interference with one's freedom and well-being into the appreciation that one must have a right to one's freedom and well-being (i.e. that others have a duty not to interfere). The third step involves converting the claim that one has a right to freedom and well-being (because one is an agent) into an appreciation that other agents have the identical right and that, concomitantly, one has a duty to respect the freedom and well-being of other agents. What Gewirth is driving at here is that the basis of one's right to freedom and well-being is that one is an agent—just that, one is an agent, not that one is an agent with particular characteristics or purposes. It follows that if being an agent grounds the right to freedom and well-being, one must accord this right to one's fellow agents and regard oneself as having a duty to respect their freedom and well-being. This duty is captured in the so-called Principle of Generic Consistency (the PGC), which enjoins that each agent should "Act in accord with the generic rights [i.e. rights to freedom and well-being] of your recipients as well as of yourself."

If the steps in this argument are valid, then Gewirth can claim to have established an objective, true principle of morality. However, the truth of the PGC does not so much reside in its correspondence with some state of affairs as in the fact that it cannot be coherently denied by an agent. In other words, provided one sees oneself as a being who fits Gewirth's description of an agent, then one cannot logically avoid the conclusion that one is bound by the PGC. There seem, therefore, to be only three escape routes. One can deny that one is an agent (which is to say that one does not perceive oneself as a being capable, in principle, of free and purposive action—but, is this perception consistent with the act of denial?). One can deny that one must submit to the dictates of logic or reason (which denial, of course, cannot be substantiated by reason or logic). Or, one can contest the validity of Gewirth's derivation of the PGC. Whilst some are inclined to dismiss Gewirth out of hand, others—critics and supporters—have subjected each step of the argument to close examination (see Regis, 1984; Beyleveld, 1991). Certainly, if Gewirth's argument is correct, it has some dramatic implications. It is not simply that the idea of human rights can be rationally grounded. It also follows that natural lawyers are right as against legal positivists (see Ch.1); that the tradition of value-free social science to which Marx, Durkheim, and Weber each subscribed must be rejected; that explanation must proceed by treating action which conforms with the PGC as the focal case; and that the PGC sets the criterion for evaluating all aspects of social, including legal, practice (*cf.* Beyleveld and Brownsword, 1986 and 1990).

However, even if the PGC were the key to evaluating law, we would still have a long way to go, for it would have to be brought to bear on all manner of concrete questions. As Charles Fried has remarked, it is a long drop from abstract moral theory to nuts and bolts legal issues (Fried, 1985). Although this is too large an issue to tackle here, we can consider in this light the question of to whom rights should be accorded.

Historically, societies have accorded different rights to different categories of persons. Roman law, for example, distinguished between Roman citizens (who enjoyed the fullest rights under the law), "Junian Latins" (an intermediate category), and slaves (who had few rights). Currently, English law accords fullest rights to its own adult citizens, but lesser rights to infants and bankrupts (e.g. they cannot vote). In England, even the right to life, classically, was limited to "any reasonable creature in being" (Coke, 3 Institutes 47). Thus, to kill a child in its mother's womb, or to use instruments or drugs to procure an abortion, was not murder (Blackstone, 4 Commentaries 197). At the present day, however, we hear much about the "rights of the unborn child" from anti-abortionists—as, for that matter, we hear claims advanced for the rights of persons who are in a persistent vegetative state, for (non-human) animals, and even for the environment. What are we to make of these various rights claims?

If we accept that human beings have rights, then presumably we take it that human beings have some particular characteristics that make them eligible to bear rights. For example, we might relate human rights to the capacity for rational thought and communication, or to the ability to participate in a regime of reciprocal rights and duties; or, we might base human rights on the capacity to experience pain and suffering; and so on. Unless we propose to draw an arbitrary distinction between humans and all other living things, and thereby invite the charge of "speciesism" (see Singer, 1979), the characteristic that we take to be critical if one is to be eligible as a rights-bearer matters a great deal. If, for instance, we take the capacity to suffer as critical (as is standard in utilitarian reasoning), then any sentient being capable of suffering must count in our moral calculations and, in the present context, is potentially a rights-bearer—from which it follows that, at a certain stage of its development, a fetus might have rights and it also follows that non-human animals might have rights. If, on the other hand, we restrict rights to those who are self-consciously capable of exercising their rights (as rights) and who are correlatively capable of responding to duties, then (unless we have seriously misinterpreted the capacities of rocks and trees, and plants and non-human animals), the moral community of rights-bearers will be restricted to developed human beings. It should be emphasised that it does not follow from this latter view that it is morally permissible to despoil the environment or to engage in wanton cruelty to non-human animals; but this view does imply that protection for the environment or for non-human animals must be largely sought by way of indirect arguments (e.g. by the argument that, in the long run, a lack of respect for non-human living things will lead to a lack of respect for human life) which may or may not be convincing (see further, Carruthers, 1992; Beyleveld and Brownsword, 1993).

We can give three examples of major debates—currently presenting the law with some of its most difficult challenges—and each of which involves the question of moral status (*i.e.* whether a particular life-form must be taken into account in a moral calculation).

The first debate, which has been raging in Europe since the late 1980s, concerns the morality (and legality) of patenting non-human animals. In the most famous test case, that of the Harvard Onco-mouse, patent offices in both the United States and Europe were asked to grant a patent on a mouse that was genetically engineered to serve as a test animal for cancer research. Some might think that such an application should be summarily rejected. For example, Dr Jeremy Rifkin (1995; 1998), the American environmentalist, takes an uncompromising stand:

"Let me ask you a question, 'What is wrong with patenting animals?' If you do not intuitively know the answer to this question, I could probably never explain it to you." (1995, p.25)

Against Rifkin, however, many see nothing wrong in principle with patenting the products and processes associated with modern biotechnology, including granting patents on genetically engineered plants and animals, and even patents on human gene sequences. In line with this view, the European Patent Office eventually granted a patent on the Onco-mouse (likewise in the US) but only after the examiners (adopting a utilitarian mode of reasoning) had carefully weighed the potential benefits (to humans) of granting the patent offset by the distress occasioned to the mice and any environmental risk. (Generally, for a range of moral and regulatory problems presented by modern biotechnology, see Brownsword, Cornish, and Llewelyn, 1998.)

Our second example is that of abortion (*cf.* Dworkin, 1993). In practice, many legal systems find that they are channelled towards granting limited authorisation for abortions. However, this is not to say that such practical accommodations of the rival pro-life and pro-choice constituencies are without any plausible credentials. For instance, if we operate with a utilitarian perspective, we might well reason that the justification for aborting in a particular case depends on two factors: the distress to the fetus that an abortion would occasion (basically, the earlier the abortion the better); and the distress that the mother would suffer if she had to carry the fetus to term. From a rights perspective, we might also arrive at a similar view. For example, in the landmark US case of *Roe v Wade* (1973), the Supreme Court established a three-trimester framework in which early–stage abortions were authorised (as an aspect of the mother's right to privacy—or, better, her right to autonomy) but in which abortion can become more densely regulated as the pregnancy proceeds and as fetal rights are recognised (so that, in the final trimester, abortions can be prohibited unless there is a threat to the life or health of the mother). Such practical accommodations, however, might be (and, in the case of the *Roe v Wade* trimester rules, have been) criticised as offering both too little and too much protection to the fetus (see e.g. Mason and McCall Smith, 1994, p.104). On the one side, proponents of the pro-life position might echo Rifkin (above) and assert that if we cannot see that there is life from the point of conception, and that it is wrong to take life, then there is little point in talking to one another. On the other side, ardent proponents of the pro-choice position might contend that potential life is not life, that a fetus has no rights, and that an abortion is no more and no less than any other surgical removal. Moreover, on this side of the debate, even if it is conceded that a fetus has rights (Gewirth, for example, recognises that a fetus has rights under a so-called principle of proportionality), the mother's competing rights may normally prevail. Thus, Judith Jarvis Thomson (1971) has famously (if somewhat bizarrely) argued that if a woman has no duty not to unplug a virtuouso violinist with a kidney complaint who has been connected to her circulatory system without her consent, then whatever the rights of a fetus, it does not follow that a mother has a duty to carry the fetus to term.

The third example is euthanasia. As we saw in our discussion of consent and the criminal law (in Ch.6), if we grant a human right to autonomy, then there is reason for thinking that individuals must be left free to determine the time and mode of their own deaths (provided, of course, that such decisions do not violate the rights of others). However, in recent years, English law has been called upon to determine the legality of withdrawing feeding and hydration from patients who are in a persistent vegetative state (and who are themselves unable to make autonomous decisions at the critical time). In the leading case of *Airedale NHS Trust v Bland* (1993), the courts ruled at all levels from trial through to the House of Lords that the termination of treatment was in the best interests of Tony Bland (who was one of the victims of the Hillsborough disaster: see Ch.5) and, thus, was lawful. Yet what kind of standing does someone like Tony Bland have in our moral calculations? Before he was caught up in the Hillsborough tragedy, Tony Bland was, on everyone's view, an agent whose interests must be fully taken into account. As an ex-agent, however, in a persistent vegetative state, do we treat Tony Bland right by speaking of his best interests (even though, as Lord Mustill remarked (at 894), the "distressing truth which must not be shirked is that the proposed conduct is not in the best interests of Anthony Bland, for he has no best interests of any kind"), or should we try to second guess what he would have wanted in such a situation, or should we take some different approach (see e.g. Finnis, 1993; Bix, 1995)?

The moral of all this is clear. Even if it is conceded that individuals may bear rights, the extent of the category of rights-bearers remains contentious, as does the scope, content, and priority of particular rights. It follows that, often, there are no easy answers. What this signifies, however, is not that we should become sceptical about the idea of human rights, or give up on morality, but that we should appreciate that moral issues, like legal issues, can be complex (see Beyleveld and Brownsword, 2006a).

4. CONSENT AND THE RISE OF HUMAN RIGHTS

As respect for human rights deepens, and as societies become more committed to the idea that individuals have the right to be treated as autonomous decision-makers (each of us responsible for making our own choices), we find that the idea of consent assumes an increasing importance in our practical thinking (see e.g. Fletcher, 1996, p.109). It follows that, as politicians and judges share this commitment to human rights and the value of individual autonomy, we will expect to find the importance of consent being registered in legal doctrine. So, to take a couple of famous examples, on one side of the Atlantic, in *Canterbury v Spence* (1972), we find the Court of Appeals of the District of Columbia embracing a doctrine of "informed consent" as it abandons physician paternalism in favour of patient-centred decision-making; and, on the other side of the Atlantic, in *R v R* (1991), the House of Lords, recognising that marriage is a partnership of equals, puts an end to the long-standing common law doctrine that a husband cannot be guilty of raping his wife (irrespective of whether the wife actually is, or reasonably appears to be, consenting to intercourse). In other words, as human rights displaces paternalistic and status-based cultures, we find the importance of individual choice emphasised and, with that, the emergence of consent as a key feature of legal doctrine (Brownsword, 2004).

Where legal thinking centres on rights, one of the more obvious roles played by consent is to give a party a response to an alleged violation of right. If it can be shown that the complainant has consented to the act or transaction in question, this puts an end to any suggestion that the complainant's rights have been violated. As George Fletcher (1996) remarks:

"When individuals consent to undergo medical operations, to engage in sexual intercourse, to open their homes to police searches, or to testify against themselves in court, they convert what otherwise would be an invasion of their person or their rights into a harmless or justified activity." (109)

In general, this seems to be on the right track. However, the function of consent is not limited to authorising actions that would otherwise involve a violation of right, for whole bodies of law (or institutions within the law), most obviously contract law, can be seen as articulations of the idea of a consensual transaction (see e.g. Barnett, 1986). Indeed, in the tradition of liberal political theory, consent is seen as the foundation for the entire politico-legal order. Accordingly, some might claim that consent is not just *in* the law; consent goes deeper than this, pointing to the basis of legal authority and perhaps to the essence of legal order itself.

Having said that the function of consent is to operate as a "green light" authorisation or empowerment of another, it might be thought that there is little more to be said. However, a harder look at consent soon throws up a host of difficult questions about such matters as who has the capacity to consent, what surrogates or proxies for consent we will accept where the individual lacks the capacity to consent, and under what conditions an ostensible consent will be recognised as authentic or valid (Beyleveld and Brownsword, 2006b. Some of these questions are reformulations of questions that we have already addressed concerning rights-bearers; but others, particularly issues relating to the conditions of consent are fresh and challenging. It is one thing to agree that, if A "consents" to hand over money to B when threatened at gun-point by B, this is not a valid consent. But, it is another thing to decide whether and, if so, when more subtle forms of pressure and influence undermine the idea of an independent unforced choice on which consent is predicated. Similarly, it is one thing to agree that, if A "consents" to hand over money to B following a fraudulent representation by B that the money will be applied for a charitable purpose, this is not a valid consent. But, it is another thing to decide how far the consent given by A must be made in the light of relevant knowledge and understanding before it will count as a valid consent. To unpack "consent" as requiring a "free and informed" consent, as many modern theorists do, is a sure sign that consent is being taken seriously; but it raises more questions than it answers.

The recent case of *R. v Jones* (2002) offers an interesting example of some of the difficulties concerning consent. In *Jones*, the defendant, who was facing charges relating to a robbery at a post-office, entered a not guilty plea at the arraignment but subsequently failed to appear for the trial. Exercising a common law discretion, the trial judge ordered that the trial should proceed and, in his absence, the defendant was duly convicted and given a long custodial sentence. Some 14 months later, the defendant was apprehended. He now claimed that the trial should not have been allowed to proceed and that, in so far as the common law permitted trial in the absence of the defendant, it was incompatible with the right to a fair trial as guaranteed by Article 6 of the

European Convention on Human Rights. Rejecting the defendant's argument, the House of Lords ruled that, irrespective of whether the defendant had waived the benefit of the right to appear and offer a defence (which is an aspect of the right to a fair trial), he had had a fair trial anyway. For present purposes, though, it is the question of the possible waiver of right (that is to say, the defendant consenting to the trial proceeding in his absence) that is of particular interest.

If we adopt the modern view that a consent (or waiver of right in this case) is valid only if it is given on a free and informed basis, was there a valid consent on the part of the defendant? Lord Bingham, following the line adopted by the Court of Appeal, had little doubt that the benefit of the right in question had been waived:

"[In] my opinion, . . . one who voluntarily chooses not to exercise a right cannot be heard to complain that he has lost the benefits which he might have expected to enjoy had he exercised it. . . . If he voluntarily chooses not to exercise his right to appear, he cannot impugn the fairness of the trial on the ground that it followed a course different from that which it would have followed had he been present and represented." (para.11)

Begging to differ, however, Lord Rodger (supported by Lord Hoffmann) was not satisfied that the right had been waived:

"Doubtless, the appellant would have been aware that, if eventually brought to justice, he would be punished for absconding to avoid trial. But I see no proper basis for going further and assuming that he would actually have known that he was liable to be tried and sentenced in his absence. I am accordingly unable to draw the conclusion that the appellant had unequivocally waived his right to be present at any trial." (para.52)

So, whereas Lord Bingham emphasised the fact that the defendant had freely (voluntarily) chosen not to appear, Lord Rodger remained to be convinced that the defendant had acted with relevant knowledge and understanding. In the final analysis, for the reasons already given, this was not to affect the outcome of the appeal. Nevertheless, if we are to protect the integrity of consent, then there is a significant issue of principle at stake. Put shortly, from a human rights perspective (signalling due process values), the State should be quick to grant the accused the right to a fair trial and slow to infer that an accused has consented to give up the benefit of that right.

One of the worrying features of *Jones* is that consent is being inferred from conduct. Of course, there is a sense in which consent is always read off conduct but, in some cases, the giving of consent is more explicit than in others. In *Jones*, it is not as though the defendant, having been read his rights, and having been counselled on the implications of waiving the benefit of any of his rights, explicitly agreed that he would not exercise his right to appear at the trial. Quite rightly, the more seriously that we take free choice and control on the part of individuals, the less comfortable we are with reliance on "consents" that are routinely obtained or read off conduct that is equivocal—hence our doubts about inertia selling techniques (which rely on acceptance by inaction or silence) and regimes that operate on a "contracting out" basis (e.g. for organ donation), and hence the reservations that many had about *DPP v Morgan* (1976) where the House of Lords held that, where a man genuinely believes that a woman is consenting to sexual intercourse, this negates the *mens rea* for rape even if the woman is not consenting and irrespective of the reasonableness of the man's belief that she is consenting (but see now the revised test in section 1 of the Sexual Offences Act 2003). Moreover, even where we have an explicit consent, respect for individual rights indicates that caution should be exercised in extending the scope of the consent by implication. So, for example, in the Canadian case of *Murray v McMurchy* (1949), it was held that a consent given to a caesarian section did not cover a secondary operation to tie the woman's fallopian tubes (while carrying out the primary operation, the surgeon found tumours in the patient's uterine wall and, fearing the risks associated with a further pregnancy, decided to carry out the secondary procedure). On the other hand, in the earlier case of *Marshall v Curry* (1933), where a surgeon removed a diseased testicle which he discovered during the course of carrying out an operation to repair a hernia, the additional surgery was held to be justified. Doctrinally, it might be possible to distinguish these cases by treating *Marshall* as an emergency or by giving the explicit consent, in its particular context, a sufficiently broad interpretation to cover the additional procedure. Beyond doctrine, however, one's reaction to these cases will depend upon whether one accepts physician paternalism (and, concomitantly, a justification along the lines that the physician acted in a way that was judged to be in the best interests of the patient); or whether one takes a utilitarian view (in which the convenience and efficiency of carrying out the additional surgery will weigh heavily towards justification); or whether one accepts a human rights perspective and, with that, the fundamental importance of acting only on the basis of explicit and specific consent.

The lesson to be taken from this is that the more a culture of human rights embeds itself, the more insistent the law will become that, in the absence of countervailing rights or public interest derogations, consent becomes the key to legitimate action. However, the restrictions imposed in the name of public interest are far from insignificant and this takes us to the emerging importance of human dignity as a value to be defended not only against human rights thinking but also against utilitarian calculation.

5. HUMAN DIGNITY AND THE NEW DIGNITARIANS

At one level, the commentary that we have offered in this book is very simple. Our view is that law cannot be understood unless its underlying ideologies are uncovered. Whether one wants to understand what makes the institutions of law tick or what is distinctive about particular doctrinal positions taken in the law, the ideologies to which law is committed at the time need to be identified. At another level, this is a demanding task because the relevant ideological patterns are constantly shifting. For much of the book, our commentary has focused on the tension between rights-based thinking and utilitarian consequentialism, a tension which, for the last half-century or so, has generated a dominant dialogue about both legal doctrine and institutional design. As we have just seen in the previous section, the reception of human rights has pretty much eliminated any traces of paternalistic or status-based thinking, in the light of which we might assume that the field has now been cleared for a two-sided contest between the proponents of human rights and their utilitarian rivals. This, however, leaves out of account the possibility of a third viewpoint, that of the "new dignitarians", asserting itself and setting up a three-cornered ideological contest (see Brownsword, 2003).

Although we are suggesting that the new dignitarians are asserting themselves in opposition to both utilitarian and human rights perspectives, the idea that human dignity is a value is not only echoed by these perspectives, in the human rights tradition it is nothing less than a founding axiom. Famously, the Preamble to the Universal Declaration of Human Rights, 1948 (and, likewise to its partner Covenants on Economic, Social and Cultural Rights, 1966, and on Civil and Political Rights, 1966) provides that "recognition of the inherent dignity and of the equal and inalienable rights of all members of the human family is the foundation of freedom, justice and peace in the world"; and Article 1 of the Universal Declaration proclaims that "All human beings are born free and equal in dignity and rights." Whether or not acceptance of respect for human dignity actually adds anything to acceptance of human rights is a moot point—for present purposes, it suffices to note that the principle of respect for human dignity is perceived to be the foundation for the modern elaboration of human rights.

Now, in a new generation of international instruments, we find appeals to human dignity playing an altogether more prominent role (see Beyleveld and Brownsword, 2001). For example, the Preamble to the Council of Europe's Convention on Human Rights and Biomedicine (1996) requires its signatories to resolve:

"to take such measures as are necessary to safeguard human dignity and the fundamental rights and freedoms of the individual with regard to the application of biology and medicine."

Similarly, the Preamble to UNESCO's Universal Declaration on the Human Genome and Human Rights (1997) states that while:

"research on the human genome and the resulting applications open up vast prospects for progress in improving the health of individuals and of humankind as a whole . . . [it is imperative] . . . that such research should fully respect human dignity, freedom and human rights."

In so far as these declarations in favour of human dignity are intended to reinforce the demand that human rights should be respected, they say little that is new. However, it is in just such declarations that we find a distinctive coalition of viewpoints (secular as well as religious) which we can portray as the new dignitarian ideology. Characteristically, it is claimed that human dignity is compromised where there is a lack of respect for the sanctity of human life (which is interpreted broadly to cover fetal and embryonic life), where human life is "commodified" (for example, where the sex or genetic make-up of a child is selected in the way that one might make a selection from a menu at a restaurant), or where the human body is commercialised (covering such matters as the sale of human organs, prostitution, commercial surrogacy, the patenting of human gene sequences), and the like. This results in some familiar calls for regulatory prohibition—for example, in relation to abortion, euthanasia, and assisted suicide; but it also encourages a deep resistance to the adoption of a range of new technologies (human reproductive cloning being the obvious example: see Brownsword, 2005a and 2005b). Crucially, the dignitarians hold their ground regardless of whether the action or practice could be supported by reference to either utilitarian or human rights criteria—in other words, if some item (say, dwarf-throwing (see below) or "reality" television programmes) is judged to compromise human dignity, it matters not that the participation is on the basis of free and informed consent nor that utility is maximised; for the dignitarians, consent cannot redeem violation of human dignity and beneficial consequences are irrelevant (or illusory).

One way of highlighting the difference between dignity-based human rights thinking and the approach of the new dignitarians is to focus on two different reference points for human dignity. First, there is the idea that human dignity speaks to what is special or specific about humans, that is to say, what is intrinsically and universally distinctive about humans. As Francis Fukuyama (2002) has recently put it, the demand made in the name of human dignity is one for equal recognition which implies "that when we strip all of a person's contingent and accidental characteristics away, there remains some essential human quality underneath that is worthy of a certain minimum level of respect. . . ." (p.149). Secondly, and by way of contrast, there is the idea that human dignity speaks less to what is special about humans *qua* humans and more to what is special about a particular community's idea of civilised life and the concomitant commitments of its members. Here, appeals to human dignity draw on what is distinctively valued concerning human social existence in a particular community—indeed, on the values and vision that distinguish the community as the particular community that it is and relative to which the community's members take their collective and individual identity. At the price of some over-simplification, we can say that, whereas the former tends to be closely associated with human rights movements aimed at giving individuals the opportunity to flourish as self-determining authors of their own destinies, the latter resonates with much new dignitarian thinking.

Perhaps the most vivid illustration of the import of new dignitarian thinking is provided by the famous French dwarf-throwing ("lancer de nain") case (1995), where the Conseil d'Etat had to rule on the legality of orders issued by two provincial authorities banning dwarf-throwing in local clubs. Significantly, the legality of the bans was challenged by, among others, one of the dwarfs, who argued that he freely participated in the activity, that the work brought him a monthly wage (as well as allowing him to move in professional circles) and that, if dwarf-throwing was banned, he would find himself unemployed again. However, the Conseil d'Etat upheld the bans, saying that dwarf-throwing compromised human dignity and that there was, thus, a threat to *ordre public* to which the authorities had rightly responded. What we see here is the elevation of the idea of human dignity as an overriding value (whether grounded in individual humans or in groups of humans), a value to be respected by all members of human society. On this view, the fact that the dwarf-throwers did not intend to demean or degrade the dwarfs, or that the dwarfs freely consented to their participation, is immaterial: *ordre public* (including respect for human dignity) sets limits to autonomy—certain expressions of free choice are, quite simply, out of bounds.

In England, the new dignitarian perspective has been pressed into service to support the sanctity of human life. So, for instance, in Dianne Pretty's case (2001) the dignitarian position resists relaxation of the law regulating assisted suicide; and in *Re A* (2001), the conjoined twins case, a dignitarian argument can be made out against authorising the separation when its certain result will be to terminate the life of one of the twins. From a rights perspective, the dignitarian position in a case like that of Dianne Pretty is badly wrong because (just as in the dwarf-throwing case) there is a failure to respect the free and informed choices of an autonomous individual. In the conjoined twins case, the situation is rather more complex. Because the twins themselves are incapable of making their own choices or signalling their consent to the procedure, rights theorists cannot make the same accusation against the dignitarians; on the other hand, if the dignitarians claim the moral high ground by arguing for the inviolability of life and the importance of protecting the vulnerable, this will incur the wrath of utilitarians who believe that it is right to save one life rather than sacrifice both lives. Finally, it is worth pointing out that the dignitarians are able to take their protective mission right back to the earliest stages of the development of a human life. For this reason, the dignitarians are resolutely opposed to the United Kingdom's permissive legal framework which authorises the Human Fertilisation and Embryology Authority to license research on human embryos and which was extended in 2001 to allow for the licensing of human embryonic stem cell research (see Brownsword, 2002).

In this light, it will be appreciated that the questions raised by the *Pro-Life Alliance* case (2002, 2003) go beyond a choice between a literal or a more purposive interpretation of the relevant sections of the Human Fertilisation and Embryology Act 1990, or beyond a choice between a restrictive or a permissive reading of Lord Wilberforce's guidance in the *Royal College of Nursing* case (1981), or even beyond deciding whether an "embryo" produced without the fertilisation of an egg by a process of cell nuclear replacement and stimulation is essentially the same as an embryo produced by sperm fertilisation of an egg. What is ultimately at stake in the case is whether developments in embryology are seen in a positive or negative way. When utilitarians monopolise the debate, the anticipated benefits of the science are highlighted and, subject to considerations of safety, the arguments will tend to be in just one direction (in favour of realising the benefits and putting in place a legal framework that facilitates the science). Rights theorists introduce a degree of friction into the debate because they insist that scientific progress should never be bought at the expense of individual humans. In practice, this means that research should not proceed without obtaining the informed consent of those who participate. With the emergence of the new dignitarians, however, the debate becomes altogether more intense. Cost/benefit calculations and respect for individual rights no longer carry the day; the dignitarian imperative is that human dignity must not be compromised. As we move into the new Millennium, with modern biotechnology (including embryology) promising to re-write the terms of human existence, we can expect dignitarian concerns to be articulated increasingly in political and legal fora (see Brownsword, 2005b).

6. QUESTIONS AND ANSWERS:
BELIEFS, DOUBTS, AND ARGUMENTS

Understanding law is a continuing process. Having broken out of the black-letter straitjacket, by asking questions about law as well as pondering questions of law, it continues by drawing on various approaches and answers available within a range of disciplines. Sooner or later, the possibility of staking a general theoretical position must be examined. It might be thought that, having identified such a position, having identified the essence of one's understanding, the task has been completed. However, this makes both unrealistic and undesirable assumptions about the confidence with which a position can be held.

In practice, taking a position will (and should) lie somewhere between indeterminacy and dogma. A position should always be adopted provisionally. Whilst one must have sufficient reason to espouse a view as one's (provisional) position, one's mind must not be closed to possible objections. Indeed, once a position has been taken, one has a duty to search all the more for its weaknesses. Of course, one may not have to search too hard, for fresh ideas and arguments are constantly rolling off the academic presses. In professing one's understanding of law, therefore, one should be cautious about believing that one has expressed the last (unproblematic) word on the matter. In this connection, one might recall the heroic honesty of the American jurist Underhill Moore who, one day, was allegedly seen turning out the contents of his filing cabinets with the wry comment: "It's my life work, all the notes I have taken in a lifetime of research—and it's all wrong". The reality, as Robert Nozick has aptly put it, is that one's understanding necessarily comprises a fragile mixture of "doubts and worries and uncertainties, as well as . . . beliefs, convictions, and arguments" (1974, p.xiv). Understanding law, therefore, is not an undergraduate, or even a post-graduate project. It is a constant process of asking questions, assessing arguments and answers, and placing and replacing one's bets as positions representing one's provisional understanding are developed, applied, modified, and sometimes (as the sad story of Underhill Moore testifies) abandoned. Understanding law, in short, is rather akin to climbing a mountain: it is an uphill task; the views can be rewarding; on occasion, one may have to retrace one's steps to make a fresh ascent; and, above all, one must be constantly sceptical that one has actually reached the summit.

BIBLIOGRAPHY

Abel, Richard (1988): *The Legal Profession in England and Wales*, Oxford, Basil Blackwell.

Abel-Smith, B., and Stevens, R. (1967): *Lawyers and the Courts*, London, Heinemann.

Ackerman, Bruce A. (1980): *Social Justice in the Liberal State*, New Haven, Yale University Press.

Adams, John N., and Brownsword, Roger (1987): *Understanding Contract Law*, London, Fontana Press (2nd ed. 1994; reprinted 1996; 3rd ed. 2000, 4th ed. 2004 London, Sweet and Maxwell).

Adams, John N., and Brownsword, Roger (1990): "Privity and the Concept of a Network Contract" 10 *Legal Studies* 12.

Adams, John N., and Brownsword, Roger (1991): "More in Expectation than Hope: The Blackpool Airport Case" 54 *Modern Law Review* 281.

Allee, Mark A. (1994): *Law and Local Society in Late Imperial China: Northern Taiwan in the Nineteenth Century*, Stanford, Stanford University Press.

Ashworth, Andrew (1994): *The Criminal Process*, Oxford, Oxford University Press.

Ashworth, Andrew (2002): *Serious Crime, Human Rights, and Criminal Procedure*, London, Sweet and Maxwell.

Atiyah, P.S. (1983): *Law and Modern Society*, Oxford, Oxford University Press.

Attenborough, F.L. (1922): *Laws of the Earliest English Kings*, Cambridge, Cambridge University Press.

Auld, Sir Robin (2001): *Review of the Criminal Courts of England and Wales*, London, Stationery Office.

Austin, John (1955): *The Province of Jurisprudence Determined*, London, Weidenfeld and Nicolson.

Baldwin, J., and McConville, M. (1979): *Jury Trials*, Oxford, Clarendon Press.

Barnard, Catherine and Hare, Ivan (1997): "The Right to Protest and the Right to Export: Police Discretion and the Free Movement of Goods" 60 *Modern Law Review* 394.

Barnett, Randy E (1986): "A Consent Theory of Contract" 86 Col LR 269.

Barry, Brian (1973): *The Liberal Theory of Justice*, Oxford, Clarendon Press.

Beale, Hugh, and Dugdale, Tony (1975): "Contracts between Businessmen: Planning and the Use of Contractual Remedies" 2 *British Journal of Law and Society* 45.

Bell, John, and Engle, Sir George (1995): *Statutory Interpretation* (3rd ed.), London, Butterworths.

Bendix, Reinhard (1959): *Max Weber: an Intellectual Portrait*, London, Methuen.

Benson Commission (1979): *Final Report of the Royal Commission on Legal Services*, Cmnd. 7648, London, HMSO.

Bentham, Jeremy (1970): *An Introduction to the Principles of Morals and Legislation*, ed. by J.H. Burns and H.L.A. Hart, London, Athlone Press (originally published 1789, London, T. Payne).

Berry, Elspeth (2004): "The EU and Human Rights: Never the Twain Shall Meet?" in Roger Brownsword (ed), *Human Rights*, Oxford, Hart.

Beyleveld, Deryck (1991): *The Dialectical Necessity of Morality: An Analysis and Defense of Alan Gewirth's Argument to the PGC*, Chicago, Chicago University Press.

Beyleveld, Deryck, and Brownsword, Roger (1986): *Law as a Moral Judgment*, London, Sweet and Maxwell (reprinted 1994, Sheffield, Sheffield Academic Press).

Beyleveld, Deryck, and Brownsword, Roger (1990): "The Implications of Natural-Law Theory for the Sociology of Law", in A. Carty (ed.) *Post-Modern Law*, Edinburgh, Edinburgh University Press, p. 126.

Beyleveld, Deryck and Brownsword, Roger (1993): *Mice, Morality and Patents*, London, Common Law Institute of Intellectual Property.

Beyleveld, Deryck, and Brownsword, Roger (2001): *Human Dignity in Bioethics and Biolaw*, Oxford, Oxford University Press.

Beyleveld, Deryck and Brownsword, Roger (2006a): "Principle, Proceduralism and Precaution in a Community of Rights" 19 *Ratio Juris* 141.

Beyleveld, Deryck and Brownsword, Roger (2006b): *Consent in the Law*, Oxford, Hart.

Beyleveld, Deryck, Kirkham, Richard, and Townend, David (2002): "Which Presumption? A Critique of the House of Lords' Reasoning on Retrospectivity and the Human Rights Act" 22 *Legal Studies* 185.

Bingham, Sir Thomas (1993): "The European Convention on Human Rights: Time to Incorporate?" 109 *Law Quarterly Review* 390.

Birkinshaw, Patrick (1991): "Complaints Mechanisms in Administrative Law: Recent Developments", in Karl J. Mackie (ed.) *A Handbook of Dispute Resolution: ADR in Action*, London, Routledge and Sweet and Maxwell.

Bix, Brian (1995): "Physician Assisted Suicide and the United States Constitution" 58 *Modern Law Review* 404.

Blackman, D.E. (1981): "On Mental Elements and Their Place in Psychology and Law", in Joanna Shapland (ed.) *Lawyers and Psychologists—The Way Forward*, Leicester, British Psychological Society, p. 20.

Blackstone, Sir William (1825): *Commentaries on the Laws of England*, 16th ed., London, Cadell and Butterworth.

Blott, A. (1917): *Legal Dispensaries* (Pamphlet in Bodleian Library, Oxford).

Bottoms, A. E., and McClean, J.D. (1976): *Defendants in the Criminal Process*, London, Routledge and Kegan Paul.

Braudel, Fernand (1973): *The Mediterranean and the Mediterranean World in the Age of Philip II*, London, Fontana Press/Collins.

Bridge, Caroline (1996): "Conciliation and the New Zealand Family Court: Lessons For English Law Reformers" 16 *Legal Studies* 298.

Brown, Paul (2001): "GM Crop Protesters Cleared in High Court Test Case" *The Guardian*, October 17, p. 12.

Browne-Wilkinson, the Right Hon. Lord (1992): "The Infiltration of a Bill of Rights" *Public Law* 397.

Brownsword, Roger (1977): "Who says that Penal Statutes are construed restrictively?" 28 *Northern Ireland Legal Quarterly* 73.

Brownsword, Roger (1979): "*Northman v. London Borough of Barnet*: Idioms and Interpretation" 42 *Modern Law Review* 562.

Brownsword, Roger (1996): "Where are all the Law Schools Going?" 30 *The Law Teacher* 1.

Brownsword, Roger (2002): "Stem Cells, Superman, and the Report of the Select Committee" 65 MLR 568.

Brownsword, Roger (2003): "Bioethics Today, Bioethics Tomorrow: Stem Cell Research and the 'Dignitarian Alliance'" 17 *Notre Dame Journal of Law, Ethics and Public Policy* 15.

Brownsword, Roger (2004a): "Introduction: Global Governance and Human Rights" in Roger Brownsword (ed), *Human Rights*, Oxford, Hart.

Brownsword, Roger (2004b): "The Cult of Consent: Fixation and Fallacy" 15 *King's College Law Journal* 223.

Brownsword, Roger (2005a): "Code, Control, and Choice: Why East is East and West is West" 25 *Legal Studies* 1.

Brownsword, Roger (2005b): "Happy Families, Consenting Couples, and Children with Dignity: Sex Selection and Saviour Siblings" 17 *Child and Family Law Quarterly* 435.

Brownsword, Roger (2005c): "Stem Cells and Cloning: Where the Regulatory Consensus Fails" 39 *New England Law Review* 535.

Brownsword, Roger, Cornish, W.R. and Llewelyn, Margaret (eds) (1998): *Human Genetics and the Law: Regulating a Revolution*, Oxford, Hart Publishing.

Cane, Peter (2002): *Responsibility in Law and Morality*, Oxford, Hart.

Cardozo, Benjamin N. (1921): *The Nature of the Judicial Process*, New Haven, Yale University Press.

Carruthers, Peter (1992): *The Animals Issue*, Cambridge, Cambridge University Press.

Cavadino, Michael and Dignan, James (2002): *The Penal System*, 3rd ed., London, Sage.

Chambliss, William J., and Seidman, Robert B. (1971): *Law, Order, and Power*, Reading (Mass.): Addison-Wesley.

Chandos, J. (1984): *Boys Together: English Public Schools 1800–1864*, London, Hutchinson.

Civil Justice Review (1988): *Civil Justice Review, Report of the Review Body on Civil Justice*, Cm. 394, London, HMSO.

Clarke, John, Cochrane, Allan, and Smart, Carol (eds) (1987): *Ideologies of Welfare: From Dreams to Disillusion*, London, Hutchinson.

Clarkson, C.M.V. (2005): *Understanding Criminal Law*, 4th ed., London, Sweet & Maxwell.

Cockburn, J.S. (1972): *A History of English Assizes, 1558–1714*, London, Cambridge University Press.

Coke, Sir Edward: *Institutes of the Laws of England*.

Collins, Hugh (1984): *Marxism and Law*, Oxford, Oxford University Press.

Conaghan, Joanne and Mansell, Wade (1998): *The Wrongs of Tort*, 2nd ed., London, Pluto Press.

Cooper, Jeremy (1983): *Public Legal Services*, London, Sweet and Maxwell.

Cooper, J. (1991): "Criminal Investigations in France" 141 *New Law Journal* 381.

Cornish, W.R. (1968): *The Jury*, London, Allen Lane.

Cotterrell, Roger (1984): *The Sociology of Law*, London, Butterworths.

Cownie, Fiona (2004): *Legal Academics*, Oxford, Hart.

Craig, Paul (2003): "Constitutional Foundations, the Rule of Law and Supremacy" *Public Law* 92.

Cunningham, John (2001): "A Plea for Life" *Guardian Society*, October 17, p.6.

Danzig, Richard (1973): "Towards the Creation of a Complementary Decentralized System of Criminal Justice", 26 *Stanford Law Review* 1.

De Sousa Santos, Boaventura (2002): *Toward a New Legal Common Sense* 2nd ed, London, Butterworths.

Deazley, Ronan (2004): *On the Origin of the Right to Copy*, Oxford, Hart.

Devlin, Patrick (1965): *The Enforcement of Morals*, Oxford, Oxford University Press.

Devlin, Patrick (1978): "Judges, Government and Politics" 41 *Modern Law Review* 501.

Devlin, Patrick (1986): *Easing the Passing: The Trial of Doctor John Bodkin Adams*, London, Faber and Faber.

Dicey, A.V. (1885) (1939): *Introduction to the Law of the Constitution* (1st and 9th eds), London, Macmillan.

Dignan, J. (1983): "Policy-Making, Local Authorities and the Courts: The 'G.L.C. Fares' Case" 99 *Law Quarterly Review* 605.

Dixon, D., Coleman, C., and Bottomley, K. (1991): "PACE in Practice" 141 *New Law Journal* 1586.

Drewry, Gavin, and Harlow, Carol (1990): "A 'Cutting Edge'? The Parliamentary Commissioner and MPs" 53 *Modern Law Review* 745.

Dworkin, Ronald (1978): *Taking Rights Seriously*, London, Duckworth.

Dworkin, Ronald (1986a): *A Matter of Principle*, Oxford, Clarendon Press.

Dworkin, Ronald (1986b): *Law's Empire*, London, Fontana Press.

Dworkin, Ronald (1993): *Life's Dominion*, London, Harper Collins.

Dyer, Clare (2002a): "Winner Takes All", *Guardian Law*, October 29, p.10.

Dyer, Clare (2002b): "Poor Face Legal Aid Crisis as Solicitors Pull Out", *Guardian* December 30, p.6.

Edgeworth, Brendan (2003): *Law, Modernity, Postmodernity*, Aldershot, Ashgate.

Edwards, Richard A (2002): "Judicial Deference under the Human Rights Act" 65 *Modern Law Review* 859.

Egerton, D. (1945): *Legal Aid*, London, Routledge and Kegan Paul.

Elton, G.R. (1991): *England Under the Tudors*, 3rd ed., London, Methuen.

English, Rosalind (1996): "The Tenant, his Wife, the Lodger and their Telly: a Spot of Nuisance in Docklands" 59 *Modern Law Review* 726.

Evans, E.P. (1987): *The Criminal Prosecution and Capital Punishment of Animals*, London, Faber and Faber.

Ewing, Keith (1999): "The Human Rights Act and Parliamentary Democracy" 62 *Modern Law Review* 79.

Ewing, Keith (2004): "The Futility of the Human Rights Act" *Public Law* 829.

Feather, J. (1980): "The Book Trade in Politics: the Making of the Copyright Act of 1710", 8 *Publishing History* 19.

Fenn, Paul, Gray, Alastair, Rickman, Neil, and Carrier, Howard (2002): *The Impact of Conditional Fees on the Selection, Handling and Outcomes of Personal Injury Cases*, London, Lord Chancellor's Department (Research Series No. 6/02).

Filmer, Sir Robert (1680): *Patriarcha; or, the Natural Power of Kings*.

Finlay Committee (1928): *Legal Aid for the Poor*, London, HMSO, Cmd. 3016.

Finnis, John (1980): *Natural Law and Natural Rights*, Oxford, The Clarendon Press.

Finnis, John (1993): "*Bland*—Crossing the Rubicon?" 109 *Law Quarterly Review* 329.

Fish, Stanley (1987): "Still Wrong After All These Years" 6 *Law and Philosophy* 401.

Fish, Stanley (1994): *There's No Such Thing as Free Speech*, Oxford, Oxford University Press.

Fisk, Milton (1975): "History and Reason in Rawls' Moral Theory" in Norman Daniels (ed.) *Reading Rawls*, Oxford, Basil Blackwell, 53.

Fletcher, George P (1996): *Basic Concepts of Legal Thought*, Oxford, Oxford University Press.

Frank, Jerome (1949): *Law and the Modern Mind*, London, Stevens.

Frank, Jerome (1950): *Courts on Trial: Myth and Reality in American Justice*, Princeton, Princeton University Press.

Franks Committee (1957): *Report of the Committee on Administrative Tribunals and Inquiries*, Cmnd. 218.

Freeman, M. (1981): "*The Jury on Trial*" [1981] CLP 65.

Fried, Charles (1985): "Rights and the Common Law" in R.G. Frey (ed.) *Utility and Rights*, Oxford, Basil Blackwell, p. 215.

Friedman, Lawrence M (2002): "One World: Notes on the Emerging Legal Order" in Michael Likosky (ed), *Transnational Legal Processes*, London, Butterworths 23.

Fukuyama, Francis (2002): *Our Posthuman Future*, London, Profile Books.

Fuller, Lon L. (1948–9): "The Case of the Speluncean Explorers", 62 *Harvard Law Review* 616.

Fuller, Lon L. (1957–8): "Positivism and Fidelity to Law—A Reply to Professor Hart", 71 *Harvard Law Review* 630.

Fuller, Lon L. (1969): *The Morality of Law*, New Haven, Yale University Press.

Galanter, M. (1974): "Why the 'Haves' come out ahead: Speculation on the Limits of Legal Change", 9 *Law and Society Review* 95.

Gale, H.P. (1956): 20 *Uganda Journal* 72.

Ganz, Gabriele (1996): "Criminal Injuries Compensation: The Constitutional Issue" 59 *Modern Law Review* 95.

Ganz, Gabriele (2001): *Understanding Public Law*, London, Sweet & Maxwell.

George, Robert P. (1988): "Moralistic Liberalism and Legal Moralism" 88 *Michigan Law Review* 1415.

Gewirth, Alan (1978): *Reason and Morality*, Chicago, The University of Chicago Press.

Gibb, Frances (2003): "The Battle to Bring Costs Under Control" *The Times*, February 25.

Gibb, Frances (2005): "It was a great day for the law, for clam and reasoned judgment" (interview with Lord Steyn) *The Times, Law*, 11 October, 5.

Goodhart, Arthur L. (1930): "Determining the Ratio Decidendi of a Case" 40 *Yale Law Journal* 161.

Goriely, Tamara, Moorhead, Richard, Abrams, Pamela (2002): *More Civil Justice? The Impact of the Woolf Reforms on Pre-Action Behaviour* (Research Study 43) London, the Law Society and Civil Justice Council.

Grant, Linda (2000): "Rough Justice" *The Guardian* (G2) April 26, 2.

Griffith, J.A.G. (1979): "The Political Constitution" 42 *Modern Law Review* 1.

Griffith, J.A.G. (1985) (1991): *The Politics of the Judiciary* (3rd and 4th eds), London, Fontana Press.

Gurney-Champion, F.C.C. (1926): *Justice and the Poor of England*, London, Routledge and Sons.

Hailsham, Lord (1976): "Elective Dictatorship", *Listener*, October 21.

Halliday, John (2001): *Making Punishment Work: Report of a Review of the Sentencing Framework of England and Wales*, London, Home Office.

Hannett, Sarah (2003): "Third Party Intervention: In the Public Interest?" *Public Law* 128.

Harden, Ian, and Lewis, Norman (1988): *The Noble Lie*, London, Routledge.

Hare, R.M. (1981): *Moral Thinking*, Oxford, The Clarendon Press.

Harlow, Carol (1987): *Understanding Tort Law*, London, Fontana Press.

Harlow, Carol (2002): "Public Law and Popular Justice" 65 *Modern Law Review* 1.

Harman, H. and Griffith, J. (1979): *Justice Deserted: The Subversion of the Jury*, London, NCCL.

Harris, D., Ogus, A., and Phillips, J. (1979): "Contract Remedies and the Consumer Surplus", 95 *Law Quarterly Review* 581.

Harris, J.W. (2002): "Retrospective Overruling and the Declaratory Theory in the United Kingdom—Three Recent Decisions" 26 *Revue de la Faculté de Droit Université Libre de Bruxelles* 153.

Hart, H.L.A. (1961): *The Concept of Law*, Oxford, The Clarendon Press.

Hart, H.L.A. (1963): *Law, Liberty and Morality*, London, Oxford University Press.

Hay, D. (ed.) (1975): *Albion's Fatal Tree*, London, Allen Lane.

Heap, Sir Desmond (1975): *The Land and the Development: Or, the Turmoil and the Torment*, London, Stevens.

Held, David (1987): *Models of Democracy*, Cambridge, Polity Press.

Held, David, and McGrew, Anthony (eds) (2002): *Governing Globalization*, Oxford, Polity Press.

Hill, Alastair M., and Griffiths, Robin C. (1982): "English Law and the Psychologist", in Joanna Shapland (ed.) *Lawyers and Psychologists— Gathering and Giving Evidence*, Leicester, British Psychological Society, p. 8.

Hilson, Chris and Cram, Ian (1996): "Judicial Review and Environmental Law—Is There a Coherent View of Standing?" 16 *Legal Studies* 1.

Hobe, Stephan (2002): "Globalisation: A Challenge to the Nation State and to International Law" in Michael Likosky (ed), *Transnational Legal Processes*, London, Butterworths 378.

Hodgson, D.H. (1967): *Consequences of Utilitarianism*, Oxford, The Clarendon Press.

Hoffmann, Leonard (2005): "Causation" 121 *Law Quarterly Review* 592.

Holdsworth, Sir William (1903–72): *History of English Law*, London, Methuen.

Holdsworth, W.S. (1923): "The New Rules of Pleading of the Hilary Term" 1 *Cambridge Law Journal* 261.

Hollis, Martin (1977): *Models of Man*, Cambridge, Cambridge University Press.

Home Office (1981): *The Brixton Disorders, 10–12 April 1981*, London, HMSO, Cmnd. 8427.

Home Office (1997): *Rights Brought Home: The Human Rights Bill*, London, HMSO, CM. 3782.

Home Office (2002): *Justice for All* (Cm 5563).

Honderich, Ted (1976): *Punishment: The Supposed Justifications* (rev. ed.) Harmondsworth, Peregrine Books.

Horwitz, Morton, J. (1977): *The Transformation of American Law 1780–1860*, Cambridge, Mass., Harvard University Press.

Hoskins, W.G. (1956): *The Age of Plunder*, London, Longmans.

Hoyano, Laura (1995): "Dangerous Defects Revisited by Bold Spirits" 58 *Modern Law Review* 887.

Hughes Commission (1980): *Report of the Royal Commission on Legal Services in Scotland*, London, HMSO, Cmnd. 7846.

Hunt, Murray (1997): *Using Human Rights Law in English Courts*, Oxford, Hart Publishing.

Hurnard, N.D. (1969): *The King's Pardon for Homicide*, Oxford, Oxford University Press.

Ingleby, Richard (1993): "Court Sponsored Mediation: The Case Against Mandatory Participation" 56 *Modern Law Review* 441.

Irving, B., and Hilgendorf, L. (1980): *Police Interrogation: The Psychological Approach* (Royal Commission on Criminal Procedure Research Study No. 1), London, HMSO.

Jenkins, Iredell (1980): *Social Order and the Limits of Law*, Princeton, Princeton University Press.

Johnson, Terry (1972): *Professions and Power*, London, Macmillan.

Justice-All Souls (1988): *Administrative Justice: Some Necessary Reforms*, Oxford, Clarendon Press.

Kairys, David (ed.) (1982): *The Politics of Law*, London, Pantheon Books.

Kamenka, Eugene, and Tay, Alice Erh-Soon (1980): "Social Traditions, Legal Traditions" in Eugene Kamenka and Alice Erh-Soon Tay (eds), *Law and Social Control*, London, Edward Arnold.

Kant, Immanuel (1948): *Groundwork of the Metaphysic of Morals*, trans., H.J. Paton as *The Moral Law*, London, Hutchinson University Library.

Kavanagh, Aileen (2005): "*Pepper v Hart* and Matters of Constitutional Principle" 121 *Law Quarterly Review* 98.

Kelsen, Hans (1967): *Pure Theory of Law* (trans. Max Knight from the 2nd revised and enlarged German ed.) Berkeley, University of California Press.

Kennedy, Helena (2004): *Just Law*, London, Chatto & Windus.

King, Michael (1981): *The Framework of Criminal Justice*, London, Croom Helm.

Koskenniemi, Martti (2002): "'The Lady Doth Protest Too Much': Kosovo, and the Turn to Ethics in International Law" 65 *Modern Law Review* 159.

Kronman, A.T. (1983): *Max Weber*, London, Edward Arnold.

Laird, Vanessa (1992): "Reflections on *R v. R*" 55 *Modern Law Review* 386.

Laird, Vanessa (1994): "*Planned Parenthood v. Casey*: The Role of Stare Decisis" 57 *Modern Law Review* 461.

Law Commission (1969): *The Interpretation of Statutes* (Law Com. No. 21).

Law Commission (1976): *Remedies in Administrative Law* (Law Com. No. 73).

Law Commission (1994): *Criminal Law: Consent and Offences against the Person*, Law Commission Consultation Paper No. 134.

Law Commission (1995): *Liability for Psychiatric Illness*, Law Commission Consultation Paper No. 137.

Law Commission (1998): *Liability for Psychiatric Illness*, Law Commission Report No. 249.

Law Commission (2005): *A New Homicide Act for England and Wales?*, Law Commission Consultation Paper No 177.

Lawrence Committee (1919): *Committee to Enquire into the Poor Persons Rules*, London, HMSO, Cmd. 430.

Laws, the Hon. Sir John (1993): "Is the High Court the Guardian of Fundamental Constitutional Rights?" *Public Law* 59.

Leader, Sheldon (1990): "The Right to Privacy, the Enforcement of Morals, and the Judicial Function: An Argument" 43 *Current Legal Problems* 115.

Lessig, Lawrence (1999): *Code and Other Laws of Cyberspace*, New York, Basic Books.

Lester, Anthony (2003): "Don't Blame the Judges" *Guardian Law* February 25, 16.

Lewis, Geoffrey (1983): *Lord Atkin*, London, Butterworths.

Lewis, Norman (1996): *Choice and the Legal Order: Rising Above Politics*, London, Lexis Nexis.

Lewis N. D. (ed) (2006): *International and Regional Organisations*, Oxford, Hart.

Lindsay, Alistair (1994): "Reasons to be Cheerful" 57 *Modern Law Review* 954.

Llewellyn, Karl N. (1940): "The Normative, the Legal, and the Law-Jobs: The Problem of Juristic Method" 49 *Yale Law Journal* 1355.

Llewellyn, Karl N., and Hoebel, E. Adamson (1941): *The Cheyenne Way*, Norman, University of Oklahoma Press.

Llewellyn, Karl N. (1960): *The Common Law Tradition: Deciding Appeals*, Boston, Little, Brown.

Locke, J. (1690): *Treatises on Government*.

Loughlin, Martin (1986): *Local Government in the Modern State*, London, Sweet and Maxwell.

Lukes, S. (1973): *Emile Durkheim*, Harmondsworth, Penguin Books.

MacCallum, G.C. (1966): "Legislative Intent" 75 *Yale Law Journal* 754.

MacFarlane, K.B. (1973): *The Nobility of Later Mediaeval England*, Oxford, Clarendon Press.

MacIntyre, Alasdair (1981): *After Virtue*, London, Duckworth.

Mackay, Lord (1991): "Litigation in the 1990s" 54 *Modern Law Review* 171.

Mackie, Karl J. (ed.) (1991): *A Handbook of Dispute Resolution: ADR in Action*, London, Routledge and Sweet and Maxwell.

Macpherson, C.B. (1973): *Democratic Theory: Essays in Retrieval*, Oxford, Clarendon Press.

Macpherson, C.B. (1977): *The Life and Times of Liberal Democracy*, Oxford, Oxford University Press.

McAuslan, Patrick (1980): *The Ideologies of Planning Law*, Oxford, Pergamon Press.

McBarnet, D. (1981): *Conviction, Law, The State and the Construction of Justice*, London, Macmillan.

Maine, Sir Henry (1883): *Early Law and Custom*, London, John Murray.

Maitland, F.W. (1901): "The Crown as Corporation" 17 *Law Quarterly Review* 132.

Marcuse, Herbert (1972): *One Dimensional Man*, London, Abacus.

Mark, R. (1973): *Minority Verdict*. The 1973 Dimbleby Lecture, London, BBC.

Martin, Robyn (1996): "Defective Premises—The Empire Strikes Back" 59 *Modern Law Review* 116.

Martin, Robyn (1997): "Diverging Common Law—Invercargill goes to the Privy Council" 60 *Modern Law Review* 94.

Marx, Karl (1974): *Capital* (Vol. I), edited by Frederick Engels, London, Lawrence and Wishart.

Mason, J.K. and McCall Smith, R.A. (1994): *Law and Medical Ethics*, London, Butterworths.

Matthews and Oulton on Legal Aid and Advice (1971), London, Butterworths.

Mawby, R., and Gill, M.L. (1987): *Crime Victims*, London, Tavistock.

Merrills, John (1993): *The Development of International Law by the European Court of Human Rights*, Manchester, Manchester University Press.

Merryman, J.H. (1969): *The Civil Law Tradition*, Stanford, Stanford University Press.

Miers, David R. (1978): *Responses to Victimisation*, Oxford, Professional Books.

Miers, David R., and Page, Alan C. (1990): *Legislation* (2nd ed.), London, Sweet and Maxwell.

Miers, David (1993): "Taxing Perks and Interpreting Statutes" 56 *Modern Law Review* 695.

Mill, J.S. (1859): "On Liberty", in J. S. Mill, *Utilitarianism*, ed. Mary Warnock (1962), London, Fontana Press.

Miller, David (1976): *Social Justice*, Oxford, Clarendon Press.

Mills, C. Wright (1956): *The Power Elite*, New York, Oxford University Press.

Montesquieu, Baron de (Charles Louis de Secondat) (1748): *L'Espirit des Lois*.

Morgan, Derek and Lee, Robert G. (1997): "In the Name of the Father? *Ex parte Blood*: Dealing with Novelty and Anomaly" 60 *Modern Law Review* 840.

Morris, D.R. (1966): *The Washing of Spears*, London, Cape.

Morris, P., White, R., and Lewis, P. (ed) (1973): *Social Needs and Legal Action*, Oxford, Martin Robertson.

Mullender, Richard (1998): "Parliamentary Sovereignty, the Constitution, and the Judiciary" 49 *Northern Ireland Legal Quarterly* 138.

Nagel, Thomas (1975): "Rawls on Justice" in Norman Daniels (ed.) *Reading Rawls*, Oxford, Basil Blackwell, 1.

Nozick, Robert (1974): *Anarchy, State, and Utopia*, Oxford, Basil Blackwell.

Oliver, Dawn (1994): "Teaching and Learning Law: Pressures on the Liberal Law Degree" in Peter Birks (ed.) *Reviewing Legal Education*, Oxford, Oxford University Press, p. 77.

Packer, Herbert L. (1969): *The Limits of the Criminal Sanction*, Stanford, Stanford University Press.

Palmer, R.C. (1976): "The Origin of the Legal Profession in England", *Irish Jurist* 126.

Parsons, Talcott (1968): "Professions" in the *International Encyclopaedia of the Social Sciences.*

Paterson, Alan (1982): *The Law Lords,* London, Macmillan.

Pearson, Lord (1978): *Royal Commission on Civil Liability and Compensation for Personal Injury,* London, HMSO, Cmnd. 7054.

Philips Commission (1981): *Report of the Royal Commission on Criminal Procedure,* London, HMSO, Cmnd. 8092.

Pipe, Gregory S. (1994): "Exemplary Damages After Camelford" 57 *Modern Law Review* 91.

Plucknett, T. (1960): *Edward I and the Criminal Law,* Cambridge, Cambridge University Press.

Posner, Richard A. (1992): *Economic Analysis of Law,* Boston, Little Brown.

Pound, Roscoe (1908): "Mechanical Jurisprudence", 8 *Columbia Law Review* 605.

Prosser, Tony (1979): "Politics and Judicial Review: The Atkinson Case and its Aftermath" *Public Law* 59.

Prosser, Tony (1983): *Test Cases for the Poor,* Child Poverty Action Group.

Putnam, B.H. (1950): *Sir William Shareshull,* Cambridge, Cambridge University Press.

Rawls, John (1972): *A Theory of Justice,* London, Oxford University Press.

Raz, Joseph (1979): *The Authority of Law: Essays on Law and Morality,* Oxford, The Clarendon Press.

Regis Jr, Edward (1984): *Gewirth's Ethical Rationalism,* Chicago, Chicago University Press.

Reid, Lord (1972): "The Judge as Law Maker", XII *Journal of the Society of Public Teachers of Law* 22.

Rifkin, Jeremy (1995): "Farm Animals and the Biotechnology Revolution: A Philosophical Overview" in Wheale, Peter and McNally, Ruth (eds), *Animal Genetic Engineering: Of Pigs, Oncomice and Men,* London, Pluto Press, p. 19.

Rifkin, Jeremy (1998): *The Biotech Century,* London, Victor Gollancz.

Roberts, Simon (1979): *Order and Dispute,* London: Penguin.

Roberts, Simon (1990): "A Blueprint for Family Conciliation?" 53 *Modern Law Review* 88.

Roberts, Simon (1993): "Alternative Dispute Resolution and Civil Justice: An Unresolved Relationship" 56 *Modern Law Review* 452.

Rock, P. (1973): *Making People Pay,* London, Routledge and Kegan Paul.

Rose, Mark (1993): *Authors and Owners: the Invention of Copyright,* London, Harvard University Press.

Roshier, Bob, and Teff, Harvey (1980): *Law and Society in England,* London, Tavistock.

Roskill Committee (1986): *Report of the Fraud Trials Committee,* London, HMSO.

Rudovsky, David (1982): "The Criminal Justice System and the Role of the Police", in Kairys (ed.) *The Politics of Law,* London, Pantheon Books, 242.

Rueschmeyer, D. (1964): "Doctors and Lawyers: a Comment on the Theory of the Professions", 1 *Canadian Review of Sociology and Anthropology* 17.

Sandel, Michael (1984): "Liberalism and the Claims of Community: The Case of Affirmative Action", in Marshall Cohen (ed.) *Ronald Dworkin and Contemporary Jurisprudence*, London, Duckworth, 227.

Sands, Phillipe (2006): *Lawless World*, London, Penguin.

Schiemann, Sir Konrad (1990): "Locus Standi" *Public Law* 342.

Sedley, the Hon. Sir Stephen (1995): "Human Rights: A Twenty-First Century Agenda" *Public Law* 386.

Shapland, Joanna *et al* (1998): *Affording Civil Justice*, London, Law Society.

Simpson, A.W.B. (1984a): *Cannibalism and the Common Law: the Story of the Tragic Last Voyage of the Mignonette and the Strange Legal Proceedings to which it gave rise*, Chicago, University of Chicago Press.

Simpson, A.W.B. (1984b): *A Biographical Dictionary of the Common Law*, London, Butterworths.

Singer, Peter (1979): *Practical Ethics*, Cambridge, Cambridge University Press.

Skolnick, J.M. (1967): "Social Control in the Adversary System", XI *Journal of Conflict Resolution* 52.

Smith, John C., and Hogan, Brian (2005): *Criminal Law* (11th ed. Ormerod), Oxford, OUP.

Smith, Roger (1986): "How Good Are Test Cases?", in Jeremy Cooper and Rajeev Dhavan (eds), *Public Interest Law*, Oxford, Basil Blackwell, 271.

Solicitor (1932): *English Justice*, London, Routledge and Sons.

Sprigge, S.J.J. (1891): *Shortcomings of the Machinery for Pauper Litigation*, London, Williams and Norgate.

Steyn, Johan (2001): "*Pepper v Hart*: A Re-Examination" 21 OJLS 59.

Steyn, Johan (2002): "Perspectives of Corrective and Distributive Justice" (John Maurice Kelly Memorial Lecture, University College Dublin).

Steyn, Lord (2005): "Deference: A Tangled Story" *Public Law* 346.

Stiglitz, Joseph (2002): *Globalization and its Discontents*, London, Penguin, Allen Lane.

Stoddart, C.N. (1979): *Law and Practice of Legal Aid in Scotland*, Edinburgh, Green and Sons.

Stone, Julius (1959): "The Ratio of the Ratio Decidendi' 22 *Modern Law Review* 597.

Street, Harry (1975): *Justice in the Welfare State* (2nd ed.), London, Stevens.

Sypnowich, Christine (1990): *The Concept of Socialist Law*, Oxford, The Clarendon Press.

Szyszczak, Erika (1992): "European Community Law: New Remedies, New Directions?" 58 *Modern Law Review* 690.

Szyszczak, Erika and Cygan, Adam (2005): *Understanding EU Law*, London, Sweet and Maxwell.

Thomson, Judith J. (1977): "A Defence of Abortion" in R.M.Dworkin (ed.), *The Philosophy of Law*, London, Oxford University Press, p. 112.

Twining, William, and Miers, David (1991): *How to do Things with Rules* (3rd ed.), London, Weidenfeld and Nicolson.

Ullmann, Walter (1975): *Mediaeval Political Thought*, Harmondsworth, Penguin.

Veall, D. (1974): *The Popular Movement for Law Reform 1640–1660*, Oxford, Oxford University Press.

Villiers, Charlotte and White, Fidelma (1995): "Agitating for Part-Time Workers' Rights" 58 *Modern Law Review* 560.

Waldron, Jeremy (1990): *The Law*, London, Routledge.

Walker, R.C.S. (1978): *Kant*, London, Routledge and Kegan Paul.

Warnock Committee (1984): *Report of the Committee of Inquiry into Human Fertilisation and Embryology*, London, HMSO, Cm. 9314.

Wasserstrom, Richard A. (1961): *The Judicial Decision*, Stanford, Stanford University Press.

Weatherill, Stephen and Beaumont, Paul (1999): *E.C. Law*, Penguin Books.

Weber, M. (1954): *Max Weber on Law in Economy and Society* (trans. M. Rheinstein and E. Shils, ed. M. Rheinstein), Cambridge, Harvard University Press.

Weber, M. (1964): *The Theory of Social and Economic Organization*, New York, The Free Press.

Weber, M. (1978): *Economy and Society*, Roth and Wittich (eds), Berkeley, University of California Press.

White, Robin C. (1999): *The Administration of Justice* (3rd ed.), Oxford, Basil Blackwell.

Williams, Andrew (2004): "The (Im)possibility of the European Union as a Global Human Rights Regime" in Roger Brownsword (ed), *Human Rights*, Oxford, Hart.

Williams, Glanville (1955): "The Definition of Crime", 8 *Current Legal Problems* 107.

Williams, Glanville (1981): "Statute Interpretation, Prostitution, and the Rule of Law" in Colin Tapper (ed.) *Crime, Proof and Punishment*, London, Butterworths, 71.

Willis, John (1938): "Statute Interpretation in a Nutshell" 16 *Canadian Bar Review* 1.

Winch, Peter (1958): *The Idea of a Social Science*, London, Routledge and Kegan Paul.

Winder, W.H. (1936): "The Courts of Requests" 52 *Law Quarterly Review* 369.

Wolfenden Commission (1957): *Report of the Committee on Homosexual Offences and Prostitution*, London, HMSO, Cmnd. 247.

Woodward, Bob, and Armstrong, Scott (1979): *The Brethren*, New York, Simon and Schuster.

Woolf, H (1996): *Access to Justice—Final Report to the Lord Chancellor on the Civil Justice System in England and Wales*, London, HMSO.

Zander, Michael (1979): *A Bill of Rights* (2nd ed.), Chichester, British Institute of Human Rights.

Zuckerman, Adrian (1994): "Quality and Economy in Civil Procedures: the Case for Commuting Correct Judgments for Timely Judgments" 14 *Oxford Journal of Legal Studies* 353.

Zuckerman, Adrian (1996): "Lord Woolf's Access to Justice: Plus ça change" 59 *Modern Law Review* 773.

CASES

INDEX

LEGAL TAXONOMY
FROM SWEET & MAXWELL

This index has been prepared using Sweet and Maxwell's Legal Taxonomy. Main index entries conform to keywords provided by the Legal Taxonomy except where references to specific documents or non-standard terms (denoted by quotation marks) have been included. These keywords provide a means of identifying similar concepts in other Sweet & Maxwell publications and online services to which keywords from the Legal Taxonomy have been applied. Readers may find some minor differences between terms used in the text and those which appear in the index. Suggestions to *taxonomy@sweetandmaxwell.co.uk*.

(All references are to page number)